App Inventor for Android:

Build Your Own Apps — No Experience Required!

App Inventor for Android:

Build Your Own Apps — No Experience Required!

Jason Tyler

A John Wiley and Sons, Ltd, Publication

App Inventor for Android: Build Your Own Apps — No Experience Required!

This edition first published 2011

© 2011 John Wiley & Sons, Ltd

Registered office

John Wiley & Sons Ltd, The Atrium, Southern Gate, Chichester, West Sussex, PO19 8SQ, United Kingdom

For details of our global editorial offices, for customer services and for information about how to apply for permission to reuse the copyright material in this book, please see our Web site at www.wiley.com.

978-1-119-99133-5

A catalogue record for this book is available from the British Library.

Set in 10/14 Chaparral by Andrea Hornberger

Printed in the United States of America by C J Krehbiel

About the Author

JASON TYLER is passionate about technology and people. Jason teaches technology professionally to help people achieve their goals using the power of technology. He plays with technology because he loves the empowerment that technology can bring, and also because he is attracted to anything shiny.

Jason is a lifetime student who considers a day wasted if he is not awed by something. His passion for technology has lead him to hold multiple certifications from Microsoft, Cisco, CompTIA, and ITIL. His passion for people led him to seek a B. A. in theology.

Jason is an avid and dedicated photographer, sailor, and gamer. Of all the things he is, Jason is proudest to be the husband of Rebecca and the father of Liam and Declan.

Credits

Some of the people who helped bring this book to market include the following:

Editorial and Production

VP Consumer and Technology Publishing Director: Michelle Leete

Associate Director- Book Content Management: Martin Tribe

Associate Publisher: Chris Webb

Publishing Assistant: Ellie Scott

Development Editor: Linda Morris

Technical Editor: Liam Green-Hughes

Copy Editor: Linda Morris

Editorial Manager: Jodi Jensen

Senior Project Editor: Sara Shlaer

Editorial Assistant: Leslie Saxman

Marketing:

Senior Marketing Manager: Louise Breinholt

Marketing Executive: Kate Parrett

Composition Services:

Compositors: Andrea Hornberger, Jennifer Mayberry

Proof Reader: Susan Hobbs

Indexer: Ty Koontz

To Rebecca Sue. This is one of the high places I promised you.
Thank you for being there in the low places, too.

Author's Acknowledgments

Rebecca, thank you for the sacrifices you made to make this book possible. I love you. Forever.

Liam and Declan, thank you for letting daddy write so much.

Jon Bartolomeo, your honesty and grounded technical knowledge were invaluable.

Bill Dwyer, thanks for the programming review and teaching. You are an amazing teacher.

Hal Abelson, thank you so much for App Inventor and the years of dedication to the ethos behind it. You have become one of the giants.

The App Inventor Google Developer team: Karen, Sharon, Liz, and Mark. There are not enough superlatives to describe your contribution to leveling the Android application playing field. Your enthusiasm, dedication, and downright rockstar-ness are unparalleled.

The AI PowerUsers: Sua Thov, Ed, Josh Turner, Shival, and Steve. I have grown and learned working with you guys.

Rachael, you are the best boss to let me work on this so much.

Chris Webb, I will be eternally grateful to you for giving me this opportunity and putting up with my author jitters.

Linda, thank you so much for making me look good.

Dennis Cohen, thanks for helping out with the Mac parts.

Dad, thanks for getting me started in technology.

Mom, thanks for educating me and making me love books, words, and excellence. I owe you the most.

Finally, thanks to the rainy days that got me through all of the hard bits.

Contents

Part II

Introduction

WHEN ANDROID WAS first introduced by Google and the Open Handset Alliance, my first thought was of how awesome it would be to have a free open-source application environment for the growing smart phone revolution. The harsh reality hit when I tried to apply my rusty programming skills to the Java and Android software development kit (SDK). The learning curve was too steep, with too few rewards to keep me going. Then Google announced the amazing App Inventor, which makes it possible for *anyone* to build Android applications. I was excited and my hope for building my own applications was renewed. As I have learned, played with, and grown with App Inventor, I have been amazed at what non-experts (including me) can build with this tool. After having spent a few months with App Inventor, I have found my journey to traditional Java and SDK development much easier, more fun, and less frustrating.

Who This Book Is For

This book is for anyone from a complete computer newbie to an experienced designer and developer. It will help anyone familiarize themselves with the App Inventor interface and components.

The really exciting news is that the world of Android applications awaits you even if you have absolutely zero programming knowledge. If you have ever had a brilliant idea for an application, App Inventor can help that idea become a reality. If you have ever been curious about how phone applications are created and function, you can learn by creating applications yourself. App Inventor is also great for rapid prototyping applications for testing and display.

This book helps you create applications for your Android device using Google's App Inventor for Android. App Inventor is a Web-based application that allows everyone from ordinary phone owners to experienced developers to create applications for Android.

App Inventor for Android: Build Your Own Apps — No Experience Required! is also great for designers or developers with great ideas and a solid background in development. App Inventor can allow very technical and experienced app developers to spend less time worrying about debugging, syntax, and development and more time making rock-star applications.

Part I: Getting Up and Running with Google App Inventor

You start with an exploration of the interface and a simple project application. In Part I, you become familiar with the interface and the basic components.

By immediately adding components and programming logic, any hesitation you may have about programming with App Inventor is eased. Each part of the App Inventor interface is explained. This allows you to move into the Part II with confidence and comfort.

Part II: Designing Your Own Apps: Step-by-Step Guides

In this part, you learn the basics of designing applications from a napkin sketch to a functioning application. I walk you through the process of creating various apps ranging from a child's alphabet tracing game to a Bluetooth chat client, and more. Many of the applications contain concepts and programming that you can use in your own applications.

Part III: Reference and Appendixes

This book also contains a Blocks and Component Reference that covers important blocks not covered in the project chapters. I explain blocks such as text blocks and demonstrate them graphically. You can use the examples to add functionality to your project or meet a specific design goal.

If you have not set up your phone to connect to the App Inventor application, you can find information for setting up your computer and Android phone in Appendix A. Appendix B shows you all of the steps needed to set up your own TinyWebDB Service. The TinyWebDB service is used throughout the book as a Web database service. With a few minutes investment, you create your own Web service for your applications to store and interchange data.

Downloadable Project Files and Bonus Content

For most of the projects, you need to download the project files and extract them to a location on your computer where you can find them easily later. When you're finished with each application, it will be fully functioning and can be loaded onto most Android devices. The project files can be downloaded from www.wiley.com/go/appinventorandroid.

Also on the Web site, you will find a Bonus Chapter called "Sprite Interaction: A Physics Primer." This more advanced chapter appears on the Web as a downloadable .PDF viewable with Adobe Acrobat Reader.

About This Book

This book follows a few typographical conventions for the sake of clarity. New terms appear in an *italic* font. URLs and special terms (such as block, event, or procedure names) appear in a monospaced font. Text you should type also appears in a monospaced font.

Part I

In Part I, you stick your toe into the waters of App Inventor. Chapter 1 gets you started right away by walking you through the creation of a simple app as a way to get familiar with the App Inventor user interface. Chapter 2 is a primer on programming and design fundamentals. In that chapter, I cover how to refine design goals, work with primitives, and introduce you to must-know programming terminology.

If you are a more advanced App Inventor user, you may want to flip right to Part II to get started building some more challenging apps.

chapter 1

Building Your First App While Exploring the Interface

APP INVENTOR IS an incredible new system from Google that allows Android applications to be designed and programmed with a Web page and Java interface. With very little programming knowledge, you can use App Inventor to create simple applications for yourself and your friends. With continuing experience with App Inventor, you can create very complex and powerful applications with App Inventor.

If you have ever had a flash of brilliance and thought, "There should be an app for that!," take heart. App Inventor makes it possible for you to create that app. If you don't yet have that incredible and exciting idea for an application, building the projects in the following chapters is very likely to spark an idea for your own Android application. I recommend keeping a notebook nearby to jot down application ideas as you do each of the projects. Many applications that are built with App Inventor are person- or group-specific. Your church, civic group, or circle of friends could well benefit from a common app that may exist but is not tailored for your group. Keep in mind that you don't have to reinvent the wheel, but you can invent a nicer custom wheel with custom engraving and nice spinners.

If you have not signed up for an App Inventor account, you need to sign up at `http://appinventor.googlelabs.com/`. You need to have a Gmail or Google Apps account to sign up.

NOTE   If you have not set up your computer and phone to work with App Inventor, turn to Appendix A and follow the steps to get set up for App Inventor programming.

Starting a New Project

To get started creating a project, start by logging into App Inventor with the account that you signed up with. If you have never logged in to App Inventor before, you see the About or Learn pages of the App Inventor Web site. Depending on whether you have logged in before and created a project, you may see the My Projects view or the Design view. If you are in the middle of building a project, App Inventor remembers the last loaded application and starts in Design view.

In this chapter and Chapter 2, you start your first project, a simple soundboard that plays a single sound when the user taps a button on the user interface. I have chosen this as a starting project instead of a traditional "Hello, World" app because App Inventor is very untraditional. It lets you do so much more, so quickly.

To start a project from the My Projects view, follow these steps:

1. From the My Projects page (shown in Figure 1-1), click the New button. This brings up the New App Inventor for Android Project dialog box.

2. When prompted, type SounDroid (or any other name you like) in the Project Name field. Keep the project name descriptive of what you are trying to do until you are completely done with all the flashy awesomeness. At the end, you can use Save As from the Design view and give your app a cool marketing-oriented name like Appzilla, but for now, a catchy name like Appzilla won't help you pick the app out of the crowd of apps and test projects you may soon have in your My Projects screen.

3. Click OK.

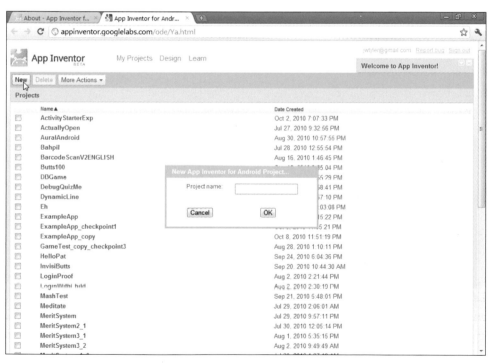

FIGURE 1-1:
Name your new project in the Project Name field

The Design view screen loads with a blank project, as shown in Figure 1-2. This is where you start placing design elements and components for your app. I explore this view thoroughly in the "Getting Familiar with Design View" section later in this chapter.

Palettes   Components   Properties

FIGURE 1-2:
The Design view
for your new
project

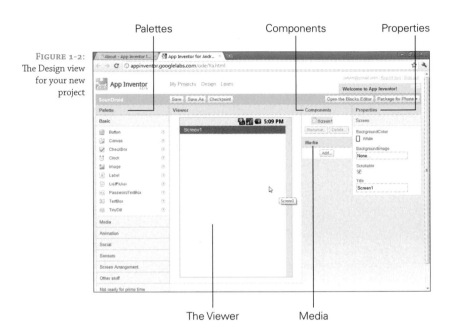

The Viewer   Media

The blank rectangle in the center of the screen is known as the Viewer. It's roughly analogous to the screen of your phone. You can see a notification bar with battery, time, and network icons in it, just like your phone has. Still, you must remember that what you see in Design view is not what you will see on your phone. This is why you should start designing your application with your phone connected to your computer and App Inventor connected to your phone. You need to test your app on a real phone. Follow these steps to connect everything and get ready to test:

1. Connect your phone to a USB port on your computer. By connecting the phone to App Inventor and then returning to Design view, you can drop buttons, pictures, and text fields onto the blank canvas and see how they will look when the application is complete.

2. Open the Blocks Editor by clicking the Open the Blocks Editor button, as shown in Figure 1-3. This launches the Java Web start program that is the Blocks Editor. Your browser downloads a Java file and, hopefully, also starts it.

NOTE   Java Web Start programs are applications that launch from your Web browser, but run as separate programs. The Blocks Editor is a part of App Inventor that runs separately from your browser. If you have trouble starting the Blocks Editor Java Web Start program, refer to Appendix A for set-up and troubleshooting help.

3. If the Blocks Editor doesn't start automatically, find the file you downloaded in the previous step and double-click to start it. If you receive a security warning, select the Always Trust Content from This Provider check box and click OK.

Open the Blocks Editor

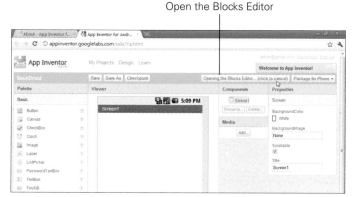

FIGURE 1-3: Clicking the Open Blocks Editor button downloads and starts the Blocks Editor

If these steps do not work for you, turn to Appendix A to find out how to set up your phone and computer. Likewise, if you have trouble starting the Blocks Editor, see Appendix A for help with setting up Java for your computer and browser.

WARNING

App Inventor application programming consists of two interfaces: the Design view and the Blocks Editor. Programming in App Inventor is done with colorful blocks that are designed to snap together like puzzle pieces. The blocks are like words that, when snapped together, form sentences of instruction to your phone. The Blocks Editor is the interface that allows you to put all those puzzle pieces . . . er, blocks . . . together. We explore the Blocks Editor in more detail later in the section, "Introducing the Blocks Editor." For now, don't be distracted by all the pretty buttons.

When the Blocks Editor launches, you see a Connect to Phone button in the ribbon at the top of the Blocks Editor window on the right side. Click the Connect to Phone button (see Figure 1-4). This starts the process of sending the necessary information to your phone to connect to App Inventor. After App Inventor is successfully connected to your phone, as you change the application in the Design view and the Blocks Editor, you see the changes both in design and functionality reflected on your connected phone. While App Inventor is connected to your phone, the Connect to Phone button changes to Restart Application. You may need to restart the application if its behavior on the phone does not match what you expect or it doesn't update appropriately.

The Connect to Phone button

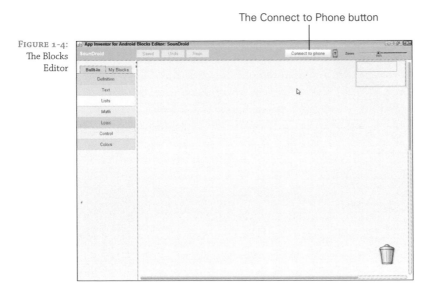

When you see the white blank screen appear on your phone, you can minimize the Blocks Editor and switch back to Design view in your browser.

Getting Familiar with Design View

Putting together a complete App Inventor application requires two major steps. First, you use the Design view to add components to your project. Some of the components you add are visible, such as buttons, labels, and text fields. These visible components make up your user interface. The user interface (or UI) is the part of the application that your user interacts with. The other kind of components you add from the Design view are functional but non-visual components, such as those for database functionality and screen arrangement. In the following sections, I help you explore the interface as you put together your first application.

The Design view is laid out in five basic columns from left to right:

○ Palette

○ Viewer

○ Components

❍ Media

❍ Properties

The Media and Components columns are stacked on top of each other. In the next several sections, I go into more detail about each of the columns in Design view, but the best way to get an idea of what these columns do is to use them. Throughout the remainder of this chapter, I guide you through an example project, step by step. Take time to understand what each area of Design view does as you build the SounDroid project.

The Palette column

The Palette column contains all the components you can add to your project. It is subdivided into groups of related components, much like you would see colors grouped on an artist's paint palette. You explore and use these components throughout this book. You can open a Palette grouping by clicking on its name. Clicking on the Social grouping of components, for example, closes the other Palette groups and exposes the Social group of components you can add to give your project social interactions such as phone calls, e-mails, and Twitter feeds. Click on each of the Palette groups to get a feel how these groups appear and disappear. As you get started, you will open and close these groups a lot until you are familiar with where the component you want is located. The Basic palette contains simpler components such as Buttons, Labels and Text fields, whereas the Animation Palette contains sprites, canvasses, and other more advanced components. For right now, click on the Basic Palette grouping to open the Basic components.

The Viewer column

Clicking on any component in the pseudo-phone display in the Viewer column makes it the active component and highlights the component name in the Components column. Making a component the active component also changes the properties that are displayed in the Properties column to the properties or settings you can set for a component.

The Components column

The Components column is a list of all the components you have added to your project. The components arrange themselves in a branching tree structure (see Figure 1-5), with screen arrangement components being the top level. When you get lots and lots of components, this structure allows you to collapse sections of the list to give freer access to some of the components.

FIGURE 1-5:
The
Components
column for a
complex project
showing the tree
structure

Media column

The Media column is located directly under the Components column (see Figure 1-6). This column lets you manage all media components for your application and add any supported media type. You can upload pictures, clip art, sounds, music, or movies to the Media column. You can also add media directly to the properties of some component that uses the media using the add file drop-down list from the property. Media that is added to your App Inventor project is uploaded from your local computer to the App Inventor server. All media files that you upload to a single App Inventor project cannot total more than 5MB. (That limitation may be increased as the App Inventor project matures.)

In the Media column, you can remove or download media from your project by clicking the media name and selecting Download or Delete. Keep the names of your media concise and meaningful because you cannot rename media after you upload it to the App Inventor server. Also, very long filenames can have a weird effect on Design view by causing the Media column to expand and squash the Viewer window.

FIGURE 1-6:
The Media
column is under
the Components
column

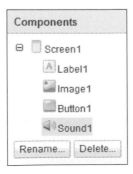

The Properties column

Every component that you add to your project has settings to change how the component looks and interacts with other components in your application. Most of the properties for your components can be set in the Properties column or changed with blocks in the Blocks Editor when a given trigger occurs in your application. For instance, when a user presses a certain button, the text content or color can be changed.

Each time you place a component that you are unfamiliar with, take a few moments to browse the fields in the Properties column. Some of the components, such as the ActivityStarter, have unique and confusing properties. Throughout this book, I explain new properties as you use them.

Adding Components to Your New Project

To add components to your application, click the component you want and drag it onto the Viewer window in Design view. The representation of your phone is labeled `Screen1`. Every project starts with a default component called `Screen1`, and its `Title` property or label is set to `Screen1`. Think of this default screen component as the blank sheet of paper on which you will design your application. All App Inventor components have settings called *properties*. Properties are set in the Properties column when a component is selected in the Viewer. The Block Editor can also be used to change component properties on the fly when events occur in your application. (More on that later, in the section called "Introducing the Block Editor.") I show you how to replace the default Screen1 title with the title of your application when you get to the Properties column in this chapter. Your application name shows up where you see the text `Screen1` in the Viewer. As you add components to the screen, the components fill in from top to bottom of the Viewer, not left to right. In Chapter 3, I show you how to arrange your components across the screen or vertically and how to simulate multiple screens for your application. For now, open the Basic palette grouping by clicking on it.

> Currently, App Inventor does not support multiple screen components. This is a limitation that many find frustrating. In Chapter 4, I show you a clever and easy way to emulate multiple screens for your application. The development team for App Inventor is hard at work on providing the multiple screen capability.

NOTE

Adding a Button component

As a demonstration, open the Basic palette and drag and drop a Button component on to the Viewer. A button shows up not only on the Viewer but also on your connected Android phone.

A button allows you to interact with the users of your application. The users tap it and things happen. Buttons, as you might well expect, play a big part in almost all applications. They provide events that you can tie actions to. Every time you drop any component onto the Viewer, a new component drawer and new blocks are added to the My Blocks tab in the Block Editor. The blocks are stored in *drawers*. The drawers are accessed by clicking the corresponding button on the left side of the Blocks Editor. Click over to the Blocks Editor to see the new component drawer and blocks: If you have minimized the Blocks Editor, it will be in your system taskbar. Click the icon to maximize it. If the Blocks Editor is closed, you need to open it by clicking the Open the Blocks Editor button. When you have the Blocks Editor open, you see two tabs labeled Built-In and My Blocks in the far left column of the Blocks Editor. Click on the My Blocks tab. All of the components you add to the Design view create a new component *drawer*. (See Figure 1-7.) Click on the Button1 rectangle to open the component drawer for your new button. All of the blocks for the button you placed on the Design view are in this drawer.

My Blocks component drawers

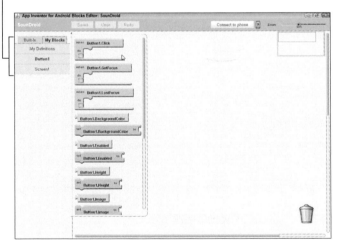

FIGURE 1-7:
The drawer for your new Button component and all of its programming blocks

Some of these blocks answer the question, "What should happen when something happens to this button?" Others manipulate and change the properties of the button, such as its size, text, or visibility. You add the button in the Design view, but you make it react and do stuff with the Block Editor. I show you how to use these blocks to add logic and function to your new application in the section, "Introducing the Blocks Editor," later in this chapter. For now, click back to the Design view to add more components.

Adding a Label component

Click on and drag a Label component from the Basic palette onto the Viewer screen. Once again, you see your new label show up on your connected Android phone. A label allows you to place text and display information on your screen. It also places blocks into the Block Editor that allow you change and manipulate the label properties and text. Just like with the button you placed, you can use blocks that change the label properties such as size, visibility, or text. Labels can be used to display information that your application generates.

By default, the label drops below the button you placed on Screen1. You can drag components around to reorder them on Screen1. Click on the label and drag it above the button. As you drag the label, you see a blue place indicator line, like the one you see in Figure 1-8, indicating where the label will drop when you release it.

FIGURE 1-8:
The blue line indicates where component will be placed when it is dropped

Blue indicator line

Adding an Image component

Drag an Image component from the Basic palette onto the Viewer and drop it on Screen1. The Image component allows you to display images and photos in your application. Just like with the previous two components, adding the Image component has created a new drawer and blocks in the My Blocks section of the Blocks Editor. The image component has dropped to last place in the viewer just like the previous component did. Click the image component and drag it until the blue place indicator is between the Label and the Button and then drop it. You set the properties for the Image component, such as what image to display and what size it should be, when you get to the Properties column.

Adding a Sound component

Some of the components you add to your App Inventor projects are not visible design elements. Some of the components add other functionality for your application but will not be something you see on your phone.

Click the Media palette in the Palette column (see Figure 1-9). The Media palette contains components that can be dragged and dropped to the Viewer to add more cool functionality to your app. Click and drag a Sound component onto the Viewer. The Sound component is dropped below the representation of a phone in the Viewer, as shown in Figure 1-10. All non-visible components are dropped to this area below the Viewer. You can still select them to change their properties, rename them, or delete them. As with the other components you added, there is now a new drawer in the Blocks Editor that allows you to programmatically use its functionality and change the sound player's properties.

FIGURE 1-9:
The Media
palette in the
Palette column

FIGURE 1-10: The non-visible components are displayed below the Viewer

The Sound component

Keeping your project neat

The names of your block drawers and the blocks are determined by what you name the components in the Components column. Remember two very important things when you're naming your components. First, you may well have many of the same components (for example, many Button components) in your project, so it's important to name the component according to what it does. It's a lot easier to read and compose the blocks when their names indicate exactly what they do. A name like btnPlaySoundButton leaves no doubt as to what happens when the button is tapped. A name like Button14, on the other hand, can easily be confused with Button41, which might close the application. Make sure your components are named not only for what they do but what they are. Some of the blocks for different components are visually similar. A name like btnPlaySoundButton helps distinguish the button that is *tapped* to play the sound from the component that actually *plays* the sound, which might be a player component known as PlaySound.

The second very important point to remember is that all the names across all components and all defined blocks in the Block Editor must be unique. When you start working in the Block Editor, you will be defining blocks that were not created by adding a component. These so-called *defined blocks* in the Block Editor cannot have the same name as other components in your App Inventor project. Duplicate names in App Inventor generate nasty errors.

At this point, your project should look like Figure 1-11, with Label, Image, Button, and Sound components. They all have default text and properties. Notice that the view on your connected Android phone is not necessarily what you see on the screen in Design view. That difference becomes even more obvious as you add more elements and arrangements to your projects. That's why it's a really good idea to have your phone plugged in and connected as you create the interface design of your application. Having your phone plugged in and connected is not a necessity for designing or editing the blocks. However, you only know what your application looks like and really does when the phone is connected and receiving real-time instruction from App Inventor.

FIGURE 1-11:
Your developing
application
interface

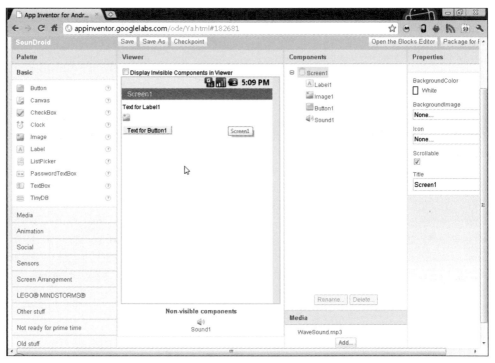

Renaming the Screen component

The Screen component is renamed slightly differently from every other kind of component. Select the Screen1 component in the Component column. Anytime you select a component in the Components column, it becomes the active component and the Properties column changes to show you the component's properties. The properties for the Screen component are fairly simple. Using the Properties column, you can set the background color, background image, whether the screen is scrollable (more on that later), and the screen title. To rename the Screen component, click in the Text field, change the screen name to SounDroid, and press Enter. Notice that the title on the Viewer and on your phone changes as soon as you press Enter.

Renaming the Image component

Make the Image component the active component by clicking it in the Viewer or in the Component column. Click the Rename button in the Component column. Rename the Image component WavPicImage and click OK. Notice that different properties are now available than were for the Screen component. You can set the image, the image width, and image height in the Properties column. Open the Blocks Editor and click the My Blocks tab, and then click WavPicImage to see the drawer for your button. There are two ways you can add an picture file for your image component. You can add the picture file directly to the image by clicking the Picture property in the Properties column and then clicking the Add button that will be displayed. Alternatively, you can add all of your pictures and other media to the Media column and then select the picture you want when you click the Picture property in the Properties column. You will add a picture for the Image component to display later, when you get to the Media column.

Renaming the Label component

Click the Label component in the Viewer or the Components column to make it the active component and then click the Rename button in the Components column. Rename the Label1 component as SoundNameLabel. You use this label to display information about your program. You can tell the label what text to display using the Text property in the Properties column, or you can add text or change the text using logic or events in the Blocks Editor.

Renaming the Button component

Make the Button1 component the active component by clicking the component in the Viewer or the Components column. Click the Rename button in the Components column and rename the button SoundPlayButton.

Renaming the Sound component

Click the Sound component below the Viewer or in the Components column to make it the active component. Click the Rename button in the Components column and rename the

Sound component WaveSound in the Rename Component pop-up box. I show you how to add a sound for the sound player and an image for the Image component next.

Adding sound for the Sound component

For each of the projects in this book, you'll need to download some project files from the companion Web site. Normally, the project files contain the application icon file and any images and sounds for the project. See this book's Introduction for more on downloading the project files. To add sound for the Sound component, follow these steps:

1. Click the Add button in the Media column.

2. Click the Browse button in the Upload File dialog box that pops up.

3. Navigate to where you saved the Chapter 01 project files.

4. Click the file wavesound.mp3 and then click Open.

5. Click the OK button on the Upload File dialog box (Figure 1-12) to upload the WaveSound.mp3 from your project file location.

   When the upload completes, you see the WaveSound.MP3 file in the listed media.

6. After the media (either pictures, sounds, or movies) is in the Media column, you can click on the media file to download it to your computer or delete it.

FIGURE 1-12:
The Upload File
dialog box

Adding images for the Image component

To add an image for the Image component, follow these steps:

1. Click the Image component to make it the active component.

   In the Properties column, you see all the properties for the Image component.

2. Click the Picture field in the Properties column that contains the text None.

   A list of available media for this component drops down, as shown in Figure 1-13. Three buttons appear at the bottom of the list: Add, Cancel, and OK.

3. Click the Add button to get the Upload File pop-up that you got in the previous section when you clicked on the Add button in the Media column.

4. Click the Choose File button, locate the WaveImage.png from your project file location, and click the file.

5. Click the Open button and then click the OK button in the Upload File pop-up.

Your file shows up in the Media column just as the media added from the Media column did. The Image component allows you to use the following image formats:

- .JPG
- .GIF
- .PNG
- .BMP

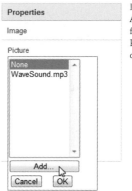

FIGURE 1-13:
Adding media
from the
Properties
column

Understanding properties

Many of the components you use in App Inventor share some common properties. These properties, such as size, color, and shape, are usually set in the Properties column and left fairly static. Keep in mind that you can change many of these later using programming blocks in the Block Editor.

Think of a component's properties as the settings that set how it looks and acts, as well as any component-specific settings such as the Picture property for the Image component. In the following section, you start setting some of these properties. The changes you make to the properties of a component may not necessarily be immediately apparent in the Viewer on the Design view.

Setting Image component properties

Make the Image component active by clicking it in the Viewer or in the Components column. The properties for the Image component are now displayed in the Properties column.

Click the Width property field and enter 150, and then click OK. This sets the width equal to 150 pixels. Click the Height property field, set the height to 100 pixels, and click OK. Clicking the text field for the Picture in the Properties column lets you select an image from the images uploaded to the Media column or upload a new image by clicking the Add button.

The Visible check box property is shared by most of the user interface components. At first, you might think it's nonsensical to add a component and then make it invisible. Remember, however, that you can change these properties with the blocks when certain trigger events occur in your application. You may have a picture, for instance, that displays a "Game Over" message, but is set to invisible in the Properties column. When the user's score in your application reaches a certain point, you display the "Game Over" image by changing the Visible property with blocks in the Blocks Editor. I cover changing properties based on Blocks Editor logic in later chapters when I delve into more advanced projects.

Any image that you upload to the Media column will have its own default size. For instance, you might upload an image that is 640 pixels by 480 pixels. The display size of most Android devices is considerably less than 640X480. You need to set the appropriate size for your images by using the Width and Height properties. Each phone has its own default pixel size and you may need to adjust the Width and Height properties to make your image look right on your application. It is a good idea to place and size images with your phone connected to your computer and connected with the Blocks Editor. This allows you to see instantly both the size of the image compared to your phone screen and how the image will look when it's resized. Try to keep the size of your images reasonable. Both space used and upload time are valuable commodities.

Resize the images on your computer *before* you upload them. Most modern digital cameras create file resolutions and file sizes far too large to be of any real use in App Inventor. NOTE

Click on the `Width` property field. A pop-up box presents you with three options:

○ **Automatic:** The Automatic button takes the image size from the default size of the image that you uploaded. If your image has a default size of 1,400 pixels by 900 pixels, your poor little Android phone will only show the tiniest part of the picture. It's best to make your images close to the size you intend to use them, but an image that's a *little* too large is okay because sizing it down in your Image component makes the image look better. On the other hand, sizing an image *up* from its native size makes it look pixelated and fuzzy.

○ **Fill Parent:** The Fill Parent option sizes your image to completely fill the screen on your phone. Currently, App Inventor does not currently allow you to "stack" images or components, so only use Fill Parent if in fact you want that component to fill the entire screen when it is visible. You might actually want to do that with our previous example of a Game Over image. Your Game Over image could fill the screen, but be set with the `Visible` property unchecked. When your user fails to win your game, you could set the Visible property to `true` and fill the user's phone screen with a "You has FAIL" image.

○ **Pixels:** The Pixels option allows to you specify the size of the component in pixels. Be careful when setting Image components manually. If you change the ratio of height to width, you could end up squashing or stretching your image in disturbing ways.

Setting Label component properties

Make your Label component the active component by clicking it in the Viewer or in the Components column. When you do so, you see a lot more properties appear in the Properties column. This label displays a name for our sound on our soundboard. The Label component has `Height` and `Width` properties as does the Image component. Set the `Width` property of the label component to 150 and leave the `Height` property set at `Automatic`. These properties act much like the Image component's `Height` and `Width` properties. When these properties are set to `Automatic`, the label expands or contracts to fit the text that the label contains.

You can see this behavior by clicking in the Text property field, typing a long string of text, and pressing Enter. The label expands to fit the text. You should see this behavior in both the Viewer and on your connected Android phone. Restricting just one dimension of the label size allows the other dimension to expand to accept the text. If you set the label width to 100 pixels and then enter a very long string of text, the label never expands wider than 100 pixels, but it will continue to expand in height to accommodate the text. The Viewer lets a really long string of text run off the edge of the Viewer if you have the Width set to Automatic. However, on your device, the label will never actually be wider than your device screen. This is another good reason to design your user interface with your phone connected to App Inventor.

Next, set the Alignment property of your label to right. The Alignment property allows you to control how the text inside your label justifies. *Justification* is a typesetter term for which side of the page the text is filled in from. In other words, selecting left alignment fills text in from the left side of your label. Center alignment centers it, and right alignment fills text in from the right. The Alignment property does not have a logic block to change justification/alignment in the Blocks Editor. Besides, it's unlikely you would want to change the alignment of a label after it is set in the Design view's Properties column.

The BackgroundColor property looks a little like a check box, but is in fact a color picker. If you click the square below the BackgroundColor property title, you get a drop-down list of colors for your button. Use it to pick a color for the background of your label. The background color can be set in the Properties column or in the Blocks Editor. You could, for instance, set a label reporting a player's health in a game to turn red when the health value drops to a critical point. For the purpose of your first application, leave the default color of None selected.

The Font settings of Bold and Italic can be set using the check boxes. When they are selected, all text that is placed in the label either from the Properties column or with the blocks in the Blocks Editor take on that font face. The Bold and Italic settings do not have Properties blocks in the Blocks Editor.

The FontSize property allows you to set the size of the text in your label. The default font size of 14.0 is a little small for most applications. Click in the FontSize property text field and replace 14.0 with 20. The size of the text shown in the Viewer and the connected phone increases.

The `Typeface` property allows you to select from a limited set of text types. You can select Serif, Sans Serif, or Monospace. Select the three options to see the differences. For the purposes of this project, use the default. There are no blocks for the `Typeface` property, so you can't change the typeface with blocks in the Blocks Editor.

The `Text` property is the critical property that allows you to place information on your label. Click in the text field, type `Relaxing Wave Sound`, and then press Enter. You should see the text on your label change both in the Viewer and on your connected phone. If you prefer, you can leave the Properties column's Text field empty and then populate it later when the application populates the `Text` property with blocks in the Blocks Editor.

The `TextColor` property offers another color picker when clicked. Click the box under the `TextColor` property label and select `Blue` to make your text blue.

The `Visible` property works just like all the other component visibility properties. It allows you to start an application with elements of your user interface invisible and to make it appear when certain conditions such as a button press occur. Likewise, you can remove components from visibility by changing the `Visibility` property with the blocks in the Blocks Editor.

Setting Button component properties

The Button component has a property that can be used much as the `Visible` property is used. The Enable button allows you to decide if you want a button to be available when your application starts or at some point later based on events in your application. Unlike the `Visible` property, a button that has the `Enable` property disabled is still visible. It is not usable, however. For this project, you leave the button enabled.

The `Alignment` property works exactly as you saw previously with the Label component. Your button text can be center-, left-, or right-aligned. Leave it centered for this project.

Buttons can be made pretty or informative by putting an image on them. The button takes the size of the image you load onto it if the `Width` and `Height` properties are set to `Automatic`. If you manually set the `Width` and `Height` properties, the image is scaled to fit the button size. It is generally a good practice to load an image slightly larger than you intend the button to be. That allows the image on the button to be crisp. You can load an image onto a button by clicking the text field in the Properties column under Image and either selecting a picture previously loaded into the Media column or using the Add button to upload an image. For this project, you won't use an image.

The BackgroundColor, TextColor, and Font properties of Bold, Italics, Size and Typeface all behave exactly as you saw with the Label component.

The text for your button is set with the Text property. Click in the Text property field and type Play. Your button must indicate clearly what it does when tapped.

> **TIP**   Your user should feel comfortable tapping a button. The default button size is usually a bit too small for larger fingers. Increase the Width property to 100 pixels and the Height property to 75 pixels. This makes for nice large button that is easy to tap.

Setting Sound component properties

The Sound component only has two properties, Source and MinimumInterval. The Source field is a selector/uploader like you saw with the Image component. Click the Source text field to select media that you have previously uploaded to the Media column. You can also click the Add button to upload a selected sound clip. Click the Source text field and then the Add button to upload the wavesound.MP3 file from your project source files location. The Sound component is best for playing very short audio clips. Any source file used with the Sound component that is longer than about six seconds will be cut off, so it is more appropriate for sound effects than for longer music or extended sounds. Longer sounds require the Player component. You can use a broad range of popular sound formats. See Table 1-1 for supported protocols and file formats.

Table 1.1   **Supported Sound Protocols and File Formats**

Protocol	Supported File Formats
AAC	.3GP, MP4, M4A
MP3	.MP3
MIDI	.MID, .XMF, .MXMF, .RTT., .RTX, .OTA, .IMY
Ogg Vorbis	.OGG
Wave/PCM	.WAV

Introducing the Blocks Editor

After you have the entire user interface (UI to the geeks) in place, it's time to add logic and flow to your application. That's where the Blocks Editor comes in.

You have placed all the visible items on the Viewer and changed the properties to make them look the way you want them to. You use the Blocks Editor to tell the application what to do when it starts, when it stops, and when the user performs an action.

Programming in App Inventor is done with blocks that are colorful and shaped to snap together like puzzle pieces (see Figure 1-14). The blocks are like words that, when snapped together, form sentences that give instructions to your phone. The text on the blocks say plainly what they are for and what they expect from you. At first, the words on the block may seem foreign and daunting, but after you've done a few projects, you will know immediately what they do and be able to read the blocks like a sentence from a finely crafted novel.

The Built-In and My Blocks tabs

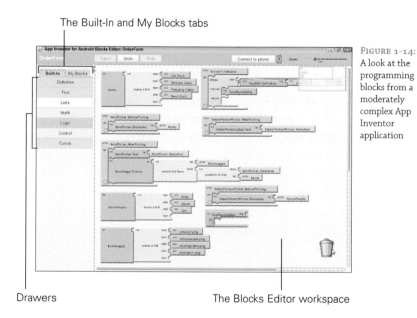

FIGURE 1-14: A look at the programming blocks from a moderately complex App Inventor application

Drawers

The Blocks Editor workspace

The blocks are stored in *drawers*. The drawers are accessed or "pulled out" by clicking the corresponding button on the left side of the Blocks Editor. The individual blocks in a drawer can then be clicked and dragged to the Blocks Editor workspace where you snap them together to represent instructions to the Android phone.

Previewing Built-in Blocks

The Blocks Editor contains two tabs: Built-In and My Blocks. Every time you drop any component onto the Viewer, a new component drawer and new blocks are added to the My

Blocks tab in the Block Editor. The Built-In blocks tab contains all the blocks drawers that have static activities and instructions. These blocks remain for you to use no matter what components you add. These blocks contain instructions such as, *make a list*. Each drawer category contains multiple blocks that you will use throughout this book. The built-in blocks work with your blocks (the ones created when you added components and the ones you create in the Blocks Editor) to create instructions for your application. The following list describes the blocks drawers found on the Built-In tab:

- ❍ **Definition drawer:** Contains blocks that allow you to define programming constructs and concepts; I explain each of these as you use them in a project throughout the book.

- ❍ **Text drawer:** Contains all of the blocks that you can use to manipulate text by creating text, joining pieces of text together, and pulling pieces of text out of other text.

- ❍ **Lists drawer:** Contains many powerful blocks that enable you to create storage containers for lists of items; traditional programmers may think of lists as arrays.

- ❍ **Math drawer:** Contains those math function blocks that you tried to avoid through high school, such as exponent, modulus, and cosine; these functions let you do nearly any mathematical function, including very advanced math.

- ❍ **Logic drawer:** Contains the blocks that help your program make rational decisions, such as Yes, No, True, False, "Are these two things alike?" and "Are these two things different?"

- ❍ **Control drawer:** Contains a wonderland of odd and peculiar-looking blocks that allow you to control the flow and progression of your application by using program "sentences" that give commands, such as "If the button is pressed, do something, but if it isn't pressed, do something else."

- ❍ **Colors drawer:** Contains blocks that allow you to easily set the color of items in your user interface; all colors for your Android application in App Inventor are represented by numbers, and these blocks make it easy to plug the right numbers for basic colors into your application.

These can be found on the My Blocks tab, which contains all the component blocks that you created when you placed components in Design view; each component you placed and named has a button to open that component's drawer:

○ **My Definitions drawer:** Contains all the blocks that you create or define using the Definitions drawer under the Built-In tab; these blocks are not created when you add a component but rather when you drag a block from the Definitions drawer.

○ **Your Components Blocks drawer:** Beneath the My Definitions drawer are the drawers for the components you have added in Design view; clicking a component name opens the drawer and allows you to drag out blocks that are events, methods, (things that happen to or with the component), or properties.

Placing Your Button Component Blocks

Make sure you are in the Blocks Editor screen. Click the My Blocks tab and then click the SoundPlayButton. This opens the drawer for the Button component you placed and renamed. Click and drag the when `SoundPlayButton.Click` do block onto the Blocks Editor workspace. This is an event button that tells you fairly plainly what it does. If you read the words on the block, you can see that it follows a pattern: `<yourcomponentname>.<event>`. With a little imagination, you can read it as, "When my button named SoundPlayButton is clicked, do what is held in this block."

All blocks shaped with the large socket can contain other blocks that are sets of instructions that are acted on when some set of conditions are met. In this case, the condition that needs to be met is "When my button is clicked." Now you need to tell your application what to do when the button is clicked. You add that instruction in the next section.

Placing Your Sound Component Blocks

To place your Sound component blocks, follow these steps:

1. Open the WaveSound drawer that contains all the blocks for your sound player by clicking it.

2. Drag the `call WaveSound.Play` block out onto the Blocks Editor workspace.

   This is a method call. A method call performs a series of more complex or prepackaged instructions. This block is prepackaged instructions on how to play the sound file you uploaded into the Media column earlier in this chapter.

3. Drag the `call WaveSound.Play` method between the arms of the when `SoundPlayButton.Click` event and drop it.

Notice that the notch in the top of the `play` method snaps into the tab on the event with a satisfying click.

Now whenever the event occurs, the method is called. In other words, "When `SoundPlayButton` is clicked, call the `WaveSound.Play`." Your Blocks Editor workspace should look like Figure 1-15.

FIGURE 1-15:
The blocks for
your SounDroid
application so
far

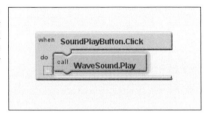

Test your application on your connected Android phone by tapping the Play button. You should hear an amazing soothing Zen-like sound from your Android phone. You have at this point built a complete Android application. Congratulations! For now, it is only on App Inventor and not loaded into your phone. Next, I tell you about your options for your completed application.

Putting the final touches on your project

Most application projects are very dynamic. They tend to evolve over time. App Inventor provides you with the tools to handle the next steps after you are happy with your project, when you want to branch your application into some new and improved application with the Checkpoint save, or of course to finally to load it onto your phone and other phones.

Click to back over to your browser where the App Inventor Design view is running. In the next section, you learn how to save, fork (a traditional programming word for changing the original intent or direction of an application), and install your application.

Saving your new application

Google is really good at making sure you don't lose your hard work accidentally. Your project work is saved every time you change anything. Your app is periodically synchronized from your browser to the App Inventor servers whenever you make a change. App Inventor has a Save button, but you will probably seldom use it. (Just in case you need to, however, the Save button is at the top center of your Design view just above the Viewer column.)

The Save As button

The Save As button, located directly above the Viewer in the Design view, allows you to save your current project with a different name. By default, it appends the text _copy to the current project name, as shown in Figure 1-16. You can, however, change the name to anything you like as long as it is unique among your projects. After you click the OK button to save a copy, you are working on the newly named copy of your project, but the old name and project still exist in the My Projects window.

FIGURE 1-16:
Save As lets you continue work on the same project but with a new name

The Checkpoint button

Unlike the Save As button, the Checkpoint button next to the Save and Save as buttons lets you save a copy of your project to a new name as it currently is but continue working on the original project. By default, the Checkpoint button appends _checkpoint# to your existing project name, as shown in Figure 1-17, and stores the check point in your My Projects window. The Checkpoint window also shows you previous checkpoints of the same project in the Previous Checkpoints area.

FIGURE 1-17:
Checkpoints are saved copies of your project that do not change your project name

REMEMBER The important distinction between the Save As and the Checkpoint button is that clicking the Save As button means that you work on the newly named project after you click OK but leave your original project in the My Projects window. Clicking the Checkpoint button, on the other hand, leaves the newly named copy of your project in the My Projects window and you continue working on your original project. The Checkpoint should be considered a "safe point" that you can roll your project back to if you break something as you develop a project. The Save As and Checkpoint buttons are very simple version-control features. Traditional programming uses versions such as 1.0, 2.0, 2.1 and so on to reflect changes in an application. You can use the Checkpoint and Save buttons to do the same thing.

Packaging your app

When your application is at a level of awesome that begs to be put on your phone or some-one else's phone, you have to package it. *Packaging* is the process of taking all of the user interface elements, all the blocks from the Blocks Editor and all of your media and turning it into code that your Android device understands. The Design view, as shown in Figure 1-18, has a Package for Phone button that allows you to select from three options for packaging your app: Show Barcode, Download to This Computer, and Download to Connected Phone. I explain these options in the next few sections. The Blocks Editor *must* be open for any of the packaging options to work. Whichever option you select, you see a message informing you that App Inventor is packaging the application. It can take a few minutes for the packaging to complete.

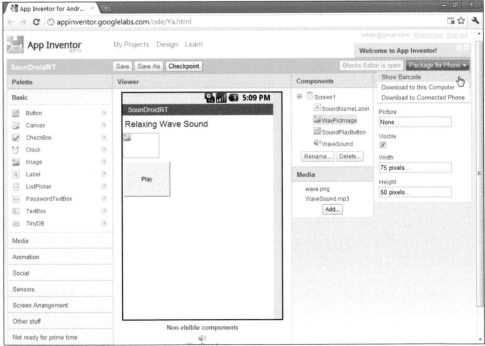

FIGURE 1-18:
The Package for
Phone drop-
down list
options

Using the Show Barcode option

When you select the Show Barcode option, your project is compiled into an .APK file. The .APK file is the final file package that will be loaded to your phone using one of the package options. With the Show Barcode option, a QR barcode pops up in the App Inventor Design view. You can then load your project onto your phone using any of the free barcode scanners for Android to scan the barcode. This method has the advantage of not needing to have your phone connected to your computer to load the application onto your phone. However, you can't share the barcode with other Android phone owners unless they too have an App Inventor account. If your phone has difficulty connecting to App Inventor or is one of the few phones that do not allow untrusted installs, you need to use this method to install App Inventor applications.

Using the Download to This Computer option

If you want to attach your application to an e-mail or load it manually to another phone, use the Download to This Computer option. Clicking the Download to This Computer option prompts you to specify a download location for your application file or automatically downloads the file to your default download folder. The downloaded file is in the format *<your project name>.apk*. The .APK files can be copied to an Android phone's SD card or e-mailed to an Android phone and installed manually. For any App Inventor .APK files to be installed, a phone must have its options set to allow installations from insecure locations. See Appendix A for more on setting up a phone to install App Inventor applications.

Using the Download to Connected Phone option

Download to Connected Phone is the option you will use most often. For this option to work, your phone must be connected to your computer and connected using the Connect to Device button on the Blocks Editor. (See Appendix A if you need a refresher on how to connect your phone.) When you select the Download to Connected Phone option, the project that is currently active is packaged and loaded onto your connected Android phone. You then receive a pop-up that informs you that the transfer was successful. It shows up like any other application in your phone's list of applications, with its name being the name of your project.

Use the Download to Connected Phone option to download the SounDroid application you created in this chapter to your phone. Congratulations! You have created and loaded your first Android application.

Managing Your Projects

App Inventor is a Web-based application. That means that your projects and all of your work stay in Google's *cloud*. Cloud computing gives you access to your work via the Internet and remote servers so that you don't have to install apps or store files on your local computer.

That way, nothing is stored on your local computer until you explicitly download your applications.

After you log into App Inventor, click the My Projects link in the upper-right corner of the browser window, as shown in Figure 1-19. This takes you to the overview of all the projects you have in your App Inventor account. From here, you can control which applications you want to open and work on, download, upload, or delete.

The My Projects link

FIGURE 1-19:
The My Projects
link that leads to
your App
Inventor
projects

From the My Projects view, you can start a new project or manage and delete old projects. This screen offers only a few options, so you can become familiar with them fairly quickly. On the My Projects views, you can

○ Create a new project

○ Delete an existing project

○ Download project source code to your computer

○ Upload project source code from a colleague into your My Project view

○ Load an existing project into App Inventor

Downloading your project source code

All App Inventor projects are saved and stored on the App Inventor servers, but you can download the source code and the application to your local computer hard drive. *Source code* is composed of all the separate instructions that make up your application before they are built into your application. When you have a project that you want to share with other app developers, you can download the source code to your local computer. You can then send the source code to other app developers to upload to their App Inventor program so that they can see your brilliance. The source code allows other app developers to see and edit the code before it is packaged into an Android application.

Don't confuse the source code you download with Java source code that SDK developers use to create applications. The source code I'm talking about here is very specific to App Inventor and can only be loaded and edited by the App Inventor program. **REMEMBER**

The option to download source code is not terribly obvious: It's hidden on the More Actions drop-down list, as you can see in Figure 1-20. If you have a project you want to download the source code for, you can download it by following these steps:

1. In the My Projects view, select the box next to the project for which you want to download the source code.

2. Click the More Actions drop-down arrow.

3. Click Download Source.

4. If your browser is set up to automatically download files to a default directory without asking you for confirmation, your source code downloads. If your browser prompts you to confirm whether you want to Save or Run the source code, you should choose Save.

The file you download is saved to your default download directory unless you choose to save it to a different location. The source code for an App Inventor project consists of one .ZIP file — a single file that contains one or more files that have been compressed to reduce the overall file size.

As I mentioned earlier, you can collaborate and share projects by downloading project source code and sending it to others to upload into their App Inventor program. It's also a good idea to occasionally download the source code for your important projects to back up your projects. This protects them from accidental deletion or the extremely unlikely event of a server losing your project.

FIGURE 1-20:
Select Download
Source from the
More Actions
drop-down list

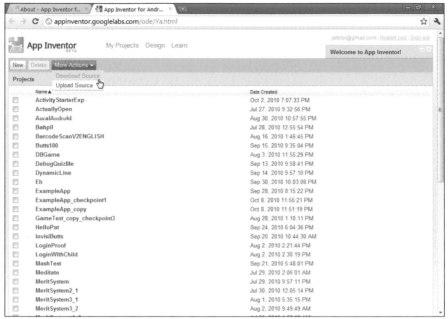

To send the source code to others, just attach the .ZIP file to an e-mail or upload it to the file-sharing site of your choice.

Uploading your project source code

When other developers send you their App Inventor projects as source code, you can see what logic they used in the Blocks Editor and learn from how they accomplished a particular goal. When you want to load source code files into your My Project view, whether from a friend or from your own backup source code, follow these steps to upload the source code from your local computer:

1. From the My Projects view, click the More Actions drop-down arrow.

2. Click the Upload Source option.

3. Click the Choose File button in the dialog box that appears.

4. Navigate to the source code you want to load. It may be in your default download directory or wherever you downloaded it from an e-mail or Web site.

5. Click the source code .ZIP file you want to upload.

6. Click Open.

The source code and all asset files are uploaded to your My Projects page. You now have a project that you can manage and edit. If a project with the same name already existed, you will get an error message when you try to upload. Change your project's name and try again.

Deleting a project

Not every project you set your hand to will turn out to be an application you want to keep around for all time. Sometime in the future, those old tutorials will probably just be in the way of all the awesomeness you have created.

Peeking inside the .ZIP file

For those of you with excessive curiosity and a love for useless trivia, the .ZIP file contains these files:

○ A folder named *Assets* that holds all your project media files.

○ A folder named src with at least one subfolder named com, which contains one additional subfolder named Gmail, which in turn contains one subfolder with your Gmail account name as its name. The folder with your Gmail account name contains a folder named after your project. If you are only familiar with a Windows-type directory structure, this structure may seem needlessly deep and complex. If you are at all familiar with the Linux operating system directory structure, however, this will be a pretty familiar structure. The directory file structure is not just about the storage location; it provides you with information about the "place" each file holds within the structure. This final folder (the one named after your project) contains the bulk of the logic part of your application. It contains a .BLK file, a .YAIL file, and a .SCM file.

○ A folder named youngandroidproject that contains a file with all the properties of your project. The Young Android Project sought to recruit and teach new programmers and was the beginning of App Inventor.

To delete a project, follow these steps:

1. From the My Projects page, check the box next to the project name.

2. Click the Delete button.

3. Verify that you want to delete the project and click OK.

WARNING Deleting a project is irreversible and you can't make something you have deleted come back, not even by begging Google really hard. I have deleted several applications accidentally, much to my chagrin and disappointment. Remember to back up your projects from time to time by downloading the source code, just in case you delete one accidentally later.

Loading an existing project

Existing projects are stored on Google's App Inventor servers. When you have lots of projects listed on your My Projects page, you can load any one of them into the App Inventor Design view and Blocks Editor by clicking the project name. When you click an existing project from the My Projects view, the source files are loaded from the App Inventor server and the screen changes to the Design view.

Programming and Design Fundamentals

THE PROJECT I detailed in Chapter 1 is known as a *soundboard*. It's a very simple sound-board, but it's a good start for our next project. It plays a short sound when a button is pushed. You built that project fairly blindly, without knowing where you were going or the reasons for the components and blocks. For the remaining projects in this book, I provide three guiding sections at the beginning of each project: a design section, a primitives section, and a progression section. Each project has these elements predesigned for you. However, for your own projects, the process of creating those statements helps you develop applications from your ideas. In this project, the design, primitives, and progression sections are broken down and each item explained.

That SounDroid application you worked on in Chapter 1 has some potential, however, so in this chapter, I show you how to take it through a design process to a second version.

In this chapter, I guide you through the thought processes and steps necessary to arrive at a list for your design goals, primitives, and progression. I explain the design goals and primitives as you move through them. Generally speaking, design goals are what you want your application to do, and primitives are the programming logic and algorithms necessary to accomplish your design goals. The progression is the order that is most logical or necessary for you to follow as you build the application.

Most of the projects in this book require that you download the project files from the book's companion site. The project files contain images such as the icons, application images, sound files, and so on. When you start a project, download the project files somewhere on your computer where you can easily find them to upload them into App Inventor. See this book's Introduction if you need instructions on how to download the project files.

Clarifying Your Design Idea

Design processes help take your awesome ideas and make them reality. There is nothing mysterious about a design process, although frequently developers give them fearsome and magical-sounding names such as *waterfall model*, *spiral model*, and *agile development*. These all refer to the same thing: logical steps that developers and programmers use to move an idea from a dream to a fully functional program. You can see a basic outline of the waterfall model in Figure 2-1. You will use a very basic and simplified form of the waterfall process in this chapter to take an idea for our SounDroid project to the next level.

All App Inventor applications start as an idea. Sometimes, the idea is born of a need, such as the firefighter in Colorado who needed an application to measure friction loss for his fire company, or the father who needed an application to track his daughter's seizures. These App Inventor apps started as a need, but sometimes, the germination of a new app is simply a desire for a certain game or communication capability. Whatever the seed of an application, it requires some fertilization and tending before it can actually be programmed.

TIP

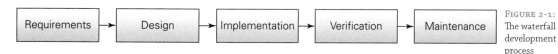

FIGURE 2-1:
The waterfall development process

○ Your design statements should clarify your original idea. So, if your original SounDroid project idea was something like "I want to create an application to play relaxing sounds," clarifying the design means identifying what you want it to do, and when and how. Begin by making a simple list of your ideas for activities and actions for your application. Your SounDroid idea might have an idea list that looks something like the following:

○ Plays relaxing sounds to aid in relaxation or meditation

○ Offers three possible sounds

○ Tracks mediation or relaxation time

These are very high-level goals that you need to turn into a design document. The first step is pencil-and-paper programming. Take your idea list, sit down with a piece of paper and pencil, and sketch what you think your application will look like. This is the classic "back of a napkin" approach that can revolutionize a market. For your SounDroid application, you might come up with something like you see in Figure 2-2.

You know that your application is going to be playing sounds, so you want a play button and a stop button for the sound next to an image. You also want a space for displaying the play time. Now you have a good starting point for refining your ideas. As you look at the sketch, you might decide that it would be more graceful and intuitive if the user could just tap the image to start the sound and tap it again to stop the sound. It would also be nice if your application had a relaxing and soothing look. Your next sketch might look like Figure 2-3.

FIGURE 2-2:
A preliminary
idea sketch for
the SounDroid
application

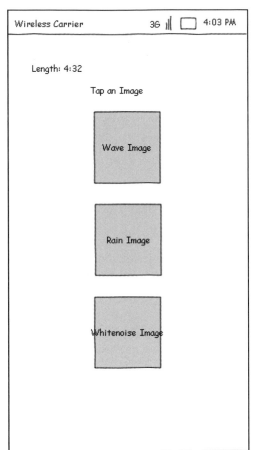

Just by giving some more thought to your idea and putting the results down on paper, you have already begun to refine the original list of ideas. Now you can flesh out that list with some specific ideas. Take the sketch and the idea and try to define with words what each element or component of the application will do. Then start listing the specific goals you have for your application. For SounDroid, you might come up with a list like the following:

○ Images that are buttons for both play *and* stop.

○ Sounds that play until stopped.

○ Three sounds to match images.

○ A timer that starts when a sound is played and stops when the sound is stopped.

○ A way to display the timer.

○ A relaxing non-intrusive background.

○ Centered orientation. (Remember from Chapter 1 that all App Inventor components fill in from the top left, so you will have to address this somehow in your implementation of your user interface. You will use a clever method for centering.)

You may go through multiple iterations of this process while developing and clarifying your idea. For more complex applications such as games or calculation applications, a single line in design requirements may be a whole bunch of primitive code when you actually design and build it. A single design goal such as "Find the greatest common denominator from two numbers" ends up being broken down into multiple mathematics operations. In this case, you are well on our way to our next step of developing the conceptual building blocks of how you as the developer will accomplish these goals.

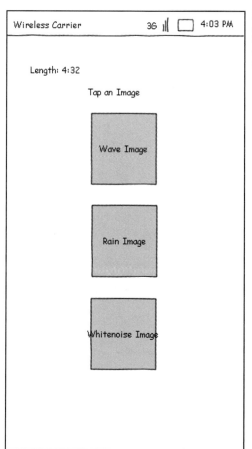

FIGURE 2-3:
A more refined
SounDroid
application
sketch

Getting Primitive with Your Design

After you know clearly what your idea really is and what your application will be expected to do, you must break it down into what each "basic" action or reaction should be. The individual ways in which your design goals are met are called *primitives*. Much like the primitive shapes — such as circles, squares, rectangles, and triangles — that are used to make up a picture, programming can be broken down to its simplest parts. See Figure 2-4. A program can be broken down into primitive steps such as an event, a reaction, or an input.

FIGURE 2-4:
Primitives used
in art
composition

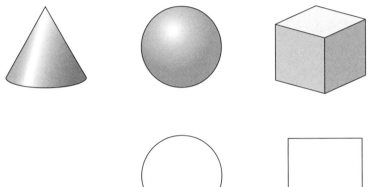

For your SounDroid project, your last idea clarification list took you pretty darn close to your primitives. In the next step, you need to clearly define what each of the design goal primitives are going to be. One way to get a grip on your primitives is to convert your list of ideas that I talked about in the last section to a bulleted list of primitives. Under each major goal, define the primitive actions to accomplish that specific goal. As you come to understand App Inventor, you will also define the App Inventor primitives here. When you're first starting on a project, you often have no idea how App Inventor will accomplish a particular task. This lack of knowing how something should be done is one of the primary reasons why you define primitives. The old saying "By the inch is a cinch, by the mile takes a while," holds true here. Take it step by step. It's far easier to figure out how to do one step, such as creating a routine to display an image and change it, for example, than it is to attempt to get your brain around an entire gallery project all at once.

Start with your previous list of ideas and begin to define the simplest possible steps to achieve that goal. Your first goal was "Images that are buttons for both play and stop." If you break that sentence down to its parts, you might get a list like this:

○ Images that are buttons for both play and stop.

    a. A button has an image.

    b. A button plays a sound.

    c. The same button should stop the sound.

The first item is obvious because we need a button that uses an image to define its shape and look. Point b and c seem to eliminate the design goal of a single button, but many times, you must start out simply and then combine simple primitives to be more complex. You have the skill to place buttons and place an image on those buttons. So after you understand how to play a sound and stop it, you can then combine those two primitives (placing an image on a button, and playing and stopping a sound) into something more complex. Frequently, how to combine simple primitives is not obvious and requires lots of troubleshooting and experimentation. Clearly defined primitives make the process easier. I guide you through the process of combining your primitives for this second version of SounDroid.

○ Three sounds to match images.

    a. Wave sound and wave image

    b. Rain sound and rain image

    c. White noise and white noise image

These primitives are pretty simple to arrive at; however, the last one does require some design decision-making. What will white noise look like on your application? For this project, I have made the decision for you (it looks like static), but this primitive would require some thought and creativity.

Your timer goal is your first real challenge. You want to display for your user the amount of time that he or she has been lulled into restful relaxing nirvana by your application. How that will be accomplished is probably pretty much a mystery to you at this point. That's okay because you can still describe an algorithm for the primitive action. An *algorithm* is just a sequence of steps to arrive at a predictable goal.

How would you as a human observer determine how long someone relaxed while sitting in front of you? Most likely, if you wanted really accurate results, you would use a stopwatch to time the passing of the seconds. So for a very accurate report on the lapsed time, you could define an algorithm that said "Start counting seconds when the sound play button is pressed. Stop counting seconds when the sound stop button is pressed. Display the total of seconds counted." That would certainly give you a very accurate view of the time, but there is usually more than one way to accomplish a goal in programming. For instance, to achieve the goal of tracking the relaxer, you might note the time they started, note the time they stopped, and subtract to find the difference. The latter is a simpler algorithm because it simply records two times and then finds the difference. Whenever you are dealing with time, timing, or dates in App Inventor, the Clock component is the root of your primitive.

So your primitive list under the timer goal might look like this:

○ A timer that starts when a sound is played and stops when the sound is stopped

    a. A record of when the sound player starts

    b. A record of when the sound player stops

    c. A record of the difference between the start and stop

○ A way to display the timer

This is an easy primitive. Displaying information on the screen is always a fairly easy primitive. With App Inventor, you use the Label component to display information on the screen. It's not the only way, but it is the primary way to display text to a user.

○ A relaxing non-intrusive background

    a. An image set as the background of the Screen1 component

NOTE The Screen1 component is a default component that every other App Inventor component is placed onto. It has properties like other components, such as background, image, and so on. You cannot place other Screen components currently with the current version of App Inventor. Throughout this book, I show you how to creatively simulate more than one Screen component. I call them VirtualScreens because they are not real screens but can be made to behave as screens.

This too is an easy primitive. You should be careful with backgrounds. Busy backgrounds can be visually distracting and keep your user from seeing important textual elements. It can also make your application look cheap and gimmicky. Backgrounds should be just that: backgrounds, not the focus of attention or distractions.

○ Centered orientation. (We need a method to counter App Inventor's default left/top down arrangement.)

   a. Padding elements to center button column

○ A centered orientation is probably the most challenging part of your design requirements. App Inventor does not easily provide for centering elements in the Viewer. However, you can use a clever technique for keeping items where you want them. It works in much the same way that Web designer's use "padding" to push elements to where they want them to be. Your primitives for pushing your centered items to the center will be empty (and therefore invisible) labels.

Your list of primitives should now be interspersed with your list of design goals. This along with your sketches of your user interface gives you a lot of guidance as you program your application. Keep in mind that goals can change and primitives can be combined or devolved even farther as you get into the nitty-gritty of making your idea come to life.

Starting Easy, Getting More Complex

As with most things in life, you're better off not attempting too much at once when developing an application. If you try to add too many features, bells, whistles, and kitchen sinks before the basic fundamentals of your program are up and running, your code and even your thinking process can get very muddled up. One of the greatest hindrances to creatively thinking about solving a programing problem is attempting to do things out of their natural progression or logical order.

Progression is the idea of starting with a basic simple level of primitives and then adding other primitives to become more complex. SounDroid 1.0 was pretty basic. Your plan for the next generation of SounDroid has several added layers and levels of complexity. To keep your thought processes clear and to keep the project moving, lay out a progressive roadmap. A *roadmap* gives you logical progression for your project. For your new design goals, you should split up the actual programming into "milestones" along the road to your completed application. The basic user interface and basic functionality should be working before you start changing them to add more functionality. Because your SounDroid project is, at its heart, a soundboard, it should first play your sounds in the way you want.

Remember that the original SounDroid only played your sound file once. Getting the sound files to loop appropriately will be enough of a challenge without adding the timer or the "pretty" parts of the user interface. SounDroid will have three major versions: SounDroid 1.0, which you built in the previous chapter as an introduction to App Inventor interface; SounDroid 2.0, which you create in this chapter; and then finally SounDroid 3.0, which you build in the next chapter following the primitives and design goals you have laid out in this chapter. Your SounDroid project should have the following milestones:

- SounDroid 2.0

  Plays the looping sound for all three sounds

  Has the basic user interface in place (buttons, labels, and centering)

- SounDroid 3.0

  Displays the time looping sound has played

- Has a polished, pretty interface

Your list of design goals and the primitive actions necessary to make them happen should look something like this:

- Images that are buttons for play and stop

  a. A button that has an image

  b. A button that plays a sound

  c. The same button should stop the sound

- Three sounds to match images

  a. Wave Sound and Wave Image

  b. Rain Sound and Rain Image

  c. White Noise and White Noise Image

- A timer that starts when a sound is played and stops when the sound is stopped

  a. A record of when the sound player starts

  b. A record of when the sound player stops

  c. A record of the difference between the start and stop

○ A way to display the timer

    a. A label for display

○ A relaxing non-intrusive background

    a. An image set as the background of screen1

○ Centered orientation

    a. Padding elements to center button column

Mastering the Fundamentals of Programming Terminology

As you move forward into completing your second version of the SounDroid project, you should get familiar with a few terms that I use consistently throughout the rest of the book. The terms I discuss in the next few section are basics and can have different inflections of meaning in different programming languages. I give you both a general and an App Inventor view of these concepts.

Events

An *event* is exactly what it sounds like: something that happens. App Inventor has event handlers that are added to many component drawers in the Blocks Editor. (See Chapter 1 for a review of drawers and components in the Blocks Editor) In programming, you use events as triggers to set off a string of reactions or calculations to process data or output something to your user. You have used an event already when you built SounDroid 1.0 in the previous chapter: the when `Button.click` do event that you used to start the sound playing. Events in App Inventor look like blocks with arms to hold other blocks, as shown in Figure 2-5, which shows some events in the Blocks Editor, with a series of instructions to be carried out when that event occurs. The proper name for these event blocks in other programming languages is *event handlers*. They "handle" the events and know what to do when they occur.

FIGURE 2-5:
A series of event
handlers in the
Blocks Editor

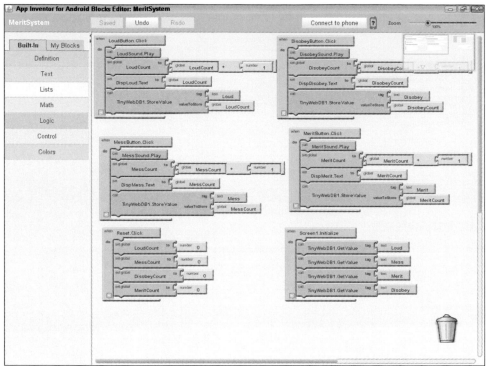

Methods

Many of the components you add to your project in the Design view have method call blocks in their Blocks Editor drawer. A *method* is a preset set of instructions and programming that allow you to use the functionality they contain, such as a set of capabilities related to playing audio. You can think of methods as miniature programs that your application accesses the functionality of and then uses to offer functions. In App Inventor, methods enable you to access a lot of functionality that a non-programmer would have a hard time implementing. When you use a method in App Inventor, you *call* it. Using a block with the *call* action word on it, as in Figure 2-6, means that you want to use that block's functionality in your application.

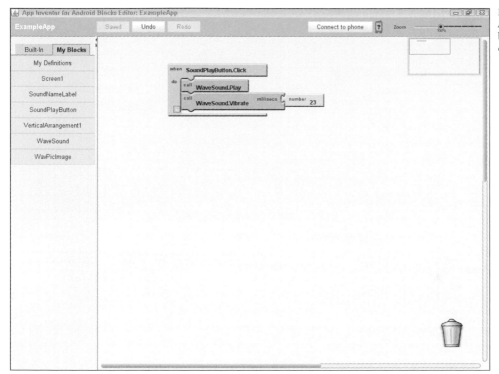

FIGURE 2-6:
A method call
being used in an
event handler

A call in App Inventor may also access functions or capabilities that are inherent to a particular component. Blocks in App Inventor can and frequently do have *sockets* that allow you to snap in other blocks. For instance, the Split At text block has a socket that allows you to define the text to split and where it should be split by snapping other blocks into it. In App Inventor, any calls to methods that are in component drawers do not have any sockets in them because they are standalone functions. Some calls have sockets that allow you to "plug in" parameters for the method call to act on or to determine the nature of how the call is activated. Many calls are to built-in App Inventor functionality. The built-in drawers in the Blocks Editor contain lots of calls to functionality such as call WaveSound.Play, which would be used to play a specific sound , as shown in Figure 2-7.

For the purposes of App Inventor, a *call* can be considered a prepackaged set of instructions **REMEMBER** that offers you functions and capabilities. Remember that the definition of a call is different in other, more traditional programming languages.

FIGURE 2-7:
Built-in call
blocks in the
Blocks Editor

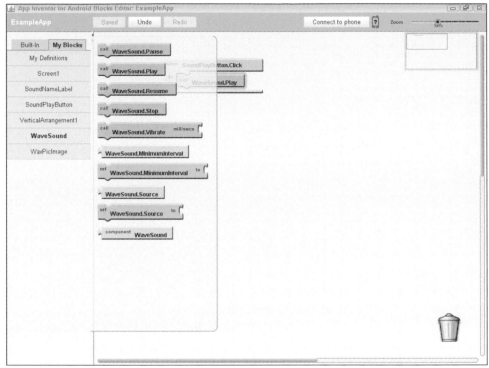

Properties

The components in App Inventor have settings that can be changed to affect the way they look, act, or interact in your application. These settings are call *properties,* and their values change the way the component functions or looks. You can for instance, change the background color using the `BackgroundColor` property in the Properties column when the Screen1 component is selected.(You saw some examples of that in the SounDroid tutorial in Chapter 1.) Some properties change the look and feel of a component, such as the `size`, `font`, and `color` properties. Some components have properties that change (make or break) the functionality of the component. Components such as the Sound player won't actually play a sound unless the sound `source` property has a correctly spelled reference to an uploaded sound file.

Some, but not all, properties can be changed by adding a block from the component's drawer and plugging the property value you wish to use into its socket. Figure 2-8 shows a sound component that has not had the `source` property value set in the Design view. Instead, the `set sound1.source to` block is used to plug a value into the sound component's `source` property. Whenever you use a property's block to change a property's settings, it overrides any value you have typed into Design view.

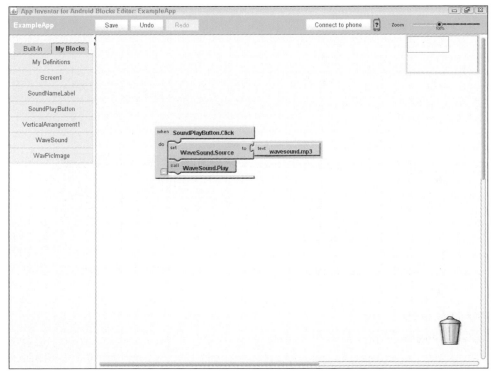

FIGURE 2-8:
A property value being set using the property set block in Blocks Editor

Variables

A variable in App Inventor is a more complex concept than any I've discussed so far. You must understand that a variable in App Inventor shares many of the same features as variables in more traditional programming languages, but is still vastly different. Variables are created or defined from the Built-In blocks drawer labeled Definition. To create a variable, drag the `variable` block from the Definitions drawer onto the workspace and give it a unique name. When you do this, it creates blocks under the My Blocks tab in the My Definitions drawer. These blocks allow you populate and reference the variable. (See Figure 2-9.)

FIGURE 2-9:
Defined
variables
populate the My
Definitions
drawer

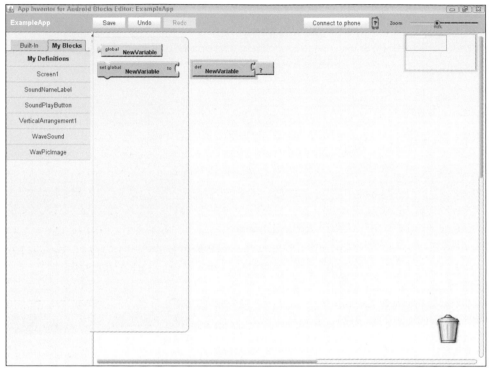

You should look at variables in App Inventor in two ways:

○ As a named storage box that we can put information into

○ As a named reference to information that is previously stored

In the first case, you are defining a variable. That is to say, you are placing words, numbers, and data into a box so you can get to them later. You could imagine a variable as a cardboard box with a masking-taped magic marker label on the side. After you label your cardboard box with a label that says something like NumberDates, you can refer to it in conversation without having to say something clumsy like "The box with 11/13/2010, 5/3/1945, and 12/25/1976 in it."

The second way of looking at variables in App Inventor is as a reference to your box with the masking tape label. The magical thing about masking tape labels is that they can be duplicated. You can tell someone, for example, to "Fetch all the pictures from a picture box that has the dates on it that match the dates listed here" and hand them a piece of masking tape with NumberDates written on it. In App Inventor, you define a variable using the Blocks Editor whenever you need to store information that you will refer to, display, or use later in your application.

Procedures

In your application, you may have a set of instructions that you want to use more than once — perhaps a mathematic series of steps to find the hours, minutes, or seconds from milliseconds stored in a variable. A *procedure* allows you to create containers of reusable instructions. A procedure is created exactly like any other definition in App Inventor: by dragging the blocks from the Definitions drawer on the Built-In tab of the Blocks Editor to the Blocks Editor workspace, as shown in Figure 2-10. Then every time you want to use that series of mathematical steps (or whatever instruction you want to reuse), you can call that procedure exactly the same way you can call a built in method. The call block is located in your My Definitions drawer.

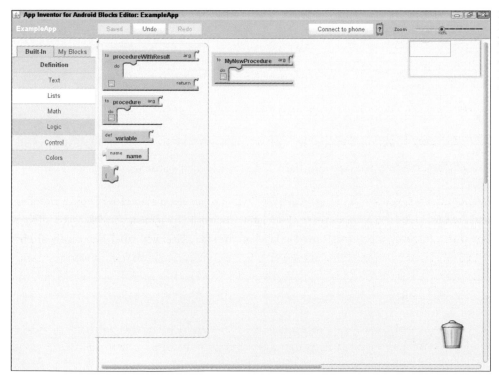

FIGURE 2-10: Defined procedures place a call block in the My Definitions drawer

A procedure then is a *subroutine* — a series of instructions that you want your application to step through and that you want to isolate for debugging or for reuse. In our previous example of using a procedure to store some mathematic steps, if the mathematical result keeps coming out wrong, you know exactly where to start troubleshooting without hunting all through all of your blocks.

There are two distinct types of procedures in App Inventor: standalone procedures, which are the kind I've already described, and procedures with arguments. Procedures with arguments behave exactly like the previous description of a standalone procedure, with one exception. A procedure with arguments allows you to pass information into the procedure and have that information processed and a value returned to your application to be used as you like. When you use a procedure with arguments, you define as many arguments as you like and blocks for those arguments are created in the My Definitions drawer.

Note: Procedures with Result has an in depth explanation and example in the second part of this book. As well as being used in projects. Procedures are important concepts and should be considered part of clean graceful programming in App Inventor.

You will use procedures, procedures with arguments, variables, and method calls throughout the following chapters as you put together a series of projects to help you become comfortable with all the incredible power that App Inventor gives you.

Part II

In Part II, you progress from dragging and dropping the simplest of components to building very complex algorithms and logic.

Each project has lots of figures to guide you through building the applications. If you are an advanced user, you can use the blocks figures to inform and guide your own application. If you are a new developer, focus on developing a good rhythm and method to your application building. Read through the design goals and sketches to get a solid understanding of what you will be trying to accomplish.

It is very important that you consider each project not an end unto itself but a demonstration of a concept and components that you can use to build your own application. Allow the process of building and seeing the completed project to inspire your own creative processes. Keep a notebook of app ideas and possible improvements for existing applications, but try not to let new ideas distract you from completing a set of design goals. You don't have to reinvent the wheel just make it better.

Most importantly, although the complexity of the applications ramps up from beginning to end, if you are not having fun building a project, move on to the next one. If you get lost or confused, refer back to simpler projects. If you aren't enjoying it, it isn't App Inventor.

chapter 3

SounDroid: Creating an Android Sound Machine

in this chapter

- Uploading and using media files in App Inventor
- Playing and looping sound files
- Arranging and placing user interface elements where you want them

IN THE PREVIOUS CHAPTER, you walked through the process of creating your design goals, primitives, and process. In this chapter, you take all of that from the previous chapter and put it into play. I also walk you through several complex algorithms.

Take special note of the method for placing and centering user interface elements on the screen. You need to reuse this method for almost any project you create. Creating user interfaces in App Inventor can be frustrating until you master the method of using invisible padding elements to adjust visible elements on the screen. You can use invisible labels or arrangements as "pusher" elements to center or move elements. I show you how to use the Fill Parent method to center components. However, remember that you can set the invisible padding components to a specific width and height to specifically place a visible element.

The use of the Clock element in this project is as both a timer and a way to mark passage of time. Take special note of both uses. The Clock component is a chameleon component that can be used for many things. You can use the method employed in this chapter to create wait states, pauses, and delay processing (more on delayed processing in a later project.)

Creating SounDroid 2.0

Your expansion of the SounDroid project takes it from a simple soundboard that plays a single sound to a looping sound machine. SoundDroid 2.0 will be able to loop sounds using a toggle button effect and track the time that the sound has played.

Using progressive milestone development makes building these sort of projects simple. Start with the easiest tasks and lowest level of functionality, as you did in the first version, and then slowly increase the features and capabilities.

Remember to download the project files for your application from the companion Web site. See the Introduction of this book if you need instructions on how to do so.

Your design

Your design sketch (see Figure 3-1) keeps your application on track with your vision of what it should look like and do. It's especially useful in the first phase of placing components and arranging them for usability.

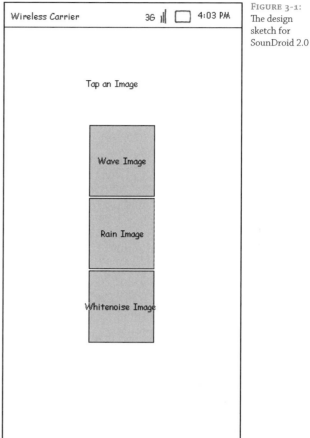

FIGURE 3-1:
The design
sketch for
SounDroid 2.0

Here are the design goals for the SounDroid 2.0 application. These are a refinement of the design goals created in the previous chapter. When you can put a check mark beside each of your design goals, you have met a milestone:

○ Images that are buttons for playing and stopping loops of relaxing sounds

○ Three unique and relaxing sounds with matching images on the buttons

○ Centered orientation of the buttons

Both design sketches and design goals are a good guideline, but they should never totally dictate your development process. They should be flexible enough to allow you to add and remove items if it is logical and efficient to do so. As you get into the development of this application, if you think that centered orientation is just too much for this version, for example, you should feel flexible enough with your design to move it to a later version.

TIP Many developers also keep a "to-do" list for inspirations that strike in the middle of creating your application. It is better to write down ideas for expansion than to try to implement them on the run. A to-do list allows you to develop later versions with greater functionality without taking from your current energy and progress.

Your primitives

Here are the logic, algorithms, and interface elements necessary to accomplish your design goals:

○ A wave, a rain, and a white noise image button

○ A way to use one button as a start and stop playing button

○ A wave, a rain, and a white noise sound file

○ A way to loop a sound file until it's stopped

○ A way to arrange the button elements on the screen

Your progression

The following list of steps is a basic (although not strict) guideline for building up the actual programming to accomplish your primitives and design goals. It is slightly more sophisticated than a to-do list but frequently fulfills the same function:

1. Create the Centering button components.

2. Place all user interface elements such as buttons, labels, and screen arrangements.

3. Upload all media, pictures, and sounds.

4. Create one looping sound algorithm.

5. Create toggle button algorithm (one button for on and off).

6. Extend the looping and toggle algorithm to all three buttons and all three sounds.

New components

These are the important new components used in this project:

○ Clock

○ HorizontalArrangement

○ VerticalArrangement

○ Padding components (empty labels)

○ Button with image

○ Player

New blocks

These are the important new blocks used in this project:

○ `IfElse`

○ `Clock1.Timer`

○ = (the comparison or equals block)

○ `Text`

Getting Started on SounDroid 2.0

Make sure that your phone is connected to your computer and can connect to App Inventor for the design phase. Remember, the Design view does not show a true representation of what your application will look like when you are finished.

Be sure you have downloaded the Chapter 3 project files from the download Web site: See this book's Introduction for details.

Although the SounDroid 2.0 project is a continuation of a previous project, it is different enough from its 1.0 version that you should start from scratch to create the 2.0 version:

1. Create a new project and name it `SounDroid2_0` (see Figure 3-2).

    App Inventor does not allow spaces or special characters such as periods in project names, so we use the allowed underscore character to make it clear what version of our project we are working with. The Design view is loaded with a blank project. You can now start with the first steps in your progression.

FIGURE 3-2:
Starting the
SounDroid 2.0
project

Begin by using a clever little trick to center all your components using horizontal and vertical screen arrangements along with empty labels.

2. Click the Screen Arrangements palette in the Palette column to expose the screen arrangement components. Drag and drop a HorizontalArrangement component from the palette to the Viewer workspace (see Figure 3-3).

FIGURE 3-3:
Placing the
Horizontal-
Arrangement
component for
the centered
buttons

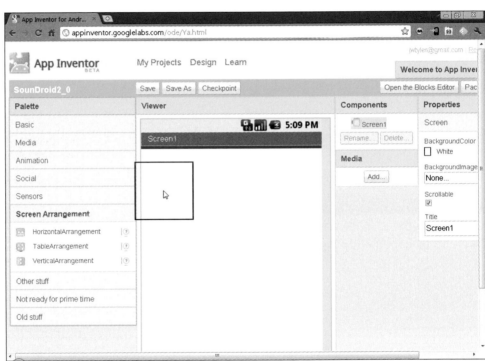

 REMEMBER HorizontalArrangement and VerticalArrangement components are containers for other components. They force the components you place in them to stack in the direction indicated. A HorizontalArrangement component forces every component that is added to it to stretch across the screen side-by-side in a horizontal direction. A VerticalArrangement component, on the other hand, forces the components you add to stack on top of each other vertically. You use these two behaviors to center your column of buttons.

3. Open the Basic palette by clicking it in the Palette column. Select a Label component and drag and drop it into the box representing the HorizontalArrangement you just placed.

This is your padding component that keeps your buttons centered. The
HorizontalArrangement component adjusts its shape and size to accommodate the
component you just placed in it.

4. Open the Screen Arrangements palette by clicking it. Drag and drop a
VerticalArrangement into the HorizontalArrangement and to the right of the label you
placed previously.

The VerticalArrangement resizes the HorizontalArrangement component again, but
stays to the right of the label you placed (see Figure 3-4). Remember the first time you
dropped two components onto the Viewer? The components stacked vertically down
the left side of the viewer. We are changing that default behavior with the Screen
Arrangement components.

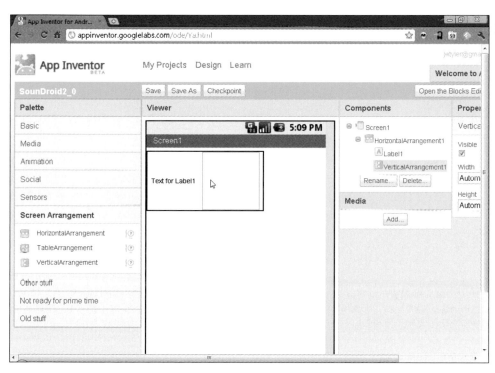

FIGURE 3-4:
Changing the
default
component
arrangements
with Screen
Arrangements

Before you go any further, you need to name the components and set their properties.
If you get too far ahead of yourself placing components, it's easy to forget what a component's name should be or what properties you wanted changed.

5. Set the name of your application as the Screen1 property so that your application is appropriately titled. Make the Screen1 component the active component by selecting it in the Components column. In the Properties column, select the Title property field and replace the Screen1 text with SounDroid 2.0. Press Enter.

The title on both the Viewer and your connected Android device should change. (If at any time the Android phone stops updating, click the Restart Phone App button in the Blocks Editor.)

REMEMBER You need to open the Blocks Editor to connect to your Android device or the emulator.

6. Select the Label1 component and name it padButtonCenterLeft.

NOTE Throughout this book, I urge you to use the pad prefix to name padding elements. The foremost reason is you should do this is that when you get to the Blocks Editor, you will likely not want to do anything with padding elements. After you set their size and behavior in the Design view, you are unlikely to move them again. Having them already named and together helps you as you search for block drawers. Using naming conventions also makes the dreaded "duplicate name error" less of a possibility. It also keeps your block structure in the Blocks Editor clear, purposeful, and easy to follow.

7. While the newly named padButtonCenterLeft component is selected, remove the default text of Text for Label1 from the text field in the Text box in the Properties column. Delete the text and press Enter. The label shrinks to practically non-existent; don't worry about, that we'll fix it in a minute. Click on the Width property text box and select Fill Parent from the three options, and then click OK (see Figure 3-5).

FIGURE 3-5:
The Fill Parent option for the padding label

The padButtonCenterLeft label's parent is HorizontalArrangement. This option tells the label to expand as much as possible and fill the parent container. For this option to work as a centering element, the parent container must be set to Fill Parent as well.

8. Select the HorizontalArrangement by clicking its name in the Component column or clicking its edge in the Viewer. Set the Width property in the Properties column to Fill Parent just as you did for the label.

You immediately see the VerticalArrangement box jump to the right side of the Viewer, although your connected Android device shows no change because arrangements are not visible components. The label obeyed the `Fill Parent` property and pushed out as far as possible, pushing the VerticalArrangement all the way to the right. This is not quite the behavior you want. You need something to exert equal pressure on the right side of that VerticalArrangement to center it.

9. Add another label by dragging and dropping it in the HorizontalArrangement on the right side of the VerticalArrangement, as shown in Figure 3-6. Select the new Label1 component in the Components column and click the Rename button. Rename the Label1 component to `padButtonCenterRight`. Select the default text in the Text field in the Properties column, delete it, and then press Enter. Select the Width property of the label now named `padButtonCenterRight` and set it to Fill Parent as you did with the `padButtonCenterLeft`.

FIGURE 3-6:
The second label, padButton CenterRight, centers the Vertical Arrangement

Now your VerticalArrangement is centered. The padding components on either side of the VerticalArrangement expand out to keep the arrangement centered no matter the width of the arrangement.

10. Drag and drop one more label above both the HorizontalArrangement and the VerticalArrangement that it contains. It should be the topmost component at the top of the Viewer workspace. Change its `Text` property to `Tap an image to begin relaxing`.

Success! You have accomplished your first full design goal. You have a centered VerticalArrangement that you can now place your buttons into (see Figure 3-7).

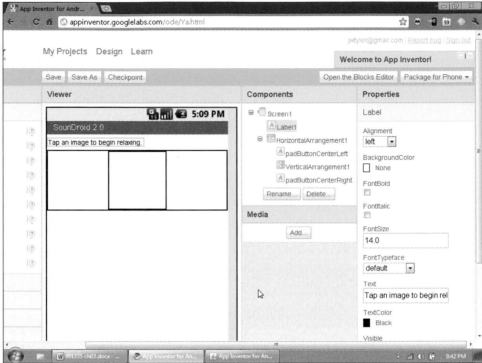

Adding components for the sound loop mechanism

You now need to add two non-visible components for the sound loop mechanism you will be creating with the Blocks Editor:

1. Drag and drop a Clock component from the Basic palette into the Viewer workspace. It drops to the non-visible components area below the viewer.

2. Open the Media palette by clicking it in the Palette column. Drag and drop a Player component to the Viewer workspace. The Player is a non-visible component.

3. Now add all the media from your project file location to the media column. If you have already determined which images, sounds, and movies will be used in your application, just upload them all at once. Click the Add button in the Media column and then click the Choose File button on the Upload File pop-up. Navigate to the folder where you downloaded and expanded the Chapter 3 project files. Click on the wavebutton.png file and then click Open. Click OK on the Upload File pop-up window to upload the wave-button.png file that you will use for the wave sound button.

Repeat for all the files you downloaded for this chapter. Be sure to let each upload complete before starting another upload. Make sure you can see the last uploaded item in the Media column before starting your next file upload. The yellow Uploading notification at the top of your browser is not always the best indicator of when the upload is completed. It gets stuck on Uploading sometimes even when the upload is completed. If the media shows up in the Media column, the upload is completed and you can start a new upload.

4. Continue with your SounDroid design phase by clicking the Basic palette in the Palette column to open it. Drag and drop a Button component into the centered VerticalArrangement in the Viewer. Repeat two more times for a total of three buttons in the VerticalArrangement. The VerticalArrangement adjusts its size for the buttons.

5. Now that you have three centered buttons, you need to set the properties for those buttons. Rename the buttons from the Components column. Having meaningful names from the outset makes programming with the blocks much easier. Click Button1 in the Components column. Click the Rename button, type btnRain, and then click OK on the Rename Component pop-up.

    I recommend that you use the btn prefix throughout this book to specify when a component name refers to a button (see Figure 3-8). Make the first button active by clicking it either the Viewer or the Components column. Select the default text in the Text field on the Properties column and delete it.

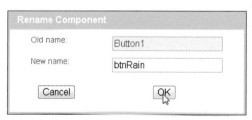

FIGURE 3-8:
Renaming your
button
components

6. Rename Button2 to btnWave using the previous steps. Rename Button3 to btnWhitenoise.

    Now add the images to your buttons. Select the btnRain component and click in the text box below the Image property, as shown in Figure 3-9.

FIGURE 3-9:
The Button
Image property
media picker

7. Select the rainbutton.png file from the list of media you upload previously to the Media column.

You should see the image appear as the button in the Viewer. You should also see it appear on the screen of the connected Android device. The image is a little large on the connected device, so we use the `Width` and `Height` properties of the button in the Properties column to constrain the image.

8. Select the `Width` property field by clicking in the field, and then click in the Pixels box in the Property picker. Enter `125` in the `Width` pixel box and click OK. Do the same thing for the `Height` pixel property, setting the height to 125 pixels, as shown in Figure 3-10.

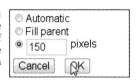

FIGURE 3-10:
Setting the
dimensions of
the image
button

Your button is now a more pleasing and reasonable size. These dimensions can always be adjusted to suite either aesthetics or functionality.

9. Continue setting your button properties. Select the btnWave component and remove the default text. Remember to press Enter after deleting the text. The Enter key registers the change and sends it to your device and the Viewer. Select the Image property and choose the wave.png file from the list of previously uploaded media. Set the Width and Height properties by clicking in the Width and Height property fields and entering 125 pixels.

10. Next, remove the default text from btnWhitenoise. Set the Image property to use the Whitenoise.png file from the Media picker. Set the Button Width and Height properties to 125 pixels.

11. Select the Clock component from the non-visible component area below the Viewer. In the Properties column, deselect the TimerEnabled check box. Set the TimerInterval numerical value to 1. The TimerInterval is the length of time in milliseconds between each cycle of the Clock1 component. You use a button click event to enable the timer. The timer then plays the appropriate sound.

12. Select the Label1 component in the Components column. Click the Rename button in the Components column and name the label labInstructions. You will use the lab prefix to denote labels throughout this book.

13. Switch over to the Blocks Editor.

    If it is not open, click the Open Blocks Editor button in Design view.

14. You know that you need to handle events whenever the buttons you created are tapped, so start by clicking the My Blocks tab. Select the btnRain drawer by clicking btnRain in the column (see Figure 3-11).

15. Drag the event handler labeled when btnRain.Click do onto the Blocks Editor workspace. This is the handler for when this button is tapped or clicked. Do the same thing for the btnWave and btnWhitenoise buttons. You end up with three event handler blocks on your workspace, as shown in Figure 3-12.

    Whenever a button is clicked, the Player1 component needs to have the correct sound file loaded into it and then played. Click back over to the Design view in your browser and click the non-visible Player1 component to make it active. You can see the Player1 component has a Source property. You don't want to set a single Sound property here because you have three different sound files that the player will need to reference at the appropriate time, so you will use property blocks from the Player1 drawer to set the Source property in the event handlers for the buttons.

FIGURE 3-11:
The btnRain
blocks drawer
opens

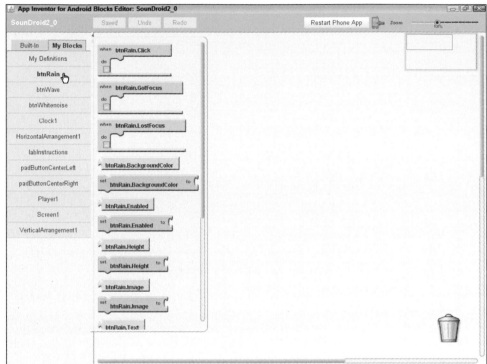

FIGURE 3-12:
The button click
event handlers
for your three
buttons

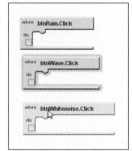

16. Click back over to the Blocks Editor. Open the Player1 drawer by clicking it in the My Blocks column. You see the set Player1.Source to block with an empty socket on the right side. You can use this block to plug in the name of the source file you want to be loaded into the Player1 component. Any sound file you set this up for must be already uploaded into the Media column in the designer. If you haven't uploaded the .mp3 files already, you need to do so now.

17. Drag a set `Player1.Source to` block and drop it between the arms of the `btn-Rain.Click` event handler. You can hear it snap into place. Now you need to populate the empty socket on the block you just placed (see Figure 3-13).

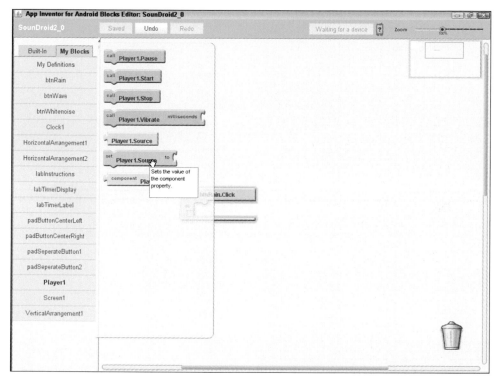

FIGURE 3-13: Dragging your .Source component onto the Blocks Editor workspace

18. Click the Built-In tab on the blocks drawer column. Open the Text drawer by clicking the word `Text` in the column. This drawer contains all the blocks that control text manipulation. You use a simple `text` block to set the source name.

19. Drag a `text` block over the workspace and onto the set `Player1.Source to` block socket. Drop it. It should socket in with a snap. Click the default word `text` on the text block. The word `text` in the `text` block highlights (see Figure 3-14).

20. Type `rain.mp3` into the text block.

The property source name you place here must be exactly the name and extension of the file that was uploaded. Putting raining.mp3 or rain in the text block won't work and the sound won't play.

FIGURE 3-14:
The text block
socketed and
ready to edit
contents

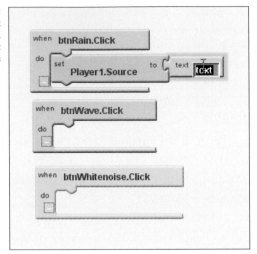

21. Place a temporary block in the btnRain.Click event handler to make sure that your source is being set and your sound can play. Activate the My Blocks drawers by clicking the My Blocks tab. Open the Player1 block drawer and drag the call Player1.Start method into the btnRain event handler. Tap the Rain button on your connected Android device. You should hear the sound play. The problem is that the sound plays only once.

The way you get the sound to loop without locking up the phone is called deferred processing. Deferred processing means that a series of blocks are executed and then there is a time in the processing of the blocks where the device can receive input or events from the user and catch up. If Android senses that your application is no longer accepting user input because a thread is processing blocks, it assumes that your application is crashed and force-closes it. You use the Clock component that is currently disabled to call the Player1.Start method. As long as the clock is enabled, it continuously runs the code held in its block, waits the time set in the properties, and run the blocks again. Therefore, you use the button event handlers to enable the Clock component.

22. Open the Clock1 drawer and drag the Clock1.Timer block onto the Blocks Editor workspace. This block name — when Clock1.Timer do — means "When the clock fires, do the blocks in this block." Place the Player1.Start method call block from the btnRain.Click event handler in the Clock1.Timer block.

23. Now you need to enable the Clock1.Timer when the button click event occurs. Open the Clock1 block drawer and scroll down the drawer until you see the set Clock1.TimerEnabled to. Drag the Clock1.TimerEnabled block into the btnRain.Click event handler block and drop it.

24. Now the Clock1.TimerEnabled block needs to have a property set in its socket. The enabled property is a true or false question, so use a true logic block from the Built-In blocks. Click the Built-In tab and open the Logic blocks drawer. Drag a true block and socket into the Clock1.TimerEnabled block (see Figure 3-15).

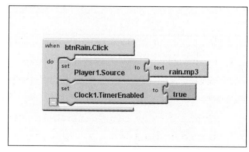

FIGURE 3-15: The Clock1. TimerEnabled block is set to true

25. Now when the Rain button is clicked, the source is set to rain.mp3 and the clock enabled property is set to true. Test it now on your connected Android device. The problem is now stopping the sound after you start it. (Note: To stop the sound from playing, click the Restart Phone App button on the Blocks Editor.)

Enabling more control over sound looping

You need to exert a little more control over that sound looping. When the buttons are clicked, you need to find out if the sound is playing and, if it is, stop it, and, if it isn't, start it. In App Inventor, you use Control blocks to direct the flow and logic of your programs code progression:

1. Click on the Built-In Tab on the Blocks Editor and open the Control blocks drawer by clicking it. The algorithm we need looks like Figure 3-16.

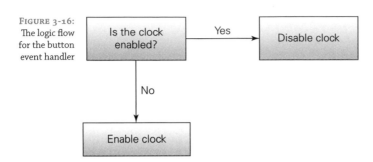

To achieve this, use the IfElse block. The IfElse block tests a condition to see if that condition is true. If it is true, the first set of blocks is executed. If the condition is not true, the second set of blocks is executed. So the IfElse block in Figure 3-17 shows a logic flow that reads like this: "If the Clock1.TimerEnabled is false, then set it to true, else (or otherwise), set the Clock1.TimerEnabled to false." This fulfills the algorithm in Figure 3-16.

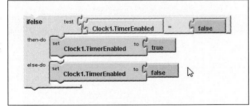

2. Build the IfElse test by dragging an IfElse block from the Control blocks drawer and dropping it below the Player1.Source block in the btnRain.Click event handler block. Now open the Logic blocks drawer on the Built-In tab by clicking it. Drag and drop the equals (=) block into the test socket of the IfElse block (see Figure 3-18).

3. The block with the equals sign (=) is the comparative block. It compares two things to see whether they are equal or the same. You know you need to compare the current enabled state of the clock with the value false, so you need to fetch the current state of the clock for the first socket in the comparative operator.

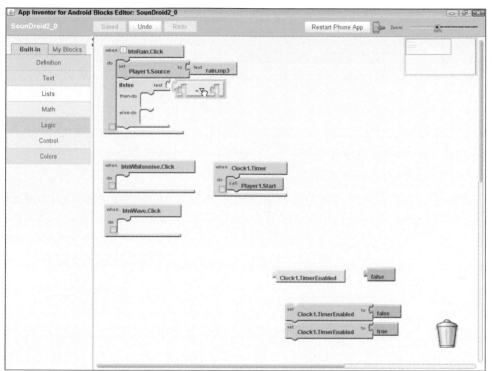

FIGURE 3-18: Socketing the test condition for the IfElse block

4. Open the Clock1 blocks drawer on the My Blocks tab and find the Clock1. TimerEnabled block that looks like it will socket into an empty socket. This block just returns the current enabled status as true or false. Drag the Clock1. TimerEnabled block and drop it into the first socket in that comparative operator that is your test condition for the IfElse block (see Figure 3-19).

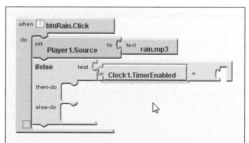

FIGURE 3-19: Setting the condition to test against it in the comparative block

5. Now open the Logic blocks drawer on the Built-In tab and drag a `false` block into the remaining socket on the comparative operator. Your test condition is built: "If Clock1. TimerEnabled equals false."

6. If the Timer.Enabled is set with a `false` block (if the timer is not enabled), the sound isn't playing and you need to enable it. Open the Clock1 blocks drawer on the My Blocks tab and drag a `set  Clock1.TimerEnabled  to` block into the first set of block space in the `IfElse` control block. Open the Logic blocks drawer from the Built-In tab and drag and drop a true block into the `set  Clock1.TimerEnabled to` socket.

7. If the test condition returns that the Clock1.TimerEnabled is already set to `true`, that means the sound is currently playing and you need to disable it. Drag another `set Clock1.TimerEnabled  to` block from the Clock1 drawer into the `else  do` set of blocks in the `IfElse` block. Then drag a `false` block from the Logic drawer into that `set Clock1.TimerEnabled to  socket`.

At this point, your `btnRain.Click` event handler should look like Figure 3-20.

FIGURE 3-20:
The completed
toggle button
routine

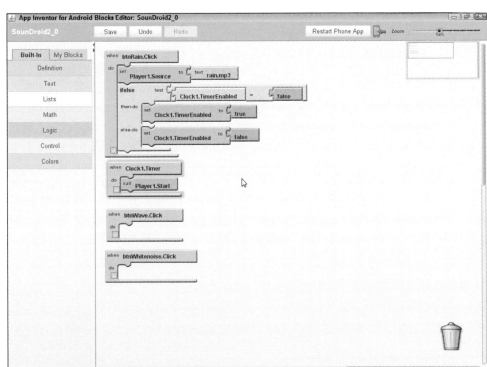

8. Test the behavior on your attached Android phone. Tap the Rain button to start the sound; tap it again to stop. If it doesn't work, compare your blocks carefully to Figure 3-19.

   Now that you have one button working like your design goal specifies, you need to set the same blocks for the other buttons. However, you don't have to build them all block by block. You can duplicate blocks in App Inventor using the keyboard cut and paste shortcuts.

9. Click on the set `Player1.Source` to block in the `btnRain.Click` event handler. You can tell if a block is selected: If it has a glow effect around it, it's selected. With the set `Player1.Source` to block selected, press Ctrl+C on your keyboard. This copies the selected block set into memory.

10. Next press Ctrl+V. A duplicate of the `Player1.Source` block and its socketed value appears. Press Ctrl+V again to create a second copy of the `Player1.Source` block. Drag one of the duplicated block sets into the `btnWave.Click` event handler. Drag the remaining duplicated block set into the `btnWhitenoise.Click` event handler.

    You will notice that the `rain.mp3` block was duplicated. You need to change the text in the text block for each event handler. Click the rain.mp3 text on the text block for the `btnWave.Click` event so that the text becomes highlighted and editable. Change the property value for the set `Player1.Source` to to `wave.mp3` (see Figure 3-21).

11. Set the text block for the `btnWhitenoise.Click` event handler to whitenoise.mp3.

12. Now you can duplicate the entire `IfElse` block from the `btnRain.Click` event handler and drag it below the set`Player1.Source` blocks in the other event handlers. Click on the `IfElse` block in the `btnRain.Click` event block. Press Ctrl+C and then Ctrl+V to duplicate the block and all the blocks socketed into it. Drag the duplicated `IfElse` block to the `btnWave.Click` block and drop it under the `Player1.Source` block. Duplicate the `IfElse` block again by pressing Ctrl+V. Drag and drop the new duplicate into the `btnWhitenoise.Click` event block. You should now have your blocks set up as in Figure 3-22.

FIGURE 3-21:
Changing the
property text
value in the
duplicated
blocks

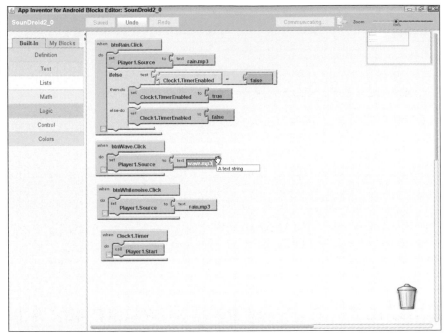

FIGURE 3-22:
The completed
button event
handlers for
your sound
looping
SoundDroid 2.0

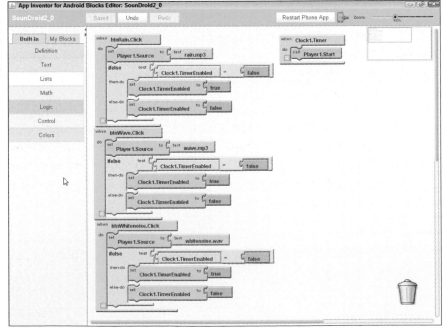

Test each of the buttons and sounds. If it doesn't work, carefully review your blocks and compare them to Figure 3-22. You have met your design goals for SounDroid 2.0:

❍ A wave, a rain, and a white noise image button

❍ A way to use one button as a start and stop playing button

❍ A wave, a rain, and a white noise sound file

❍ A way to loop a sound file until stopped

❍ A way to arrange the button elements on the screen

Click back to the Design view and click the Checkpoint button above the Viewer. Change the default checkpoint name to SounDroid2_0final. Now you have a copy of the SounDroid 2.0 project in its current functioning state. Enjoy your app for a moment and then get ready to go on down the road to the next milestone!

Expanding the SounDroid Project: SounDroid 3.0

In building this milestone, you learn more about how to meet design goals and create a pleasing user interface. Remember that many of the properties you will set in the Properties column can be set from the Blocks Editor. That means that the padding elements you use for creating visual space and arrangement can be changed later based on an event or some other programmatic logic. Arranging and placing components on the design interface is all about placing invisible elements and setting the sizes and shapes in such a way as to "push" your visible elements into the right place.

The Clock component is used in the next milestone in a completely different way. The Clock component has functionality that enabled you to create a timed event with the .Timer. Now you use the functionality of the Clock component that lets you record and mark time. The Clock component with its Timer and Time and Date functionality is a very important component in any project you build.

Your design

The design sketch for version 3.0 is shown in Figure 3-23.

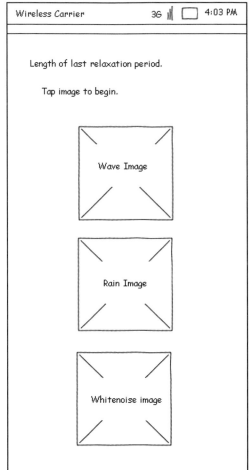

FIGURE 3-23:
The design
sketch for
SounDroid 3.0

Design goals

These are your goals you need to achieve to improve the SounDroid application. This could be considered a list of goals before a "milestone" release.

- ○ A timer that starts when a sound is played and stops when the sound is stopped
- ○ A way to display the timer
- ○ A relaxing non-intrusive background
- ○ Slightly separated buttons for visual distinction

Your primitives

These are the pieces you build to accomplish your goals. The most challenging will be the timing logic:

○ A record of when the sound player starts

○ A record of when the sound player stops

○ A record of the difference between the start and stop

○ An image set as the background of Screen1

○ A label for display

○ Padding labels between the buttons

Your progression

As usual, you begin by placing new user interface components and the move to the Blocks Editor to give the components functionality.

1. Place a timer label and timer display label.

2. Place padding labels between buttons.

3. Set a background image.

4. Create the logic for displaying play time in timer display label.

New components

Here are the new components you'll explore in this project:

○ Clock as a timer

○ Background image

New blocks

Here are the new blocks you'll need to create this app:

○ Procedure

○ If

○ Variable

Getting Started on SounDroid 3.0

Begin by placing the new components in the Design view. Later you move back to the Blocks Editor.

A milestone is a good place to do a "checkpoint" save from the Design view. If you mess up the functional application by attempting to add to it, you have a spot to go back to and try again.

---

1. From the Design view, click to open the Screen Arrangements palette and drag a HorizontalArrangement to just under the labInstructions label with the text Tap image to begin relaxing above the buttons.

    Don't worry about the arrangement pushing the buttons down. Drag two labels from the Basic palette into the HorizontalArrangement you just placed (see Figure 3-24).

FIGURE 3-24:
Placing the
timer labels

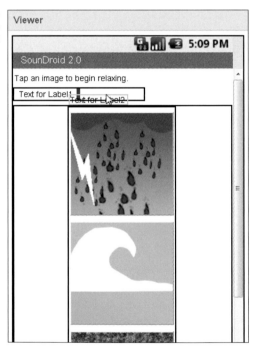

2. Make the Label1 component active by clicking on it in the Viewer or the Components column. Check the FontBold property box in the Properties column and set the TextColor to yellow. Replace the default text in the Properties column with

Length of last relaxation: and press Enter. With Label1 still the active component, click the Rename button in the Components column and rename the label labTimerLabel.

3. Make the Label2 component active by clicking on it and delete the default text, leaving the label blank. Check the FontHold property box in the Properties column and set the TextColor to yellow. This label displays the time. Rename the label component labTimerDisplay.

4. Select the labInstructions label in the Components column. Set the TextColor to white so that it will be clear against your background.

If you lose "invisible" elements in the Design view, you can always select them by clicking on the component name in the Components column. That way, the component is highlighted in the Design view. **NOTE**

Now use two labels as padding to separate the buttons so they are visually more appealing on the phone screen.

5. Drag a label component between the Rain button and the Wave button and drop it. Rename the component padSeperateButton1. Remove the default text from the Text property. Set the padSeperateButton1 Height property to Fill Parent.

6. Drag a second label component between the Wave and Whitenoise buttons. Rename the component padSeperateButton2. Remove the default text from the Text property. Set the padSeperateButton2 Height property to Fill Parent. (See Figure 3-25.)

The two padSeparate elements adjust themselves to space the buttons equally no matter the screen size.

7. Select the Screen1 component in the Components column. Click the BackgroundColor property to bring up the color picker. Select None as the color. Deselect the Scrollable check box. The background will not display properly on a scrollable screen or with a color and a BackgroundImage set. In the Properties column, click on the BackgroundImage property box to bring up the media picker. Select the soundroid_background.png uploaded to the Media column earlier in the SounDroid 2.0 project.

You may need to click the Restart App on Phone button on the Blocks Editor to get the background to show up on the connected Android device. **TIP**

FIGURE 3-25:
Setting your padding elements to arrange user interface components

Building the logic for the timer counter

Switch over to the Blocks Editor to get ready to build the logic for the timer counter. The first thing you will likely need to do is to move the workspace to the right, away from your button event handlers. You can click and drag on an empty part of the Blocks Editor workspace to drag your view of the workspace to an uncluttered area. When you click and drag the workspace, a "mini-map" of your workspace in the upper-right corner of the Blocks Editor illustrates where your view is on the workspace. You can use that map to navigate your view of the workspace. Get familiar with using this drag behavior to move back and forth between areas on your workspace. Your workspace grows horizontally as you add blocks to the left of your starting position on the Blocks Editor.

1. Drag your Blocks Editor workspace to the right to give yourself a clear workspace for building the timer for SounDroid 3.0 (see Figure 3-26). You will be able to see your blocks in the Block Editor minimap.

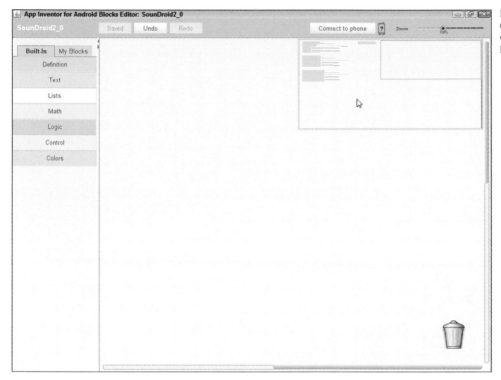

FIGURE 3-26:
Creating added
workspace in the
Blocks Editor

The algorithm you are going to use is to record the system time of the phone when the
sound starts playing. When the sound stops playing, the stop time will be recorded.
Subtracting the start time from the stop time will tell you the amount of time passed.

As I mentioned in Chapter 2, whenever you know you are going to be storing something to access later, you use a variable. A variable is a storage location to put data in
for reference or processing. You are going to be storing two values: the start time and
the stop time.

2. When you create a variable, you are said to be defining the variable. To define a variable
   in App Inventor, click on the Built-In tab on the Blocks Editor. Open the Definition
   block drawer by clicking it. Click and drag two variables out onto your Blocks Editor
   workspace.

Variables must have unique names just like all the other components. Change the first ▶ **REMEMBER**
variable name by clicking on the text name `variable`. The existing name is highlighted and
you can change it by typing a new name. Change the first variable name to `varPlayStart`.

I suggest that you use the `var` prefix for all variables throughout the exercises in this book. This helps assure unique names and help you find the variable blocks when you are setting or retrieving the information stored in a variable. Rename the second variable `varPlayStop` (see Figure 3-27).

NOTE   The prefix names you use for components in AppInventor are important for three reasons. First, they ensure that your components all have unique names. Second, when you are sorting through a lot of component drawers, it places all the similarly named components together because the component drawers are organized alphabetically. Third, it helps when you have a screen full of mysterious blocks all connected to easily see that a particular block is doing something to a variable or a list picker, and so on. In other programming languages, you may use other naming conventions for variables and functions and subroutines, but the important thing is to use a clear and easily repeatable naming methodology.

FIGURE 3-27: Renaming your global variables for storing start and stop times

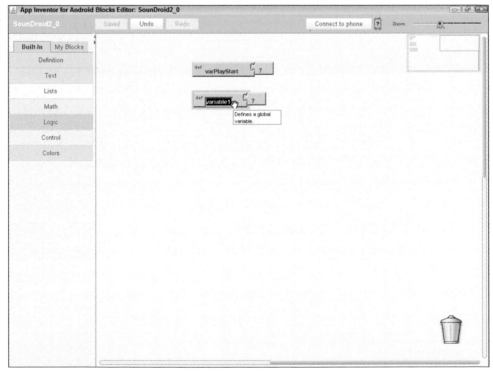

3. Currently the variables have a block socketed with a question mark on it. Select the question mark block and press Delete on your keyboard. The Blocks Editor asks you if you want to delete the selected blocks. Select Yes on the Delete Blocks pop-up. Delete both question mark blocks. You will replace these with empty number blocks.

App Inventor does a good job of indicating what kind of information you are storing in a variable, whether, text, number or a Boolean value (true/false). However, you should still define your variables with the type of information they will store. When you move from developing with App Inventor to any other language, variables must be defined to include what type of data they contain.

4. Open the Math blocks drawer by clicking it on the Built-In tab. The first block is labeled number and contains the default numbers 123. Drag and drop a number block from the drawer onto your workspace. Click on the default 123 numbers to make the number block editable and replace them with a 0. Duplicate the 0 block by selecting it and then using Ctrl+C to copy it and then Ctrl+V to paste.

5. Drag and drop the 0 number blocks into the sockets on the varPlayStart and var-PlayStop variables.

You now have two variables for storing start and stop times, but you need a way to record those times into the variables no matter what button is selected in the user interface. There are three possible user generated events in the SounDroid application, or three button clicks, to be exact. In the SounDroid 2.0 project, we reused the same code in all three event handlers. For the timer, we use a procedure that does the work of recording the start and stops. We can then call that procedure from each button click with a single block. It also calculates and displays the result. A procedure is a subroutine or a reusable program within your application. Your procedure needs to determine whether the sound is being started or stopped and record the time in the appropriate variable. The algorithm logic flows as shown in Figure 3-28.

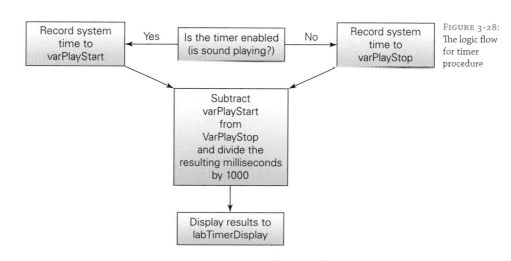

FIGURE 3-28:
The logic flow
for timer
procedure

Defining the stop and start timer procedures

To define your procedure, follow these steps:

1. Open the Definition drawer on the Built-In tab of the Blocks Editor. Drag and drop a procedure out onto your workspace. Two types of procedures are available: a procedure with arguments and a return and a plain procedure. Choose the procedure without the return socket. Click on the procedure name and change the name text to procTimer. The prefix proc is used for all procedures in this book.

2. Now build the procedure according to the logic in Figure 3-28. For decision-making, you already know to use an IfElse block. Open the Control blocks drawer on the Built-In tab and drag and drop an IfElse block into the procTimer procedure.

   IfElse blocks always test something. The test we are building is "Is the Clock currently enabled or disabled?" If you think back to the SounDroid 2.0 project, you'll remember that the clock, when enabled, continuously plays a sound. Therefore, if the clock is enabled, sound is currently playing. You will be calling or executing the procTimer subroutine the very last thing every time a button is clicked, so our test needs to determine if the clock is enabled by the button click or disabled.

3. Drag a comparative operator (the equals block) from the Logic drawer and socket it into the IfElse block that is in the procTimer. The Clock1 has a block that reports the state of the clock whether enabled or disabled. You used that block previously when creating the logic for the toggle buttons.

4. Open the Clock1 blocks drawer on the My Blocks tab. Scroll down until you see the Clock1.TimerEnabled block. Drag the Clock1.TimerEnabled block into the first socket on your equals block (see Figure 3-29).

5. You need to know if the Clock1.TimerEnabled block is reporting true, so drag a logic block from the Logic drawer into the second socket on the equals block.

   Now you must build to two cases. If it is true that the button click just enabled the timer, you need to record the time. When you defined a variable to store the play start time, it created two blocks in the My Definitions drawer on the My Blocks tab. The first block delivers the contents of the variable into whatever socket it is plugged. The second block allows you to put information into the variable.

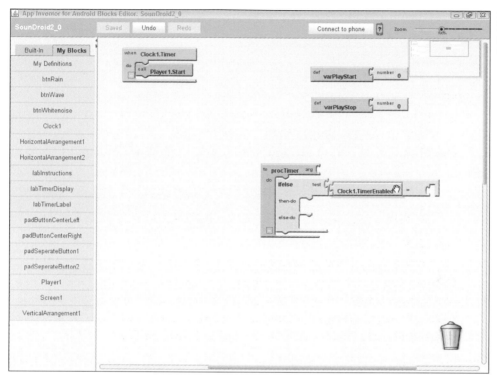

FIGURE 3-29:
Building the test
conditions for
the procTimer

6. Open the My Definitions drawer and drag out the set global varPlayStart to
block and snap it into the first case of your IfElse block. That's the then-do portion
of the IfElse block. The set block allows to set what the contents of a variable are.
We want to set this variable to the system time.

All time and date operations are handled by the Clock component. The Clock component
has a lot of methods or built in functionality that you can utilize. One of those methods is the
system time block. The system time block reports the time of the phone or device on which
it is called.

REMEMBER

7. Open the Clock1 drawer and locate the block that says call Clock1.SystemTime.
This is a call to the SystemTime method. It will dump the system time into whatever
socket you put it into. Drag the call Clock1.SystemTime block and socket it into
the set globalPlayStart to block in your first case of the IfElse block (see
Figure 3-30).

FIGURE 3-30:
The varPlayStart
variable will be
set to the
system time
when these
blocks are
processed

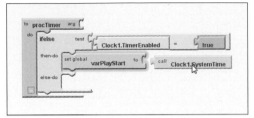

FIGURE 3-30:
The varPlayStart
variable will be
set to the
system time
when these
blocks are
processed

Now, you need to set the second case logic. If the test condition is not true that the Clock1.
TimerEnabled equals true, you need to record the stop time varPlayStop. Remember, you
will be calling the procTimer procedure right after each button press on your SounDroid
application. So, if the Clock is disabled when the procTimer checks it, the toggle button has
just set it to disabled and you need to have the procTimer update the varPlayStop and
display the total lapsed time:

1. Open the My Definitions drawer and drag the set global varPlayStop to block
   into the else-do on your IfElse block. Then just duplicate the Clock1.
   SystemTime block in the block above by selecting it and pressing Ctrl+C followed
   by Ctrl+V. Drag the duplicated Clock1.SystemTime call into the socket of the set
   global varPlayStop to block.

   The only other thing left is to do the math and update the TimerLabel when the two
   times have been recorded.

2. Open the blocks drawer for the labTimerDisplay by clicking it in the My Blocks tab.
   These blocks allow you to manipulate the properties of the label. You will use the set
   labTimerLabel.Text to just like you used the set global blocks for the variables. Anything you plug into the socket of the set labTimerLable.Text is displayed on the label. Drag the set labTimerLabel.Text to block and snap it in
   just below the varPlayStop block in your procTimer procedure.

   The time is reported by the SystemTime blocks in milliseconds, so you need to do
   some massaging of the data in your variables. The math is pretty easy, but you need to
   get it in the right order. The math formula will be the stop time in milliseconds minus
   the start time in milliseconds divided by the number of milliseconds in a second:

   (varPlayStop – varPlayStart)/1000

3. To build this into your labTimerDisplay.Text block, open the Math blocks drawer
   on the Built-In tab and drag out a divide (/) block. The divide block has a slash on it
   (see Figure 3-31).

4. From the Math blocks drawer, drag out a minus (–) block and socket it in the first socket on the divide block.

5. Now open the My Definitions drawer on the My Blocks tab and drag out both the global PlayStart and the global PlayStop blocks. Drag and socket the PlayStop block into the first socket on the minus block. Drag and socket the PlayStart block into the second socket on the minus block.

6. Click on any blank area of the workspace and type the number 1000 on your keyboard. Press Enter. A number block with the number 1000 is created. Drag the number block into the final socket on the divisor block. The procTimer procedure should now look like Figure 3-31.

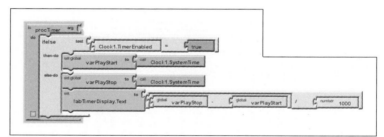

FIGURE 3-31:
The completed procTimer procedure

Adding the procTimer procedure to the button event handlers

The only thing left to do is to utilize your shiny new procedure in each of your button event handlers:

1. Open the My Definitions blocks drawer on the My Blocks tab. For every procedure you create, a call for that procedure is created in the My Definitions drawer. This call does exactly what a built-in method call does: It references a stored set of instructions.

2. Drag the call for the procTimer and drop it below the IfElse call in the btnRain. Click event handler. Do the same for the btnWave.Click and the btnWhitenoise.Click event handlers.

The completed SoundDroid 3.0 project blocks should look like Figure 3-32.

FIGURE 3-32:
The completed
blocks for
SounDroid 3.0

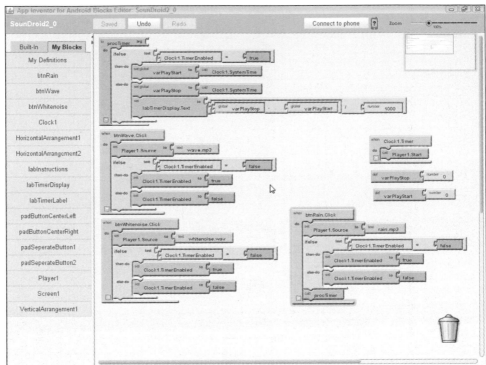

FIGURE 3-32:
The completed
blocks for
SounDroid 3.0

Congratulations: You have just finished your first multi-version application! You have taken an idea from its birth to completion. Along the way, you learned about the process of creating design documents and some new blocks and components in App Inventor. Now, on to even greater applications in the next project.

chapter 4

OrderDroid: A Maintainable
Mobile Commerce App

ONE OF THE QUESTIONS App Inventors ask most often is, "How do I get data out of my application?" In this chapter, you build an application that takes user data and e-mails it to a given address. This is a good method for gathering field data and storing it elsewhere. In a later project, you see how to use the TinyWebDB component to get data in and out of your applications. The e-mail method you learn in this project could be used to send data to an e-mail scraping application or be archived in a document management system such as Microsoft's SharePoint.

The other major limitation of the current App Inventor version is that it has only one Screen1 component and no easy way to create more. In this project, you learn how to create multiple screens for your App Inventor applications. This enables you to have settings screens, multiple output screens, and so on. For the purposes of this book, I call these "imitation" screens VirtualScreens. You can use VirtualScreens whenever you want to create more than one user interface view for your applications.

The method you use to send e-mails in this project uses the ActivityStarter to call the built-in default e-mail handler. The ActivityStarter can be used to call other applications on the Android device. The ActivityStarter requires very specific properties to function correctly.

> **NOTE**　*VirtualScreens* are the name I give in this book to the method of "faking" multiple App Inventor screens. The term is used in other applications and other types of programming to mean vastly different things. Future versions of App Inventor will very likely contain a built-in method for creating multiple screens. For the time being, you'll need to use the method I outline here.

Creating the OrderDroid Application

The OrderDroid application will be used by a salesperson in the field to take a customer's name, address, and purchase info and e-mail it to a predetermined processing address for fulfillment. An important design qualification is that it be maintainable because you anticipate rapidly expanding usability requirements.

Your design

The design goals for the OrderDroid application are simple statements that contain a great deal of complex algorithm to accomplish. Future versions should not have to be significantly redesigned to add functionality. The design sketch is shown in Figure 4-1.

FIGURE 4-1:
The design
sketch for
OrderDroid 1.0

The following design goals are your first milestone. When you can check these off, you have reached a performance and functionality point that you could release and use. You will have another set of design goals for the next milestone:

○ A form that accepts input of data such as customer name, address, items sold, and payment options

○ The ability to e-mail the order to an address for processing

○ Easy maintainability

Your primitives

These are the algorithms and logical pieces to accomplish your design goals. Each primitive is built to achieve a piece of an overall completion goal:

○ A form to get the customer's name and address

○ A list of products to select for purchase

○ A way to select, store, and display a single product selection

○ A way to record payment options

○ A way to send the complete order via e-mail to a fixed address, while maintaining the possibility of supporting variable addresses in the future

Your progression

This is the a logical way to move through your events, primitives, and design goals. However, remember to be flexible enough to quickly move to a different primitive or goal if the flow is natural and logical.

1. Create the form with the customer name and address input, item selection, payment check boxes, and a button for submitting the order.

2. Create blocks to populate a list of product items.

3. Store selected purchase items in a variable.

4. Create a procedure to e-mail the entire form to a predetermined address.

New components

These are the important new components introduced in this project:

○ ActivityStarter

○ ListPicker

○ CheckBox

○ TextBox

○ Notifier

New blocks

These are the important new blocks used in this project:

- ○ `ActivityStarter.DataUri`
- ○ `Notifier1.ShowMessageDialog`
- ○ `Make a List`
- ○ `Listpicker.AfterPicking`
- ○ `Make Text`

Getting Started on OrderDroid 1.0

The OrderDroid application should be built with maintainability foremost in your mind. Applications frequently go through usability changes after their first release and making changes should not require a complete redesign or major rethinking of your algorithms. Even more importantly, you will very likely want to add capabilities to your applications someday.

One way that developers keep maintainability in their applications is to compartmentalize the functionality. In the last project, you used a procedure to create code that you could reuse for multiple events in your application. In this project, you use procedures again, with a slightly different emphasis for maintainability. Not only will your procedures exist for reusability, but they will be used as expansion and scalability points. In other words, a procedure for e-mailing the form may be not only for reusability but also to isolate the e-mailing logic so it can be expanded on or changed in a later version.

Here's how to get started on the OrderDroid project:

1. From the My Projects window, start a new project and name it OrderDroid1_0.

2. Drag and drop a new VerticalArrangement onto the viewer from the ScreenArrangements palette.

3. Change the default VerticalArrangement1 name to VirtualScreen1 using the Rename button in the Components column.

   For this version of the app, you will only be using a single VirtualScreen. (More on VirtualScreens later.) With your emphasis on maintainability, you want to keep all of version 1.0's functionality constrained within a single VerticalArrangement so that later you can add other screen arrangements to contain new functionality.

4. Change the VirtualScreen1 Width property in the Properties column to Fill Parent.

5. Make the Screen1 component active by selecting it in the Components column. Change the Title property in the Properties column to OrderDroid 1.0.

6. Set Screen1 BackgroundColor to dark gray by clicking the square color picker.

TIP For this application, clarity and usability are of greatest importance. A dark gray background provides a good background for high contrast text without being glaring or too gloomy.

---

7. Deselect the Screen1 Scrollable property.

   The Scrollable property is less important in this version, but when you move on to 2.0 and use multiple virtual screens, you need to have the scrollable property off.

8. Drag and drop a label into the VirtualScreen1. Change its name to lblCustomerInfoText using the Rename button in the Components column.

9. Replace the default text in the Properties column Text property field with Customer Information. To increase visibility and contrast, change the text color of labCustomerInfoText to white. This label is static and acts as an identifier for the content of the form below it.

10. Drag a text box from the Basic palette and drop it below Customer information label in VirtualScreen1. Text boxes allow you to capture user text input and then process or use it.

    Text boxes are the primary way you get information from your application user.

TIP For our OrderDroid application, text boxes are important because you are creating a form that is filled out and submitted via e-mail. Remember that naming your components with easy-to-read names that specify their purpose makes building the blocks much easier. Good naming conventions also help with our overarching goal of maintainability. In large-scale developments, more than one developer may well be working on the same code. Easily understood names help everyone debug and maintain code.

---

11. Rename the TextBox1 component txtCustomerName using the Rename button in the Components column. Set the Width property to Fill Parent.

    Note the txt prefix at the beginning of the component name. I use the txt prefix to denote text entry boxes throughout this book.

12. In the Properties column, change the `Width` property to `Fill Parent`. You should see the text box fill out to the width of your screen on your connected Android phone. Change the `Hint` property to `Enter customer's name`.

Hint text is very useful for saving space and letting your user know what to enter into a text box. Adding a label for every text element in our form takes a lot of screen space. Instead, use the Hint text to label clearly what each text space is used for.   **TIP**

---

13. Drag three TextBox components directly below the Customer Name text box.

14. Make TextBox1 active by clicking it in the Components column. Click the Rename button and change the name to `txtAddress`. In the Properties column, change the `Hint` property to `Enter Address`.

15. Select TextBox2 and rename it as `txtCityState`. Change the `Hint` property to `City, State`.

16. Select TextBox3 and rename it as `txtZip`. Change the `Hint` property to `ZIP Code` (or `Postal Code`).

17. From the Basic palette, drag a ListPicker component and drop it below the txtZip text box.

A list picker looks like a button on the interface, but when it's tapped, it allows you select an item from a predefined list. Although you can define the items in the list picker with the `Elements from String` property in the Properties column, for this project, define the list of items to be picked from within the Blocks Editor.

18. Rename the ListPicker1 component to `lstpItems`. You will use the `lstp` prefix to denote a list picker through this book. When the list picker is clicked by your user, you set the text on the button to indicate the item they have chosen. However, the button for the ListPicker starts with some text to prompt the user to select an item. Change the `Text` property in the Property column to `Select an Item`.

19. Drag two CheckBox components from the Basic palette and drop them under the item list picker.

Check boxes are a two-state reporter. A check box is always one of two states: true or false. A state of true means that the check box is currently checked. False means that the check box is not checked. You can use the "true or false" nature of the check box to report on your form whether it is true that the customer has paid in full or will pay cash on delivery.

20. Make the CheckBox1 component active by clicking on it in either the Viewer or the Components column. Rename CheckBox1 to `chkPaidFull`. In the Properties column, change the `Text` property to `Paid in full`. Change the `TextColor` property to `white` by using the color picker.

---

21. Make the CheckBox2 component active by clicking it in either the Viewer or the Components column. Rename CheckBox2 as `chkCOD`. In the Properties column, change the `Text` property to `COD`. Change the `TextColor` property to `white` by using the color picker.

22. Drag and drop a button component below the COD check box. Change the name to `btnSendEmail` in the Components column. In the Properties column, change the `Text` property to `Submit Order`.

The Submit Order button is the last thing the user taps to send the completed form to a predetermined address.

23. Open the Other Stuff palette in the Palette column. Drag and drop a Notifier component onto the Viewer workspace.

The Notifier component gives you the ability to have several different types of notifications:

- ShowAlert: Displays a simple text pop-up at the bottom of the device screen

- ShowChooseDialog: Puts up a pop-up text box with a message, title, and two buttons

- ShowMessageDialog: Displays a pop-up text box with a single button

- ShowTextDialog: Gives you a pop-up message with a text box for the user to enter text

You use the third option, ShowMessageDialog, after a check to make sure that a customer name has been entered in the form fails. The notifier alerts the user to an empty text box.

Adding New Components to OrderDroid 1.0

The next steps guide you through adding the e-mail functionality. If you have your own application that you want to add e-mail to, this is where you should start. You use the *type-block* method of creating most of your blocks in this section. Typeblocking is a good way to speed up development. Simply start typing the name of the block you want and a list of possible blocks appears on the Blocks Editor workspace. When you see the block you want, press Enter and the block is created on the workspace. This is a significant speed-up from opening each component or block drawer and dragging out the desired blocks.

Along with typeblocking, you can use the Tab key to change the active selected block. A combination of typeblocking, using the Tab key, and copying/pasting with keyboard shortcuts allows you, in time, to program in App Inventor without a lot of mouse movement.

However, whenever you see typeblock in a step, you can always open the required block or component drawer and drag out the component.

1. Drag and drop an ActivityStarter component from the Other Stuff palette onto the Design view.

2. In the Properties column, set the `Action` property field (the `Action` field is the first property field in the Properties column) value to `android.intent.action.VIEW`.

TIP

The ActivityStarter component allows your application to start other applications on your phone while handing them data to process. For the OrderDroid application, you use ActivityStarter to send a standard mailto link to the built-in Android browser. The browser in turn starts the default e-mail handling application. The properties of the ActivityStarter are complex and arcane. They are the closest to the underlying code that makes up the instructions to your Android phone. Because of the relatively low-level nature of the ActivityStarter, it is fairly sensitive to any errors in its usage. The ActivityStarter usually responds to being used incorrectly by ungracefully forcing your application to close. If your project is causing force close errors and it has an ActivityStarter in it, you should suspect the ActivityStarter first and foremost.

REMEMBER

No ActivityStarter actions work while the phone is connected to the App Inventor: In other words, when your project is running in Development mode and connected via USB. Any attempt to use the ActivityStarter functions while connected and running your project via App Inventor results in the project crashing on your phone. ActivityStarter applications must be packaged and installed on the phone before they can be tested. That includes your OrderDroid application, so don't try to send the e-mail while the phone is connected to a computer.

At this point, the visual user interface components should be in place. The Design view should look like Figure 4-2. Your connected Android phone will look considerably different — like Figure 4-3.

FIGURE 4-2:
The Customer
Information
form takes
shape

3. Switch to the Blocks Editor. If it is not open, click the Open Blocks Editor button on the Design view.

When you need to do something before anything else happens in your application, use the `Screen1.Initialize` block. The `Screen1.Initialize` is a special event handler. The event that it handles is the startup of your application. Anything that needs to occur when your application starts should be placed in the `Screen1.Initilize` block.

You have a list picker in your application that needs a list of items populated as selection options. The ListPicker component gives you the block `set lstpItems.Elements to` block, but you need an event to execute the block.

FIGURE 4-3:
The phone view
of the
OrderDroid user
interface

4. Open the Screen1 blocks drawer by clicking the Screen1 text on the My Blocks tab. Locate and drag the Screen1.Initilize block onto the workspace.

5. Open the lstpItems blocks drawer, locate the set lstpItems.Elements to block, and snap it into the Screen1.Initialize event handler.

   Now you need to make a list of items in that set lstpItems.Elements to socket.

6. Open the Lists blocks drawer on the Built-In tab of the Blocks Editor.

   List blocks allow you to manipulate arrays of data in App Inventor. For now, you are only concerned with the first block in the drawer. Drag a Make a List block and socket it into the set lstpItems.Elements to socket. Each time you place something into a socket on the Make a List block, it expands and places a new item socket.

7. Click any blank spot on your Blocks Editor workspace. Type the word text and press Enter.

App Inventor creates a text block and highlights the default text, making it ready for you to replace default text with whatever you like. This is called typeblocking and you saw it in action in Chapter 3 when you typeblocked the number 1000. Throughout this book, I show you how to use typeblocking to save yourself time and to aid in learning efficiency. Any time a project refers to typeblocking, start typing the name of the block. If similarly named blocks exist, a drop-down list of possible blocks appears. You can use the arrow keys on your keyboard to highlight the desired block; then press Enter. You can also use the mouse to click the desired block's name in the drop-down list.

8. Replace the default text in your typeblocked text block with 'Andy' Android Figurine. Drag the text block into the Make a List block and socket it in the item socket. The block expands and adds a new socket.

9. Typeblock a new text block by clicking in the empty workspace, typing the word text, and pressing Enter.

> **TIP** Remember you can also drag a text block from the Text blocks drawers on the Built-In tab. Typeblocking is just a little faster and more efficient.

10. Replace the default text in your new text block with Android Laptop Decal. Socket your new text block into the open socket on the Make a List block (see Figure 4-4).

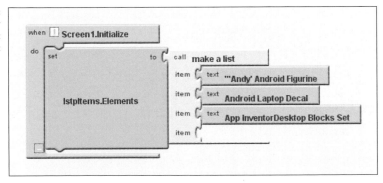

FIGURE 4-4:
The ListPicker
Elements set
with Make a List

11. Typeblock one more text block and set its text to App Inventor Desktop Blocks Set. Socket that text into the Make a List block as well.

12. You can test your list picker now on your phone. Tap the Select Item button on the connected Android phone to see the list of items pop up. Selecting one of the items has no effect yet. Close the list picker to return to the application.

    When one of the items is picked from your ListPicker, you need to keep it stored until it is sent in an e-mail. Remember that storing information temporarily in App Inventor means that you use a variable. Because you foresee adding multiple items to the order form in future versions, you are going to define a storage container for all the items that will be purchased. You will define a variable to be the shopping cart for the order form.

13. Typeblock a new variable by clicking on a blank spot on the workspace, typing vari, and then pressing Enter. A list of possibilities appears in a drop-down list. As you type, App Inventor filters through all of your defined components and blocks. When the component or block you wish to typeblock is at the top of the drop-down list, you can press Enter and that block is created (see Figure 4-5). The newly created variable block has its default text of variable highlighted and ready for you to change. Rename the variable varShoppingCart. A variable cannot have an empty socket, so you need to typeblock a text block by typing text and pressing Enter. Clear the text from the created block and socket it in the new variable.

FIGURE 4-5:
Typeblocking a
new variable
block

    You can open the My Definitions drawer to see the two new blocks created by type-blocking the new variable. The global varShoppingCart block is for pulling infor-mation out of the variable and the set varShoppingCart to block is for putting information into the variable.

14. Now that you have a place to store the selected item, you need to handle the event of a user picking an item from the list picker. The AfterPicking event allows you to exe-cute instructions when a user picks something from a list picker.

15. Open the lstpItems drawer on the My Blocks tab and drag and drop the lstpItems. AfterPicking event from the lstpItems drawer. After your user selects an item from your list picker, the blocks in this event are executed.

16. You store the item picked in your `varShoppingCart` variable. Open the My Definitions drawer on the My Blocks tab, drag out the `set VarShoppingCart to` block, and socket it into the `AfterPicking` event handler. The ListPicker component has a block that reports the results of the user's selection. You socket that block into the `set VarShoppingCart to` block. This sets the contents of your variable to the item that the user selected.

17. Open the lstpItems drawer and locate the `lstpItems.Selection` block. Drag the `lstpItems.Selection` block and socket it into the `set varShoppingCart to` block.

TIP   To test your blocks up to this point, you need to know about *watching* your blocks. Watching is the primary way you use to debug and learn about your applications in Google App Inventor. Right-click the `def varShoppingCart` block and select the Watch option from the menu that appears. An empty Watch "balloon" pops up. This balloon populates in real time with whatever that variable currently holds, as shown in Figure 4-6. On your connected Android phone, tap the Select Item button and select one of the items that appears. The Watch balloon in the Blocks Editor populates with your selection. If the Watch balloon seems to disappear, click the Watch square on the watched block to stick it open.

FIGURE 4-6:
Watch balloons
are invaluable in
troubleshooting
your application
projects

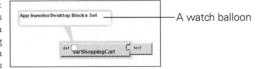
A watch balloon

18. You want the ListPicker button to reflect the user's selection. When a user selects `App Inventor Desktop Blocks Set`, you want the button that once said `Select an Item` to reflect the user's choice. You can change the text property of the ListPicker button by using the `set lstpItems.Text to` block.

19. Open the lstpItems drawer and locate the `set lstpItems.Text to` block. Drag and drop it under the `set varShoppingCart to` block in the AfterPicking event handler. Open the lstpItems drawer and locate the `lstpItems.Selection` block again. Drag and socket the `lstpItems.Selection` into the `set lstpItems.Text to` block (see Figure 4-7).

You used the `lstpItems.Selection` block previously to store the list picker selection into our shopping cart variable. This time it is pumping the same information, the user's selected item, into the text of the ListPicker button.

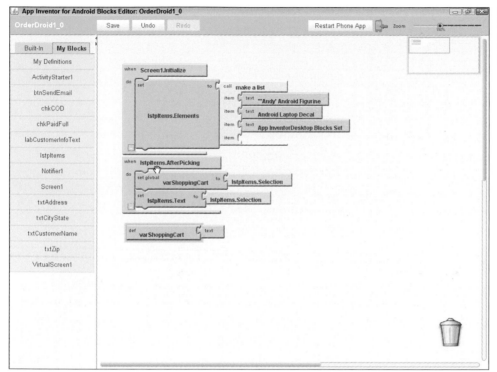

FIGURE 4-7:
The ListPicker
and
ShoppingCart
blocks

Gathering your form data to be e-mailed

Now you need to gather up all of the form data and e-mail it to a preset order processing
address. Keep in mind that in the future, this process for e-mailing the order form needs to
accommodate multiple items and variable addresses:

1. You named your submit order button btnSendEmail, so open its drawer on the My
   Blocks tab and drag out the event handler for btnSendEmail.Click. Drop it on to
   the workspace.

   You will place the blocks to execute when the user thinks the order is ready to send. An
   easy way to identify event handlers is the when keyword they are all labeled with. An
   event handler always says "when something happens, do something."

   Many times, you need to include logic to make sure that data a user has entered fits
   your requirements (for example, a ZIP code must be a number instead of a text string).
   You may also want to verify that certain fields have data. In traditional programming

terminology, this kind of logic is called validation. It validates user input and sometimes sanitizes it so that it can be used. In App Inventor, these kinds of checks utilize the built-in control blocks.

You build logic into the `button click` event to make sure that the name and the address field have content before you allow the e-mail to be sent. Your algorithm requires the kind of logic that says, "If the address field is empty, don't send the e-mails; otherwise, go ahead and send the e-mail." You use the `IfElse` block to accomplish this validation task. In this case, you use a nested `IfElse`. You place one `IfElse` block in the socket of another `IfElse` block. You can do this to ask multiple questions about data test or conditions. You check first for the Name field for content and, if that passes, you check the Address field.

2. Open the Control blocks drawer on the Built-In tab of the Blocks Editor and drag an `IfElse` block into the `btnSendEmail.Click` event handler.

   Now you build the test condition. If the Name field is empty, you use the Notifier component to warn the user. If it's not empty, you proceed to checking the Address field.

3. Typeblock a comparison operator by typing an = and pressing Enter. Socket that comparison operator into the test socket on the `IfElse` block. You want to compare the contents of the Customer Name text field with a blank `text` block.

4. Open the txtCustomerName drawer and locate the `txtCustomerName.Text` block. This block reports the contents of the text box. Drag the `txtCustomerName.Txt` block and socket it into the first socket on the comparison operator (see Figure 4-8).

5. Typeblock a `text` block by typing `text` and pressing Enter. Delete its default value, leaving an empty `text` block. Snap the empty `text` block into the second socket on the comparison operator.

   This test condition tests whether the Customer Name text box is equal to " " or nothing. If the user has neglected to populate the customer name field, the condition evaluates as `True` and execute the blocks in the `then-do` of the `IfElse` block.

   You use the Notifier component to clearly indicate to the user the lack of data in the form.

6. Open the Notifier1 blocks drawer on the My Blocks tab. Locate the `Notifier1.ShowMessageDialog` block. Drag the `Notifier1.ShowMessageDialog` block and snap it into the `then-do` socket on the `IfElse` block (see Figure 4-8).

The ShowMessageDialog has three sockets that require text. They are a little out of
logical order:

- The first, message, is the text that is displayed in the dialog pop-up box. Typeblock
a text block by typing text and pressing Enter. Replace the default text with
Please enter a Customer Name... and press Enter. Snap the text block into
the message socket on the Notifier1.ShowMessageDialog block.

- The second socket on the ShowMessageDialog block, title, will be the text at
the top of the dialog box pop-up. Typeblock a text block. Replace the default text
in the text block with Attention and press Enter. Drag the text block into
the title socket on the ShowMessageDialog block.

- The third socket on the ShowMessageDialog block is button text. This is the
text on the button to dismiss the notification. Typeblock a new text block and
change the default text to OK. Drag the text block and socket it into the but-
tonText socket on the Notifier1.ShowMessageDialog block.

The btnSendEmail.Click event handler should now look like Figure 4-8.

7. Test your application behavior by tapping the Submit Order button on your connected
Android phone, with no text in the Customer Name field. You should get the notification pop-up.

If the Customer Name field is populated, you want to move on and perform the exact
same evaluation on the address field.

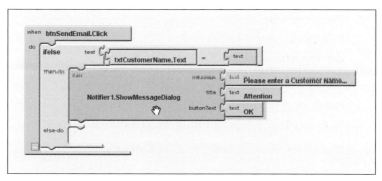

FIGURE 4-8:
The completed
notification
block

8. Drag another `IfElse` block from the Control blocks drawer on the Built-In tab and socket it in the `else-do` of your first `IfElse` block. This creates nested `IfElse` blocks. Typeblock a comparison operator by typing an = (equals sign) and pressing Enter. Socket the comparison operator into the `test` socket of your nested `IfElse` block.

9. Open the txtAddress blocks drawer by clicking it on the My Blocks tab. Locate the `txtAddress.Text` block. This block reports the contents of the text box. Drag the `txtAddress.Text` block and socket it into the first socket on the comparison operator in your nested `IfElse` block.

10. Typeblock a `text` block and delete the default text to leave an empty `text` block. Drag the empty `text` block into the second socket in your comparison operator.

    If this test evaluates as `true`, it means that the user neglected to put any information in the address field, so you need to notify them of this. The address field is important enough that you want to get the address from the user immediately. Having an order with no deliverable address is a disaster. For this task, you use a different `Notifier` block. The `ShowTextDialog` prompts the user to enter the address before it is dismissed.

11. Open the Notifier1 blocks drawer by clicking it on the My Blocks tab. Locate the `Notifier1.ShowTextDialog` block and drag it into the `then-do` socket in your nested `IfElse` block (see Figure 4-9).

    You have taken care of the first notification with the previous steps. Now you need to provide the text for the second notification.

12. Typeblock a `text` block and change the default text to `Please enter a customer address`. Snap the `text` block into the `message` socket on the `Notifier1.ShowMessageDialog` block.

13. Typeblock another `text` block and change the default text to `Attention`. Drag the `text` block into the `title` socket on the Notifier1 block.

14. The `ShowTextDialog` block generates a pop-up dialog box, as shown in Figure 4-10. There is a text box for the user to enter text. When the OK button is tapped, an event is generated and the text from the dialog box can be handled any way you like.

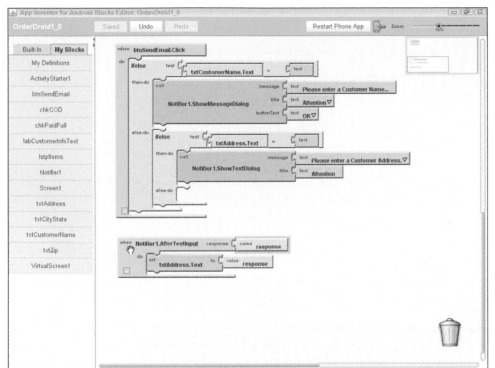

FIGURE 4-9:
The Notifier1.
ShowTextDialog
block

FIGURE 4-10:
The
ShowTextDialog
notification and
text box

15. To control and take advantage of this text box in the dialog box, open the Notifier1 blocks drawer and locate the `Notifier1.AfterTextInput` event handler. Drag the event handler onto the Blocks Editor workspace (see Figure 4-11).

FIGURE 4-11:
The
AfterTextInput
event handler

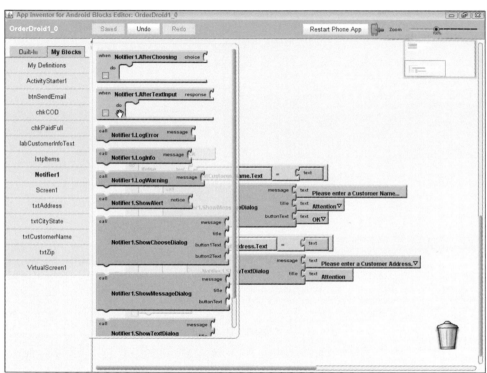

16. After a user inputs the address in the dialog box, you want to populate the Customer Address field on your main form with the entered text. Open the My Definitions blocks drawer.

You will see a new block that was created when you dragged out the `Notifier1.AfterTextInput` event handler. The `value response` block contains the text the user inputs in the text box.

17. Open the txtAddress blocks drawer and locate the set `txtAddress.Text to` block. Drag and drop it into the `Notifier1.AfterTextInput` event handler.

18. Open your My Definitions drawer and drag the `value response` block and socket it into the set `txtAddress.Text to` block (see Figure 4-12).

19. Test your application behavior on your connected Android phone. Populate the Customer Name text box with some text but leave the Address text box empty. Tap the Submit Order button. When the dialog box pops up, enter some text into the dialog text box and tap OK.

You should see the text you entered in the dialog text box appear in the Address text box.

At this point in your project, you have accomplished the following goals:

○ Created the form for gathering customer data

○ Created a list picker with items for selection

○ Created validation checks for critical fields in the form

Your `btnSendEmail.Click` event handler should look like Figure 4-12. The only socket left empty is the final `else-do` in your nested `IfElse` block. In the next section, I show you how to create a procedure to handle the e-mail creation and sending and then call the procedure in this `else-do` socket.

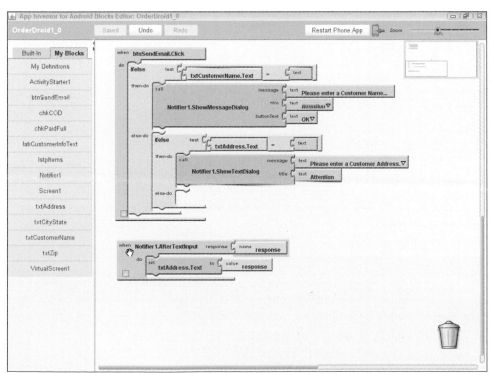

FIGURE 4-12: The validation checks in the btnSendEmail. Click event handler

Creating an e-mail

The ActivityStarter uses its DataURI property to pass a mailto link to the Android built-in link handler. You will define a procedure to handle the gathering and building of the e-mail text and the actual sending of the e-mail. You use a standard mailto link to send your e-mail. The e-mail mailto syntax is fairly simple, but it requires a strict adherence to a preset format. Mailto links are those links on Web pages that launch your e-mail client and automatically populate an e-mail message with address and subject information. The format is as follows:

```
mailto:address@email.com?subject=Subject text&body=body text%0AA
   new line.%0AThirdline
```

The important parts to remember are

- The `mailto:`, which is needed to tell the built in browser to call the default client
- The single `?` after the e-mail address
- The subject and body keywords used to prepopulate the e-mail in the default client
- The ampersand (`&`) between the keywords
- The `%0A`, which indicates a new line for the e-mail body text

You use text function blocks to build up the mailto link and then use the ActivityStarter to call the default link handler on the Android device. Remember that the ActivityStarter cannot be tested while in development mode (that is, while it's connected to App Inventor). It will crash the application. To test this part of your application, you need to package and install your application. Refer to Chapter 1 for a refresher on how to package and install your applications. Here's how to get started creating the e-mail:

1. Open the Definitions blocks drawer on the Built-In tab. Drag a `Procedure` block onto the Blocks Editor workspace. Rename the Procedure `procSendMail`.

 WARNING Make sure you do not grab a `Procedure with Result` block by mistake. I show you how to work with the `Procedure with Result` in Chapter 10.

The first thing you have to do is set the `DataURI` property of the ActivityStarter with the complete mailto link. The mailto link contains all of the text for the e-mail address, and the subject and body of the e-mail.

2. Open the ActivitStarter1 blocks drawer on the My Blocks tab. Locate the set ActivityStarter1.DataUri to block and drag and socket it into the procSend-Mail procedure.

3. Open the Text blocks drawer on the Built-In tab. Drag a make text block on the Blocks Editor workspace.

   The make text block is an expanding block. Every time you socket something into its text socket, it creates another text socket. You can build a text up from various elements such as variables, text boxes, and text blocks. It reports the result of all of its text sockets in a single text string. You build up the mailto string in such a way that it can be easily maintained and expanded in a later version upgrade point.

4. Typeblock a text box by typing text and pressing Enter. You will be using several text blocks, so select the newly created text block and copy it into memory by pressing Ctrl+C on your keyboard. Press Ctrl+V to paste the text block onto the workspace whenever you need a new text block.

5. Change the default text of your first text block to mailto: without the quotes. Snap the mailto block into the text socket on the make text block. A new text socket will be created.

6. Use Ctrl+V to create a new text block. Change the text to the e-mail address you want to send the completed form to. You might want to use your own e-mail address so you can see the result when you test the completed application. Snap the e-mail text block into the new text socket on the make text block.

   In a future version, you might want to replace this block with an address from the contacts or from a text field that you allow the user to input.

7. Use Ctrl+V to create a new text block. Replace the default text with ?subject=A new order from OrderDroid. Snap the Subject block into the next text socket on the make text block.

8. Use Ctrl+V to create a new text block. Replace the default text with &body=. Snap the Body block into the next text socket on the make text block. You will separate the body= tag from the actual body text so that it can be changed later with variables or information from future versions of the OrderDroid application.

9. To prepare for creating the body of the e-mail, drag all the necessary blocks and place them on the workspace for when you need them. You create a nicely formatted e-mail from all of the text entered into the text boxes on your form. So, you will need the .Text blocks from all of your text boxes and the .Value blocks from your check boxes (see Figure 4-13).

10. Open the txtCustomerName drawer on the My Blocks tab and drag out the `txtCustomerName.Text` block.

   Open the txtAddress drawer and drag out the `txtAddress.Text` block.

11. Open the txtCityState drawer and drag out the `txtCityState.Text` block.

   Open the txtZip drawer and drag out the `txtZip.Text` block.

12. Open the chkCOD drawer and drag out the `chkCOD.Value` block.

   Open the chkPaidFull drawer and drag out the `chkPaidFull.Value` block.

13. Open My Definitions drawer and drag out the `global varShoppingCart` variable block.

FIGURE 4-13:
Preparing to
build the body
of the mailto
link

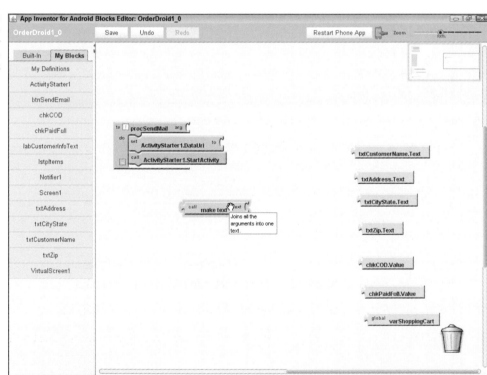

If you get lost or confused while building this long make text block, just flip ahead to Figure 4-14.

14. Typeblock a new `text` block and change the default text to `Customer Name:%0A`. Remember that the `%0A` creates a new line, so you are creating the text `Customer Name:` and then a new line. Drag the `text` block with `Customer Name:%0A` and plug it into the `text` socket on the `make text` block.

15. Snap the `txtCostumerName.Text` block you placed on the workspace earlier into the next `text` socket.

    Typeblock a `text` block and replace the default text with `%0A`. Place the newline block in the next `text` socket.

16. Typeblock a new `text` block and change the default text to `Customer Address:%0A`. Snap the `Customer Address%0A` block into the next `text` socket on the `make text` block.

    Snap the `txtAddress.Text` block into the next `text` socket on the `make text` block.

17. Typeblock a `text` block and replace the default text with `%0A`. Place the newline block in the next `text` socket.

18. Snap the `txtCityState.Text` block into the next text socket.

    Typeblock a `text` block and replace the default text with `%0A` without the quotes. Place the newline block in the next `text` socket.

19. Snap the `txtZip.Text` block in the next text socket.

    Typeblock a `text` block and replace the default text with `%0A`. Place the newline block in the next `text` socket.

20. Typeblock a `text` block and replace the default text with `Purchased Items:%0A`. Drag the `Purchased Items` block and socket it in the next `text` socket.

21. Snap the `global varShoppingCart` block into the next `text` socket.

    Typeblock a `text` block and replace the default text with `%0A`. Place the newline block in the next `text` socket.

22. Typeblock a `text` block and replace the default text with `Payment Type:%0A`. Snap the `Payment Type` block into the next `text` socket.

23. Typeblock a `text` block and replace the default text with `COD=`. Drag this `text` block into the next `text` socket.

    Snap the `chkCOD.Value` block into the next `text` socket.

24. Typeblock a `text` block and replace the default text with `%0A`. Place the newline block in the next `text` socket.

Typeblock a `text` block and replace the default text with `Paid in Full=`. Place this block in the next `text` socket.

25. Snap the `chkPaidFull.Value` block in the next `text` socket.

Typeblock a `text` block and replace the default text with `%0A` without the quotes. Place the newline block in the next `text` socket.

26. Finally, drag the entire `make text` block and socket into the `ActivityStarter1. DataUri` block in your `procSendMail` procedure (see Figure 4-14).

FIGURE 4-14:
The completed
procSendMail
with make text
block for the
mailto link

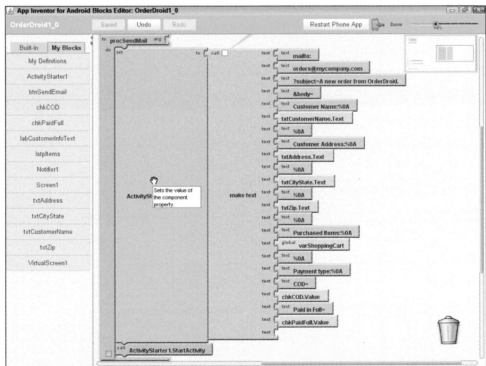

Because you set the `Action` property in the Properties column of the Design view, all that is left for you to do is to call the ActivityStarter in your `procSendMail` procedure:

1. Open the ActivityStarter1 drawer and drag and drop the `call ActivityStarter.StartActivity` block below the `ActivityStarter1.DataUri` block in the `procSendMail` procedure block. (Refer back to Figure 4-14.)

2. Open the My Definitions drawer on the My Blocks tab. Drag the `call procSendMail` block and socket it into the final `else-do` in the `btnSendEmail` event handler. See Figure 4-15.

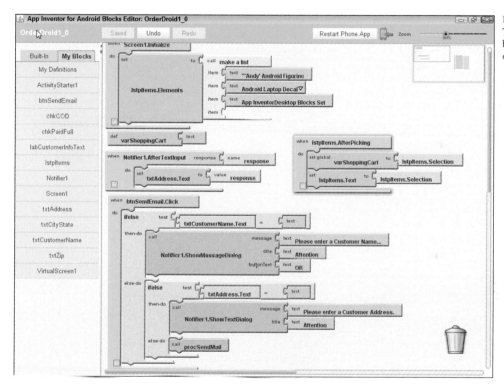

FIGURE 4-15: The completed btnSendEmail event handler.

The completed OrderDroid 1.0 blocks are shown in Figures 4-14 and 4-15.

3. Click back over to your Design view to package and install the application to your phone for testing. If you get a force close error, make sure that the ActivityStarter `Action` property is correctly set.

Creating OrderDroid 2.0

OrderDroid 2.0 progresses from the 1.0 version to include new functionality and bring OrderDroid to the high level you want for an app you're going to deploy. Building the previous version with maintainability in mind makes the expansion of the OrderDroid project smoother and allows for future expansion as well.

Your design

The 2.0 version of OrderDroid changes both the look and the functionality of the application. With OrderDroid 2.0, you learn how to create and use multiple VirtualScreens. Multiple VirtualScreens allow you to include more components and organize your applications logically. Although the second version of this project will not include a whole bunch of new blocks or components, you learn more about creating logic flow and algorithm logic to solve seemingly complex problems. The challenge of keeping all the product items in the shopping cart and formatting them once for display and again for e-mailing takes up most of your time in version 2.0.

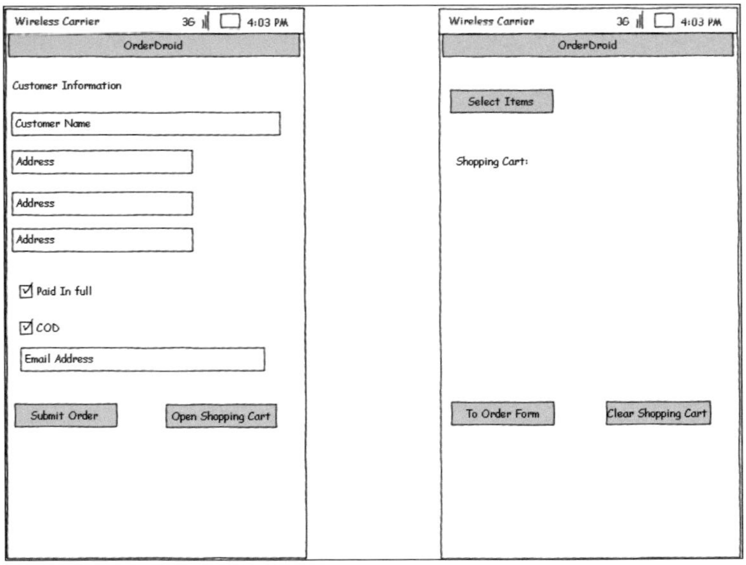

FIGURE 4-16: Design sketches for VirtualScreens 1 and 2 for OrderDroid 2.0

These are your design goals for moving the OrderDroid app to the next milestone:

1. Add a screen for multiple items to be added to the shopping cart.

2. Add the ability to set the address to send e-mail.

3. Include a variable address for order processing.

4. Add the ability to view or clear shopping cart.

Your primitives

These are the primitive programming steps required to achieve your goals:

○ A field to enter e-mail addresses to send the order form to

○ A new VerticalArrangement to be used as VirtualScreen2

○ Navigation buttons to move between VirtualScreens

○ A way to keep multiple items in the `varShoppingCart` variable

○ A way to format and display the shopping cart

○ Organizational elements to make the layout usable and attractive

○ A way to format the shopping cart for the mailto link

Your progression

This is the basic order for accomplishing your design goals and primitives:

1. Create a second VirtualScreen.

2. Create an e-mail field.

3. Create navigation buttons.

4. Create the shopping cart display.

5. Create the shopping cart Clear button.

6. Create the navigation logic.

7. Create the shopping cart logic.

8. Change the e-mail procedure.

New components

The new concept of VirtualScreens is important for future applications:

○ VirtualScreens

New blocks

These are the new blocks used for building version 2.0:

○ ForEach

○ Add Item to List

You will be expanding the previous version of the OrderDroid application, but you do not want to lose the current version, so you should save a copy and work on the copy:

1. Open the OrderDroid1_0 project.

2. Select the Save As button in Design view above the Viewer.

   The default Save As name is OrderDroid1_0copy.

3. Change the Save As name to OrderDroid2_0.

   A copy of the 1.0 version is made and renamed OrderDroid2_0. You will be editing the newly named OrderDroid2_0 copy.

The first VerticalArrangement that you placed in the OrderDroid 1.0 project was renamed to VirtualScreen1 in preparation for a version with more virtual screens. You use another VerticalArrangement to act as a holder for all of the elements meant to show up for VirtualScreen2.

App Inventor does not currently support multiple screens in the traditional sense of the idea. However, you simulate the exact same effect using virtual screens. VirtualScreen1 starts with the `Visible` property set to `true`. VirtualScreen2 starts with its `Visible` property set to `false`. The result is that all the components in VirtualScreen1 are visible and all the components in VirtualScreen2 are invisible. You can harness this behavior by having a button event that changes the two states so that the invisible becomes visible and vice versa. If you get lost or confused while setting up the user interface for OrderDroid 2.0, flip forward to Figure 4-17 for clarification.

Getting Started on OrderDroid 2.0

The VirtualScreens are VerticalArrangements that you repurpose as containers for all the required elements for a given user interface screen. Pay close attention to the following steps so you can reproduce them for your own applications:

1. To begin, drag and drop a VerticalArrangement from the Screen Arrangement palette below the existing VirtualScreen1. Rename this VerticalArrangement as `VirtualScreen2`.

2. In the Properties column, uncheck the `Visible` property. Because you will be using the component centering method you used in the SounDroid project, make sure the `Width` and the `Height` property on both VirtualScreens is set to `Fill Parent`.

    The second virtual screen is the Shopping Cart screen. From this screen, the user can select items to add to the cart. The ListPicker component named lstpItems needs to be moved to the second virtual screen.

3. Click on the ListPicker component in the Viewer and drag it down into VirtualScreen2.

    Most of the screen space on VirtualScreen2 is taken up with item listings for the shopping cart. You need a label to indicate what you are displaying.

4. From the Basic palette, drag a label below the ListPicker in VirtualScreen2. In the Components column, rename the label `lblShoppingCartLabel`. Set the `TextColor` property to `white` and then change the default text to `Shopping Cart Contents:`.

    Drag a second label from the Basic palette and drop it below the `lblShoppingCart-Label`. In the Components column, rename the label to `lblShoppingCartDis-play`. In the Properties column, change the `TextColor` property to `white`. Delete the default text, leaving an empty label. Set the `Width` and `Height` property to `Fill Parent`. Refer to Figure 4-17 for layout reference.

Adding navigational elements

After you have your shopping cart display set up, you need to put in place the navigation elements that allow users to move back and forth between the virtual screens by toggling the visibility of the VirtualScreen components:

1. Drag a HorizontalArrangement from the Screen Arrangement palette and drop it directly below the Shopping Cart display label. Set its `Width` property to `Fill Parent`.

    This acts as a container for two buttons: one to navigate back to the Order form and the other to clear the contents of the shopping cart.

2. Drag a button from the Basic palette into the HorizontalArrangement you just placed. This is the button to go back to the main order form screen. Change the name to `btn-BackToForm`. Change the default text to `Back to Order Form`.

Next you use an empty label as padding between the Back button and the Clear Shopping Cart button.

3. Drag a label next to the Back button. In the Components column, rename the label `padButtonSpace2`. Delete the default text and leave the label blank. Set the `Width` property to `Fill Parent`.

The label keeps the buttons equally spaced at the bottom of the Virtual Screen.

4. Drag and drop another button next to the padding label. In the Components column, rename the button `btnClearCart`. Change the default text to `Clear Shopping Cart`.

Your VirtualScreen2 is complete. Now you need to add a navigation button on VirtualScreen1 to enable VirtualScreen2. You need a HorizontalArrangement to keep the Submit button and the navigation button arranged nicely.

5. Drag a new HorizontalArrangement below the Submit Order button. In the Properties column, set the `Width` property of the HorizontalArrangement to `Fill Parent`.

6. Drag and drop the Submit Order button into the HorizontalArrangement.

You will use a padding label as in Virtual Screen2 to separate the two buttons. Drag a label from the Basic palette and drop it into the HorizontalArrangement. Rename the Label `padButtonSpace1`. Delete the default text leaving an empty label. Set the `Width` property to `Fill Parent`.

7. Drag a new button to the right of the padding label in the HorizontalArrangement. Rename the button `btnToCart`. Change the default text to `Open Shopping Cart`.

On your connected Android device, you will notice that there is space below the Submit and Navigation buttons. To keep VirtualScreen1 and VirtualScreen2 consistent and looking nice, put a HorizontalArrangement above them and set it to `Fill Parent`. The HorizontalArrangement also holds the text box for the user to enter an e-mail address to send the order form to:

1. Drag and drop a new HorizontalArrangement between the COD check box and the HorizontalArrangement holding the buttons. In the Properties column, set both the `Width` and `Height` property of the arrangement to `Fill Parent`.

2. Drag and drop a label into the new HorizontalArrangement. In the Components column, rename the label `lblEmailAddressLabel`. Change the default text to `Receiving Email:`. Change the default text color to white.

3. Drag and drop a text box from the Basic palette to the `lblEmailAddressLabel`. Change the name of the text box to `txtEmailAddress`. Change the default Hint text to `Enter Email Address`. This will be the text box in which your user enters the e-mail address for the mailto link.

At this point, your component layout should look like Figure 4-17.

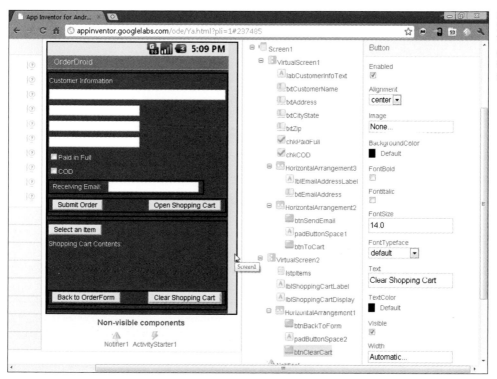

FIGURE 4-17: Both VirtualScreens of the OrderDroid 2.0 user interface

Make sure your Blocks Editor workspace is scrolled to a clean workspace area away from the programming blocks that give your OrderForm its current functionality. Hover your mouse over the mini-map in the upper right of the Blocks Editor and click on an empty space to move your current workspace to that spot.

Switch over to the Blocks Editor. Your first task is to set up the logic for the two navigation buttons that allow the user to move between VirtualScreen1 and VirtualScreen2. Use the `.Click` event handlers for the `btnToCart` and the `btnBackToForm` to toggle the visibility property on the VirtualScreens.

1. Open the btnToCart blocks drawer by clicking it on the My Blocks tab. Drag the when `btnToCart.Click` do event handler out onto the workspace.

2. Open the btnBackToForm blocks drawer and drag the when `btnBacktoForm.Click` do event handler to the workspace.

3. Open the VirtualScreen1 blocks drawer and drag out the `set VirtualScreen1.Visible to` block. Select the block so that it is highlighted and press Ctrl+C to copy the block into memory. Then press Ctrl+V to paste a copy of the block. You should now have two `set VirtualScreen1.Visible to` blocks.

4. Open the VirtualScreen2 blocks drawer and drag out the `set VirtualScreen2.Visible to` block. Copy and paste the block so that you have two `set VirtualScreen2.Visible to` blocks.

5. Drag one of the `set VirtualScreen1.Visible to` blocks into the `btnToCart.Click` event handler, and then drag one of the `set VirtualScreen2.Visible to` blocks into the `btnToCart.Click` event handler (see Figure 4-18).

6. Drag the two leftover `VirtualScreen.Visible` blocks into the `btnBackToForm.Click` event handler.

You now need to provide a value for the `.Visible` blocks. The `btnToCart.Click` handler is for the To Shopping Cart button. Tapping it should make VirtualScreen1 invisible and VirtualScreen2 visible.

1. Typeblock a `false` block by clicking on a blank area of the workspace, typing `false` on your keyboard, and pressing Enter. Snap the `false` block into the `set VirtualScreen1.Visible to` in the `btnBackToForm.Click` block.

2. Type block a `true` block by typing `true` and pressing Enter on your keyboard. Snap the `true` block into the socket on the `set VirtualScreen2.Visible to` block in the `btnToCart.Click` event handler block.

   The `btnBackToForm.Click` event handler is for the Back to Order Form button on VirtualScreen2. Tapping it should do the exact opposite of the previous event handler.

3. Typeblock a `true` block and socket it into the `set VirtualScreen1.Visible to` block in the `btnBackToForm.Click` event handler.

4. Typeblock a `false` block and socket it into the `set VirtualScreen2.Visible to` block in the `btnBackToForm.Click` event Handler (see Figure 4-18).

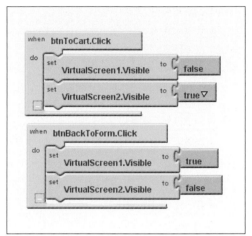

FIGURE 4-18: The completed Navigation button event handlers for the VirtualScreens

Test the navigation buttons on your connected Android device. The buttons should now move you back and forward between the two virtual screens. Voilà! Your application now gives the impression of having two distinct areas of user interface elements. You can use this method to create a wide variety of application functionality.

Storing multiple items and formatting them for display

The design goal of storing multiple items and formatting them for display is the most challenging goal in this project. In the version 1.0 of the OrderDroid project, you just dropped whatever the ListPicker selected into a variable and then e-mailed the contents of the variable. The algorithm for the process looked something like Figure 4-19.

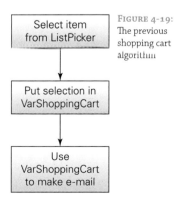

FIGURE 4-19: The previous shopping cart algorithm

For storing multiple items and then displaying them, you need a more complex process. You will make use of a variable as a list, a temporary formatting variable, and a `ForEach` block to create the logic in Figure 4-20.

FIGURE 4-20:
Algorithm for
the shopping
cart in
OrderDroid 2.0

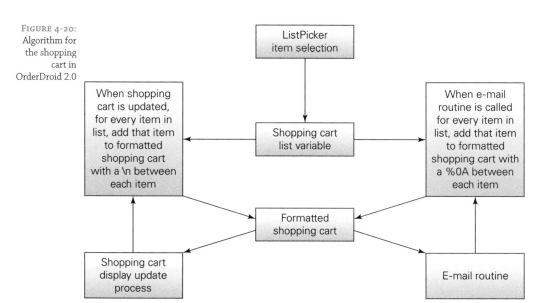

When an item is selected from the ListPicker, it is written to a variable as an item in a list. In App Inventor, a list is a variable that has been defined as a list by using blocks from the List drawer. The `varShoppingCart` doesn't change unless the shopping cart is cleared or an item is added with the ListPicker. The `varShoppingCart` list can be used by either the Shopping Cart Display routine or the Email routine to format and then use the formatted text in the formatted shopping cart variable. Another way to think of it is that the `varFormattedShoppingCart` is a piece of scrap paper that the two routines use to organize the list text the way they need it. The Display routine needs each list item to be on a new line, so it will use the "\n" newline character to format the text. The Email routine needs each list item on a new line as well but must use the `%0A` e-mail@@ndspecific newline character.

So breaking that logic down piece by piece, you let the `ListPicker.AfterPicking` event handle the updating of the `varShoppingCart` variable list. You build a new procedure for the display update, and then you update the existing e-mail procedure to utilize the new shopping cart as a list.

1. In the Blocks Editor workspace, locate the `def varShoppingCart` block. It currently has a null or empty `text` block in it. Delete the `text` block.

You can delete blocks by dragging them to the trash can icon in the lower right corner of the ◄ **REMEMBER** screen or by highlighting them and pressing Delete on your keyboard.

---

2. Open the List blocks drawer on the Built-In tab of the Blocks Editor. Drag out a `Make a List` block and socket it into the `varShoppingCart` block (see Figure 4-21).

   Locate the `lstpItems.Afterpicking` block in the Blocks Editor workspace. This is the event that handles what happens after an item is selected from your ListPicker. Currently it sets the value of the `varShoppingCart` to the selected Item from the ListPicker. That will not work with multiple items. Each time an item is selected, it overwrites the previous item that was in the variable. Because we turned the `varShoppingCart` into a list, we can now add an item to that list each time an item is selected.

3. Remove the `lstpItems.Selection` block from the `varShoppingCart` block and set it aside — you will reuse it in a moment.

4. Delete the `set global varShoppingCart to` block from the `lstpItems.Afterpicking` event.

5. Delete the `lstpItems.Text` block that is in the `lstpItems.Afterpicking` event block.

   This was the block that turned the ListPicker text to the text of the selected Item. This time, you are displaying the list of select items in `lblShoppingCartDisplay`.

6. Open the Lists blocks drawer by clicking it on the Built-In tab. Drag out an `add items to list` block and snap it into the `lstpItems.AfterPicking` event handler (see Figure 4-21).

   The `Add Items to List` block has two sockets: one for the list you want to add items to, and one for the items to add to the list. Populating the `item` socket generates another `item` socket on the block.

7. Open the My Definitions drawer on the My Blocks tab. Drag out the `global varShoppingCart` block and socket it into the `list` socket on the `Add Items to List` block. The `varShoppingCart` global variable is where your list of items will be stored.

8. Now grab the `lstpItems.Selection` block that you set aside earlier (or you can get a new one from the lstpItems blocks drawer) and socket it into the `item` socket of the `Add Items to List` block (see Figure 4-21).

You will also call the Shopping Cart display procedure in the `lstpItems.AfterPicking` event handler, but you haven't built it yet.

FIGURE 4-21: The rebuilt blocks without the display procedure

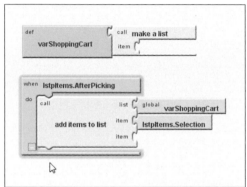

Building the display procedure for the varShoppingCart list

Next, build the display procedure to utilize the items stored in the `varShoppingCart` list:

1. Open the Definition blocks drawer from the Built-In tab. Drag a `procedure` block onto the Blocks Editor workspace. Click on the `procedure` text to rename the procedure. Rename the procedure `procUpdateCartDisplay`.

2. Now you need that temporary place to format the list from the `varShoppingCart` before displaying it. Open the Definitions blocks drawer on the Built-In tab. Drag out a variable and rename it `varFormattedShoppingCart`. Typeblock a `text` block by typing the word `text` and pressing your Enter key. Socket the empty `text` block into the variable you just created.

This is the temporary holding place for the formatted shopping cart before it is displayed or e-mailed.

Because your procedure and the `varFormattedShoppingCart` will be used repeatedly, you need to clean the `varFormattedShoppingCart` up before repopulating it.

3. Open the My Definitions drawer on the My Blocks tab. Drag out the `set varFormattedShoppingCart to` block and snap it into the `procUpdateCartDisplay` procedure.

4. Typeblock a `text` block by typing the word `text` and pressing Enter. Delete the default text on the block and snap the empty block into the `set varFormattedShoppingCart` block that is now in your `procUpdateCartDisplay` procedure.

   This clears the variable of any leftover formatted text from previous calls to the procedure.

   For every item in the `varShoppingCart` variable, we want to display that item, create a new line, display the next item and a new line, and so on. To do this kind of an iterative task, you use a `ForEach` block.

5. Open the Control blocks drawer on the Built-In tab. Locate and drag out the `ForEach` block. Snap the `ForEach` block into the `procUpdateCartDisplay` block underneath the `set global` block.

   The `ForEach` block defines its own parameter variable where it places each item from the list while it works on it. You tell the `ForEach` block what list you want it to work on in the socket in the lower arm labeled `in list`. The `ForEach` block then loads each item in the list into the variable defined in its upper arm and does to that item whatever blocks you put between the two arms. When it reaches the last item, your application goes on executing. You can change the name of the parameter variable, but usually you won't have to.

   You need to tell the `ForEach` block what list it will be working with.

6. Open the My Definitions drawer, pull out the global `varShoppingCart` block, and snap it into the `in list` socket in the lower arm of the `ForEach` block (see Figure 4-21) Now that the `ForEach` block knows what items it will be working with, you need to tell it what to do with each item.

7. You want to take each item and write it to the `varFormattedShoppingCart` variable and then write a new line. If you don't do that, App Inventor lists look like this:

   (Item1 Item2 Item3)

   Just a bunch of list elements held in parentheses: not very readable at all.

8. Open the My Definitions blocks drawer and drag out the `set varFormattedShoppingCart to` block and snap it between the arms of the `ForEach` block (see Figure 4-22).

You could just plug in that parameter variable called `var` into the variable set block, but that would just write one item from the list to the `varFormattedShopping-Cart` variable. Each pass of the `ForEach` block would write the current contents of the parameter variable over the contents of the `varFormattedShoppingCart`. You need to take all of what is in the formatted shopping cart variable and add to it the current contents of the parameter variable. You want all the previous items and newlines plus each item plus a newline. You will use the `join text` block to join the contents of the formatted shopping cart variable with your parameter variable and a newline character. Another way to think about what you are doing is "layering" the information into the `varFormattedShoppingCart` by taking what is in the variable and layering the new item and newline on top of the contents, and then placing it all back in the variable.

9. Open the Text blocks drawer on the Built-In tab and drag out a `join` block and snap it into the `set varFormattedShoppingCart to` block that is in the `ForEach` block. You are joining the contents of the formatted shopping cart, so open the My Definitions drawer, pull out the `global varFormattedShoppingCart` block, and snap it into the first open socket on the `join` block.

   You want to join to that variable contents the current contents of the parameter variable and a newline.

10. Open the Text blocks drawer on the Built-In tab, drag out a `make text` block and snap it into the second socket on the join block.

11. Open the My Definitions drawer and pull out the `value var` block. The `value` block reports the contents of the parameter variable `var`. Snap the `value var` block into the socket on the `make text` block. A new socket is created.

12. Typeblock a new `text` block by typing `text` and pressing Enter on your keyboard. Change the default text to \n. (Make sure the slash is a back slash.)

Updating the shopping cart display

Now the `ForEach` block adds all the items in the `varShoppingCart` to the `varFormat-tedShoppingCart` one at a time followed by a newline character. Now you have to update the shopping cart display with your newly formatted content. Because there may already be formatted content on the display, first you need to clear it:

1. Open the lblShoppingCartDisplay blocks drawer. Drag out the `set lblShopping-CartDisplay.Text to` block and snap it under the `ForEach` block. Copy and paste

another `set lblShoppingCartDisplay.Text to` block or drag it from its drawer.
Place the second block under the first (see Figure 4-22).

2. Typeblock a `text` block and delete the default `text`. Snap the blank text block into
   the first `lblShoppingCartDisplay.Text block`. This clears any text currently in
   the display.

3. Open the My Definitions drawer and locate the `global varFormattedShopping-`
   `Cart` block. Drag it out and snap it into the second `lblShoppingCartDisplay.`
   `Text` block. This populates the display label with the current contents of the formatted shopping cart.

Your `procUpdateCartDisplay` procedure should be completed and look like Figure 4-22.

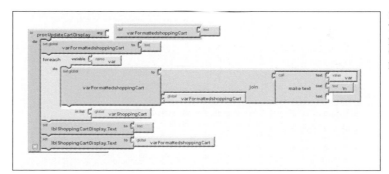

FIGURE 4-22:
The completed
procUpdate
CartDisplay
procedure

Finishing the shopping cart

The only thing left to do for your shopping cart is to call the `procUpdateCartDisplay`
procedure in the `lstpItems.AfterPicking` event:

1. Open the My Definitions drawer and drag out the `call procUpdateCartDisplay`
   block. Snap it in as the very last block into the `lstpItems.AfterPicking` event
   that is already on your workspace.

   If your user makes a mistake or needs to start all over again selecting items, they can
   click the Clear Shopping Cart button. The Clear Shopping Cart button clears both the
   shopping cart variable and the shopping cart display.

2. Open the btnClearCart blocks drawer and drag out the `when btnClearCart.Click`
   `do` block.

3. Open the My Definitions blocks drawer and drag out the set varShoppingCart to block and snap it into the when btnClearCart.Click do event handler.

4. Typeblock a Make a List block and snap the Make a List block into the set varShoppingCart to block. When the block is executed, this clears the variable.

NOTE

> When you are clearing a variable used as a list, you must use a Make a List block to clear it. If you clear with a text block, you get an error when you attempt to use it as a list again.

---

5. Open the lblShoppingCartDisplay blocks drawer. Drag out the set lblShopping-CartDisplay.Text to block and snap it into the btnClearCart.Click block.

6. Typeblock a text block and delete the default text. Snap the empty text block into the set lblShoppingCartDisplay.Text to block on your keyboard (see Figure 4-23). This clears the Shopping Cart display.

FIGURE 4-23:
The clear button
event handler

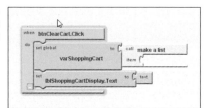

Test the item selection, display, and shopping cart clearing on your connected Android device. If you experience any trouble, go back carefully over all the figures in the 2.0 version to spot any differences.

The e-mail procedure

The process of formatting the shopping cart for display is almost exactly duplicated in the e-mail procedure, except the newline character will be different. The e-mail procedure formats all of the selected items and the customer information to be so it can be sent with the mailto link and the ActivityStarter. The mailto only recognizes the %0A as a newline. You use a ForEach loop to create the items in the varShoppingCart with the %0A character. Then you partially dismantle the make text that makes up the mailto link text. You replace the varShoppingCart variable with the varFormattedShoppingCart and replace the e-mail address with the text from the e-mail address text box on VirtualScreen1.

Just as you did in the update display procedure, you should flush out anything that might have been put into the `varFormattedShoppingCart`:

1. Locate the `procSendMail` block in your Blocks Editor workspace. Open the My Definitions blocks drawer, drag out the `set varFormattedShoppingCart to` block, and snap it into the `procSendMail` above the `ActivityStarter1.DataUri` with the long `make text` block in it (see Figure 4-24).

2. Typeblock a `text` block and delete the default text. Snap the empty `text` block into the `set varFormattedShoppingCart to` block. This clears anything left over in the variable.

   In the next step, be sure to use a new `ForEach` block instead of copying the existing `ForEach` in the `procUpdateCartDisplay`. Just as with all of the other components, the parameter variable's name must be unique.

3. Open the Control blocks drawer on the Built-In tab, drag a `ForEach` block, and snap it below the `set varFormattedShoppingCart to` block you just placed (see Figure 4-24).

4. Open the My Definitions blocks drawer and drag out the `global varShoppingCart` block. Socket it into the `in list` socket on your `ForEach` block. Each item in the shopping cart variable is written one by one into the parameter variable `var1` for processing.

5. Open the My Definitions drawer and locate the `set varFormattedShoppingCart to` block. Drag and snap it into your new `ForEach` block. You use this variable as a temporary formatting location as you did in the display update procedure.

   Join the contents of the formatted shopping cart variable with each item in the `varShoppingCart` list variable.

6. Open the Text blocks drawer on the Built-In tab. Drag out a `join` block and socket it into the `varFormattedShoppingCart` variable in your ForEach block.

7. Open the My Definitions drawer and drag out the `global varFormattedShoppingCart` block. Snap that block into the first open socket on the `join` block.

   The goal is to add to whatever is in the formatted shopping cart variable the current contents of the `var1` parameter variable and a newline character.

8. Open the Text blocks drawer and drag out a `make text` block. Snap the `make text` block into the second open socket on the `join` block.

Open the My Definitions blocks drawer and locate the `value var1` block. Snap the `var1` value block into the `make text` block that is nested in the `join` block (see Figure 4-24).

9. Typeblock a new `text` block and replace the default text with `%0A`. Snap the `text` block with the newline character in the open socket on the `make text` block.

Your new blocks in the `procSendMail` procedure shown in Figure 4-24 now clear the formatted shopping cart variable, and then iterate through the `varShoppingCart` and write each item followed by a newline character into the `varFormattedShoppingCart` variable.

FIGURE 4-24:
The new
formatting
blocks for the
procSendMail
procedure

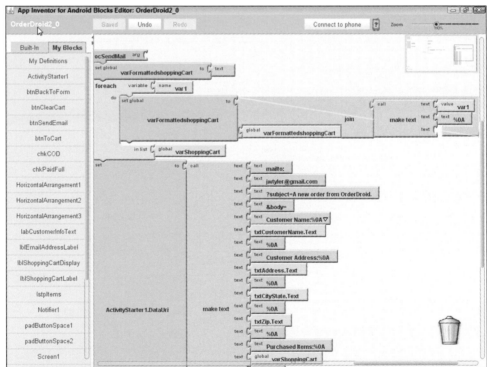

You can now use the `varFormattedShoppingCart` variable in the `make text` block in the `procSendMail` procedure that makes the mailto link. Refer to Figure 4-25 to clarify the following directions.

You now alter the long `make text` block that is socketed into the `ActivityStarter1.DataUri` block. Work from the bottom of the `make text` up, removing the following blocks. You remove the `text` block with the e-mail address in it and replace it with the text from the txtEmailAddress text box. You also replace the `varShoppingCart` block and then replace all of the removed blocks.

Remove all of the blocks in the following list from the `make text` block, working your way up. Set them to the side as you will resocket them in just a minute:

- ⭕ chkPaidFull.Value
- ⭕ Paid in Full= text
- ⭕ chkCOD.Value
- ⭕ COD= text
- ⭕ Payment type:%0A text
- ⭕ The %0A text
- ⭕ Remove the varShoppingCart block and delete it (see Figure 4-25)
- ⭕ Purchased Items %0A: text
- ⭕ %0A text
- ⭕ txtZip.Text
- ⭕ %0A text
- ⭕ txtCityState.Text
- ⭕ txtAddress.Text
- ⭕ Customer Address:%0A text
- ⭕ %0A text
- ⭕ txtCustomerName.Text
- ⭕ Customer Name:%0A text
- ⭕ &body= text
- ⭕ ?subject=A new order from OrderDroid. text
- ⭕ Remove the e-mail address block and delete it

After removing all of the preceding blocks and deleting the `varShoppingCart` and `email@ example.com` text block, your `make text` and all the blocks that were in it should look like Figure 4-25.

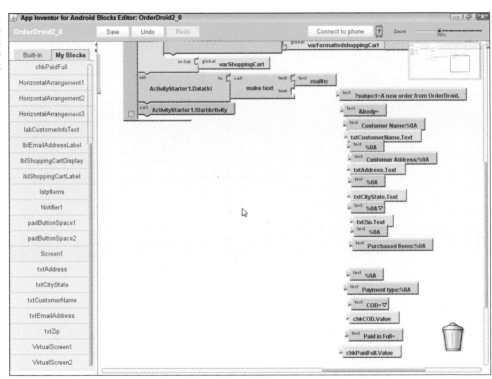

FIGURE 4-25:
Rebuilding the
make text block
for the mailto
link

Open the txtEmailAddress blocks drawer on the My Blocks tab. Locate the `txtEmail Address.Text` block. Drag it out and snap it in under the `mailto:` text block in the make text block you just cleaned out (see Figure 4-25).

Resocket the following blocks below the `txtEmailAddress.Text` block in this order:

○ `?subject=A new order from OrderDroid. text`

○ `&body= text`

○ `Customer Name:%0A text`

- ⭘ `txtCustomerName.Text`

- ⭘ `%0A text`

- ⭘ `Customer Address:%0A text`

- ⭘ `txtAddress.Text`

- ⭘ `%0A`

- ⭘ `txtCityState.Text`

- ⭘ `%0A text`

- ⭘ `txtZip.Text`

- ⭘ `%0A text`

- ⭘ `Purchased Items %0A: text`

Open the My Definitions drawer and drag out the global `varFormattedShoppingCart` block. Snap it into the `text` socket (see Figure 4-26).

Continue replacing the following blocks:

- ⭘ `%0A text`

- ⭘ `Payment type%0A text`

- ⭘ `COD text`

- ⭘ `chkCOD.Value`

- ⭘ `Paid in Full= text`

- ⭘ `chkPaidFull.Value`

Refer to Figure 4-26 to make sure your blocks are in the right order.

FIGURE 4-26:
The rebuilt make
text mailto
blocks

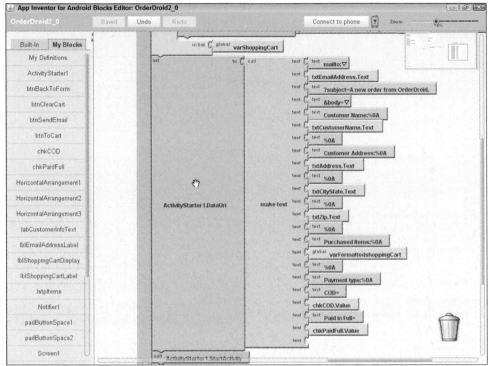

Congratulations! You have successfully moved the OrderDroid project to its 2.0 version. Go back to the Design view and package the application to your phone. Test it by filling out the form, selecting a few items, and then submitting the order. The order should show up at whatever address you put in the Receiving E-mail Address field.

chapter 5
AndroidDown: A Location-Aware Panic Button

in this chapter

- ○ Using LocationSensor for GPS location information
- ○ Using TinyDB for persistent data
- ○ Using SMS texting capabilities
- ○ Using deferred processing to avoid force closures while in a wait state

THE ANDROIDDOWN APPLICATION gives you a solid introduction to utilizing the LocationSensor to pull GPS coordinates for your application. The LocationSensor component can use GPS, network, or Wi-Fi location systems. In this application, you use the GPS provider. The LocationSensor needs to have a "lock" on the signals from GPS satellites before it can provide coordinates. If you just told the application to wait until the LocationSensor had a strong enough signal, the Android operating system would very likely decide your application had crashed.

When an application does not accept input from the user, it assumes the application is dead and force-closes the application. To avoid this, you will learn how to use deferred processing. *Deferred processing* uses a Clock timer component and a procedure to check for the desired state (in this case, the GPS lock) on a timed basis. As your application attempts to get a signal lock for the LocationSensor, it bounces back and forth between a timer and a procedure. Each time the timer calls the procedure, you increment a counter. Incrementing a counter is an important programming concept that is used to count repeated events. You can use the incrementing steps found in this project to count the number of times a certain thing happens. You can also use incrementing to break out of a loop. In other words, you can count every time a certain thing happens and put a limit on the number of times it can happen.

The AndroidDown project is your first introduction to persistent data using the TinyDB component. The TinyDB component is a simple database that can store key/value pairs. TinyDB stores data with an index word called a tag. The tag is attached to the data you place in TinyDB. Your data can then be recalled from the database using the tag word. TinyDB is simple but also very powerful. Using the `text split` blocks, you can store multi-dimensional arrays or lists of data in TinyDB. For the AndroidDown application, you use TinyDB to store the applications settings. This is a common use of TinyDB; however, you can store and retrieve data in TinyDB for anything you can imagine. The only limitation of TinyDB is the storage memory on your device.

The Texting component gives you complete control over sending and receiving text messages via the SMS (Short Message Service) standard. The Texting component accesses the phone's native SMS texting capability with simple function calls. Use this project to learn how to incorporate SMS capabilities into your applications. The ability to send and receive SMS texts is a valuable level of functionality to many applications.

You need to download the Chapter 5 project files from the companion Web site. See this book's Introduction for more details on the Web site.

Creating the AndroidDown Application

The AndroidDown application is a panic button program. The 1.0 version sends the phone or device's physical address to a contact selected from the device contacts. It uses the LocationSensor to report the address. The LocationSensor uses the GPS coordinates of the device to determine the physical address. It does this by sending the coordinates via network (either the phone data network or Wi-Fi) to Google Maps, which returns the address to the component. The SMS component is used to send a text message with the information gathered from the LocationSensor.

Be careful while building and testing this application. If your carrier or data package charges for SMS text messages, you will be charged when the SMS component sends a message.   **NOTE**

Use your device's SMS number or a Google Voice SMS number to test panic messages. Sending a flurry of SOS and panic messages to a friend or relative may not be advisable. (Or if you do, at least tell them what you're doing first!)

Your design

Figure 5-1 shows the design sketch for the first user interface of AndroidDown. You can use the design sketch to help you while beginning the process of building the user interface.

The AndroidDown application is a location-aware panic button. It records your current address using a GPS sensor and a network data connection to Google. When the panic button is pushed, it lets the user pick a contact to send a pre-built panic SMS (Short Message Service, or text) message with the user's location. It keeps the panic button disabled until it gets a solid fix on the current location: If there is no data in the LocationSensor, there is nothing to send in the panic message. It also lets the user know that it is still actively attempting to get a location fix.

FIGURE 5-1:
The design
sketch for
AndroidDown
1.0 user
interface

FIGURE 5-1: The design sketch for AndroidDown 1.0 user interface

Your primitives

These are the simple logic and algorithms needed to accomplish your design goals:

- ❍ A phone number picker
- ❍ A way to get physical address of device
- ❍ A way to disable panic button until a fix on address is obtained
- ❍ A way to track the phones attempt to get a fix and update user
- ❍ A way to notify the user that an SMS message has been sent
- ❍ A way to send SMS messages

Your progression

These are the logical or easiest steps to build the major design goals and primitives:

1. Build the PhoneNumberPicker to select the number to which to send an SMS panic message.

2. Build the centering methods you have learned to center the AndroidDown user interface (UI) components.

3. Build the LocationSensor component to access the GPS signal and retrieve the user's current physical address.

4. Build the process to use deferred processing to keep the phone number picker disabled until the user's position is known.

5. Build the labels and a sequence of button image updates to keep the user informed of the status of the app.

New components

These are the new components introduced in the AndroidDown application:

❍ LocationSensor

❍ Texting

❍ PhoneNumberPicker

Getting Started on AndroidDown 1.0

You should design your user interface first. Your design sketches are always a good way to start the process of putting the user interface elements onto the Viewer. You can refer to them to get an idea of what buttons, labels, and components your interface requires. Keep this version of the AndroidDown application flexible for future improvements. The primary interface element of the AndroidDown application is the giant Help button in the middle of the screen. That button not only plays an integral part in the user interaction, but it's also a primary status indicator to the user. As the AndroidDown application is looking for the current location of the user, it changes the image for the PhoneNumberPicker button to indicate it is still looking. When the location is found and fixed, the PhoneNumberPicker is enabled and the button image is changed.

Here's how to get started on the interface:

1. Start a new project from your My Projects view and name the project `AndroidDown1_0`.

2. Select the Screen1 component in the Components column. In the Properties column, change the `Title` property to `AndroidDown 1.0`.

3. Drag a VerticalArrangement from the Screen Arrangement palette and drop it into the Viewer. In the Components column, rename the VerticalArrangement as `VirtualScreen1`.

   This VerticalArrangement you have renamed VirtualScreen1 will be the primary container for all of the user interface elements. Using VirtualScreens provides for future expansion into more VirtualScreens for your 2.0 version — all you will need to do is add a new VerticalArrangement for a new virtual screen.

4. In the Properties column, set the `Width` and `Height` properties to `Fill Parent`.

   When you use padding elements to center components, the Screen1 `Width` and `Height` of all Arrangement containers should be set to `Fill Parent` for the centering and padding elements to work. This is the easiest way to get dynamic centering of components on App Inventor interfaces.

5. Next, drag and drop a HorizontalArrangement into the VirtualScreen1.

   This HorizontalArrangement is the container for the large panic button. You use the empty padding labels trick to keep it centered on the screen. In the Properties column, set the `Width` and `Height` properties to `Fill Parent`.

6. Drag a Label component from the Basic palette into the HorizontalArrangement.

   This is your left side padding element. In the Components column, rename the Label1 component to `padLabel1`. For this project, you simply sequentially number all the padding elements.

   Wait until your PhoneNumberPicker is in place before changing the properties on this padding element. If you remove the default text from the `Text` property, the HorizontalArrangement shrinks down until it's almost impossible to place your other components into it.

7. Open the Social palette, drag out a PhoneNumberPicker, and place it next to the padLabel1 component.

For this project, because you are learning the PhoneNumberPicker component and   **TIP**
activities, you should leave its name unchanged. The PhoneNumberPicker is not available
unless the location has been determined by the LocationSensor component. In other words,
the starting state of the PhoneNumberPicker is visible but not enabled.

8. Deselect the Enabled property check box for the PhoneNumberPicker in the Properties
column.

The PhoneNumberPicker takes its shape and look from the image that is loaded into
the button. However, the PhoneNumberPicker Image property is populated by the
property blocks in the Blocks Editor. For any image to be used as a property in the
Blocks Editor, it must be first uploaded into the Media column.

9. Go ahead and upload the images for the PhoneNumberPicker button now. Click the
Add button in the Media column. Click the Choose button in the Upload pop-up.
Navigate to where you downloaded the project files for Chapter 5. Select the getloc.png
image and click the Open button. This is the image for when the AndroidDown app is
attempting to get the current location.

10. Click the Add button again and upload the help.png image file. When you see getloc.
png and help.png in the Media column, you know that the files have been added to
your project and will be available to assign to the PhoneNumberPicker from the property blocks.

11. Set the BackgroundColorPicker to None.

This allows the PhoneNumberPicker button to take its shape from the nice rounded
edges of the images you just uploaded. At least, they have the appearance of nice
rounded edges. In reality, the images you uploaded were made with a transparent
background and rounded edges on the visible part of the image. If a background color
is set on the button, it won't look as nice. So, wherever there is no image, the button
doesn't appear to be there. You can use this effect to create visually striking buttons
for your user interfaces in App Inventor.

12. Delete the default text in the Text property. The text for your button is in the images
you uploaded.

13. In the Properties column, set the Width property of the PhoneNumberPicker to 200
pixels. Set the Height property to 250 pixels.

14. Drag a new Label component from the Basic palette to the right side of the PhoneNumberPicker. Rename this Label component as padLabel2. Remove the default text in the Text property. Set the Width property to Fill Parent. Do the exact same thing for the padLabel1. Remove the default text and set the Width property to Fill Parent.

REMEMBER If one of your padding elements becomes hard to select because it is not visible or it is too small, you can always make a component active to change its properties by clicking on it in the Components column.

You should see your PhoneNumberPicker is nicely centered left and right now, but it's a little scrunched up at the top of the phone screen. We can use two padding elements above and below the HorizontalArrangement that contains PhoneNumberPicker to center it up and down:

1. Drag a Label from the Basic palette into the VirtualScreen1 above the HorizontalArrangement. You may need a couple of tries to get it in the right place. Remember to watch the blue line indicator to judge where on the Viewer your component will drop. Refer to Figure 5-2 if you get confused about component placement.

2. Rename the Label to padLabel3. In the Properties column, remove the default text from the Text property. Set the Height property to Fill Parent.

3. Drag another Label below the HorizontalArrangement. Rename the Label padLabel4. Remove the default text from the Text property. Set the Height property to Fill Parent.

4. Your PhoneNumberPicker in its HorizontalArrangement should be centered left and right and up and down.

Refining the interface

Your user interface is shaping up nicely, but you need the labels for status updates and labels for tracking how many times AndroidDown has tried to get a fix on its location. User interface design requires thinking about how a user might feel or think while using your application. We have disabled the panic send button until the device has a fix on the address so a "null" address isn't sent in the panic message. Because the user cannot select who to send the panic message to until the phone has a location, you need to give some real-time feedback to the user about your application's status:

1. Drag a HorizontalArrangement below the padLabel4 component on the Viewer. Watch where the blue line is when placing the component. Make sure it is below the padLabel4 component but still inside the VirtualScreen1 container (see Figure 5-2).

   Depending on your computer screen resolution, you may have to scroll the Viewer down to see the bottom of the padLabel4 component.

2. Drag a Label component into the HorizontalArrangement2. Rename the Label as lblStatusLabel. Change the Text property to read Last Message Sent:.

3. Drag a Label component to the right of the lblStatusLabel component. Rename the Label lblStatusDisplay. Remove the default text in the Text property.

Now you place the screen arrangement for the location fix counter and buttons:

1. Drag a new HorizontalArrangement below HorizontalArrangement2. Make sure it stays within the VirtualScreen1 container.

2. Drag a new Label component into the HorizontalArrangment3 that you just placed. Rename the label lblTrysLabel. Change the default text in the Text property to read Try number:.

3. Drag a second Label component to the right of the lblTrysLabel. Rename the Label lblTriesDisplay. Delete the default text in the Text property.

Now you need to place the non-visible components:

1. Drag a Clock component from the Basic palette and drop it on the Viewer. Make sure it is the active component by clicking it below the Viewer or in the Components column. In the Properties column, deselect the TimerEnabled property. You will control when and how the clock fires from the blocks. Set the TimerInterval component to 5000. Leave the TimerAlwaysFires property checked.

   When the Clock is enabled, it waits 5,000 milliseconds (5 seconds), fires off whatever instructions the Clock1.Timer component has snapped into its block, and then waits 5,000 milliseconds and does it again.

2. Open the Social palette, drag out the Texting component, and drop it on the Viewer.

3. Open the Sensors palette, drag out the LocationSensor, and drop it on the Viewer.

Your user interface for AndroidDown 1.0 is completed. It should look like Figure 5-2. Notice that the indention of the component names in the Components column indicates their relationship with each other. You can clearly see that VirtualScreen1 is the container for HorizontalArrangement1, 2, and 3 because they are each indented to the same level beneath the VirtualScreen1. Use this behavior when troubleshooting complex or very troublesome App Inventor interfaces.

FIGURE 5-2:
The completed
AndroidDown
1.0 user
interface

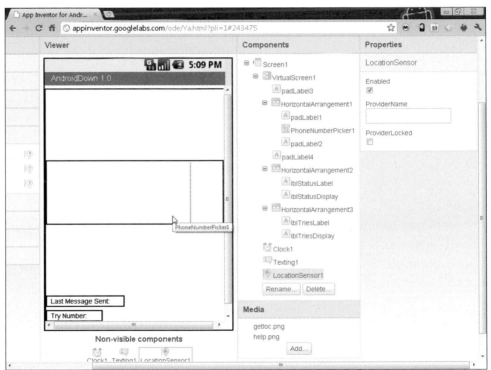

Locating the user's position with LocationSensor

The LocationSensor has the capability to use multiple location methods. You use the following method to wake up the GPS sensor and see whether it has a location fix. Remember that when you use the LocationSensor, you need to tell the sensor which provider to use (in this case, GPS) and then wait for that provider to get a location fix.

1. Switch over to the Blocks Editor.

   When the user starts the AndroidDown application, it needs to immediately start attempting to get a fix on its position. The `Screen1.Initialize` block is the starting gate for any App Inventor application. When you need to do something when the application starts, the `Screen1.Initilize` block is the block you will use.

2. Open the Screen1 blocks drawer on the My Blocks tab. Drag the `Screen1.Initialize` block out onto the Blocks Editor workspace.

The LocationSensor component must have its source set. The Android operating system **▶ REMEMBER**
can use a combination of Wi-Fi and carrier network location awareness and GPS coordinates
to determine location. The carrier location awareness is not very accurate because it relies
on rough triangulation of your carrier signal. Wi-Fi location awareness requires a Wi-Fi signal
that has been placed previously and the location remembered. For greatest accuracy, you'll
use GPS to get location for this application. The AndroidDown application depends on the
user having the GPS turned on in the Location settings of his phone. Currently, App Inventor
does not allow you to turn on the GPS functionality of the phone if it has been disallowed by
the user.

---

3. Open the `LocationSensor1` blocks. Drag the set `LocationSensor1.ProviderName to` block and snap it in the `Screen1.Initialize` block. Typeblock a text block and replace the default text with gps. Snap the gps text block into the set `LocationSensor1.ProviderName to` block.

When this block sequence is activated, the provider block is set to gps. The GPS activates and attempts to lock onto the GPS signal. (You use this sequence again in your deferred processing procedure to keep GPS on and attempting to lock.) If you right-click the set `LocationSensor1.ProviderName to` block and then select the Do It option from the menu that appears, you should see the GPS indicator on your phone. If you do not see the GPS indicator, check to make sure that GPS is enabled in your phone's settings.

If you do not specify GPS as the provider, LocationSensor attempts to use any location- **◀ NOTE**
aware method, including Wi-Fi and carrier network triangulation.

When the application first starts, you want to notify your user that the application is currently attempting to get an address and location fix. You do this using the getloc.png image file you uploaded into the Media column. Set the `Image` property of the PhoneNumberPicker1 to the getloc.png file using the `Screen1.Intialize` event.

4. Open the PhoneNumberPicker blocks drawer. Locate the set `PhoneNumberPicker1.Image to`, drag it out, and snap it into the `Screen1.Initialize` block. Typeblock a text block and change the default text to `getloc.png`. Drag the text block with the filename and snap it into the socket on the set `PhoneNumberPicker1.Image to` block.

The button displays the Getting Location image on start-up. You use a procedure to determine when the location has been fixed and then set the button image to the Help image.

The procedure checks the status of the `LocationSensor1.CurrentAddress` to see if there is currently a fix on the address of the device. If the phone does not have a fix on the address, it enables the Clock component, which takes further steps to activate the GPS and attempt to get a fix on the address. The Clock component disables itself and activates the procedure, which checks the status of the current address again. The clock and the procedure bounce back and forth until the procedure determines that there is a good fix on the address. Because these two components will do most of the work, you should place them on the workspace and build them together.

5. Open the Definitions blocks drawer on the Built-In tab. Drag a new procedure onto the workspace. Rename it `procLocationWait`.

6. Open the Clock1 blocks drawer, drag out the `when  Clock1.Timer  do` block, and place it on the workspace.

REMEMBER The Clock component is a multifunction component, a bit of "Swiss army knife" component. It has many built-in methods to call to get dates, times, and make calculations. The Clock component also has an event handler. The event is, "When the clock timer counts down, do this stuff." The amount of time that the timer counts is set with the `TimerInterval` property. When the clock is enabled, it starts counting the number of milliseconds set in the `TimerInterval` property. If the `TimerAlwaysFires` property is enabled, it immediately starts the countdown again after counting down. If the `TimerAlwaysFires` property is not enabled, it only counts down once.

You use the `procLocationWait` procedure to repeatedly enable the clock, which counts down, attempts to make the phone get a location fix, disables itself, and calls the procedure again. The `procLocationWait` needs to check whether the address has been found yet. To do this, use the familiar `IfElse` control block.

7. Open the Control blocks drawer on the Built-In tab. Drag an `IfElse` block and snap it into the `procLocationWait` procedure.

The test for the `IfElse` block checks the `LocationSensor1.CurrentAddress` block. If the `LocationSensor` does not have a fix on the address, it reports `No Address Available` in the `LocationSensor1.CurrentAddress` block. Because this is an condition that will never change, we can easily test for it changing using a comparison operator.

Now to learn some advanced typeblocking and continue the deferred process method. Read through the following sequence before you do it and try to get the feel of typing entire blocks of code blocks without using the mouse:

1. Make the IfElse control block active by clicking it on the workspace. You can tell which block is active by the orange halo effect around the block. With the IfElse block active, typeblock a comparison operator by typing = and pressing Enter.

   The comparison block is created and automatically snapped into the test socket on the IfElse block. Now the comparison operator block is active and highlighted. Without clicking anything, typeblock the LocationSensor1.CurrentAddress block.

   Because you know what block you want to use in the comparison operator, you can start typeblocking it, starting with its component name. Remember that your blocks start with the component name you gave them in the Design view.

2. Start typing the component name LocationSensor1. As you start typing, the dropdown box starts to narrow down the choices of blocks. Keep typing up to the LocationSensor1.C. The only option left is LocationSensor1.CurrentAddress. At this point, press the Enter key.

   The LocationSensor1.CurrentAddress block is created and automatically snapped into the first empty socket on the comparison operator.

   Now the LocationSensor1.CurrentAddress block is active, but it's in a comparison operator block and App Inventor knows that you need something to compare the LocationSensor1 block to.

3. Without clicking anything, typeblock a text block by typing text and pressing Enter. The text block is automatically created and socketed in to the last open socket on the comparison operator. The default text is automatically highlighted and you can fluidly and without stopping continue typing the text for the text block. Type No address available and press Enter.

   You just typeblocked an entire block sequence.

Making the most of typeblocking

Typeblocking can make your block creation and editing very fast and efficient. As you get more familiar with the blocks and components you are using in a project, you will find that typeblocking familiar and repeatedly used blocks is easier than dragging and dropping the blocks from their drawers. As you get more familiar with App Inventor, you end up using the drawers only when you are unsure of a block's name or are looking for functionality that you cannot remember the name of. For most of the remainder of this book, I show you how to use a combination of dragging newer blocks that you might not be familiar with and type-blocking familiar blocks as you build your projects.

If your comparison operator evaluates as `true`, the `Location.Sensor` does not have an address fixed. Then you enable the Clock1.Timer for another cycle:

1. Open the Clock1 blocks drawer. Scroll down through the blocks in the drawer. Notice the `set Clock1.TimerEnabled to` block. It's right next to the `Clock1.TimerEnabled` block. The first block, `Clock1.TimerEnabled`, reports the state of the property. The `set Clock1.TimerEnabled to` block puts a value in the property.

2. Click on the workspace and start typeblocking `Clock1.TimerEnabled`. Typeblocking either the `reporting` block or the `setting` block starts with the block name. In other words, to typeblock the `set` block, you do not start by typing `set`. Instead, you start with the name of the block. The block that sets a property has the component and property name appended with `[to]`.

   To get a property setting block when typeblocking, use the name of the block and property and a square bracket. Alternatively, when you get to only the two options left in the drop-down block, you can use the arrow keys or mouse to select the block you want to create.

 NOTE From this point on, I indicate the `set` blocks as you see them when typeblocking, like this: Typeblock a `"Clock1.TimerEnabled [to]"` block. (Notice that there is a space between the component name and the first square bracket.) This allows you to rapidly typeblock the required blocks by following the text.

3. Continue building your `procLocationWait` and `Clock1.Timer` blocks by type-blocking a `Clock1.TimerEnabled[to]` block. Snap the `Clock1.TimerEnabled [to]` block into the `then-do` socket on your `IfElse` block.

4. Make sure the `Clock1.TimerEnabled` block is active and typeblock a Boolean `true` block by typing the word `true` and pressing Enter. The `true` block should snap into the `to` socket on the `Clock1.TimerEnabled` block.

   If your comparison operator evaluates as `false`, something other than `No address available` is being reported by the `LocationSensor1.CurrentAddress` block. When that happens, you want the PhoneNumberPicker to be enabled so that the emergency SMS can be sent.

The `enable` block is the same no matter what the component name is, so you can typeblock the set `PhoneNumberPicker1.Enabled to` by starting to type `PhoneNumberPicker.Enabled [to]` and pressing Enter. (You can actually press Enter after you enter the first square bracket because there are no other blocks with that name and a `to`.) **REMEMBER**

---

5. Snap the `PhoneNumberPicker1.Enabled [to]` block into the second case else-do of your `IfElse` control block. Typeblock a `true` block and snap it into the `to` socket on the `PhoneNumberPicker` block.

6. When your LocationSensor gets a location fix and enables the PhoneNumberPicker, you need to indicate the status change to the user. Do so by changing the `Image` property on the PhoneNumberPicker button.

7. Typeblock a `PhoneNumberPicker1.Image [to]` block. Snap the `PhoneNumberPicker.Image` block into the else-do under the `PhoneNumberPicker1.Enabled` block.

8. Typeblock a `text` block and replace the default text with `help.png`. This is the name of the image that you uploaded to the Media column. Remember that no matter what the text in a `text` block will be, you always typeblock a `text` block by typing the word `text`.

9. Snap the `help.png` text block into the `PhoneNumberPicker1.Image [to]` block. Now when the PhoneNumberPicker1 is enabled, its button is changed to the help.png button image.

Finalizing the location and phone number functionality

You will use the `PhoneNumberPicker1.AfterPicking` event to handle what happens after a user selects a phone number. First, however, you need to build the clock routine to continue attempting to get the GPS signal and address fix. When the `Clock1.Timer` counts down, you want the GPS to be activated and to attempt to get a location lock. You do this by using the `set provider` block for the `set LocationSensor1.ProviderName to` block:

1. Drag out the `set LocationSensor1.ProviderName to` block and snap it into the `Clock1.Timer` block on your workspace. Typeblock a `text` block and replace the default text with `gps`. Snap the `gps text` block into the `LocationSensor1.ProviderName to` socket.

   Every time the clock counts down and processes its blocks, the first thing it does is to set the location provider to `gps`. When you set the `provider`, the location sensor turns on the provider and attempts to get a position fix. Unfortunately, if it doesn't get a fix the first time, it tends to stop trying. This is why we use the `procLocationWait` procedure to check for location fix and then try again.

   After setting the ProviderName, you don't want the clock processing again until the `procLocationWait` has checked the status, so you disable the `Clock1.Timer` with the `Clock1.Timer`.

2. Typeblock a `Clock1.TimerEnabled [to]` block and snap it in below the `LocationSensor1.ProviderName` block in the `Clock1.Timer` block.

3. Typeblock a `false` block and snap it into the `to` socket on the `Clock1.TimerEnabled [to]` block.

You want to allow your user to see that the application is actively attempting to get a lock. When you designed the user interface, you created a label called `Try Number`. Each time the clock processes, you need to advance a count and display that count. To do so, you use a variable that keeps track of the number of times the process has run. I show you how to increment a variable with this `Try Number` process. Incrementing a variable is incredibly useful in many ways. You will often find yourself needing to count, sum, or otherwise track data in your applications. You can use some form of the process that you are using here to increment the `Try Number` variable:

1. Typeblock a new variable by typing the word `variable` and pressing Enter. A new variable is created and the variable name is highlighted, ready for you to change the variable name. Rename the variable to `varTryNumber`.

2. Typeblock a number block by typing the number `0` and pressing Enter. Snap the number block into the `varTryNumber` block.

You can typeblock your My Definitions blocks as well, although sometimes it is easier to drag them from the My Definitions drawer. To typeblock the set varTryNumber to block, start typing varTryNumber. The drop-down box populates with your defined blocks with that name just like any other block. The block to set the variable has the square brackets just like property set blocks.

3. Typeblock the varTryNumber [to] block and snap it in the Clock1.Timer event handler below the Clock1.TimerEnabled [to] block.

Each time the Clock1.Timer block processes, you want to take whatever number is in the varTryNumber variable and add one more number to it. To do so, use the varTryNumber reporting block socketed into an addition operator block with a number block:

1. Make the varTryNumber [to] block active by clicking it. Typeblock an addition operator by typing + and pressing the Enter key. The + addition operator block should be created and socketed into the varTryNumber [to] block.

2. With the addition operator block active, typeblock the varTryNumber global value block.

   When you start typing the varTryNumber text, the global value reporting block is the one that does not have the [to] next to it. The square bracketed to means that is a set to block.

3. When you typeblock the global varTryNumber, it should automatically snap into the first socket on the addition operator (see Figure 5-3). If it doesn't, drag it and snap it into place.

4. Typeblock a number 1 block by typing the numeral 1 on your keyboard and pressing Enter. Snap the numeral 1 block into the second socket on the addition operator.

Now whenever the Clock1.Timer blocks process, the varTryNumber variable is incremented by one. You can now display the contents of the varTryNumber variable in the Try Number status label to indicate how many times AndroidDown has attempted to lock its position:

1. Open the lblTriesDisplay blocks drawer and locate the set lblTriesDisplay.Text to block. This block allows you to set what is displayed in the label. Snap the block directly below the varTryNumber [to] block. (See Figure 5-3.)

2. Typeblock the `varTryNumber global` block by typing `varTryNumber` and pressing Enter. Snap the `global varTryNumber` block into the `lblTriesDisplay.Text` `[to]` block. Now after the `varTryNumber` variable is incremented by one, the `Try Number` status label is updated with the new number.

The very last thing the `Clock1.Timer` does after it counts down is call the `procLocationWait` procedure so the address lock can be checked. If no address is available, run the process all over again.

3. Open the My Definitions blocks drawer and drag out the `call procLocationWait` block. Snap it in as the last block in the `Clock1.Timer` event handler.

4. Drag out another `call procLocationWait` block and snap it in as the last block in the `Screen1.Initialize` block.

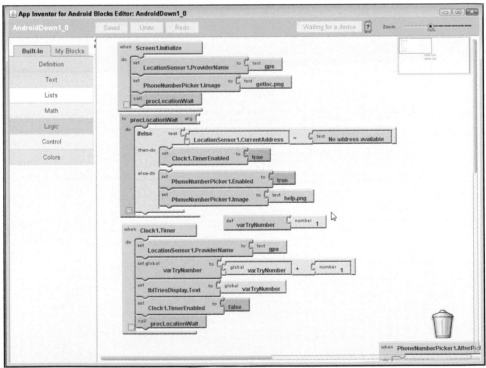

Now you have two processes that bounce back and forth until the current address is available with address information. When the address has been established, the PhoneNumberPicker component is enabled. The user can tap it to select the phone number to send the text SMS message to. Next, you need to build the event handler to handle what your application will do after the user has selected a phone number:

1. Open the PhoneNumberPicker1 blocks drawer. Locate the when `PhoneNumber Picker1.AfterPicking do` event handler. Drag it out on a clean workspace area.

    You could also typeblock this block by typing `PhoneNumberPicker1.A` and pressing Enter.

    `PhoneNumberPicker1.AfterPicking` is the event that you will use; however, most of the functionality in the event comes from the Texting1 component. Basically, you are using the picking of the phone number as an event to do all the stuff you want to do with the texting component.

2. Open the Texting1 blocks drawer. Drag out the `set Texting1.PhoneNumber to` block. Snap it into the `PhoneNumberPicker1.AfterPicking` event handler block.

    Just like the list picker you used in the previous project, the PhoneNumberPicker has a block that holds and reports the number the user selected. You use that block to set the Texting component's `PhoneNumber` property with the `Texting1.PhoneNumber [to]` block.

3. Open the PhoneNumberPicker1 blocks drawer. Scroll down through the drawer and drag out the `PhoneNumberPicker1.PhoneNumber` block. Snap this block into the `set Texting1.PhoneNumber to` block in your event handler.

    Next, use `text` blocks to assemble and send the message to be sent when the number is picked.

4. Open the Texting1 blocks drawer and locate the `set Texting1.Message to` block. Drag it out and snap it under the `Texting1.PhoneNumber` block in the `AfterPicking` event handler.

5. Typeblock a `call make text` block by typing `make text` and pressing Enter. Snap the `make text` block into the `to` socket on the `Texting1.Message` block.

6. With the `make text` block active, typeblock a `join` text block by typing `join` and pressing Enter. Snap the `join` block into the `make text` block open socket. The `make text` block create a new socket.

7. With the `join` block active, typeblock a `text` block and replace the default text with `HELP! I am at `. Make sure to leave a trailing space at the end of the text. The `text` block should snap into the first open socket on the `join` block.

NOTE You will be expanding on this panic message significantly in the next version of AndroidDown. Try to think ahead when planning for feature expansion.

You want the text phrase you just created to be followed by the address where the `LocationSensor` block has determined the user is.

8. Open the LocationSensor1 blocks drawer. Locate the `LocationSensor1.CurrentAddress` block. Drag the block out and snap it into the second socket on the `join text` block. A text string like "Help! I am at 14 Any Street, Anytown, OH 44235" is stored in preparation for being sent.

   Before sending the message, you want to make sure the message has an embedded time stamp so that the recipient knows when the message was sent out from the person signaling for help. Use the `make text` to add a newline character and then a line indicating the time from the Clock1 component.

9. Typeblock a `text` block and replace the default text with \n. This is the newline character. Snap the newline `text` block into the next open `text` socket on the `make text` block.

10. Typeblock a `join text` block snap it into the next `text` socket on the `make text` block. Typeblock a `text` block and replace the default text with `Sent at:`. Again, make sure you have a trailing space after the text so that the formatting looks nice. Snap the `text` block into the first socket on the join `text` block.

    Now use another of the Clock1's functions. Not only does the Clock1 component provider an event handler that will tick down milliseconds and execute blocks, but it also allows you to format times and dates.

11. Open the Clock1 block drawer and locate the `call Clock1.FormatDateTime instant` block. Drag it out onto the workspace. The calls to the Clock component in App Inventor tell the Clock component to return a certain formatting of time and date. But Android needs to know not only how you want the time and date formatted, but what time and date.

NOTE App Inventor uses an *instant* to mark a specific point in time. The `.Now` block creates an instant at the point in time that the block is executed. You can also create your own "instant" by using the `Make Instant` blocks and specifying a particular point in time. The `.Now` block is the one most commonly used to capture a time or date.

The way it asks for this information is called an instant. You can create and manipulate
different instants for some pretty complex behaviors. But in this situation, you just
need the instant returned in the form of a time and date.

12. Open the Clock1 blocks drawer again and locate the `call Clock1.Now` block. Drag
out the `Clock1.Now` block and snap it into the `instant` socket on the `Clock1.`
`FomatDateTime` block. Drag the `Clock1.FormatDateTime` with its connected
instant block and snap it into the second open socket on the `join` block.

Now you need to update and send the message you have built and update the status message
to indicate that you have successfully sent the message:

1. Open the Texting1 blocks drawer and locate the `call Texting1.SendMessage`
block. Drag the `SendMessage` block and snap it in below the `make text` block in your
`AfterPicking` event handler. This block takes whatever text has been placed in the
`Texting1.Message` block and sends it using Android's native SMS capability.

Now you need to update the status label to show the panicking user that their message
has been sent.

2. Open the lblStatusDisplay blocks drawer and drag out the `set lblStatusDis-`
`play.Text to` block. Snap it into the `PhoneNumberPicker1.AfterPicking`
event handler below the `Texting1.SendMessage` block.

3. Copy the entire `make text` block and all its attached blocks and paste a copy. Make
the `make text` block that is socketed in the `Texting1.Message` block active by
clicking on it. Press Ctrl+C. This makes a copy of the blocks in memory. Now, press
Ctrl+V to paste a copy of the blocks. Drag the copy of the `make text` and all its blocks
and snap it into the socket on the `lblStatusDisplay.Text [to]` block.

Your `PhoneNumberPicker1.AfterPicking` event should now look like Figure 5-4.

Package the AndroidDown 1.0 application to your phone from the Design view. Make sure
the GPS settings have GPS enabled. Test the functionality of AndroidDown. If AndroidDown
has difficulty getting a fix on the location, be patient: It can take a few minutes. Remember
that some cell phone carrier plans charge for SMS text messages. Know your smartphone
plan and be aware that you could incur charges testing the AndroidDown application.

Now, time to move on to making the AndroidDown application a more practical, full-fledged,
and usable panic button application.

FIGURE 5-4:
The completed
PhoneNumber
Picker1.
AfterPicking
event handler

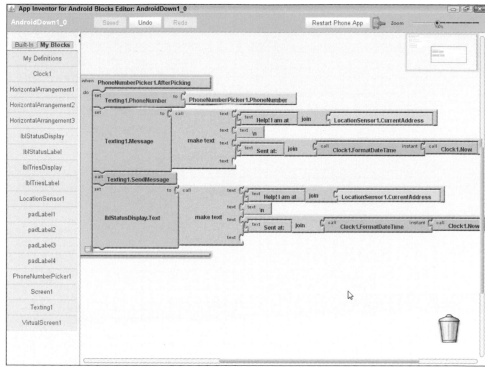

Creating AndroidDown 2.0

AndroidDown 2.0 adds to the functionality of the previous version. AndroidDown 2.0 sends its emergency SMS text message as soon as the application is started. The first time the application starts it will ask for and stores the contact number that the user designates as the emergency contact, as well as storing the way the user wants the application to behave (such as whether the application should send the SMS at application start). The 2.0 version retains all of the functionality of the previous version, with the ability to select a contact from the address book and send the SMS emergency message to the selected contact.

Your design

AndroidDown 2.0 (Figure 5-5) ramps up the usability of the application. It also introduces a level of complexity you haven't experienced yet. It uses multiple state checks to determine the application's process flow. You will see how you can create the ability to store settings for your applications. AndroidDown 2.0 allows the user to select the behavior they desire. Using the TinyDB component, you store the user's selections between sessions of the AndroidDown application. The idea of storing data for your application between instances of the application running is known as *data persistence*. AndroidDown 2.0 is your first exposure to data persistence with App Inventor. I cover local data persistence and network data persistence in Chapter 7.

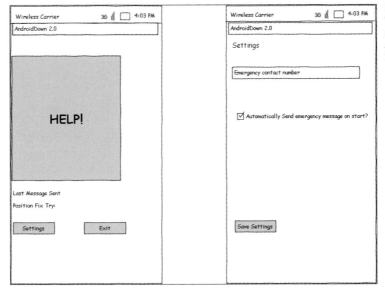

FIGURE 5-5:
The design
sketch for
AndroidDown
2.0

The complexity of AndroidDown 2.0 requires that you build a fairly involved logic flow. This chart isn't a literal yes/no decision chart, nor is it to build from, but instead shows you the relationship of each part of the application's logic flow. Read through it carefully before you start and refer back to it to keep in mind a good overall view of what you are trying to accomplish while you are building the individual block components. Come back to this flow chart when you have finished the project and read through it again. Both the flow and the project will be clearer. Unlike previous applications, this application has some fairly non-linear decisions and flow. After you complete this project, you should have an understanding of some of the things you will need to take into account when building very complex applications. When you are designing applications with lots of functionality, your job is easier if you take the time to sit down and create a logic flow chart like the one in Figure 5-6. A better flow chart would map each decision and the actual flow of the programming. The chart in Figure 5-6 is a polished recreation of a hand-drawn flowchart I sketched out while designing the AndroidDown application. Without this hand-drawn logic flow, I would have been lost fairly quickly when building the AndroidDown 2.0 application.

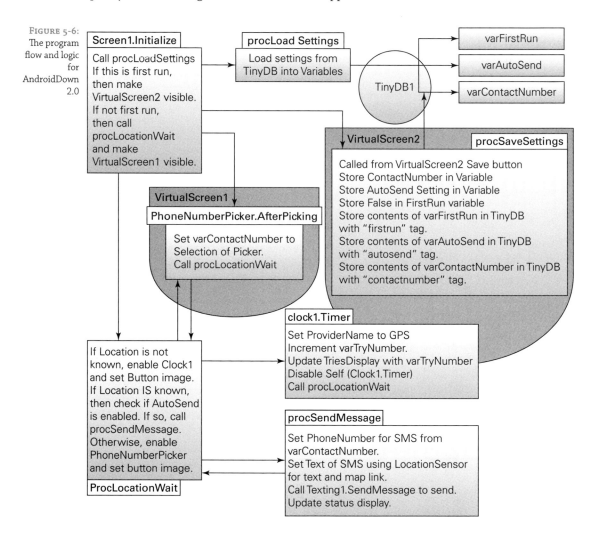

FIGURE 5-6: The program flow and logic for AndroidDown 2.0

Your primitives

These are the new pieces of functionality you will build into the AndroidDown application:

- ❍ A new VirtualScreen for the Settings screen
- ❍ A way to store the Emergency contact number

❍ A way to store and detect the AutoSend setting

❍ A database to store settings

❍ An algorithm to set settings only on the first run

❍ An algorithm to check and load settings on subsequent runs

❍ AutoSend message delay

❍ An algorithm to send a Google Maps link to device current location

Your progression

The following is a list of basic steps towards creating the new primitives, algorithms, and logic:

1. Create the VirtualScreen2 settings screen.

2. Add user interface elements to VirtualScreen1 and VirtualScreen2.

3. Create variables to store settings.

4. Create button events for Save Settings DB.

5. Create button events for Open settings.

6. Create button event for the Exit button.

7. Create `Screen.Init` to check for settings and load settings or to start the main app.

8. Create a procedure for `SendMessage`.

9. Create a procedure for `SaveSettings`.

10. Create a procedure for `LoadSettings`.

11. Alter `procLocWait`.

New components

Only one new component is introduced in this version of the app:

❍ TinyDB

New blocks

Only one new block is introduced in this version of the app:

❍ `If`

Getting Started on AndroidDown 2.0

You will build AndroidDown 2.0 a little bit differently than you built previous projects in this book. The goal with AndroidDown 2.0 is to begin to think holistically to understand how various individual parts of an application work in relationship to each other to accomplish the application's design goals. Instead of building a complete procedure or event before moving on to the next one, you define all of the procedures and variables initially as barebones programming structures with no instructions in them. Then, you move through each defined procedure or event handler, fleshing it out with the instructions it needs to accomplish the design goals. This allows you to both see the program grow organically and also allows you to call a procedure before it is completely built.

The AndroidDown 1.0 application changes fairly radically in its 2.0 version. However, you still use the procedures and logic already in place in version 1.0. You adjust and change them somewhat as you move along:

1. Begin by opening the AndroidDown 1.0 application and saving a copy by using the Checkpoint button in Design view. Change the default checkpoint name to `AndroidDown2_0`.

2. Drag a HorizontalArrangement onto the VirtualScreen1 below the `lblTriesDisplay` label. This HorizontalArrangement holds the buttons at the bottom of your main application screen. One button is to open to the Settings screen. The other is to exit the AndroidDown program entirely.

3. Drag a Button component from the Basic palette into the new HorizontalArrangement. Rename the button `btnSettings` in the Components column. Change the `Text` property to `Settings`.

4. Drag a second Button component to the right of the Settings button. Rename the Button component `btnExit` in the Components column. Change the default `Text` property to `Exit`.

   Now create the second VirtualScreen to act as the settings page for your AndroidDown application. The settings for AndroidDown 2.0 consist of the emergency contact number and the setting for whether to auto-send when the application starts. Your application checks on startup to see whether the settings have been set. If they have been set, VirtualScreen1 is visible; if the settings have not been set, VirtualScreen2 is visible. This enables the AutoSend feature and the emergency contact to be set from the first time the application ever runs. You store the settings in TinyDB.

5. Drag a new VerticalArrangement onto the Viewer below the VirtualScreen1. Rename the VerticalArrangement `VirtualScreen2`.

6. Drag a Label into the VirtualScreen2. Rename the Label component `lblContact-Display`. Change the default text in the `Text` property to `Emergency Contact Number`.

7. Drag a TextBox component into the VirtualScreen2. Rename the text box `txtContactNumber`. This text box is where your user enters the number they want the emergency SMS text number sent to when AndroidDown starts. You store the user's entry in this text box, first in a variable and then in TinyDB.

8. In the Properties column, change the `Hint` property to `Enter Emergency Contact`. This prompts your user for the number when the setting screen is open.

   Ask the user if she wants the AndroidDown application to automatically send the emergency message on application startup. For a yes/no question, you can use a CheckBox component.

9. Drag a new CheckBox component below the txtContactNumber text box. Rename the CheckBox component `chkAutoSend`. Change the default text in the `Text` property to `Automatically send panic message at app start?`.

   Now you need a button to save the user's setting choices. The single Save button saves the settings and exits back to VirtualScreen1.

10. Drag a new Button component onto the VirtualScreen2 below the chkAutoSend check box. Rename the button `btnSaveSettings`. Change the text in the `Text` property to `Save`.

11. Drag a TinyDB component from the Basic palette and drop it onto the Viewer. It drops below the Viewer in the Non-Visible Components area.

    The TinyDB component is a very simple database storage component. It allows you to store data with a *tag*. The tag can be used to retrieve the data. In other words, you could store the emergency contact number with the tag number. When the program starts again, instead of the user having to reenter the number, your application calls the number up from the TinyDB storage area using the tag number. TinyDB is a very simple and very effective way to store small amounts of data and settings. TinyDB can contain as much data as you have memory on in your phone in plain text and numbers. That data exists from one session of your application to the next session.

Your user interface changes have been made at this point. You should have the elements as you see in Figure 5-7.

FIGURE 5-7:
The user
interface
components for
AndroidDown
2.0

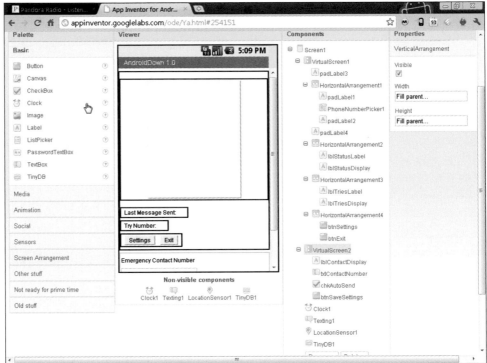

Building your button event handlers

Launch and switch over to the Blocks Editor. You will build all the button event handlers first. However, to do that, you need to have all your procedure calls available. You do this by creating procedures and leaving them empty for the moment. That way, you can put the procedure calls into the button event handlers. When the procedures are built, the calls will be in the right place. As you place the procedure calls, you can refer back to the application logic flow diagram to see how you are creating the skeleton of the flow that you will flesh out with its muscles later.

1. Scroll the Blocks Editor workspace to an empty place. Typeblock a procedure by typing `procedure` and pressing Enter. Rename the procedure `procSaveSettings`.

2. Typeblock a new procedure and rename it `procLoadSettings`.

3. Typeblock a new procedure and rename it `procSendMessage`.

4. You should now have a total of four defined procedures and their `call` blocks in your My Definitions drawer. One is from the AndroidDown 1.0 version named `procLocationWait`, which you continue to use in the AndroidDown 2.0 application (see Figure 5-8).

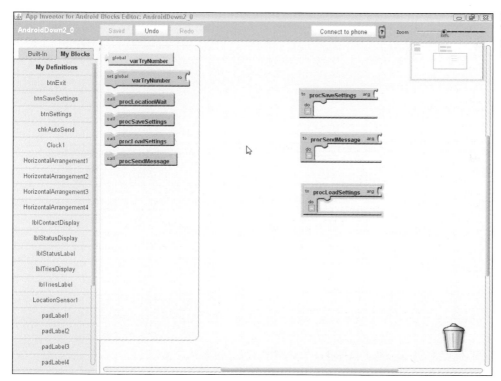

FIGURE 5-8:
Your skeletal
procedures and
their calls

Now you can use the calls from the skeletal procedures to build up your button event handlers. The logic of your application says that the application should check on start up to see whether the program has ever had the contact number and AutoSend settings set before. You use a variable to store the answer to the question, "Is this the first time AndroidDown has ever run?" If the answer is `true`, the Settings page on VirtualScreen2 is shown so that the contact number and AutoSend settings can be set. When the settings are set the first time, the variable is set to `false`. If the answer to the preceding question is `false`, depending on whether the `AutoSend` variable is set to `true` or `false`, the main VirtualScreen1 is activated and the emergency SMS is sent.

When you are making decisions related to your application's logic flow, you always use some form of a `Control` block from the Control drawer on the Built-In tab.

The following steps use the `Screen1.Initialize` block to query TinyDB and then the first start variable. You rebuild the `Screen1.Initialize` and make the changes to query and load settings from TinyDB:

1. Locate the `Screen1.Initialize` block on your workspace. Currently it sets the LocationProvider name, sets the PhoneNumberPicker button image, and calls the `procLocationWait`. These steps significantly change `Screen1.Initialize`.

2. Remove and delete the `call LocationWait` block from the `Screen1.Initialize` block.

3. Remove and delete the `set LocationSensor1.ProviderName to` block.

4. Leave the `set PhoneNumberPicker1.Image to` block in the `Screen1.Initialize` block.

Now you start to rebuild the `Screen1.Initialize` block. Refer to Figure 5-9 if you get confused or lost while working through the steps. The very first thing the application should do after setting the PhoneNumberPicker button image is load the settings from TinyDB, if the settings are available:

1. Drag the `call procLoadSettings` block from your My Definitions drawer and snap it into the `Screen1.Initialize` block below the `PhoneNumberPicker` block. Currently the `procLoadSettings` is empty and doesn't do anything, but you change that when you build up the `procLoadSettings` block.

   Next, your application needs to decide based on the settings that have been loaded whether this is the first time the application has been run. It does that by evaluating the settings that have been loaded into your variables. Currently you don't have any variables defined. Take this opportunity to think through what settings need to be stored and to define all the variables you will need for the AndroidDown 2.0 application.

   You need to store all the user input from VirtualScreen2 in your Settings page: the Emergency contact number and the AutoSend settings.

2. Typeblock a new variable by typing `variable` and pressing Enter. Rename the variable `varContactNumber`. Typeblock a `text` block by typing `text` and pressing Enter. Remove the default text from `text` block, leaving an empty `text` block. Snap the empty `text` block into the `varContactNumber` block.

You now need to store whether the value of the AutoSend check box is `true` or `false`.

3. Typeblock a new variable and rename it `varAutoSend`. Typeblock a `false` block by typing `false` and pressing Enter. Snap the false block into the `varAutoSend` block.

You need to track one unseen setting and that is whether this is the first time the application has been run. You store this `true` or `false` value in a variable as well.

Typeblock a variable and rename it `varFirstRun`. Typeblock a `true` block by typing `true` and pressing Enter. Snap the `true` block into the `varFirstRun` block. The `varFirstRun` variable now read as `true`, indicating it is the first run of the application unless the `procLoadSettings` process has loaded a `false` value into the `varFirstRun`.

You should now have three new variables defined:

○ `varContactNumber`

○ `varAutoSend`

○ `varFirstRun`

You evaluate the `varFirstRun` variable as the next step in the `Screen1.Intialize` block:

1. Drag an `IfElse` block from the Control blocks drawer on the Built-In tab and snap it in below the `procLoadSettings`.

    With the `IfElse` block selected, begin to build the test condition.

2. Typeblock a comparison operator by typing = and pressing Enter. The comparison operator block should snap into the `test` socket on the `IfElse` block.

3. With the Comparison block selected, typeblock the `global varFirstRun` block by typing `varFirstRun` and pressing Enter. The `varFirstRun` block should snap into the first socket on the comparison operator.

4. With the comparison operator selected, typeblock a `false` block. The `false` block should snap into the final empty socket on the comparison operator. You are now comparing the contents of the `varFirstRun` variable with the value `false`. If the contents of the variable are `false`, the then-do blocks execute. The `varFirstRun` being `false` means that this is not the first time AndroidDown has run and you should start the process of establishing location. You also want to enable the VirtualScreen1 main screen.

5. Drag the `call procLocationWait` block from the My Definitions drawer and snap it into the then-do socket in your `IfElse` block. The `procLocationWait` procedure is the procedure from AndroidDown 1.0 that begins the process of establishing and fixing address and location.

6. Typeblock the set `VirtualScreen1.Visible` to block by typing `VirtualScreen1.Visible [to]` and pressing Enter. Snap the `VirtualScreen1.Visible` block under the `call LocationWait` block in the then-do socket on your `IfElse` block.

7. With the `VirtualScreen1.Visible` block still selected, typeblock a `true` block. The `true` block should snap into the `VirtualScreen1.Visible` block.

8. Typeblock the set `VirtualScreen2.Visible` to block by typing `VirtualScreen2.Visible [to]` and pressing Enter. Snap the `VirtualScreen2.Visible` block under the `VirtualScreen1.Visible` block.

REMEMBER   You can press Enter as soon as the block you want is the only one left in the Typeblock drop-down list. Usually, by the time you type the [, you can press Enter.

9. With the `VirtualScreen2.Visible` block selected, typeblock a `false` block. The `false` block should snap into the `VirtualScreen2.Visible` block.

At this point, if the application starts and the `varFirstRun` reports a value of `false`, the `procLocationWait` is started. The VirtualScreen2 is made invisible and VirtualScreen1 is made visible.

Now you need to set up the case for when the `varFirstRun` has a value of `true`, indicating a first-time run. If this is the first run, you need to make the Settings page visible so the AutoSend and emergency contact settings can be set and saved to TinyDB:

1. Typeblock `VirtualScreen1.Visible [to]` and press Enter. Right after you press Enter, start typeblocking a `false` block and press Enter. This should create the set `VirtualScreen1.Visible` to block and then immediately created a `false` block and socket it into the `VirtualScreen1.Visible` block.

2. Snap the `VirtualScreen1.Visible` block with its `false` block and into the `else-do` socket on your `IfElse` block.

3. Typeblock a `VirtualScreen2.Visible [to]` block and immediately typeblock a `true` block into it. Drag the `VirtualScreen2.Visible` block under the `VirtualScreen1.Visible` block in the `else-do` socket.

4. If the test condition determines there is anything other than `false` in the `varFirstRun` variable, it enables the Settings screen on startup.

At this point, your completed `Screen1.Initialize` block should look like Figure 5-9.

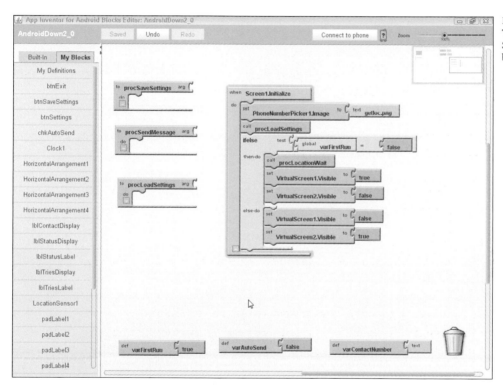

FIGURE 5-9:
The completed
Screen1.Intialize
block

Creating your button events

You have three buttons on your user interface. On VirtualScreen2, you have the Save settings button that saves the contact number and AutoSend settings to the database and makes VirtualScreen1 visible. On VirtualScreen1, you have a Settings button to access the Settings screen. You also have an Exit button to gracefully leave AndroidDown without it continuing to attempt to locate itself and send its SMS text:

1. The Settings button on the VirtualScreen1 makes VirtualScreen2 visible. It also loads whatever is stored in the `varContactNumber` into the TextBox component and whatever value is in the `varAutoSend` into the CheckBox component. That way, if there are stored settings, the user sees what they are.

2. Open the btnSettings blocks drawer. Drag out the `when btnSettings.Click do` event handler onto your workspace. You use the VirtualScreens `.Visible` blocks to make VirtualScreen1 invisible and VirtualScreen2 visible.

3. Typeblock a `VirtualScreen1.Visible [to]` block by typing `VirtualScreen1. Visible [` and pressing Enter. Without a pause, continue typing a `false` block. The `false` block should socket into the `VirtualScreen1.Visible` block. Snap the `VirtualScreen1.Visible` block into the `btnSettings.Click` block. (See Figure 5-10.)

4. Typeblock a `VirtualScreen2.Visible [to]` block and a `true` block into the `VirtualScreen2.Visible` block. Snap the `VirtualScreen2.Visible` block under the `VirtualScreen1.Visble` block.

5. Typeblock the `txtContactNumber.Text [to]` block and, without pausing, start typeblocking the `varContactNumber` global variable block into it. Snap the `txt- ContactNumber.Text` block with its `varContactNumber` block into the `btnSet- tings` event handler under the `VirtualScreen` blocks.

6. Typeblock the `chkAutoSend.Value [to]` block and immediately typeblock the `varAutoSend` global variable block into it. Snap the `chkAutoSend.Value` block into the `btnSettings` event handler under the `txtContactNumber.Text` block.

7. Open the btnExit blocks drawer. Drag out the `when btnExit click` event handler.

8. Open the Control blocks drawer on the Built-In tab. Locate the `call close screen` block. Snap the `close screen` block into the `btnExit.Click` event handler. Whenever the btnExit button is tapped, it closes all the AndroidDown processes and exits the program.

The Save Settings button from VirtualScreen2 is a little more complex. When the button is tapped, it stores all the settings from the screen into their respective variables and then save the contents of the variables into TinyDB. The Settings button event also sets the varFirstRun variable to false because if the settings have been set, it can't continue to say that AndroidDown has never run before. The varFirstRun variable contents also must be saved to TinyDB. All of these actions, however, are handled by the procSaveSettings procedure. For now, you simply call the procedure in the button event.

9. Open the btnSaveSettings blocks drawer on the My Blocks tab. Drag the when btnSaveSettings.Click do onto your Blocks Editor workspace.

10. With the btnSaveSettings.Click block selected, typeblock the call procSaveSettings block by typing procSaveSettings and pressing Enter. The procSaveSettings block should snap into the btnSaveSettings.Click event handler.

After the settings are saved, the user exits back to the VirtualScreen1 main screen:

1. With the btnSaveSettings.Click block selected, typeblock a VirtualScreen2.Visible [to] block and immediately typeblock a false block. The VirtualScreen2.Visible block should auto-snap into the btnSaveSettings.Click event handler and the false block should auto-snap into the socket on the VirtualScreen2.Visible block.

2. Typeblock a VirtualScreen1.Visible [to] block and typeblock a true block into the VirtualScreen1.Visible block. Make sure that the VirtualScreen1.Visible block is snapped in below the VirtualScreen2.Visible block in the btnSaveSettings.Click event handler.

At this point, you should be getting fairly proficient at typeblocking chains of blocks. **WARNING** Remember, though, that sometimes auto-snap snaps a block into the wrong socket and either generates an error or winds up in the wrong place. Always double-check typeblocked blocks visually.

All of your button events should be handled at this point.

FIGURE 5-10:
All of the button
events for
AndroidDown
2.0

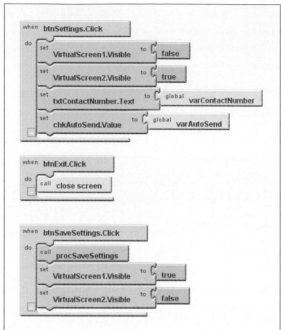

Sending the message

Next you alter the PhoneNumberPicker.AfterClicking event. In the AndroidDown 1.0, the PhoneNumberPicker.AfterClicking event handled the task of sending the SMS. In the 2.0 version, the PhoneNumeberPicker.AfterPicking event only sets the SMS number. Your procSendMessage procedure is the workhorse of your SMS activity. Your procSendMessage is responsible for sending the SMS when appropriate, so you strip the logic from the AfterPicking event and place it in the procSendMessage. When you get to the procSendMessage procedure, you significantly alter these blocks. Because you have most of the SMS logic built in, moving the blocks to the procSendMessage saves you time when it's time to build the procSendMessage procedure:

1. Drag the empty procSendMessage procedure close to the PhoneNumberPicker1. After picking block.

2. Click on the first block in the AfterPicking event handler (it should be the Texting1.PhoneNumber block), drag and snap it into the procSendMessage block.

All of the blocks in the `AfterPicking` event should drag over to the `procSendMes-`
`sage` block and snap in. All of the blocks that were in the `PhoneNumberPicker1.`
`AfterPicking` event should now be in the `procSendMessage` procedure block.
(See Figure 5-11.)

When the user taps the Help button on the VirtualScreen1 main screen, you want
whatever phone number they picked to be stored in the `varContactNumber` so the
`procSendMessage` procedure can use it as the SMS contact number.

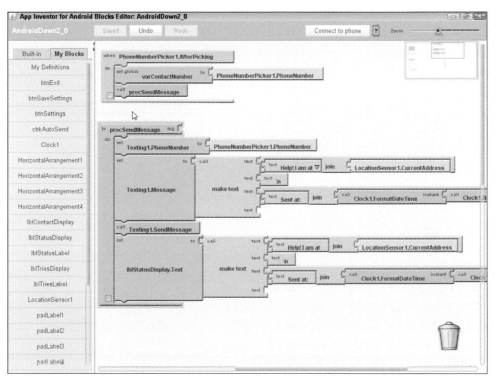

FIGURE 5-11:
The incomplete
procSend
Message and
completed
AfterPicking
event handler

3. Make the `PhoneNumberPicker1.After` picking event handler active by clicking it.

4. Typeblock the `set varContactNumber to` by typing `varContactNumber [to]`
and pressing Enter. Immediately typeblock the `PhoneNumberPicker1.`
`PhoneNumber` block. It should auto-snap into the `varContactNumber [to]` block.

The set `varContactNumber` to block should have auto-snapped into the `PhoneNumberPicker1.AfterPicking` event handler.

5. Typeblock the `call procSendMessage` block by typing `procSendMessage` and pressing Enter. Snap it in below the `varContactNumber [to]` block in the `AfterPicking` event handler.

Now, when a user clicks the PhoneNumberPicker button with the word `Help` on it, the selected phone number is placed in the `varContactNumber` and the `procSendMessage` process is called to send the emergency SMS.

Next, start fleshing out the internal logic and instructions for your procedures:

1. Locate the `procSaveSettings` procedure and drag it to a clean workspace. If your workspace gets cluttered, make use of the Organize All Blocks function. Right-click any empty workspace on the Blocks Editor and click the Organize All Blocks option.

   The `procSaveSettings` procedure takes the settings from `txtContactNumber` and `chkAutoSend` and stores them in their variables and then saves them to TinyDB.

2. Make the `procSaveSettings` procedure block active by clicking it.

3. Typeblock the `varContactNumber [to]` block. It should auto-snap into the procedure. Typeblock the block to report the contents of the `txtContactNumber` TextBox. Type `txtContactNumber.Text` and press Enter. It should auto-snap into the `varContactNumber [to]` block.

4. Typeblock the `varAutoSend [to]` and make sure it snaps in under the previous variable `set-to` block. Typeblock the block to report the value of the `chkAutoSend` CheckBox by typing `chkAutoSend.Value`. Snap the `chkAutoSend.Value` block into the `varAutoSend [to]` block.

5. Typeblock the `varFirstRun [to]` block and snap it under the previous two variable setting blocks. Typeblock a `false` block and snap it into the `varFirstRun [to]` block. See Figure 5-12 for the variable block configuration.

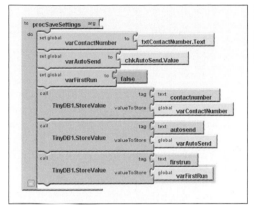

FIGURE 5-12:
The completed
procSave
Settings
procedure

Next you use the `Store.Value` block from TinyDB to store the contents of the variables for long-term storage. TinyDB uses a tag for every value you store in it. You can retrieve that value by using the `.GetValue` block and referencing the tag it was stored under. The tag is just a `text` block with text in it that you choose to reference the data you store. You use a tag that refers to the data you stored. When stored, your data will look like Table 5-1:

Table 5.1   Tags and Values for the AndroidDown TinyDB

Tag	Value
contactnumber	varContactNumber
autosend	varAutoSend
firstrun	varFirstRun

Follows these steps for building up the procedure and using TinyDB to store the contact number and auto send settings.

1. Open the TinyDB1 blocks drawer on the My Blocks tab. Drag out the `call TinyDB1.StoreValue` block and drop it on your workspace. Copy the block by selecting it and press Ctrl+C to copy. Press Ctrl+V twice to paste two copies.

   You should now have three `call TinyDB1.StoreValue` blocks. When you want to store something in TinyDB, use a `.StoreValue` block.

2. Snap the three `.StoreValue` blocks into the `procSaveSettings` procedure block (see Figure 5-12).

3. Select the first `TinyDB1.StoreValue` block. Typeblock a `text` block. It should auto-snap into the `tag` socket on the `TinyDB1.StoreValue` block and be ready to receive the tag name for this `StoreValue`. Replace the highlighted text in the `text` block with `contactnumber` and press Enter.

4. Without clicking anything, typeblock the `global varContactNumber` block by typing `varContactNumber` and pressing Enter. The `varContactNumber` reporting block should auto-snap into the `valueToStore` socket on the `TinyDB1.StoreValue` block.

5. Select the next `.StoreValue` block. Typeblock a `text` block and change the default text to `autosend`. It should auto-snap into the `tag` socket on the `.StoreValue` block.

6. Typeblock the `global varAutoSend` block by typing `varAutoSend` and pressing Enter. It should auto-snap into the `valueToStore` socket below the tag.

NOTE   You can make the next `TinyDB1.StoreValue` block active by pressing Tab on your keyboard.

---

7. Make the next `.StoreValueBlock` active. You can click it or press Tab if the previous block is still active.

8. Typeblock a `text` block and change the default text to `firstrun`. It should auto-snap into the `tag` socket.

9. Typeblock the `global varFirstRun` block by typing `varFirstRun` and pressing Enter. It should auto-snap into the `valueToStore` socket.

Now whenever the `procSaveSettings` procedure is called, it takes the settings from the Settings screen and store it first in the variables and then in TinyDB for long-term retrieval.

After the data has been stored in TinyDB, it can be retrieved at any point instantaneously using the `.GetValue` blocks. Follow these steps to build up the procedure for loading the application settings from TinyDB:

1. Locate the `procLoadSettings` procedure in your Blocks Editor workspace.

   The TinyDB `.GetValue` blocks can be used to store the contents of a tag directly into a variable or process. In other words, using the `.GetValue` blocks with a tag of contactnumber immediately returns the result of whatever was stored with that tag.

2. Make the `procLoadSettings` block active. In quick succession, typeblock `varContactNumber` [to] and press Enter. Typeblock `varAutoSend` [to] and then press Enter. Typeblock `varFirstRun` [to] and press Enter.

   All three blocks `set` blocks for your variables should auto-create and auto-snap into the `procLoadSettings` block.

3. Open the TinyDB1 blocks drawer and drag out a `call TinyDB1.GetValue tag` block and place it on your workspace. Select the block and copy it by pressing Ctrl+C. Make two copies of the `.GetValue` block by pressing Ctrl+V twice.

   You should now have three `TinyDB1.GetValue` blocks. Snap a `TinyDb1.GetValue` block into each of the variable `set-to` blocks in the `procLoadSettings` block.

   This block configuration places into each of the variables whatever value is returned from the `.GetValue` blocks. The `.GetValue` blocks return whatever was stored under the `tag` that is socketed into the `.GetValue` blocks.

4. Select the `.GetValue` block in the `varContactNumber` block. Typeblock a `text` block and replace the default text with `contactnumber`. This is the tag you used to store the contact number variable.

5. Select the `.GetValue` block in the `varAutoSend` block. Typeblock a `text` block and replace the default text with `autosend`. This is the tag you used to store the `AutoSend` variable.

6. Select the `.GetValue` block in the `varFirstRun` block. Typeblock a `text` block and replace the default text with `firstrun`. This is the tag you used to store the `varFirstRun` variable. The completed `procLoadSettings` should look like Figure 5-13.

FIGURE 5-13:
The completed
procLoad
Settings
procedure block

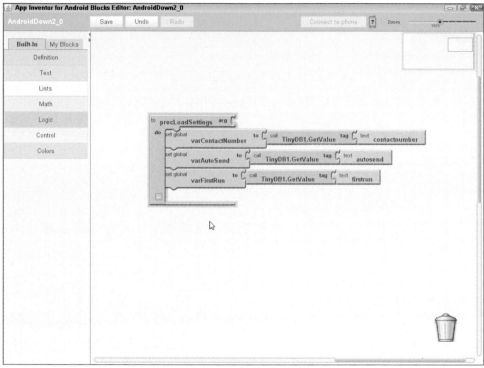

Next, build up the `procSendMessage` procedure that is called whenever a message needs to be sent:

1. Locate the `procSendMessage` procedure block on your Blocks Editor workspace and drag it to an open area of your workspace. If you begin to run out of workspace, moving a block to the farthest right side of the workspace increases the workspace horizontally.

   The current `procSendMessage` block contains the blocks that were in the `AfterPicking` event handler. The `set Texting1.PhoneNumber to` block should be the first block in the `procSendMessage` block. It should have the `PhoneNumberPicker1.PhoneNumber` block snapped into its socket.

2. Remove the `PhoneNumberPicker1.PhoneNumber` block from the `Texting1.PhoneNumber` block and delete it.

3. Make the `Texting1.PhoneNumber` block active and typeblock `varContactNumber`. Press Enter. The `global varContactNumber` block should be created and auto-snapped into the `to` socket on the `Texting1.PhoneNumber` block.

You expand the `Texting1.Message` block to include a Google Maps link to the devices current location. The URL for the Google Maps link must conform to the following format:

`http://maps.google.com/maps?q=latitude,longitude`

You use `text` blocks to build up this link with `text` blocks and the latitude and longitude from the LocationSensor.

4. Typeblock a `text` block and change the default text to `\n` — this is the newline character. Socket the newline `text` block in the open `text` socket on the `make text` block.

5. Typeblock a `text` block and change the default text to `Map link:` . Make sure to leave a trailing space after the text. Snap the `Map link:` text block into the open `text` socket on the `make text` block.

6. Typeblock a `text` block and change the default text to `http://maps.google.com/maps?=`. Snap the URL block into the next open `text` socket on the `make text` block.

7. Open the LocationSensor1 blocks drawer and locate the `LocationSensor1.Latitude` block. Drag the `LocationSensor1.Latitude` block and snap it into the next text socket on the `make text` block.

8. Typeblock a `text` block and change the default text to a single comma (`,`). Snap the comma text block into the next `text` socket on the `make text` block.

9. Open the LocationSensor1 blocks drawer and locate the `LocationSensor1.Longitude` block. Drag the Longitude block and snap it into the next `text` socket on the `make text` block.

Now remove the `make text` block directly below the one you just altered:

1. Select the `make text` block that is socketed into the `lblStatusDisplay.Text` block. Delete the entire `make text` and all its blocks. You will duplicate the previous `make text` you have altered.

2. Select the `make text` block socketed into the `Texting1.Message` block. Press Ctrl+C to copy the block and then press Ctrl+V to paste it.

3. Drag the copied `make text` block and snap it into the socket on the `lblStatusDisplay.Text` block.

Your completed `procSendMessage` procedure should look like Figure 5-14.

FIGURE 5-14:
The completed
procSend
Message
procedure

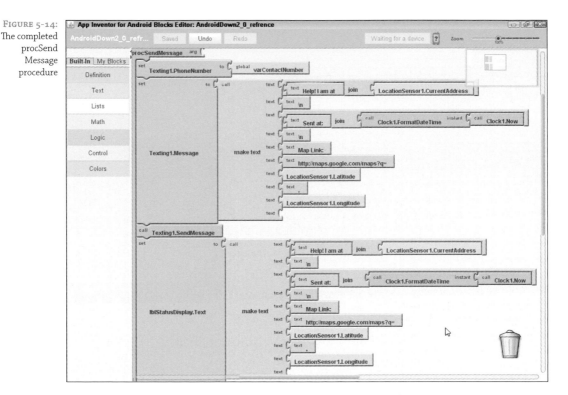

Finalizing the procLocationWait procedure

The `procLocationWait` procedure needs to be altered slightly. If the test for the `IfElse` block in the `procLocationWait` evaluates to `true`, the location has been fixed, in which case we need to send the message if the AutoSend setting is set to `true`. Use a simple `If` block to test whether the `varAutoSend` is indeed set to `true`. If it is not, the application acts just as it did in AndroidDown 1.0. Regardless of whether the AutoSend is enabled, the `procLocationWait` still enables the PhoneNumberPicker and changes its button image:

1. Locate the `procLocationWait` procedure on your Blocks Editor workspace and drag out an `If` block from the Control blocks drawer on the Built-In tab. Snap the `If` block into the `else-do` socket on the `IfElse` block in the `procLocationWait` procedure.

2. With the `If` block selected, typeblock a comparison operator by typing = and pressing Enter. The comparison operator should snap into the `test` socket on the `If` block.

Continue building the If test by typeblocking the varAutoSend global variable block. Make sure it snaps into the first open socket on the comparison operator.

3. Typeblock a true block and make sure it snaps into the second socket on the comparison operator.

4. If varAutoSend is true, you need to call the procSendMessage procedure. Typeblock a callprocSendMessage block by typing procSendMessage. Snap the procedure call block into the If block.

Your altered procLocationWait block should look like Figure 5-15.

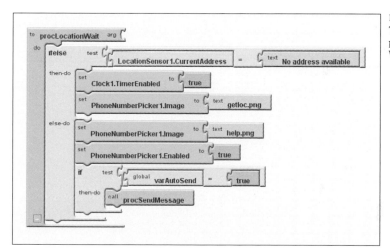

FIGURE 5-15:
The altered
procLocation
Wait block

Package your AndroidDown application (see Chapter 1 for more on packaging and installing applications) and install it on your phone. Test each level of functionality. Make sure that is saving settings and restoring them when you exit the application and restart it. Store a string of text such as qwerty, rather than a number, in the Emergency Contact setting to keep the application from sending an SMS while testing.

You explored three important concepts in this application. The first concept is that of persistent data. You can store settings, user input, application state, or whatever you like in TinyDB using a simple tag system, thus making data persist. As you create more applications, TinyDB becomes more and more useful. The second very useful concept is that of cycling through processes until you obtain a desired result. You used the Clock1.Timer and the procLocationWait to keep the phone looking for its location without locking up the application or the phone. This is known as *deferred processing* and is a concept you will use many times.

The third concept you used is that of incrementing a counter variable. The variable increment can be used in tasks such as breaking out of a loop after a certain number of passes or keeping score in a game.

Congratulations! You have completed a very complex application that you can now give to your teenagers, your girlfriend, or mother, or anyone else. It will prove useful in situations as diverse as avoiding a creepy stalker to getting rescued from a bad party.

AlphaDroid: An Alphabet Tracing Game

THE CANVAS COMPONENT is a versatile component that allows the user to interact with your application through touch and drag. Although the way you use the Canvas component events in this project is fairly straightforward, you can use the input from the canvas for everything from control input for games to hotspot touch buttons.

The Canvas and sprites make up most of the interface elements for most game designs. Use the AlphaDroid application in this chapter to become familiar with canvas and sprite programming. Another core component of many games is animation. In this chapter, you learn a sprite animation technique that comes in handy for event animation such as explosions, collisions, and so on.

You need to download the Chapter 6 project files from the companion Web site. See this book's Introduction for more information on how to download the files.

Creating AlphaDroid 1.0

The AlphaDroid application starts with a canvas to accommodate the user interaction events such as touch and drag. The canvas is also used to display a series of images of the alphabet. The method you employ uses long lists of image filenames. The algorithm keeps tabs on the index number of the filename being used to display the current alphabet character. Pay close attention to the list handling for future projects of your own.

The randomization used for the canvas paint color is important for many aspects of gaming as well. A similar algorithm could be used to randomize a list of sprites for a scrolling shooter game or to randomize speed, headings, or other aspects of sprite interaction. Remember that every list in App Inventor has an index number indicating its position in the list. You can use the randomizing blocks in conjunction with lists to randomize the selection of list items.

Your design

The design sketch for the AlphaDroid application is shown in Figure 6-1.

The idea behind AlphaDroid is to provide a toddler-friendly alphabet tracing game. The game features the 26 letters of the alphabet and allows the user to trace the shapes of the letters with multicolored lines, dots, and circles. The user interface consists of a large display canvas where the alphabet is displayed. It has three buttons to change between drawing random colored lines, circles, and dots. The buttons should be designed so that a non-reading toddler can understand them. Tapping the alphabet display canvas changes the letter to the next letter in the alphabet. Tapping the screen to change the alphabet also changes the background to a random color. The application should start with a splash screen with basic instructions.

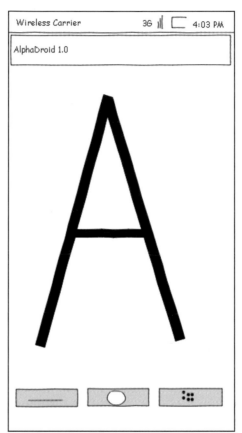

FIGURE 6-1:
The AlphaDroid
design sketch

Your primitives

These are your simple parts and algorithms to accomplish your design goals:

○ A canvas that will respond to touch and drag events

○ A method to change the canvas image when it is tapped

○ A method to draw on the canvas

○ A way to distinguish what should be drawn: a line, circle, or point

○ A way to randomize the color of the background

○ A way to randomize the color of drawn objects

○ Buttons and events to change drawn objects

○ A splash screen image and a way to display it

Your progression

These are the suggested steps for building up the interface and logic to accomplish your design goals:

1. Place the canvas for the user interface.

2. Place the buttons for the user interface.

3. Upload all media for the application.

4. Change the icon for the application.

5. Create lists for the alphabet and colors.

6. Create variables for tracking randomization.

7. Create event handlers for canvas taps.

8. Create event handlers for canvas drags.

New components

These are the important new components and introduced in AlphaDroid:

○ Canvas

New blocks

○ Pick random item

Getting Started on AlphaDroid 1.0

The first version of AlphaDroid explores the use of the Canvas component in App Inventor. The Canvas in App Inventor allows you to track users touching the canvas and location of the touches as well. You can use the X/Y coordinates reported by the Canvas component to do both graphical things, such as drawing lines, and programmatic things, such as handling events. For the first version, you use basic functionality of touch and drag events offered by Canvas.

In this chapter, you also explore some of the advanced things you can do with lists. Lists can be used to help track which item is currently being used in a list or which item should be used from a list of files. Every list item in App Inventor has an index number associated with its place in the list. For instance, if an item is the first item in a list, its index is 1; but if an item is the twelfth item, its index is 12. This allows you to pull items from or identify items based on their *index* or position in a list. You learn how to use the index marker from lists in a very simple form in AlphaDroid.

You also learn more about using variables to track states, conditions, and processes in your application. You use the three buttons on the user interface to change whether the user draws with lines, circles, or dots. A variable is set using three buttons. The draw event checks the variable to see what should be drawn.

Here's how to get started:

1. Start a new project from the My Project window. Name the project `AlphaDroid_1.0`. Deselect the Scrollable check box.

2. From the Design view, select the Screen1 component and change the `Title` property to read `AlphaDroid 1.0`.

3. Click in the `Icon` property field. A file picker pops up. Click the Add button and navigate to the AlphaDroid project files. Double-click the alphaico.png file to upload the icon image.

4. Drag a new VerticalArrangement onto the Viewer. Rename the VerticalArrangement `VirtualScreen1`. Set the `Width` and `Height` properties to `Fill Parent`.

Most of the screen is taken up by the canvas where the alphabet characters will be displayed. The Canvas component can be sized just like any other component.   **TIP**

---

5. Drag and drop a Canvas component from the Basic palette onto the Viewer. Leave the `PaintColor` and `BackgroundColor` properties set to their defaults. You will be setting those properties with their associated properties' blocks. Set the `Width` and `Height` properties to `Fill Parent`.

6. Drag and drop a HorizontalArrangement below the Canvas component. This arrangement holds your buttons for changing the drawing type.

7. Drag three button components into the HorizontalArrangement. Each of these buttons correspond to a type of drawing. You will place an image on each button to indicate to a non-reading toddler what the button does.

8. Rename Button1 as btnLine. Remove the default text from the Text property. Click in the Image property field. Click the Add button in the drop-down list that appears when you click in the Property field. Navigate to your AlphaDroid project files and double-click the btnLine.png. You should see the button show up on your Viewer and connected Android phone.

9. Rename Button2 as btnCircle. Remove the default text from the Text property. Click in the Image property field. Click the Add button and double-click the btnCirc. png file in your AlphaDroid project files.

10. Rename Button3 as btnPoint. Remove the default text property Text. Click the Image property field and add the btnPoint.png file.

You've now created all of your user interface components; however, you still need to upload all the images for your application. Each of the letters of the alphabet and the program opening splash screen are represented by separate .png image files.

In the Media column, click the Add button and start uploading the images from the AlphaDroid project files. Upload all 26 .png alphabet image files. You should see files for a.png through z.png. Upload the splash.png image as well. Splash.png is the splash screen image that is displayed before anything else happens on the phone. You should already have the button images and icon uploaded from setting the Image properties.

Your user interface for AlphaDroid should look like Figure 6-2.

Picking colors

You use two fairly long lists of items in AlphaDroid: lists of alphabet characters and colors. The list of colors is selected randomly for the drawing paint color and for setting the background of Screen1 to a random color when the alphabet character changes. You use two different methods for randomly picking the color.

Pay close attention to the splash screen method introduced in the following steps. You frequently want a splash screen to introduce your application. These steps also start building your color and canvas changes.

FIGURE 6-2:
The AlphaDroid
1.0 user
interface
components

1. Switch to or start the Blocks Editor.

   When the AlphaDroid application starts, you want to see a splash screen with a simple set of instructions and the application name. The image (splash.png) that you uploaded into the Media column needs to be placed as the background image of Canvas1 one when the application first starts. Later, I show you how to set up logic that changes that background image to the alphabet graphics when the screen is tapped.

2. Typeblock the `Screen1.Initialize` event handler. Open the Canvas1 blocks drawer and locate the `set Canvas1.BackgroundImage` to block. Drag it out and snap it into the `Screen1.Initialize` block.

3. Typeblock a `text` block and replace the default text with `splash.png`. Whenever the application is started, the `Screen1.Initialize` event is called and the background image of the application is set to the splash.png graphic.

4. Next, define the two long lists of items starting with the list of alphabet characters. Define a new global variable by typeblocking `variable` and pressing Enter. Rename the variable `varAlphabet`.

5. Typeblock a `make a list` block by typing `make a list` and pressing Enter. Snap the `Make a List` block into the `varAlphabet` variable socket.

6. Typeblock a `text` block and replace the default text with a. Snap the a `text` block into the first `item` socket on the `make a list` block. Continue typeblocking `text` blocks and replacing the default text with letters of the alphabet until you get all 26 letters of the alphabet in the `Make a List` block, as in Figure 6-3.

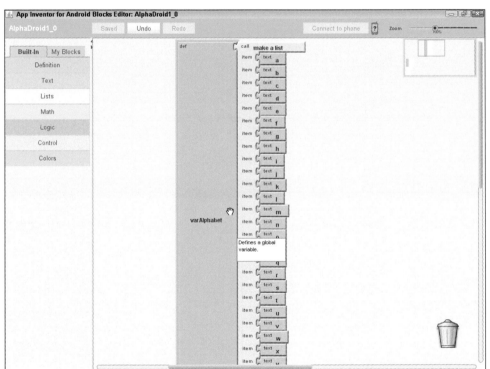

FIGURE 6-3:
The Alphabet
character list

Next, define the list of colors for the color randomization:

1. Typeblock a new variable and replace the default text with `varColors`. Typeblock a `make a list` block and snap it into the `varColors`.

2. Open the Colors blocks drawer on the Built-In tab and drag out the `Blue` color block. Snap the `Blue` block into the `item` socket on the `Make a List` block socketed into your `varColors` variable.

3. Color blocks in App Inventor are preformatted number blocks. All colors in App Inventor are designated using numbers representing red, blue, green, and transparent

(alpha channel). Each color `channel` is represented by a number from 1 to 255 — pretty standard stuff for representing colors on computers. For instance, the `Blue` block you just used is in reality just a block that reports a value of -16776961 to the phone as the color requirement. But because most of us don't think in terms of blocks of 8-bit numbers to represent colors, App Inventor uses the handy predefined color blocks. Many Web sites can help you mix RGB colors and find the numbers you need to represent the color you want. Color Tools (`www.colortools.net`) offers a color mixer and several other helpful color-related tools.

For an even more in-depth look into colors and color mixing for Android, check out the App Inventor documentation pages on the subject at `http://appinventor.googlelabs.com/learn/reference/blocks/colors.html`. **NOTE**

---

4. Continue socketing all the color blocks from the Colors blocks drawer on the Built-In tab. Don't use the `Black` or `None` colors. The `Black` color block won't show up against the black alphabet characters and obviously neither will the `None` block.

When you finish the `varColors` list, it should look like Figure 6-4.

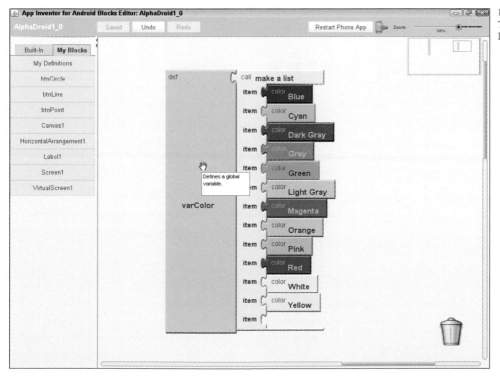

FIGURE 6-4: The varsColors list

Understanding dragging and touching events

Open the Canvas1 blocks drawer on the My Blocks tab. Two event handlers are provided by the Canvas component: one is for when something is dragged on the canvas and one for when something is touched on the canvas.

Whenever something (such as a finger or a sprite, which I explain later on in "Creating AlphaDroid 2.0") is dragged on the canvas, the Canvas1.Dragged event is fired. The event records and reports the position and movement of the drag event. Three sets of coordinates are reported by the Canvas1.Dragged event:

- ◯ **Start:** This is the location where the drag event begins. The start value remains constant throughout a single event occurrence.

- ◯ **Previous:** This is the location just before the current location. The value changes as the drag event occurs.

- ◯ **Current:** This is the location of the drag event currently. In other words, this is where the finger is currently in a drag event. By giving instructions that reference the Start or Previous and Current, we can do things like draw or indicate movement and direction.

The Canvas1.Dragged event reports the Start, Previous, and Current coordinates in X/Y numbers. The coordinates blocks are defined when you place a Canvas1.Dragged event handler on your workspace. Just as defining a variable creates blocks in the My Definitions drawer, a Canvas1.Dragged event handler creates blocks that report the values gathered by the Canvas in a dragged event. When you view the event handler in its drawer, all of the value sockets are empty. It can be intimidating because you think, "I don't know what to plug in all of those sockets!" However, when you drag the event to the workspace, all of those sockets are populated with a name block. The accompanying value block is placed in the My Definitions drawer. You can then use the value blocks in the Canvas1.Dragged event or in any other process.

The Canvas1.Touched event reports only one set of coordinates. It reports the location of where the canvas was touched. Whenever the canvas is tapped as opposed to dragged, the Canvas1.Touched event is fired and whatever blocks are socketed in the event are executed.

Drag a Canvas1.Touched event handler out onto your workspace. Whenever your young user taps the canvas, you want the letter image to change. You can accomplish this in either of two ways: One way is to use two variables, one to track what letter of the alphabet is currently displayed and another to track what one should be next. When your user taps the canvas, display the varNext and record which letter was just displayed in the varCurrent and increment the VarNext to varCurrent plus one.

The second method of changing the letter image is a little more elegant in that it eliminates one variable. When the user taps the canvas, it displays varCurrent +1 and then sets varCurrent to varCurrent +1. That may be confusing now, but it will become clearer as you build the Canvas1.Touched event handler.

Because you are incrementing a variable, the application continues to increment that variable to infinity every time the canvas is tapped. However, you have only 26 characters to display. At some point, you want to loop back to the beginning of the alphabet. First, set up the canvas background image and the screen background color to change appropriately, then you can worry about controlling the loop:

1. Typeblock a new variable and rename it varCurrent.

   This variable will always hold the currently displayed alphabet character. However, it actually holds the index position number in the varAlphabet list. (This will make more sense as you move forward.) Typeblock the numeral 0 and snap the number block into the varCurrent block. You want the numeral block to have a zero so that when you tell the varCurrent to increment for the first time, it displays the 1 position index from your varAlphabet.

2. Set Screen1.BackgroundColor to randomly select a color when the screen is tapped. You will use the first and most straightforward randomization method for the background color. You are setting the Screen1 background color instead of the Canvas background color because the Canvas can display an image or a color but not both. The alphabet letter graphics have a transparent background so the Screen1 background will be visible through them.

3. Typeblock the Screen1.BackgroundColor [to] block and snap it into the Canvas1.Touched event handler.

4. Open the Lists blocks drawer on the Built-In tab. Drag out a call pick random item block and snap it into Screen1.BackgroundColor block. This block randomly picks an item from the list you specify and reports it back to whatever you have it socketed into. In this case, we want it to randomly pick a color.

5. With the pick random item block selected, typeblock the varColor global variable block. It should auto-snap into the random block.

Now when the screen is tapped, the `Canvas1.Touched` event fires and the background changes colors. You can test the behavior on your connected Android device. (Flip ahead to Figure 6-5 to see the final result.)

Changing the BackgroundImage property

Next, build the logic for changing the `BackgroundImage` property of the Canvas1.

1. Open the Canvas1 blocks drawer and locate the `set Canvas1.BackgroundImage to` block. Drag it out and snap it under the `Screen1.BackgroundColor` block in the `Canvas1.Touched` event handler.

   You will use the `make text text` block to build up a filename. The `BackgroundImage` block needs a `text` block with a filename that has been uploaded in the Media column. You want these blocks to execute each time the next alphabet file is loaded.

2. Typeblock a `make text` block by typing `make text` and pressing Enter. Socket the `make text` block into the `Canvas1.BackgroundImage` block.

3. Open the Lists blocks drawer on the Built-In tab and locate the `call select list item` block. This block returns the item from a list based on the numerical value snapped into the `index` socket. Remember that every list item has an index number equivalent to its position in the list, so you can retrieve the `a` character by retrieving index position 1 from the `varAlphabet` variable list.

4. Drag out the `Select List Item` block and snap it into the socket on the `make text` block.

Now you need to define which list the `Select List Item` block will use. Typeblock the `varAlphabet` global variable block and snap it into the `list` socket on the `Select List Item` block.

Each time the `Canvas1.BackgroundImage` block executes, you need to pull the next index number from the `varAlphabet` variable. You can do that by saying, "Select the list item from varAlphabet that is at the index of varCurrent +1":

1. Typeblock the addition operator by typing + and pressing Enter. Socket the addition operation into the `index` socket on the `select list item` block. With the addition operator selected, typeblock the `varCurrent` global variable block.

   It should auto-snap into the first socket on the addition operator. Typeblock a numeral 1 block by typing 1 and pressing Enter. Drag the number 1 block into the second socket on the addition operator.

2. Typeblock a `text` block and replace the default text with .png. This is the file extension of your alphabet images. Snap the `text` block into the next `text` block on the `make text` block.

   Now each time the `Canvas1.Touched` event is triggered, the `Canvas1.BackgroundImage` block will be changed by selecting the next index number based on the `varCurrent` number and appending that list item with .png. For example, the first time it runs, `varCurrent` contains the number 0. The select list item block increments by 1, making the index position it pulls the index position 1 and therefore the letter A. However, the next time the `Canvas1.Touched` event is triggered, the `varCurrent` variable needs to reflect the new currently displayed index number.

3. Typeblock the `varCurrent   [to]` block and snap it in below the `Canvas1.BackgroundImage` block. With the `varCurrent  [to]` block selected, typeblock the addition operator. Next, typeblock the `varCurrent` global variable block. It should auto-snap into the first open socket on the addition operator. Typeblock a numeral 1 number block and snap it into the second socket on the addition operator.

Now each time the `Canvas1.Touched` event is triggered, after the current image is cycled to the next index number, the `varCurrent` variable is incremented for the next go-round.

Further refining the Canvas1.Touched event handler

You still have a slight problem with the `Canvas1.Touched` event handler. After your young user has tapped the canvas 26 times, the `varCurrent` increments to index number 27 and the background image tries to pull index number 27. There are only 26 index places, however, so your application will crash with an error.

You need to check the `varCurrent` variable first thing when the `Canvas1.Touched` event occurs. If the variable contains the number 26, the currently displayed graphic is the z character and the `varCurrent` variable can be reset to 0. That way, when the set `Canvas1.BackgroundImage` block executes, the index number it pulls is 0+1. Any time you need to compare the contents of a variable and make a decision based on the contents, you use a control block.

1. Open the Control blocks drawer on the Built-In tab. Drag out an `If` block and socket it at the very top of the `Canvas1.Touched` event handler. Test the contents of the `varCurrent` and see if it contains the number 26.

2. With the `If` block selected, typeblock the comparison operator by typing a = and pressing Enter. Make sure it snaps into the `test` socket on the `If` block. With the

comparison operator selected, typeblock the `varCurrent` global variable block. It should auto-snap into the first socket on the comparison operator. Typeblock the numeral 26 and press Enter. The Number block with 26 in it should auto-socket into the second socket on the comparison operator.

3. With the `If` block selected, typeblock the `varCurrent [to]` block. It should auto-snap into the `then-do` socket on the `If` block. With the `varCurrent [to]` block selected, typeblock a number 0 block. It should auto-snap into the `varCurrent [to]` block.

Now the first thing the `Canvas1.Touched` event does is check the `varCurrent` variable to make sure that the current index number in use isn't the last one, number 26. Your completed `Canvas1.Touched` event should look like Figure 6-5. You should be able to tap the canvas on your connected Android device and cycle through the alphabet images.

FIGURE 6-5:
The completed
Canvas1.
Touched event
handler

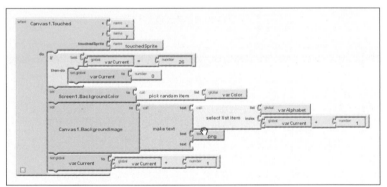

To prepare for building up the `Canvas1.Dragged` event handler, you need to define a variable for tracking what kind of drawing will be done. You gave your young user three buttons with three options for drawing lines, circles, and points.

The following list sets up your variable for tracking the drawing type. It contains one of three values to indicate the three different possible drawing types:

1. Typeblock a new variable by typing `variable` and pressing Enter. Rename the variable `varDrawType`.

    This variable is changed to represent which button has been pressed on the user interface. You want a default value, however, so that even if the user doesn't select a button, something is drawn.

2. Typeblock a number 1 block and snap it into the `varDrawType` variable.

Setting up button event handlers

You need to set up the button event handlers to change the `varDrawType` when they are tapped:

1. Open the btnLine blocks drawer and drag out the `btnLine.Click` event handler.

    When the Line button is clicked, you want to set some value in the `varDrawType` variable so the `Canvas1.Dragged` event handler can check on what kind of drawing to do.

2. Typeblock the `varDrawType [to]` block and snap it into the `btnLine.Click` event handler.

3. With the `varDrawType [to]` block selected, typeblock a numeral 1 block by typing the number 1 and pressing Enter. Make sure the number block auto-snaps into the `varDrawType [to]` block.

    You use numbers from 1 to 3 to indicate which type of drawing that should be done, with 1 being a line, 2 being a circle, and 3 being a point (see Figure 6-6).

4. Open the btnCircle blocks drawer and drag out the `btnCircle.Click` event handler. Typeblock the `varDrawType [to]` block and snap it into the event handler. Typeblock a numeral 2 block and snap it into the `varDrawType [to]` block.

    The `btnCircle` event sets the `varDrawType` variable to a value of 2, indicating that a circle should be drawn.

5. Open the btnPoint blocks drawer and drag out the `btnPoint.Click` event handler. Typeblock the `varDrawType [to]` block and snap it into the event handler. Typeblock a numeral 3 block and snap the number block into the `varDrawType [to]` block.

FIGURE 6-6:
The button
event handlers

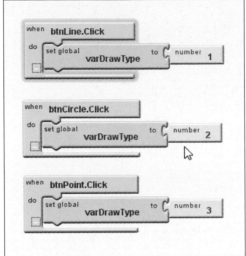

FIGURE 6-6:
The button
event handlers

Putting the finishing touches on the drawing functionality

1. Open the Canvas1 blocks drawer and drag out the Canvas1.Dragged event handler. When you drop it on your workspace, you see all the parameter sockets fill with name blocks.

2. If you open your My Definitions drawer, you see that all of the accompanying value blocks were created as well.

    First you need to define what color of paint is used for the drawing activity. The color is randomized using a slightly different method than we used previously. Using the index numbers, you choose a random integer between the highest and the lowest index.

3. Open the Canvas1 blocks drawer and locate the Canvas1.PaintColor [to] block. Drag it out and snap into the Canvas1.Dragged event handler.

4. This block sets the color for the paint each time the dragged event occurs.

5. Open the List blocks drawer and locate the Call Select List Item block. Snap it into the Canvas1.PaintColor block. You need to define what list you will be selecting an item from. With the Select List Item block selected, typeblock the varColor global variable block.

    Make sure it snaps into the list socket on the Select List Item block.

6. Open the Math blocks drawer on the Built-In tab and locate the Random Integer block. This block selects a random number from a range you specify whenever it is executed. Drag the Random Integer block and snap it into the index socket on the Select List Item block. Delete the two default number blocks in the Random Integer block.

7. You are going to select a random index number. With the Random Integer block selected, typeblock a numeral 1 block and snap it into the from socket. Typeblock a numeral 12 number block and snap it into the to socket on the Random Integer block. A random index number is selected each time the Canvas1.PaintColor block is processed.

Now you need to have a case for everything that might happen when the "dragged" event occurs. In some cases, a line should be drawn; other times, a circle or a point should be drawn. The determining factor is what the value of varDrawType variable currently is. You need an If block for each possibility:

1. Typeblock an If block by typing If and pressing Enter. Repeat until you have three If blocks. Snap each If block into the Canvas1.Dragged event handler below the Canvas1.PaintColor block.

   You set the first If block up to test if the varDrawType variable has the number 1 value, thus indicating a line should be drawn.

2. Typeblock a comparison operator (=) and snap it into the test socket of the first If block. Typeblock the varDrawType global variable block and snap it into the first socket on the comparison operator. Typeblock a numeral 1 block and snap it into the second socket on the comparison operator.

   If the value of varDrawType is 1, this test evaluates as true and the blocks in this If block execute.

You want the method call Canvas1.DrawLine to be what executes if the varDrawType is 1. You use the call Canvas1.DrawLine with the value of where the dragging event is occurring. You use the X and Y value blocks created by the Canvas1 event to let the Canvas1.DrawLine know where it should draw the line:

1. Open the Canvas1 blocks drawer and drag out the call Canvas1.DrawLine method.

---

2. Snap the `Canvas1.DrawLine` method into the first `If` block.

   You need two sets of X and Y values for the `Canvas1.DrawLine`. The first set inform the method where to draw a line from. The second set inform it where to draw the line to. The `Canvas1. Dragged` event created the previous and current X/Y values that we can use.

3. Open the My Definitions drawer and locate the value `prevX` block. Drag the `prevX` block and snap it into the `x1` socket on the `Canvas1.DrawLine` method.

4. Open the My Definitions drawer and locate the value `prevY` block. Drag the `prevY` block and snap it into the `y1` socket on the `Canvas1.DrawLine` method. You should now have the `X1` and the `Y1` sockets filled with the `Previous` X/Y coordinates.

5. Open the My Definitions drawer and drag out the value `currentX` and the value `currentY` blocks. Snap the `currentX` block into the `x2` socket on the `Canvas1.DrawLine` method. Snap the `currentY` block into the `y2` socket on the `Canvas1.DrawLine` method.

You should now have the `x2` and `y2` blocks on the `Canvas1.DrawLine` block populated.

Next create the `If` block for the case where the `varDrawType` contains the value 2:

1. Select the second `If` block and typeblock a comparison operator. With the comparison operator selected, typeblock the `varDrawType` global variable block. It should auto-snap into the first socket on the comparison operator. Typeblock a numeral 2 number block and snap it into the second open socket on the comparison operator.

   When the second `If` block tests to true, it means that the dragged event needs to create a circle. A method provided by the Canvas1 component creates a circle for you at the coordinates specified.

2. Open the Canvas1 blocks drawer and locate the `call Canvas1.DrawCircle` method block. Drag out the `Canvas1.DrawCircle` and snap it into the second `If` block.

   The `Canvas1.DrawCircle` method only accepts one set of X/Y coordinates. You use the current coordinates to tell the method to draw a circle every time the current coordinates change.

3. Open the My Definitions blocks drawer and locate the `currentX` block. Drag the `currentX` block and snap it into the `x` socket on the `Canvas1.DrawCircle` block.

4. Open the My Definitions drawer and locate the `currentY` block. Drag the `currentY` block and snap it into the `y` socket on the `Canvas1.DrawCircle` block.

The other parameter that the `Canvas1.DrawCircle` needs is the radius of the circle in pixels. The `r` socket requires a number that indicates how large you want the circle to be drawn. Open the Math blocks drawer and drag out a `random integer` block. Snap it into the `r` socket on the `Canvas1.DrawCircle`. Change the number range on the `random integer` block to 5 and 20, indicating a random number of pixels from 5 to 20.

Your final `If` block tests to see if the `varDrawType` contains the value 3, which indicates the Point button was tapped:

1. Select the third `If` block and typeblock a comparison operator. With the comparison operator selected, typeblock the `varDrawType` global variable block. Make sure it auto-snaps into the first socket on the comparison operator. Typeblock a numeral 3 number block. Snap the number block into the second socket on the comparison operator.

2. When the third `If` block evaluates as true, it means that the Point button has been tapped and the user wants to draw a series of points. The Canvas1 component provides you with a `DrawPoint` method that handles this nicely.

3. Open the Canvas1 blocks drawer and locate the `call Canvas1.DrawPoint` block. Drag the `Canvas1.DrawPoint` block and snap it into the third and final `If` block. The `DrawPoint` method only takes one set of coordinates. You use the current coordinates of the dragged event to create a single pixel of random color when the current coordinates change.

4. Open the My Definitions drawer and locate the `currentX` and `currentY` blocks. Drag both blocks out onto the workspace. Snap the `currentX` block into the x socket on the `Canvas1.DrawPoint` block.

Now whenever the user taps the Point button and drags a finger on the canvas, a series of points are drawn. You can test this behavior on your connected Android device.

Your completed `Canvas1.Dragged` event handler should look like Figure 6-7.

FIGURE 6-7:
The blocks for
the completed
Canvas1.
Dragged event
handler

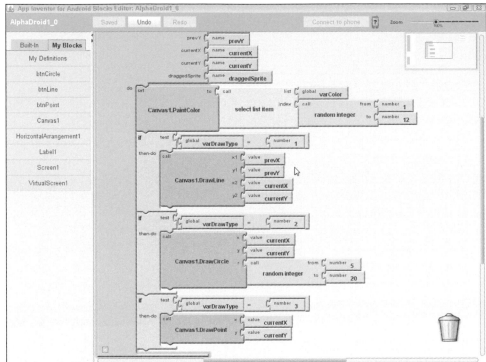

Creating AlphaDroid 2.0

AlphaDroid 2.0 (see the design sketch in Figure 6-8) builds on the solid functionality of the 1.0 version and adds some fun and levity to the mix. The Canvas component that allowed your user to interact with the screen image also allows image sprites to be placed on the screen and animated. The main change from the 1.0 version to the 2.0 version is the addition of an animated Andy the Android to the canvas. As the user plays and draws on the canvas, Andy runs around in random directions and, when tapped, jumps and yells.

Your primitives

These are the basic algorithms and logical pieces to achieve your design goals for the improvements to your application.

○ A canvas to allow the placement of sprites (already in place from the 1.0 version)

○ A sprite with a preloaded image of Andy the Android

○ A series of sequential images for animation of the sprite

○ A method of detecting when the sprite is touched

○ A sound for when the image is touched

○ A method for handling sprite movement, bounds, and so on

○ A method for sequential animation

FIGURE 6-8:
The AlphaDroid
2.0 design
sketch

Your progression

These are the basic logical steps to approach the new design goals:

1. Update the user interface with the sprite.

2. Upload the sprite images and sound.

3. Create the sprite movement logic.

4. Create the sprite touched animation sequence.

New components

These are the new components and blocks you use to introduce added functionality to your application. These are mostly about or involved with your sprite Andy and his movement and animation.

- ○ ImageSprite
- ○ New blocks
- ○ Not
- ○ ImageSprite.Touched
- ○ ImageSprite.EdgeReached
- ○ ImageSprite.Heading
- ○ ImageSprite.Speed
- ○ ImageSprite.Interval
- ○ ImageSprite.Picture

The Canvas component that you used in the AlphaDroid 1.0 application allowed you to handle user interaction with the touch screen interface. The Canvas component is also an integral part of sprite animation. You cannot have moving interactive elements in App Inventor without the Canvas. Even if the Canvas events are not used, the Canvas component is required to place sprites and use the sprite events.

You use the previously existing canvas to allow you place and animate a small Andy the Android figure. *Sprites* are the primary component in most games and animated movement on the Android. The sprite component provides the methods and capabilities for movement and touch and drag interaction for the sprite. However, the App Inventor sprites do not currently allow for animation natively. You use a programmatic method to animate the Android figure. This project familiarizes you with the basics of sprite use. In Chapter 11, I show in more depth how the sprites can be used for interaction.

Beginning AlphaDroid 2.0

Create a copy of the AlphaDroid application using the Save As button in Design view. Name your new project AlphaDroid 2.0. The Save As button lets you edit your new project when you click OK.

Follow these steps to add the images and components necessary to have an interactive Andy the Android sprite in your application. You upload all of the images and then animate them a bit later.

1. Select the Screen1 component in the Components column and change the Title property in the Properties column to reflect your new application name.

2. Drag an ImageSprite component from the Animation palette and drop it on the Canvas1 component. You cannot place an ImageSprite unless you have a Canvas component. The ImageSprite component shows up as a small icon on the canvas component.

3. In the Components column, rename the ImageSprite component as sprtAndy. Use the sprt prefix for all ImageSprites throughout this book. With the sprtAndy component selected in the Components column, click on the Picture property field in the Properties column. A media picker box drops down. Click the Add button and then click the Choose File button to navigate to your AlphaDroid project files. Double-click the image called andy.png and then click OK on the File Upload pop-up.

   The image sprite on the canvas should populate with the little green Android as soon as the image is uploaded.

4. Set the Interval property in the Properties column to 1.

The Interval property determines how often and quickly the canvas updates the position   **TIP**
of the sprite. Lower numbers make animation smoother but can take up processing time.
Higher numbers update the screen less often and make the sprite appear to skip from
position to position. For some kinds of sprite that are not intended to move smoothly, this
behavior is fine. Our little Android is going to glide smoothly around the canvas, so the interval
needs to be set low. Leave the Heading, X, Y, and Speed properties at their defaults. You set
these with the property blocks from the Blocks Editor.

---

5. Click on the sprtAndy sprite in Design view and drag him around the canvas.

   The X and the Y coordinates change as you drag. You can place image sprites in their initial or start positions on the Design view. Make sure you check the actual position on your connected Android device. The position isn't always where you think it is in relation to your phone screen. You can use the readout of the X and Y position to aid you in programming your application. If you want a certain zone to be a "score" zone or "kill" zone, you can use the X and Y read-out on the properties to inform your programming. Drag the sprite until it is where you would like a zone to be located and then write down the X/Y coordinates and use it in your blocks. Make sure that when you do this, you check the position on your connected device too or your application may have completely unexpected results.

6. With the sprtAndy still selected, change the `Width` property to `100` pixels and the `Height` property to 75 pixels.

7. Drag a Clock component from the Basic palette onto the Designer screen. In the Properties column, set the Clock1 components `TimerInterval` property to 65.

The Clock1 `TimerInterval` property in this case is the amount of time between each image being changed on your sprite. When animating your own sprites, you may need to use some trial and error to find the smoothest, most realistic interval for your image change speed.

This is the time between instances of the clock timer firing. You will use the clock as you have in past projects for deferred processing. Specifically, you use it to time the changes of the sprite images to animate it when touched.

8. Uncheck the `TimerEnabled` property for the Clock1 component.

9. From the Media palette, drag a Sound component and drop it on the Design view.

This Sound component does much the same thing as the Player component you used previously. The difference is that it plays very short sounds, typically no longer than 5–7 seconds. Longer sounds loaded into the Sound component play only about 6 seconds of the sound. You use the Sound component for a single purpose: The Sound component plays the andyouch.mp3 sound file when Andy is touched.

10. With the Sound1 component selected, click on the `Source` property field in the Properties column. A media picker drops down. Click the Add button and then the Choose File button to navigate to your AlphaDroid project files. Double-click the andyouch.mp3 file and then click OK in the File Uploader pop-up.

11. Leave the `MinimumInterval` property value at `500`.

This property determines how long before the same sound component plays the sound. If a request to play the sound is generated in the time specified by the `MinimumInterval` property, the sound doesn't play. This keeps the sound from being played several times at once, creating cacophony.

12. In the Media column, click the Add button and navigate to your AlphaDroid project files. Double-click the first andyjump1.png files. Repeat until all the andyjump images are showing in the Media column.

Making Andy move

Switch over to the Blocks Editor; if it's not open, click the Blocks Editor button on the Design view. Your first task is to get Andy moving. You use randomized speed and directions for this little application. The Andy figure darts around the screen, changing directions when the canvas is tapped.

1. Locate the `Canvas1.Touched` event handler on your Blocks Editor workspace. Remember to use the Organize All Blocks and Collapse All Blocks functions when your workspace gets disorganized. You can access these by right-clicking any open workspace area.

2. Make sure the `Canvas1.Touched` event is expanded. Clicking the small white plus sign (+) on collapsed blocks expands them. When they are expanded, you can click the minus sign (-) at the bottom of the blocks to collapse them. (See Figure 6-9.)

3. Open the sprtAndy blocks drawer on the My Blocks tab. Locate the `set sprtAndy.Speed to` block. Drag the `set speed` block out and snap it in to the `Canvas1.Touched` event handler above all the other blocks.

   The `sprtAndy.Speed [to]` block sets the speed at which Andy moves from place to place. You want to randomize Andy's movement, including the speed.

4. Typeblock a `random integer` block by typing `random integer` and pressing Enter. You can actually press Enter right after you type the `I` in `integer`. Snap the `random integer` block into the socket on the `sprtAndy.Speed [to]` block. Typeblock a numeral 5 number block. Make sure the number 5 block auto-snaps into the `from` socket on the `random integer` block. Typeblock a numeral 15 block and snap it into the `to` socket on the `random integer` block. Now whenever the canvas is tapped, the speed of the Andy sprite is set to a random speed between 5 and 15.

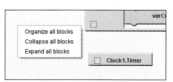

FIGURE 6-9: The collapse and expand hotspot and right-click options

These blocks then set the sprite named sprtAndy to a random speed between 5 and 15 when they are executed. The speed number is an arbitrary number from 0 to 100 — 100 is incredibly fast and 0 is no movement at all. For your project sprites, you might well have a sprite speed set at a constant rate or have it change based on user input.

You also need to randomize the heading or direction of the sprite:

1. Open the sprtAndy blocks drawer and locate the sprtAndy.Heading [to] block. Drag out the heading block and snap it in under the sprtAndy.Speed block.

2. With the sprtAndy.Heading block selected, typeblock a random integer block. After it auto-snaps into the to socket on the sprtAndy.Heading block, typeblock a numeral 1 block and snap it into the from block on the random integer block. Then typeblock a numeral 360 block into the to block on the random integer. If you started by typeblocking the random integer and did not click anything between blocks, you be able to type block the whole string fairly quickly.

3. The Canvas1.Touched event now activates Andy to head in a new random direction from 1 to 360 degrees and at a random speed. Your altered Canvas1.Touched event should look like Figure 6-10.

FIGURE 6-10:
The altered
Canvas1.
Touched event
handler with the
sprtAndy blocks
in it

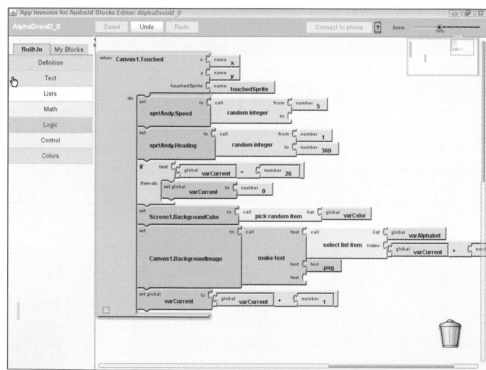

Managing the sprite at the edge of the canvas

On your connected Android device, whenever you tap the canvas, the background image should change and Andy should start moving in a random direction. However, you notice that when Andy reaches the edge of the canvas, he is stuck unless a canvas tap moves him off in a new direction. The ImageSprite gives you an event handler to handle what happens when your sprite reaches the edge of the canvas. The event handler is called every time a sprite reaches an edge. You can do different things depending on which edge is reached. When an edge is reached, the particular edge is reported using a numerical value from the following list:

❍ If the north edge is reached, the number 1 is returned.

❍ If the northeast edge is reached, the number 2 is returned.

❍ If the east edge is reached, the number 3 is returned.

❍ If the southeast edge is reached, the number 4 is reached.

❍ If the south edge (the negation of north) is reached, the number -1 is returned.

❍ If the southwest edge (the negation of northeast) is reached, the number -2 is returned.

❍ If the west edge (the negation of east) is reached, the number -3 is returned.

❍ If the northwest edge (the negation of southeast) is reached, the number -4 is returned.

For this project, you don't care which edge is reached, but in future projects, this will be important. Flip back and review this information when you need it. Here's how to handle the sprite at the edge of the canvas:

1. Open the sprtAndy blocks drawer and drag out the `sprtAndy.EdgeReached` event handler.

   You will notice that the `edge` socket is populated with a `name` block. A matching `value` block was created in your My Definitions drawer. This is the value block that reports which edge the sprite touches. For your AlphaDroid project, all you want is for the sprite to not stick at the edge. The ImageSprite component provides a method for a "bounce" behavior that bounces the sprite away from the edges.

2. Open the sprtAndy blocks drawer and locate the `call sprtAndy.Bounce edge` method call. Drag the bounce method call and snap it into the `sprtAndy.EdgeReached` event handler. The method call needs to know which edge was reached.

3. Open the My Definitions drawer and locate the value edge block. If you had more than one sprite, you might change the name block in the .EdgeReached event handler to be more specific, such as AndysEdge. That would make it easier to pick the value edge block out of the drawer because the value block would also change to value AndysEdge. For this project, the generic name edge is good enough. Drag the value edge block and snap it into the sprtAndy.Bounce [edge] block (see Figure 6-11).

FIGURE 6-11:
The sprtAndy.
EdgeReached
block

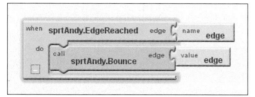

Now whenever any edge is reached, the .EdgeReached block is executed and Andy bounces away from the edge. Tap the canvas on your connected Android device to see Andy exhibit this behavior.

Handling sprite touch events

The only behavior left to program is when the Andy sprite is touched. The ImageSprite component provides an event handler to handle touch events. You set up the .Touched event handler to call a procedure that then bounces back and forth between the procedure and a clock timer changing the image of the sprite. The appearance is of Andy jumping as the images are rapidly changing. The concept is much like the animated flip books of childhood, where each image you load onto the ImageSprite is just a little different than the previous one.

You still have to overcome two challenges. The first is how to keep all the images from being changed at once. If you were to put a series of five sprtAndy.Picture [to] blocks in a procedure and call it, the procedure would update the Image property of the sprite five times before the screen ever updated. The processor on your phone is fast enough to do that between screen refresh cycles. So you have to introduce enough delay between updates to allow the image on the sprite to actually change.

The second challenge is to come up with an algorithm to change the andyjump#.png image sequentially. Your algorithm needs to keep track of what the current image is and be able to break out of the update loop when the last image is updated. You build procAnimateAndy and the Clock1.Timer to handle the algorithm shown in Figure 6-12.

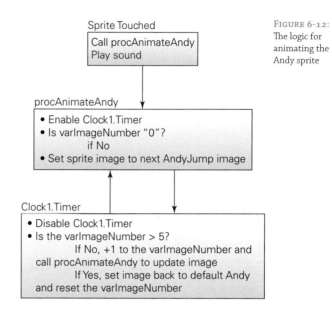

FIGURE 6-12:
The logic for
animating the
Andy sprite

To start, define the variable that tracks which image is currently being displayed. Your images are sequentially numbered. Use the sequential numbers plus static text to create the file name in the procAnimateAndy procedure:

1. Typeblock a variable and rename it varImageNumber. Typeblock a numeral 1 and snap the number block into the varImageNumber block. This initializes the variable with the number 1.

2. Typeblock a new procedure by typing procedure and pressing Enter. Rename the procedure procAnimateAndy.

3. Typeblock the .Timer block from the Clock1 component by typing Clock1.Timer and pressing Enter. Drag the Clock1.Timer near the procAnimateAndy procedure. You will be building these two blocks together.

   The first thing the procAnimateAndy block needs to do is enable the Clock1 timer. The .Timer introduces a slight delay (65 milliseconds) and increment the varImageNumber variable during the animation process.

4. With the procAnimateAndy block selected, typeblock the Clock1.TimerEnabled [to] block. Immediately typeblock a true block. The .TimerEnabled block should auto-snap into the procedure and then the true block should auto-snap into the .TimerEnabled block (see Figure 6-13).

The next step builds the logic that says, "If the `varImageNumber` hasn't yet reached the last image number, update the sprite image with the next image":

1. Typeblock an `If` block by typing `If` and pressing Enter.

2. Typeblock a `not` block. The `not` block can be very useful for determining the opposite of a control block's test. The test we want is, "If `varImageNumber` is not greater than or equal to 5 (the last image number), execute the following blocks." If you are having difficulty building a particular logic test, remember to ask yourself if you need to use a `not` block. For this test, you could use a simpler test. But, for the sake of learning it, use the `not` block.

3. With the `not` block selected, typeblock a "greater than or equal to" comparison operator by typing `>=` and pressing Enter.

4. Typeblock the `varImageNumber` global variable block. Make sure it auto-snaps into the first socket on the `>=` block. Typeblock a numeral 5 block and snap it into the second socket on the comparison operator.

   Your test should look like the one in Figure 6-13.

5. Open the sprtAndy blocks drawer and locate the set `SprtAndy.Picture` to block. Drag out the `sprtAndy.Picture [to]` and snap it into the socket on your `If` block. This is the block to change the image on the image sprite. If the `varImageNumber` has not reached the limit, this block needs to use the number in the `varImageNumber` to assign the next andyjump image to the sprite.

6. With the `sprtAndy.Picture` block selected, typeblock a `make text` block. Typeblock a `text` block. It should auto-snap into the `text` socket on the `make text` block. Replace the default text with `andyjump`.

7. Make sure the `make text` block is still selected and typeblock the `varImageNumber` global `variable` block. Make sure it snaps into the next `text` socket on the `make text` block. This block reports the number in the `varImageNumber` variable. That number and the two `text` blocks are joined to create the filename for the `sprtAndy.Picture` block.

8. Typeblock a `text` block and replace the default text with `.png`. Snap the file `text` block into the `text` socket underneath the `varImageNumber` block.

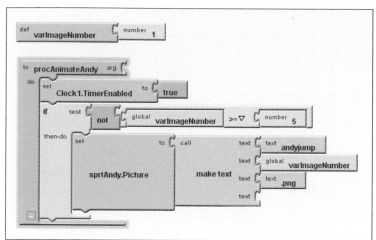

FIGURE 6-13:
The proc
AnimateAndy
procedure

Next build the Clock1.Timer that increments the varImageNumber variable and decides if the procAnimateAndy needs to be called again:

1. Locate the Clock1.Timer on your Blocks Editor workspace.

   The first thing the Clock1.Timer does is to disable itself so it does not run again until it is enabled by the procAnimateAndy procedure.

2. Select the Clock1.Timer event handler and typeblock the Clock1.TimerEnabled [to] block. It should auto-snap into the event handler. Continue by typeblocking a false block and making sure it auto-snaps into the Clock1.TimerEnabled block, as shown in Figure 6-14.

   The clock timer decides whether the varImageNumber has incremented high enough to display the last animation image. If not, it increments the varImageNumber and then calls the procAnimateAndy. If the varImageNumber has incremented far enough, it sets the sprite image back to its default image and resets the variable.

3. Typeblock an IfElse block and snap it into the Clock1.Timer block under the Clock1.TimerEnabled block.

4. Continue typeblocking a "less than" comparison operator by typing < and pressing Enter. Make sure it auto-snaps into the test socket on the IfElse block.

5. Typeblock the `varImageNumber` global variable block and snap it into the first socket on the comparison operator.

6. Typeblock a numeral 5 block and snap the number block into the second socket on the comparison operator. This test checks to see if the `varImageNumber` is still less than 5.

   If the test evaluates to `true`, the final number 5 image has not yet been displayed and the `varImageNumber` needs to be incremented by 1.

7. Typeblock the `varImageNumber [to]` block and snap it into the `then-do` socket on the `IfElse` block. You build the standard variable incrementing string that you have used before.

8. Typeblock the addition block by typing `+` and pressing Enter. Make sure it snaps into the `to` socket on the `varImageNumber [to]` block.

9. Typeblock the `varImageNumber` global variable block. Snap it into the first socket on the addition block.

10. Typeblock a numeral 1 block and snap the number 1 block into the second socket on the addition block.

11. Typeblock the `procAnimateAndy call` block. Snap it in under the incremented variable blocks in the `then-do` socket of the `IfElse` block.

Next you need to fill the `else-do` socket with the blocks to execute when the `varImageNumber` variable has reached its highest number. When the last animation image is displayed, you want Andy to return to his normal self, so you set the `sprtAndy.Picture` property back to the default image.

1. Typeblock the `sprtAndy.Picture [to]` block and snap it into the `else-do` socket on the `IfElse` block. Typeblock a `text` block and replace the default text with andy. png. Snap the `text` block into the `sprtAndy.Picture` block.

2. Typeblock the `varImageNumber [to]` block and snap it in under the `sprtAndy.Picture` block in the `else-do` socket. Typeblock a numeral 0 block and snap the number block into the `varImageNumber [to]` block.

Your completed `Clock1.Timer` block should look like Figure 6-14.

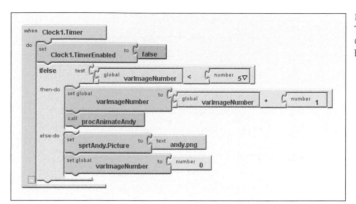

FIGURE 6-14:
The completed
Clock1.Timer
blocks

The final step is to set up the sprtAndyTouched event handler.

1. Open the sprtAndy blocks drawer and locate the sprtAndy.Touched event handler. Drag the event handler out onto the workspace.

2. With the sprtAndy.Touched block selected, typeblock the procAnimateAndy call block. Make sure it auto-snaps into the event handler.

3. Continue typeblocking the Sound1.Play block. This block plays the andyouch.mp3 file that was uploaded into the Media column. Make sure that you set the Source property in the Design view Properties column to point to the andyouch.mp3 file.

The completed sprtAndy Touched block should look like Figure 6-15.

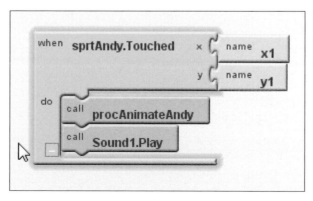

FIGURE 6-15:
The completed
sprtAndy.
Touched event
handler

Test your application by packaging it onto your connected Android device. (Review Chapter 1 for packaging instructions.) More importantly, test it by handing your precious Android device to a toddler and letting them try it out to see whether they like the application. The true test of an application's design goals is whether the user accepts the final result.

chapter 7

PunchDroid: An Android Punch Bug Game

in this chapter

- Using the TinyWebDB component for multi-handset communication
- Using a timer to poll a datasource to keep apps up-to-date
- Employing a `choose` block for variable situations
- Implementing a multiplayer game between handsets
- Using check boxes as radio buttons

REMEMBER PLAYING THE PUNCH BUG game back in the day when Volkswagen Beetles were a rare sight? You know the game. Whenever someone sees the distinctive little car, she would punch the other player on the arm and yell "Punch Bug!" and get a point. Well, the game you played as a child is about to get an update. The PunchDroid project allows your user to play the same game regardless of the distance between the players. Whether you're looking for VW Beetles or Android phones, PunchDroid is a fun little game that can be played between two phones.

This application introduces the TinyWebDB component. Previously you used the TinyDB component to store data between application settings. TinyDB stores its data on the local device as an .XML file in the Settings section of the Android file system. *TinyWebDB*, by contrast, uses either Wi-Fi or cell phone networks to communicate with a database running on a Web server. The TinyWebDB service runs on a Web server, accepts incoming data, and responds to requests for stored data from your application. TinyWebDB is an important part of your skill set for creating connected applications and devices.

NOTE   The TinyWebDB component uses a service URL to connect to the TinyWebDB service running on a Web server. Google has provided a test TinyWebDB service that is used in this project. You share that TinyWebDB service with every other person testing the TinyWebDB service. If you want a TinyWebDB service to use for just yourself and your applications, set up your own TinyWebDB service using the instructions in Appendix B. If you do not set up your own TinyWebDB service, you can expect to have someone else using this project chapter to overwrite your data.

Creating the PunchDroid Application

The key concepts I introduce in this project include

- ○ Using the TinyWebDB service

- ○ Handling returns from the TinyWebDB service

- ○ Creating test conditions and multiple test conditions for complex tests

- ○ Creating check boxes that act as radio buttons to force a choice

- ○ Keeping and storing data between multiple handsets

The TinyWebDB service as it is used in this project can be used for multiplayer games, reference applications, or data mining applications. The advanced use of the TinyWebDB service is integral to taking advantage of the networked nature of Android smartphones. Think of the TinyWebDB not just as a data storage component, but as a thread that can tie multiple devices together and as a gateway to other devices. Advanced hacks are available on the Google App Inventor forums that turn the TinyWebDB service into an even more powerful gateway to other data sources. Learning the basic fundamentals of how TinyWebDB works is the first step towards more advanced uses of the component.

Your design

Figure 7-1 shows the sketched user interface for the PunchDroid application. The application has two VirtualScreens: One for the main play interface and one for the Settings interface.

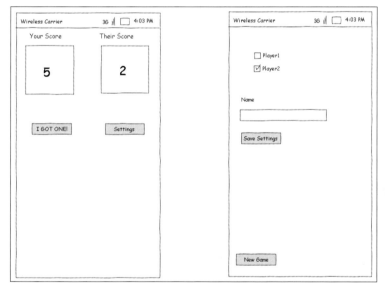

FIGURE 7-1:
The PunchDroid
design sketches

The PunchDroid application is a multiplayer game that can be played by two players across the Internet. The user inputs their name and player number to identify themselves uniquely. The user then has a button to tap whenever the user sees a VW Bug.

Your primitives

These are the core programming concepts for this app, broken down into simple statements to aid in programming the design goals:

○ A button that increments the user's score

○ A method to distinguish between the local and the remote player

○ A method to transmit data to the opposing player's phone

○ A method to store the user's name and player number between sessions

○ A method to start a new game

○ A method to display the local and remote players' scores

○ A method to keep both players' scores up to date

Make sure you download the Chapter 7 project files from the companion Web site for this book and save them somewhere where you can find them easily during the project build. See this book's Introduction for more on downloading the files from the Web site.

Your progression

These are the basic steps you take in order to build the application:

1. Place the VirtualScreen1 user interface elements.

2. Place the VirtualScreen2 user interface elements.

3. Define the variables required for local information storage.

4. Build out the `Screen1.Initialize` event.

5. Build blocks to handle the events on the Settings page.

6. Build blocks to handle the events on the main play page.

Getting Started on the PunchDroid Application

The PunchDroid application introduces you to a major component for interacting with data across the Internet: TinyWebDB. TinyWebDB is very useful for getting information to multiple handsets and allowing data to persist beyond the state of the local application. The PunchDroid application is a fun proof-of-concept application that can be expanded to fit any number of entertaining game ideas. The PunchDroid app only allows for two players, Player1 and Player2. The user determines when they start the application for the first time whether they are going to be Player1 or Player2.

1. Start a new project from the My Projects window. Name the project `PunchDroid1_0`.

2. Select the Screen1 component in the Components column. Uncheck the Scrollable property and change the Title property to PunchDroid 1.0.

NOTE Make sure the Display Invisible Components in Viewer check box is selected. That keeps even your invisible screen arrangements visible in the Design view.

3. Click on the Icon property field to bring up the drop-down list. Click the Add button to bring up the Upload File pop-up. Click the Choose File button and navigate to your Chapter 7 project files. Double-click the punchdroid_ico.png file to select the icon file for upload. Click OK on the Upload File pop-up.

   The PunchDroid application will have two screens. VirtualScreen1 is the main play screen, where the user can tap the I Got One! button to increment their score. VirtualScreen2 is the Settings screen, where the user can set whether they are Player1 or Player2 and enter their name.

4. From the Design view, drag and drop two VerticalArrangements onto the Viewer. Rename the first VerticalArrangement VirtualScreen1. Rename the second VerticalArrangement VirtualScreen2.

TIP As you build the user interface, remember to refer to the design sketches or Figure 7-2 if you get confused.

5. Uncheck the Visible property for both VirtualScreens. The Screen1.Intialize event decides whether the user should set their settings first or proceed to the main play screen. Set the Width and Height property of both VirtualScreens to Fill Parent.

6. Drag a HorizontalArrangement into the VirtualScreen1 component. This holds the two score boxes that display the score for the two players. Each score box is a VerticalArrangement that displays the player's name label above their score label.

7. Set the Width and Height property of the HorizontalArrangement1 to Fill Parent.

8. Drag and drop two VerticalArrangements into the HorizontalArrangement1. These are the boxes to hold the labels for score display.

9. Set the Width and Height property on the VerticalArrangements1 and 2 to Fill Parent.

10. Drag and drop another HorizontalArrangement below the HorizontalArrangement1 that contains the score boxes. Set the `Width` property to `Fill Parent`. Don't set the `Height` property to `Fill Parent`. You want the buttons pushed to the bottom of the screen. This arrangement holds the I Got One! button and the button used to access the settings page.

Now place all the Basic palette components:

1. Drag and drop a label into the VerticalArrangement1 that is the left box for your score display. (See Figure 7-2.) Rename the label `lblThisPlayerName`. Change the default `Text` property to `Your Score:`. This label is changed programmatically when your user inputs their name, but having this default text to begin with helps you if you have to troubleshoot. It also helps you get a feel for the overall layout as you build the user interface.

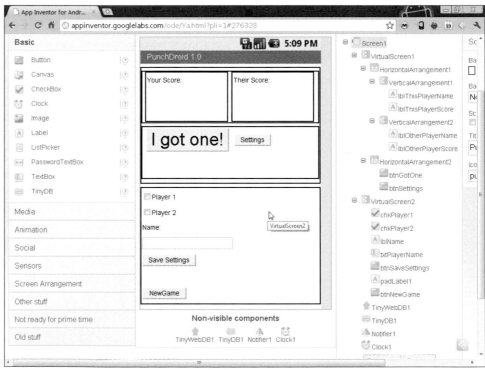

2. Drag and drop a second label below the label you just named `lblThisPlayerName`. Rename the new label `lblThisPlayerScore`. Change the `Alignment` property to

Center with the Property drop-down list. Check the FontBold property check box. Set the FontSize property to 75 and the FontTypeFace to monospace. Delete the default text in the Text property field. This label displays the score of the local user.

Now set up the right score box in the same way:

1. Drag and drop a label into the VerticalArrangement2 that is the right score box in VirtualScreen1. Rename the label lblOtherPlayerName. Change the default Text property to Their Score:. Again this is mostly for your benefit as the actual text changes to the name of the other player.

2. Drag and drop a label directly below the lblOtherPlayerName label. Rename the new label lblOtherPlayerScore. Change the Alignment property to Center with the Property drop-down list box. Check the FontBold property check box. Set the FontSize property to 75 and the FontTypeSpace to monospace. Delete the default text in the Text property. This label displays the remote player's score whether he is Player1 or Player2.

Now place the buttons for play and for the Settings screen:

1. Click on the HorizontalArrangement2 to highlight it in the Design view. Drag and drop a button into the Horizontal Arrangement2 component. Rename the Button btnGotOne. Set the FontSize property to 35. Change the default Text property to I Got One!.

2. Drag and drop another button to the right of the btnGotOne button. Rename the button btnSettings. Change the default Text property to Settings.

VirtualScreen1 is now completed and should look like VirtualScreen1 in Figure 7-2.

Follow the next steps to set up VirtualScreen2. VirtualScreen2 is the screen for your player settings. It contains check boxes to allow your user to specify whether they are Player1 or Player2. It also contains the Player Name setting and the Reset Game button:

1. Drag and drop a CheckBox component into the VirtualScreen2. Rename the CheckBox component chkPlayer1. Change the default Text property in the Properties column to Player1.

2. Drag and drop a second CheckBox component into the VirtualScreen2 below the chkPlayer1 check box. Rename the CheckBox component chkPlayer2. Change the

default `Text` property to `Player2`. These two check boxes allow the user to select whether they are Player1 or Player2. Because they must be one or the other but cannot be both, you set up special logic that requires one to be checked but does not allow both to be checked.

3. Drag and drop a label below the chkPlayer2 check box. Rename the label `lblName`. This label marks the following text box as the spot for your user to put their player name. Change the default `Text` property to `Name:`.

4. Drag and drop a TextBox component below the lblName label. Rename the TextBox `txtPlayerName`. Set the `Hint` property to `Enter Player Name`. Change the default `Hint` property to `Enter Player Name`. This is the TextBox where the user can enter her name. That name is stored locally and uploaded to TinyWebDB.

5. Drag and drop a button below the txtPlayerName TextBox. Rename the button `btnSaveSettings`. This button is a major event in your application. It stores all the settings and initializes the game. You need one more button to give the players the option of resetting the score and starting a new game. However, you don't want it to be accidently hit, so you use a little vertical space to separate it from the other elements on the Settings screen.

6. Drag and drop a label below the btnSaveSettings button. Rename the label `padLabel1`. This label acts as padding between the buttons. Remove the default text in the `Text` property. Set the `Height` property to `Fill Parent`. This pushes the maximum vertical space between the two buttons on the Settings screen.

Now you need to place all of the application's non-visible components. You need to add TinyWebDB as the data component for communication between the player's phones. You also need to add a TinyDB component to store the local user's name and player number locally. You must add a notifier to provide pop-up notifications for several different application events you will program later. Finally, you should add a Clock component for keeping both players' games up-to-date on a reasonable schedule.

1. Drag and drop a TinyWebDB component from the Not Ready for Prime Time palette. The TinyWebDB component makes URL calls against a Web database application running on a Web server. The TinyWebDB component has one very important property: The `ServiceURL` property tells the TinyWebDB component where the Web database and application are located.

NOTE The component has a default `ServiceURL` property value of `http://appinvtinywebdb. appspot.com`. This URL points to a testing Web database that Google has set up on the Google AppSpot servers. The testing database is for testing and development, not for apps you actually want to use. It is subject to going down frequently. It is also used by anyone else testing a TinyWebDB component in an application. This makes it slow sometimes and means that your data can accidently be overwritten. Appendix B shows how to set up your own private WebDB to work in conjunction with TinyWebDB.

For the purposes of learning and creating the PunchDroid application, the testing database at `http://appinvtinywebdb.appspot.com` is sufficient.

2. Drag and drop a TinyDB1 component from the Basic palette.

3. Drag and drop a Notifier component from the Other Stuff palette.

4. Drag and drop a Clock component from the Basic palette.

Your user interface should look like Figure 7-2. Make sure that the VirtualScreens do not have the `Visible` property checked. Make sure the Display Invisible Components in Viewer check box is selected. Check that all arrangements have the `Fill Parent` property set as the `Width` and `Height` properties.

Handling the Settings page events

Switch over to the Blocks Editor. Click the Open the Blocks Editor button if the Blocks Editor isn't already open. The PunchDroid programming logic is almost entirely event-driven. The application does most of the work and then communicates the result to TinyWebDB for the PunchDroid application running on another device to download. You need to handle each of the button events on the user interface as well as one special event from TinyWebDB that is not user-generated.

You need to make provisions for storing several pieces of information locally on your application. For local storage, you use variables. When a variable value changes, you have to communicate it to TinyWebDB so that it can be accessed by the other player. You also need to make provisions for some information to be locally persistent. In other words, you use variables for storing immediate data locally, TinyDB for storing long-term user data, and TinyWebDB for storing persistent game information.

First you have to create all of the needed variables. You use typeblocking predominately in this project. I use the App Inventor syntax to represent the blocks. A quick review of App Inventor typeblock syntax: The `set Label1.Text to` block is referred to in App Inventor typeblocking as `Label1.Text [to]`.

Typeblock and create the following variables.

REMEMBER You create a new variable by typeblocking the keyword `Variable` and pressing Enter. You can then change the name to a unique name that is memorable to you. You need to plug a default value (usually a blank value) into the newly created variables.

- ○ `varPlayerName`: This stores the name of the player who is using the phone. Snap in a blank `text` block.

- ○ `varPlayerName1`: This stores Player1's name, whether he is on this phone or another. Snap in a blank `text` block.

- ○ `varPlayerName2`: This stores Player2's name, whether she is on this phone or another. Snap in a blank `text` block.

- ○ `varPlayerNumber`: This stores the user's player number (Player1 or Player2).

- ○ `VarPlayerScore1`: This stores Player1's score.

- ○ `varPlayerScore2`: This stores Player2's score.

Because a single game may well last across multiple instances of the application, you need to store the user's player number and name locally in TinyDB. Otherwise, the user would have to initialize those settings every time the application starts.

The `Screen1.Initialize` event checks to see whether TinyDB has player number information stored. If it does, the user has set his settings previously. If the user has not set their settings, the settings page needs to be displayed. If the user has set their settings, all the variables need to be initialized and the main game screen displayed. Some of the variable information comes from TinyDB, such as PlayerName and PlayerNumber. The others are initialized with calls to TinyWebDB.

First build an `IfElse` block to test if TinyDB has stored information. The `IfElse` block handles two cases. The first directs the user to the Settings page; the second initializes the variables:

1. Typeblock the `Screen1.Initialize` event handler block.

   The `IfElse` control block is your test decision-maker for the `.Initilize` event. With the `.Initialize` block selected, typeblock an `IfElse` block and snap it into the `.Intialize` event block.

2. Build the test for the `IfElse` block to test whether any data is stored in TinyDB. You do this by posing the question, "Does the contents of a specific TinyDB tag equal nothing?"

   Throughout this project, you use the variable names for all of the database tags minus the variable prefix. So, `varPlayerNumber` stored in a database uses the tag `player-number` and `varPlayerName` uses the tag `playername`. TinyDB and TinyWebDB tags are not case-sensitive, but using all lowercase characters can help differentiate them from variable names in your head.

3. Select the `IfElse` block and typeblock the equals comparison operator (=) and snap it into the `test` socket on the `IfElse` block. Typeblock a `TinyDB1.GetValue` block by typing `TinyDB1.GetValue`. Make sure it snaps into the first socket on the comparison operator. Now it needs a tag to try to pull data with. If the user has entered any settings, the `playernumber` tag contains data. Typeblock a `text` block and replace the default text with `playernumber`. Snap it into the `.GetValue` block. Typeblock a `text` block and remove the default text, leaving a blank `text` block. Snap the blank `text` block into the second socket on the comparison operator.

   The `then-do` first case of the `IfElse` block is fairly straightforward to build. If the user needs to set their player information, you need to make the Settings screen visible and create a pop-up to inform the user what is expected of them.

4. Typeblock the `VirtualScreen2.Visible [to]` block and snap it into the then-do socket on the `IfElse` block. Typeblock a `true` block and snap it into the `.Visible` block.

5. Typeblock the `Notifier1.ShowMessageDialog` block and snap it into the then-do socket on the `IfElse` block. This block is set up to notify the user that they need to enter their player information. Typeblock a `text` block and replace the default text with `You need to set your player information`. Snap the `text` block into the message socket on the `.ShowMessageDialog` block. Typeblock another `text` block and set its text to `First run!`.

Snap that `text` block into the `title` socket on the `.ShowMessageDialog` block. Typeblock a third `text` block and set its text to OK. Snap this text box into the `but-tontext` socket on the `.ShowMessageDialog` box.

The Notifier component has a special event handler for whenever you use a notification that has a button to press. The `Notifier` block you just placed has an OK button. Clicking the OK button signals the Settings screen to become visible. You build the instructions for the OK button press in the `Notifier1.AfterChoosing` event handler.

6. Typeblock the `Notifier1.AfterChoosing` event handler. Just to keep everything clean and symmetrical, you handle both VirtualScreens with the `AfterChoosing` event handler.

NOTE   The `.AfterChoosing` block is the event called when the OK button is clicked. It is also the event that is called if you use a Yes/No or other multi-button notification. The `.AfterChoosing` event has a parameter that contains the results or choice that your user selected. In this notification, the user has only one choice: OK. In multi-button notifications, the user's choice is contained in the parameter `value` block named whatever is snapped into the `choice` socket.

TIP   App Inventor should automatically populate the `choice` socket on the `.AfterChoosing` event. However, sometimes the Blocks Editor glitches and that `socket` winds up empty. When that happens, you can populate the `choice` socket with a `name` block and change the `name` block name to something memorable. The default `name` block is named `choice`.

---

7. Typeblock the `VirtualScreen1.Visible [to]` block and snap it into the `.AfterChoosing` event handler. Typeblock a `false` block and snap it into the socket on the `VirtualScreen1` block.

8. Typeblock the `VirtualScreen2.Visible [to]` block and snap it in below the previous block. Typeblock a `true` block and snap it into the `VirtualScreen2` block.

9. Now whenever the OK button on the notification is tapped, the Settings screen becomes visible to enable the user to set the player settings.

That's the complete first case of the `IfElse` block that is executed on start-up. Flip ahead to check out Figure 7-3 if you have any issues.

Next, you need to build the second case `else-do` socket on the `IfElse` block. If the settings have been set and stored in TinyDB, that information as well as whatever information exists in the TinyWebDB needs to be used to initialize your variables. You set the main play screen to visible and then start initializing variables with database calls:

1. Typeblock the `VirtualScreen1.Visible [to]` block and snap it into the else-do socket on the `IfElse` block in the `Screen1.Initialize` block. Typeblock a `true` block and snap it into the `VirtualScreen1.Visible` block.

2. Now for your first variable initialization call: Typeblock the `varPlayerNumber [to]` block and snap it under the `VirtualScreen1` block.

3. To pull information out of TinyDB and place it into a variable or label, use the `TinyDB1.GetValue` block socketed directly into where you want the data to go.

4. Typeblock the `TinyDB1.GetValue` block and snap it into the `varPlayerNumber [to]` block. Now you need to tell the `.GetValue` block what tag to pull the data from. Typeblock a `text` block and replace the default text with `playernumber`. Snap the `text` block into the `.GetValue tag` socket. You populate the tag `playernumber` with the correct data when you handle the Save Settings button event on the VirtualScreen1.

5. When the user enters their player number and name, your Save Settings event stores all the information under the correct tags.

Now you will initialize the `varPlayerName` variable. Typeblock the `varPlayerName [to]` block and snap next in the else-do socket. Typeblock a `TinyDB1.GetValue` block and snap it into the `varPlayerName [to]` socket. Typeblock a `text` block and replace the default text with `playername`.

Now you need to create a series of calls to the TinyWebDB for the other variable values. TinyWebDB works differently than TinyDB. TinyDB stores information on the local handset in the Settings location for applications on your phone. TinyWebDB, on the other hand, is a simple database that runs on a server located on the Internet. (See Appendix B for information on how to set up your own private Web database.) That means that when you submit a call for data to the TinyWebDB, the request is sent over the Internet to the URL placed in the `ServiceURL` property. The response is then sent over the Internet back to the phone.

The upshot of this is that data calls to TinyWebDB are not instantaneous as they are with TinyDB. Whenever you use TinyWebDB, you make calls for data, but you can't actually place that data or process that data until it actually comes back to the phone. You handle the responses to data request to the TinyDBWeb service using a special event provided by the TinyWebDB component. The `TinyWebDB1.GotValue` event is used to process any incoming data requested from any other blocks in your application. You build that event later; for now, you are just going to tell the TinyWebDB component to get the data for the variables based on the appropriate tags. You actually place that data in the variables in the `.GotValue` event handler.

You continue building the `Screen1.Initialize` event in the following steps by placing all of the `.GetValue` blocks in the `IfElse` block:

1. Typeblock a `TinyWebDB1.GetValue` block and snap it in the `else-do` socket on the `IfElse` block. Typeblock a `text` block for the tag and replace the default text with `playername1`. Snap the `text` block into the `tag` socket on the `.GetValue` block. This block sends the request across the Internet for the data stored under the tag `playername1`, which is the name of the player who declared himself as Player1.

2. Typeblock a `TinyWebDB1.GetValue` block and snap it in. Typeblock a `text` block for the tag and replace the default text with `playername2`. Snap the `text` block into the `tag` socket on the `.GetValue` block. This block sends the request for the data stored under the tag `playername2`.

3. Typeblock a `TinyWebDB1.GetValue` block and snap it in next. Typeblock a `text` block for the tag and replace the default text with `PlayerScore1`. Snap the `text` block into the `tag` socket on the `.GetValue` block.

4. Typeblock a `TinyWebDB1.GetValue` block and snap it in next. Typeblock a `text` block for the tag and replace the default text with `PlayerScore2`. Snap the `text` block into the `tag` socket on the `.GetValue` block.

After you've built all the calls to the TinyWebDB for the `Screen1.Initialize` block, you need to place the user's player name in the Label in their score box.

Typeblock the `lblThisPlayerName.Text` [to] block and snap it in as the last block in the `Screen1.Initialize` event handler block. Typeblock the `varPlayerName` global variable block and snap it into the `text` block. This sets the score label in the score box on the right side to represent the local player's name.

Your completed `Screen1.Intialize` block should look like Figure 7-3.

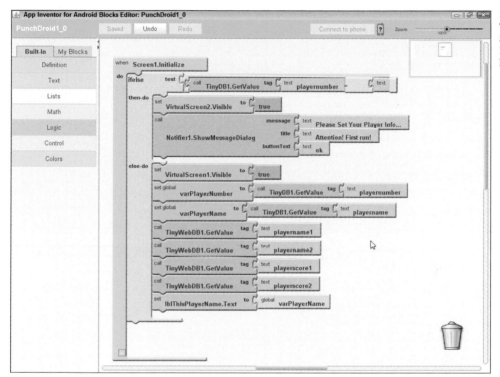

FIGURE 7-3:
The completed
Screen1.
Initialize event
handler

Next, get ready to build the programming logic for the components and events on the Settings screen of your application. You have several components to handle and two buttons to handle events for on the Settings page. You need to handle the Save Settings button event, and you also need to set up logic that ensures that one check box is selected but not both. You also need to handle the event for the New Game button.

The logic for the check boxes seems complex, but the check boxes come with a very useful event handler, the CheckBox.Changed event. This event is called whenever the value of the check box is changed. A check box is always either true or false. If that value changes, you can build logic to check on and or change the other check box. You need to build logic that says, "When the check box is changed, set the other check box to the opposite value."

1. Typeblock the chkPlayer1.Changed event handler. With the chkPlayer1. Changed block selected, typeblock the chkPlayer2.Value [to] block.

This is the .Value [to] block opposite of the event handler. Make sure the .Value [to] block snaps into the event handler. The ChkPlayer1.Changed has the chkPlayer1. Value block and vice versa.

NOTE

2. Typeblock a not block and snap it into the to socket on the chkPlayer2.Value block. Now typeblock the chkPlayer1.Value reporting block and snap it into the not block. The logic of these blocks now reads, Set the Value of chkPlayer2 to the opposite of chkPlayer1 whenever chkPlayer2 is changed. (See Figure 7-4.) You set up the same thing for the chkPlayer2 check box next.

3. Typeblock the chkPlayer2.Changed event handler. Typeblock the chkPlayer1.Value [to] block and snap it into the event handler. Typeblock a not block and snap it into the to socket on the .Value block. Typeblock the chkPlayer2.Value reporting block and snap it into the not block. Your Player1 and Player2 selection check box event handlers should now look like Figure 7-4.

Whenever one check box is selected, the other is automatically set to the opposite value, ensuring that one but not both are always selected.

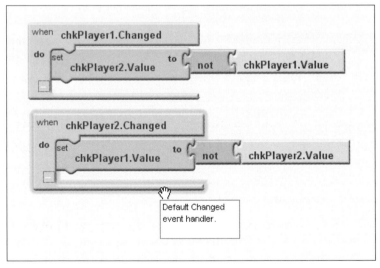

FIGURE 7-4:
The completed
.Changed event
handlers

You use a new block to create the logic in the event handler for the Save Settings button. The choose block allows your blocks to make a choice about which value to use in a string or logic pattern. In this case, you use the choose block to choose which number to store with the playernumber tag in TinyDB. If the user has selected the Player1 check box, your blocks will store the value 1 in with the tag playernumber. If the user has selected the Player2 check box, your blocks store the value 2 with the tag playernumber. That way, when the Screen1.Initialize event pulls the information from TinyDB, your application has the correct value in the varPlayerNumber variable:

1. Start off by typeblocking the btnSaveSettings.Click event handler. Typeblock a TinyDB1.StoreValue block.

   The TinyDB1.StoreValue block allows you to save any data with a tag so that it can be retrieved later. You store the player number with the tag playernumber.

2. With the TinyDB1.StoreValue block selected, typeblock a text block and replace the default text with playernumber. Make sure the text block is snapped into the tag socket on the .StoreValue block.

3. Typeblock a choose block and snap it into the valueToStore socket on the .StoreValue block. The choose value block chooses which number to return to the valueToStore socket based on a test much like an IfElse block.

Now build the test for the choose block. The logic of your test goes like this: If the chk-Player1 value is set to "true" then return the value in the first return socket; otherwise, return the value in the second return socket.

1. Typeblock an equals comparison operator (=) and snap it into the test socket on the choose block. Typeblock the chkPlayer1.Value reporting block and snap it into the first socket on the comparison operator. Typeblock a true block and snap it into the second socket on the comparison operator.

   Now you need to set the values that the test case will choose between. If the test evaluates true, you want the value 1 to be stored because that is the number the player chose. If the test case evaluates to false, you want to return the value 2. You know that if chkPlayer1.Value is false, chkPlayer2.Value must be set to true because one of the check boxes must be checked.

2. Typeblock a numeral 1 block and snap it into the then-return socket on the choose block.

3. Typeblock a numeral 2 block and snap it into the else-return socket on the choose block.

Now you use the value just stored in TinyDB to set the value of the variable varPlayer-Number so the player can start playing.

1. Typeblock the varPlayerNumber [to] block and snap it in under the TinyDB1.StoreValue block. Typeblock a TinyDB1.GetValue block and snap it into the varPlayerNumber block. Typeblock a text block and replace the text with the tag

text `playernumber`. Snap it into the `tag` socket on the `.GetValue` block. Because TinyDB instantly stores and returns data, we can populate the variable with TinyDB data immediately after storing it.

Next, store the text from the `txtPlayerName` text box in TinyDB so your application can remember your player's name.

2. Typeblock a `TinyDB1.StoreValue` block and snap it in next in the `btnSaveSettings.Click` event handler. Typeblock a `text` block and replace the default text with `playername`. Snap it into the `tag` socket on the `.StoreValue` block. Typeblock the `txtPlayerName.Text` reporting block. Snap the `text` block into the `valueToStore` socket on the `.StoreValue` block. The text from the `txtPlayerName` text box is stored in TinyDB under the tag `playername`.

    Next, place the player name in the `varPlayerName` variable and set the label on the main play screen to the player's name.

3. Typeblock the `varPlayerName   [to]`   block and snap it in next under the `.StoreValue` block. Typeblock a `TinyDB1.GetValue` block and snap it into the `to` block on the `varPlayerName` block. Typeblock a `text` block and replace the text with `playername`. Snap the `text` block into the `tag` socket on the `.GetValue` block.

4. Now set the lblThisPlayerName label on the main play screen to represent the name just entered. Typeblock the `lblThisPlayerName.Text   [to]` block and snap it in under the previous block. Typeblock the `varPlayerName` variable reporting block and snap it into the `lblThisPlayerName.Text` block.

Next, you need to store the player's name in TinyWebDB under the tag that represents the player's number. In other words, if the player chose to be Player1, the player's name should be stored under the tag `playername1` and `playername2` if the player chose to be Player2. To accomplish storing the local player's name with their selected player number, use a text join block to join the text `playername` with the value of the variable `varPlayerNumber` and use the resulting text string as the tag to store the value of the `varPlayerName`. If that is confusing, look at Figure 7-5. You can see that the player's name is joined with the player's selected number. That string is used to store the player's name. For instance, if the player has entered his name as `Joe` and selected the Player2 check box, the following would be stored:

`playername2 = Joe`

The application uses TinyWebDB to retrieve the tags `playername1` and `playername2` and place them in the correct variable. In the `Screen1.Intialize` event, you created the TinyWebDB calls that retrieve those values. You handle those returns when you set up the `.GotValue` event a little later:

1. Typeblock a `TinyWebDB1.StoreValue` block and snap it into the `btnSaveSettings` event handler. Typeblock a `join` block and snap it into the `tag` socket on the `.StoreValue` block. Typeblock a `text` block and replace the text with `playername`. Snap the `text` block into the first socket on the `join` block. Next, typeblock the `varPlayerName` block and snap it into the second socket on the `join` block.

2. Typeblock the `varPlayerName` global variable block and snap it into the `valueToStore` socket on the `.StoreValue` block.

   Now the player's name is stored with the tag `playername#` with the number depending on what number is stored in the `varPlayerNumber`.

   When the user taps the Save Settings button, you want to also retrieve the values stored in the TinyWebDB for both tags, `playername1` and `playername2`. That way, no matter what player this player is, the variables are populated with the player's name. Remember that for TinyWebDB, we can only make the calls to TinyWebDB with the tags. We must actually handle the data later when it is returned from the TinyWebDB service on the Internet.

3. Typeblock a `TinyWebDB1.GetValue` block and snap it in below the `.StoreValue` block in the `btnSaveSettings.Click` event. Typeblock a `text` block and replace the text with the tag text `playername1`. Snap the `text` block into the `tag` socket on the `.GetValue` block.

4. Typeblock another `TinyWebDB1.GetValue` block and snap it in next in the `.Click` event handler. Typeblock a `text` block and replace the text with `playername2` this time. Snap it into the `tag` socket on the `.GetValue` block.

After storing all the user settings in the appropriate variables and databases, you need to make the main play screen appear and the Settings screen disappear:

1. Typeblock the `VirtualScreen1.Visible [to]` block and snap it in under the previous `.GetValue` block. Typeblock a `true` block and snap it into the `.Visible` block.

2. Typeblock the `VirtualScreen2.Visible [to]` block and snap it in as the last block in the event handler. Typeblock a `false` block and snap it into the `.Visible` block.

Your completed `btnSaveSettings.Click` event handler should look like Figure 7-5.

FIGURE 7-5:
The completed
btnSaveSettings.
Click blocks

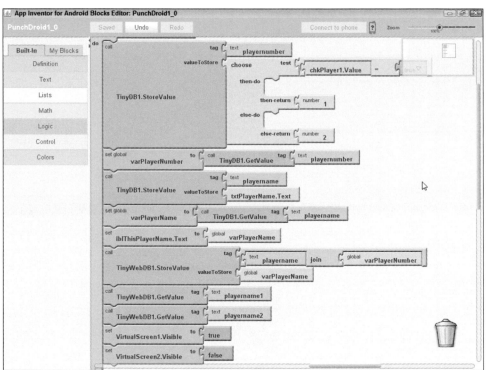

The `btnNewGame.Click` event handler is fairly easy to set up. To start a new game, you just have to reset all the score information stored locally in variables and stored in the TinyWebDB:

1. Typeblock the `btnNewGame.Click` event handler. Typeblock the `varPlayer-Score1 [to]` block. Snap the variable block into the event handler. Snap a numeral 0 block into the `to` socket.

2. Typeblock the `varPlayerScore2 [to]` block and snap it in next in the `btnNew-Game.Click` event handler. Snap a numeral 0 block into the `to` socket.

3. Typeblock the `TinyWebDB1.StoreValue` block and snap it next in the `btnNew-Game` event handler. Use a `text` block to set the `tag` to `playerscore1`. Use a number block to set the `value` socket to 0.

4. Typeblock another `TinyWebDB1.StoreValue` block and snap it in under the previous block. Use a `text` block to set the `tag` to `playerscore2`. Use a number block to set the `value` socket to 0.

Now you need to reset the score display labels on the main play screen to display zero:

1. Typeblock the `lblOtherPlayerScore.Text` [to] block. Snap it in after the last TinyWebDB block. Use a numeral 0 block snapped into the `to` socket to set the variable to zero.

2. Typeblock the `lblThisPlayerScore.Text` [to] block and snap it in next. Use a numeral 0 block to set the variable value to zero.

Your completed `btnNewGame.Click` event handler should look like Figure 7-6.

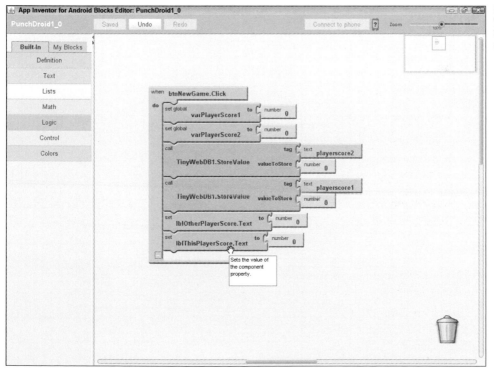

FIGURE 7-6:
The completed
btnNewGame.
Click blocks

Handling events on the main play screen

Now that you have handled the events on the Settings screen, it's time to handle the events on the main play screen. There are two user events to handle on the main play screen: the Settings button, which allows the user to bring up the Settings screen, and the I Got One button, which is the main play event. Clicking the I Got One! is the digital equivalent of punching your friend on the shoulder and yelling "Punch Bug!"

To handle the Settings button, make the main play screen invisible and make the Settings screen visible.

1. Typeblock the `btnSettings.Click` event handler. If necessary, move it to a clear area of your workspace. Remember to right-click on the workspace to organize and handle your blocks.

 TIP   Using the "Right-click, select Collapse All Blocks, right-click again, and select Organize All Blocks" routine should become habit when you are dealing with a large number of large event handlers or long block routines.

    With the `btnSettings.Click` block selected, typeblock the `VirtualScreen1.Visible [to]` block. Typeblock a `false` block and snap it into the `.Visible` block.

2. Typeblock the `VirtualScreen2.Visible [to]` block and snap it in under the previous block. Typeblock a `true` block and snap it into the `.Visible` block.

    If the user has reopened the PunchDroid application from a previous game, the `txtPlayerName` text box might not have any text in it even though database calls have been used at the start of the application to populate the variable. You need to place the contents of the variable in the TextBox component so the user gets the sense of data and player persistence.

3. Typeblock the `txtPlayerName.Text [to]` block and snap it under the previous `.Visible` block. Typeblock the `varPlayerName` global variable block and snap it into the `to` socket on the `text` block.

Your completed `btnSettings.Click` event handler should look like Figure 7-7.

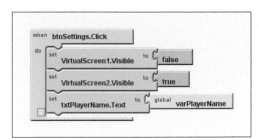

FIGURE 7-7:
The btnSettings.
Click blocks

The most important event on the main play screen is the I Got One! button that the user taps to indicate that they have just spotted whatever item the game is centered around. When the user taps the I Got One! button, the appropriate player score variable should increment and the appropriate score display label should display the new score. Also, the new score needs to be sent to the TinyWebDB. Before you increment the score, you use the event as an opportunity to send a request to the TinyWebDB for any updates to the other players score. You use the choose block again to determine which call should be made. In reality, you could just send a call for both PlayerScore1 and PlayerScore2, but for the purpose of this project, you use the choose block again for a little extra practice in using it:

1. Typeblock the btnGotOne.Click event handler and drag it to a clear workspace.

2. First build the TinyWebDB call to check on the other player's score. Typeblock the TinyWebDB1.GetValue and snap it into the event handler. Typeblock a make text block and snap it into the tag of TinyWebDB1.GetValue. The make text block creates a single string for the tag from the text PlayerScore and the opposite of whatever number is in varPlayerNumber. Typeblock a text block and replace the default text with PlayerScore. Snap it into the text socket on the make text block. Typeblock a choose block and snap it into the next text block on the make text block.

   Now build the test for the choose block that says, "If the varPlayerNumber value is 1, return the numeral 2 to the make text; otherwise, return the numeral 1."

3. Typeblock an equals comparison operator (=) and snap it into the test socket on the choose block. Typeblock the varPlayerNumber global variable block and snap it into the first socket on the comparison operator. Typeblock a numeral 1 number block and snap it into the second socket on the comparison operator.

4. Now typeblock a numeral 2 number block and snap it into the then-return block.

5. Typeblock a numeral 1 block and snap it into the else-return block on the choose block.

   Now the make text block concatenates the text PlayerScore and either the numeral 1 or 2 and uses it as one string for the TinyWebDB tag.

Next you need to increment the appropriate variable so that the player's score goes up when the I Got One! button is clicked. If the varPlayerNumber is 1, varPlayerScore1 should increment. If the varPlayerNumber is 2, the varPlayerScore2 should go up. You can use a simple IfElse block to increment the right variable and then store the result in the TinyWebDB:

1. Typeblock an IfElse block and snap it into the btnGotOne.Click event handler. Build the test condition to check if the varPlayerNumber contains the value 1. If it does, the first case then-do socket should increment the varPlayerScore1. Otherwise, the second case else-do socket should increment the varPlayer-Score2 variable.

2. With the IfElse block selected, typeblock an equals comparison operator. Typeblock the varPlayerNumber global variable block and snap it into the first socket on the comparison operator. Typeblock a numeral 1 number block and snap it into the second socket on the comparison operator.

   Now build the then-do case for when the test evaluates to true. If the test is true, increment varPlayerScore1 and send the new value to the label and the TinyWebDB.

3. Typeblock the varPlayerScore1 [to] block and snap it into the then-do socket on the IfElse block. Typeblock an addition operator by typing a plus sign (+) and pressing Enter. Snap the additive operator into the to socket on the varPlayer-Score1 block. Typeblock the varPlayerScore1 global reporting block and snap it into the first socket on the additive operator block. Typeblock a numeral 1 number block and snap it into the second socket on the additive operator block. This takes the value of varPlayerScore1, adds one, and stores it back into the variable.

4. Now update the label with the new score. If this player is Player1, you use the lblThisPlayerScore to display the new score.

5. Typeblock the lblThisPlayerScore.Text [to] block and snap it in under the varPlayerScore1 incrementing block. Typeblock the varPlayerScore1 global variable reporting block and snap it into the lblThisPlayerScore.Text block. This updates the label with the latest score.

Now store the value of the `varPlayerScore1` because it has changed in TinyWebDB:

1. Typeblock the `TinyWebDB1.StoreValue` block and snap it in under the label set block. Typeblock a `text` block for the tag and replace the default text with `PlayerScore1`. Snap the `text` block into the `tag` socket on the `.StoreValue` block. Typeblock the `varPlayerScore1` reporting block and snap it into the `value-ToStore` block on the `.StoreValue` block. This sends the contents of the `varPlayerScore1` variable to the TinyWebDB to be stored under the tag `PlayerScore1`.

   Your first case `then-do` socket should look like Figure 7-8.

   If the `IfElse` block test evaluates to `false`, you want to increment the Player2 score and update the label and store it as well.

2. Typeblock the `varPlayerScore2 [to]` block and snap it into the `else-do` socket on in the `IfElse` block. Typeblock the additive (+) block and snap it into the `to` socket on the `varPlayerScore2` block. Typeblock the `varPlayerScore2` global variable block and snap it into the first socket on the additive block. Typeblock a numeral 1 number block and snap it into the second socket on the additive block. Again, this is the typical variable increment routine.

   Now update the label with the new score. In the previous case for the `then-do` socket, if the local player was Player1, the `lblThisPlayerScore.Text` would be populated with the value of the `varPlayerScore1`. If this player is Player2, you want to set the `lblThisPlayerScore.Text` to the value of the `varPlayerScore2` variable.

3. Typeblock the `lblThisPlayerScore [to]` block and snap it into the `else-do` socket under the `varPlayerScore2` block. Typeblock the `varPlayerScore2` global variable block and snap it into the `lblThisPlayerScore.Text` block.

Now store the changed variable in the TinyWebDB. Typeblock the `TinyWebDB1.StoreValue` block and snap it last into the `else-do` socket on the `IfElse` block. Typeblock a `text` block for the tag and replace the text with `PlayerScore2`. Snap the `text` block into the `tag` socket on the `.StoreValue` block. Typeblock the `varPlayerScore2` global variable block and snap it into the `valueToStore` socket on the `.StoreValue` block.

Your completed `btnGotOne.Click` event handler should look like Figure 7-8.

FIGURE 7-8:
The completed
btnGotOne.
Click event
handler blocks

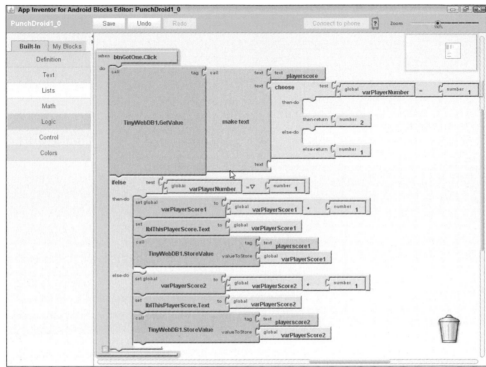

FIGURE 7-8:
The completed
btnGotOne.
Click event
handler blocks

Every time you make a TinyWebDB call, the Web service eventually returns the requested tag
and data. The `TinyWebDB1.GotValue` event handler has two special name/value blocks
associated with it. When the TinyWebDB service returns the value that has been called for, it
returns it in one package made up of two pieces: the *tag* and the *value*. The first piece is represented by the `tagFromWebDB1` value block. This value block contains the tag that was called
for that initiated the tag/value return. If the tag that was used to initiate the call was
`PlayerName1`, the contents of the `tagFromWebDB1` are `PlayerName1`. The second piece
of the return package is the actual data that was stored with the tag. This piece of the package
is represented by the `valueFromWebDB1` value block. If the tag that was used to initiate the
call has the `PlayerName1` data stored under that tag, it is returned in the `valueFrom-`
`WebDB1` block.

This method of handling data returning from the TinyWebDB1 service is an *asynchronous*
service fulfillment. That means that the order you request tag/value combinations is not
necessarily the order they return in. Because of delays with servers and Internet pathways,
you cannot assume that data arrives in the order it was requested. The tag/value pairing
allows you to open a return package and say "Aha! This is the `PlayerName1` tag I requested!

I want to place the value I stored with that tag in a certain variable." When that data returns, you need to decide what data has been returned and what you want to do with it. You use a series of nested `If` and `IfElse` blocks for every possible tag and data pair that might be returned. So far, you have stored information in the TinyWebDB under the following four tags:

○ `PlayerName1`

○ `PlayerName2`

○ `PlayerScore1`

○ `PlayerScore2`

The player name tags test whether the returned value is the same as the name in `VarPlayerName`. If it is the same, you don't want to do anything with the data. But if the value of the returned data for a player name tag is not the same as the name stored in `VarPlayerName`, `lblOtherPlayerName` should be set to the value.

For the player score tags, you need to check whether the returned value is empty. App Inventor doesn't like to do calculations on variables that have a `null` value. If you set the value of one of the `varPlayerScore` variables to `null`, when the application tries to increment the value, the application crashes. If there is no data in the value returned from the TinyWebDB service, you want to discard the data. If there is in fact a value in the returned response, you should update the appropriate variable.

Finally you set the `lblOtherPlayerScore.Text` to the appropriate score using the contents of the appropriate variable:

If the `TinyWebDB1.GotValue` does not have name blocks in the `tagFromWebDB` and `valueFromWebDB` sockets on the `.GotValue` event handler, you need to populate the sockets with name blocks from the Definitions drawer and change their names accordingly.

NOTE

---

1. Typeblock the `TinyWebDB1.GotValue` event handler. With the `TinyWebDB1.GotValue` block selected, typeblock an `If` block. Build the test for the `If` block by typeblocking an equals comparison operator and snapping it into the `test` socket of the `If` block. With the comparison operator selected, typeblock the `tagFromWebDB1` value block and snap it into the first socket on the comparison operator. Typeblock a `text` block and replace the default text with `playername1`. Snap it into the second socket on the comparison operator.

This test checks to see whether the incoming tag is the `PlayerName1` tag. If it is, you need to decide what to do with the value that is connected to the tag.

If the test in the `If` block evaluates to `true`, you need to test to see whether the current player name stored in `varPlayerName` is the same as the value coming in from the TinyWebDB service. If it is the same, you can discard it. This is information your application already knows.

You use an `IfElse` block in a special way for this operation. You can use an `IfElse` block to say, in essence, "If this is true, do nothing; otherwise, do something." You do this by leaving one of the cases without any blocks to execute. If the value from the Web database is the same as the value in `varPlayerName`, you do nothing with the value.

2. With the `If` block selected, typeblock an `IfElse` block and make sure it snaps into the `If` block. Typeblock the equals comparison operator (=) and snap it into the `test` socket on the `IfElse` block. Typeblock the `valueFromWebDB1` block and snap it into the first socket on the comparison operator. Typeblock the `varPlayerName` global variable block and snap it into the second socket on the comparison operator. This tests to see whether the contents of `valueFromWebDB` and `varPlayerName` are the same.

    If the test evaluates to `true`, you don't want to do anything with the data, so leave the then-do socket empty on the `IfElse` block.

    If the test evaluates to `false`, the incoming name is the name of the other player and you want to place it the `lblOtherPlayerName` label on the main play screen.

3. Typeblock the `lblOtherPlayerName.Txt [to]` block and snap it into the else-do socket of the `IfElse` block. Typeblock the `valueFromWebDB1` value block and snap it into the `lblOtherPlayerName` block. These blocks set the label to the other player's name.

Next you set the exact same series of blocks again, but this time for when the incoming `tagFromWebDB1` is PlayerName2:

1. Typeblock an `If` block and snap it in below your first `If` block. With the `If` block selected, typeblock the equals comparison operator (=). Typeblock the `tagFromWebDB1` value block and snap it into the first socket on the comparison operator. Typeblock a `text` block and replace the default text with `PlayerName2`. These blocks test to see whether the incoming tag is the `PlayerName2` tag.

With the If block selected, typeblock an IfElse block and make sure it snaps into your second If block.

2. Select the IfElse block and typeblock an equals comparison operator. Typeblock the valueFromWebDB1 value block and snap it into the first socket on the comparison operator. Typeblock the varPlayerName global variable block and snap it into the second socket on the comparison operator. Again, if the value incoming from the Web database is the same as that stored in the PlayerName variable, you discard it.

3. Leave the then-do socket empty on the second IfElse block.

4. Typeblock the lblOtherPlayerName.Text [to] block and snap it into the else-do socket on the second IfElse block. Typeblock the valueFromWebDB1 block and snap it into the socket on the lblOtherPlayerName.Text block.

Your next two nested If blocks check whether the incoming tag is the PlayerScore tag and then check to see whether the value is empty. You could handle the incoming PlayerScore tag/value in much the same way as you handled PlayerName; instead, you use nested If statements with a not block. So instead of building the logic as, "If the value from the WebDB is empty, do nothing; otherwise, do something," you build the logic as, "If the value from the WebDB is *not* empty, do this." You see that the method you use here is a slightly neater and more graceful way to handle the situation:

1. Typeblock an If block and snap it in as the third If block down in your TinyWebDB1. GotValue event handler. Build the test for the If block by typeblocking a comparison operator and snapping it into the test socket on the If block. Typeblock the tagFromWebDB1 value block and snap it into the first socket on the comparison operator. Typeblock a text block and replace the text with PlayerScore1. Snap the text block into the second socket on the comparison operator.

   This test checks to see if the incoming tag is the PlayerScore1 tag. If it is, you need to make sure that the data content isn't a null value. App Inventor hates doing math on a variable with a null value.

2. With your third If block selected, typeblock another If block and make sure it snaps into your third If block's then-do socket.

   You use the not block to execute this nested If block only when the value from the WebDB is not null.

3. Typeblock a `not` block and snap it into the `test` socket of your nest `If` block. Typeblock an equals comparison operator and snap it into the `not` block. Typeblock the `valueFromWebDB1` block and snap it into the first socket on the comparison operator. Typeblock a `text` block and delete the default text, leaving an empty `text` block. Snap the `text` block into the second socket on the comparison operator.

4. This test says, "If the valueFromWebDB1 is not null, the test is true." If the test is true, you want to store the value in the `varPlayerScore1` variable. Typeblock the `var-PlayerScore1 [to]` and snap it into your nested `If` block. Typeblock the `value-FromWebDB1` value block and snap it into the `varPlayerScore1` block.

   If the incoming tag is `PlayerScore1` and the incoming value is not blank, the value is placed in the `varPlayerScore` variable.

As you can probably see, you can write this same logic in a third way that is even tighter. You can use an `And` block to chain conditions. You can create a test that says, "If this test *and* this test *and* this test are true, execute these blocks." You can create as many and clauses as you need. As you build this `If` block, refer to Figure 7-9 for this slightly more complex but neater way to check for two things at once:

1. Typeblock a fourth `If` block and snap it in below the third `If` block. Typeblock an and block and snap it into the `test` socket of your fourth `If` block. Typeblock an equals comparison operator and snap it into the `test` socket on the and block. It creates another `test` socket for every test you put in it. With your first comparison operator selected, typeblock the `tagFromWebDB1` value block . Typeblock a `text` block and replace the text with PlayerScore2. Snap the `text` block into the second socket on the comparison operator.

2. Select the and block and typeblock a not block. Make sure it snaps into the next `test` socket. Typeblock an equals comparison operator (=) and snap it into the `not` block. Typeblock the `valueFromWebDB1` value block and snap it into the first socket on the comparison operator. Typeblock a `text` block and delete the default text. Snap the empty `text` block into the second socket on the comparison operator.

   Now you have a test that asks that two conditions evaluate as true before the contained blocks are executed.

3. Typeblock the `varPlayerScore2 [to]` and snap it into the then-do socket on your fourth `If` block. Typeblock the `valueFromWebDB1` value block and snap it into the `varPlayerScore2` block.

At this point, you have handled every possible incoming tag from the TinyWebDB component. When you are building large projects, it is sometimes helpful to keep a list of the tags/values you use throughout your application. Every time you request data from the TinyWebDB component, it has to be handled with the .GotValue event when it arrives from the Web database.

Finally, set the OtherPlayerScore label with the appropriate variable value:

1. Typeblock an IfElse block and snap it into the .GotValue block as the last block. Typeblock an equals comparison operator. Snap it into the test socket. Typeblock the varPlayerNumber global value block and snap it into the first socket on the comparison operator. Typeblock a numeral 1 number block and snap it into the second socket on the comparison operator. If the player number is 1, the lblOtherPlayer-Score.Text should be set to the value of the varPlayerScorc2. If the varPlayer-Number is not 1, the label should be set to the value of varPlayerScore1.

2. Typeblock the lblOtherPlayerScore.Text [to] block and snap it into the then-do case of your IfElse block. Typeblock the varPlayerScore2 global variable block and snap it into the lblOtherPlayerScore.Text block.

3. Typeblock another lblOtherPlayerScore.Text [to] block and snap it into the else-do socket of your last IfElse block. Typeblock the varPlayerScore1 global block and snap it into the lblOtherPlayerScore.Text block.

    Your completed TinyWebDB1.GotValue event handler should look like Figure 7-9.

To keep your player opponents and scores up-to-date, create a clock timer event that regularly polls the TinyWebDB service to have it return an updated score. Reuse blocks you already have built to make the database call.

Locate the btnGotOne.Click event handler on your workspace. The first block in the btn-GotOne.Click event handler is the TinyWebDB1.GetValue block, which uses a choose block to decide what tag to request. Click on the TinyWebDB1.GetValue block and copy it to memory by pressing Crtl+C. Close the btnGotOne.Click event handler. Click on an empty workspace and typeblock the Clock1.Timer event handler. Press Ctrl+V to paste a copy of the TinyWebDB1.GetValue block from the btnGotOne.Click event handler.

FIGURE 7-9:
The complete
TinyWebDB1.
GotValue event
handler blocks

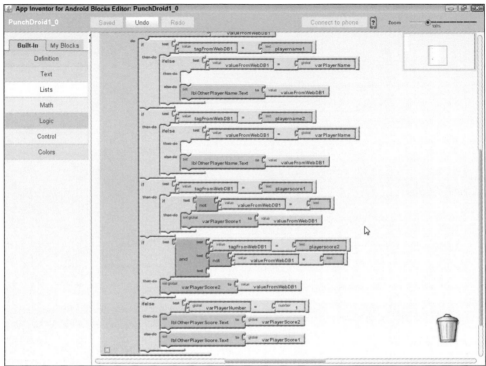

Snap the copied blocks into the Clock1.Timer event handler. Your Clock1.Timer event handler should look like Figure 7-10.

Based on the timer value you entered in the TimerInterval property in the Design view, the Clock1 component periodically executes the .GetValue for the opponent's score. A lower TimerInterval value means the application is more up-to-date, but repeated calls to the TinyWebDB service use up data and battery power on the phone.

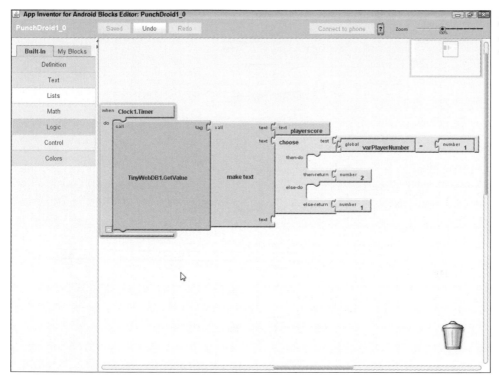

FIGURE 7-10:
The completed
Clock1.Timer
event handler

Installing the PunchDroid Application

You have completed the PunchDroid application. Install the application on your phone by clicking the Package for Phone button in Design view. Use the Download to this Computer option when you click the Package for Phone button to download the .APK file and send it to a friend with an Android device. The friend must have the Untrusted Install Locations setting enabled on their phone. (Setting the Allow Untrusted Install Locations option varies from Android device to device. Check your device manual or look for online instructions.) You can also test PunchDroid between your phone and the emulator. You can start the emulator by clicking the New Emulator button on the Blocks Editor. The emulator can connect to the Internet through your computer's Internet connection.

The PunchDroid application has a lot of room for improvement. Some of the features you could include in future versions are

❍ Support for more players

❍ Checking to see whether a player number slot is taken already

❍ Adding sound or vibration when an opponent scores

❍ Adding a goal or win game target

If you've worked your way through all of the previous apps in this book, you should have enough knowledge to create some pretty incredible multiplayer games that are based on the concepts in this project but have nothing to do with the silly childhood Punch Bug game. Consider a timer-based resource management game or a location-based scavenger hunt, for example. The possibilities are limitless.

chapter 8

Collection Assistant: A Barcode and Database Application

in this chapter

- ◯ Using the Barcode Scanner component
- ◯ Creating multidimensional arrays
- ◯ Developing and using traditional database functions

THE COLLECTION ASSISTANT application replicates the functionality of some of the popular barcode scanner applications available on the market. Its basic function is to scan a barcode and store the location and name of the scanned object in a local database. You can use scanner applications for many different things. The Collection Assistant could be used to catalog and keep track of a media collection such as a DVD or CD collection, for example. It could also be used as part of an organizational system where boxes or storage containers are labeled with printed barcodes.

In building the Collection Assistant, you learn how to utilize the functionality of the Barcode Scanner component. The Barcode Scanner is a fairly simple component with just a few component blocks that provide a lot of functionality. The Barcode Scanner uses the device camera to scan barcodes. The Barcode Scanner component can scan not only traditional barcodes, but can scan the increasingly popular *matrix* (sometimes called *QR* or *Quick Response*) codes as well. QR codes have the capability of storing far more information than traditional barcodes and open up a lot of interesting applications for using the Barcode Scanner component.

Creating Collection Assistant 1.0

The Collection Assistant takes your usage of the TinyDB component to the next level. One of the most frequently asked questions about TinyDB is "How can I select an item or tag in TinyDB and retrieve that item?" In this chapter, I show you how to use the technique of storing all used tags in TinyDB itself so that pulling data from the database is controllable.

In creating the Collection Assistant, you find out more about an advanced technique that allows you to create quasi-multidimensional arrays in App Inventor. Lists in App Inventor are single-level arrays in traditional programming. *Array* is just another way of saying *list*. Using some clever (albeit complex) text parsing, you can create multi-dimensional arrays in App Inventor. A multi-dimensional array increases the number of values that a single variable list can have. A *multi-dimensional array* is best understood if you visualize them as a table. Each tag has two separate pieces of information stored together with a comma separating them. The Collection Assistant stores the item name and its location in a two-dimensional array that can be visualized using Table 8-1.

Table 8-1   A Simple Two-Dimensional Array

Barcode (Tag)	Name, Location (Value1)
123456789	Dire Straits, Shelf1
987654321	Pink Floyd, Shelf4

Each row represents an individual item and each column some property or attribute of that item. Retrieving the barcode retrieves both the name and the location of the item. This is a very simple example, but the principle can be used in far more complex data structures. For instance, each tag could have ten or twenty values separated by commas.

You use the scanned barcode as the tag for each item and, under that tag, you store both the name and location separated by a comma. Then you can use App Inventor's text parsing blocks to iterate through the data using a `ForEach` block when it is returned from TinyDB.

Refer back to Chapter 4 for a refresher on the `ForEach` block.

Your design

Figure 8-1 shows the design sketches for the Collection Assistant app.

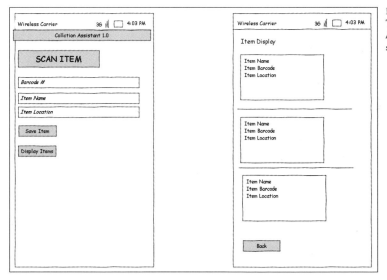

FIGURE 8-1:
The Collection
Assistant design
sketches

Collection Assistant 1.0 starts with the most basic functionality. The application scans a barcode and stores the code along with user-entered information. The storage framework is local using TinyDB. The 1.0 version of the application is able to display all the contents of the application in a formatted and readable display.

Your primitives

Use these basics for building the Collection Assistant:

○ A method of scanning barcodes and populating a text field with the scan results

○ Text boxes to collect the barcodes, names, and locations of items

○ Buttons for initiating the scanning, saving, and display of items

○ A method for storing multiple attributes of a single item

○ A method for retrieving, parsing, and formatting multiple attributes from TinyDB

○ A method for cleanly displaying all items in the database

New components

This app uses only one new component:

○ Barcode Scanner

New blocks

Here are the new blocks you'll use to build this app:

○ Add item to list

○ Split

○ Select list item

Your progression

These are the steps you take to build up the 1.0 version. It's always a good idea to have a rough idea of what order you intend to tackle your primitives. After one primitive is handled, you can move on to the next one:

1. Build the main item entry screen.

2. Build the database display screen.

3. Handle the Scan/Add Item button event.

4. Handle the Save Item button event.

5. Handle the Display Items/Database button event.

6. Handle the Back to Main Screen button event.

Your toughest primitive is the method for parsing and formatting the data in the multi-dimensional array out of TinyDB. After you get that algorithm nailed down, however, you reuse it in the 2.0 version of the application when you build search functionality into the application.

Getting Started on Collection Assistant 1.0

Start a new project and rename it `Collection_Assistant1_0`. Set the Screen1 Title property to `Collection Assistant`. Upload the CA_icon.png file for the `Icon` property and set the `Icon` properties with the icon file from the project files you downloaded from this book's companion Web site. (See this book's Introduction if you need instructions for downloading the project files.)

You need to build up the user interface to accept both input from the Barcode Scanner component and the user before it is saved to the database. Your user interface uses two VerticalArrangements as VirtualScreens. VirtualScreen1 is used for the main data entry screen. VirtualScreen2 is used for the database display screen:

1. Place two VerticalArrangements onto the Viewer.

2. Rename the VerticalArrangements `VirtualScreen1` and `VirtualScreen2`.

3. Set the `Width` and `Height` properties for both VirtualScreens to `Fill Parent`.

You need to create VirtualScreen1 with a large, easily seen button for scanning a barcode at the top of the main screen. It should be followed by three text fields.

The first text field is populated by the return data from a successful Barcode Scanner scan. Because you do not want the code to be accidently bungled up by the user after it is scanned, deselect the `Enabled` property on the text field. The Barcode Scanner can still populate the text box and you can still utilize the contents of the text box programmatically. The user will not, however, be able to manually populate the text box. You can exert this sort of control over text boxes when they are programmatically populated. You might also use this functionality when a text box is populated as a result of a calculation done on numbers or text entered in other text fields.

The second and third text boxes are enabled and accept input from the user to specify a scanned object's name and location:

1. Drag a button onto the Viewer and drop it into the VirtualScreen1.

2. Rename the button btnAddItem in the Components column.

3. Change the FontSize property to 25.

4. Change the Text property to Scan Item to Add.

Next is the text box that is populated when the barcode is scanned. You disable the text box so the user can not alter the number after it has been scanned:

1. Drag a TextBox component and drop it below the Scan Item button.

2. Rename the TextBox component txtBarCode.

3. Uncheck the Enabled property.

4. Set the Hint property to Scan Barcode.

5. Set the Width property to Fill Parent.

The next two text boxes are where the user enters the name and location of the scanned barcode. Whether the item is a collectible *Star Wars* figurine or a DVD, the name and location need to be stored in a meaningful way. You use the Hint property to indicate what information the user should enter rather than label the text boxes:

1. Drag and drop two TextBox components under the txtBarCode component.

2. Rename the first text box txtName and set its Hint property to Item Name.

3. Rename the second text box txtLoc and set its Hint property to Item Location.

4. Set both the Width property to Fill Parent for both text boxes.

Next, place the button to save both the scanned code and the entered text items into TinyDB:

1. Drag and drop a button below the last text box.

2. Rename the button btnSave.

3. Set the Text property of the button to Save Item to Database.

The Display Items button lets your user can see that a scanned item has been placed in TinyDB. It is also the event that handles pulling the items out of TinyDB and parsing them onto the VirtualScreen2:

1. Drag and drop a button below the bntSave button.

2. Rename the button btnDisplay.

3. Set the Text property of the button to Display Items.

Those are all of the user interface items for VirtualScreen1. VirtualScreen2 is composed primarily of a label to display TinyDB items and a button to return the user to the main VirtualScreen1.

The label you place onto the VirtualScreen2 is populated with descriptive text. This is in place primarily as placeholder text for troubleshooting. If the text is unchanged when you attempt to display TinyDB items, you know to check the label update blocks.

1. Drag and drop a Label component onto VirtualScreen2.

2. Rename the Label component lblDBDisplay.

3. Set the Text property to DB Display.

The final user interface element is the button to return the user to the main screen to continue entering items after displaying items. In the 2.0 version, you will have a similar button to return from the item search screen. Planning ahead can keep you from having to rename components:

1. Drag and drop a button below the lblDBDisplay label.

2. Rename the Button component btnDisplayBack. Set the Text property to Back.

   Next you add the two non-visible components: Collection Assistant uses the Barcode Scanner and the TinyDB components.

3. Drag and drop the Barcode Scanner component from the Other Stuff palette.

4. Drag and drop the TinyDB component from the Basic palette onto the Design view. Remember: It is a non-visible component and shows up only under the Design view.

That's it for the user interface of Collection Assistant 1.0. Your user interface should look like Figure 8-2.

FIGURE 8-2:
The completed
Collection
Assistant 1.0
user interface

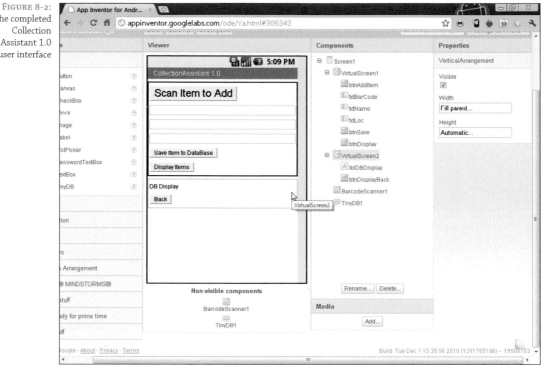

Select the VirtualScreen2 component and deselect its Visible component. The VirtualScreen2 disappears from the Viewer. To make adjustments, you can recheck the visible component to make it visible in the Viewer again.

Start with the Blocks Editor by handling the Scan Item to Add button named `btnAddItem`. The btnAddItem calls the Barcode Scanner built-in method that starts up the built-in Barcode Scanner. When the user scans a barcode, an event is generated that contains the result of the scan. When you're building event-driven applications, it helps to follow the event trail and build up the events as they would occur. Call the scanner from the `btnAddItem` event handler and then build the `BarcodeScanner` event that is generated after scanning:

1. Typeblock the `btnAddItem.Click` event handler.

2. Typeblock the `BarcodeScanner1.DoScan` method call and snap it into the event handler.

The `.DoScan` method call contains all of the code and instructions for your event. It launches the barcode scanner and waits for a barcode to pass in front of the phone's camera. When a

successful scan is recognized, the value that is scanned is passed back to the
`BarcodeScanner1.AfterScan` event handler. The result of the scan is passed to the
event handler as an argument named `result`. That argument can be renamed by renaming
the name block in the `result` socket on the event handler. Although you will not normally
change the name of the `result` name block, you sometimes need to do so if App Inventor
does not automatically create the block that is plugged into the `result` socket.

When the event occurs, you add the result to a list of scanned codes. This list is the key list.
Because you store all of the information using the barcode as the tag, this list is important
for retrieving all data entered into the database. You also need to remember to load this list
with the `Screen1.Intialize` event.

After each scan, you save the entire list to TinyDB. That way, you can retrieve all of the barcodes that have been scanned. You can then use the barcodes as tags for retrieving data from
TinyDB.

You also set the text of the disabled (not invisible) txtBarcode text box to the result of the
scan.

First, create the variable list to be used for storing the barcodes:

1. Typeblock a variable and rename it `varBarcodelist`.

2. Typeblock a `make a list` block and snap it into the `barBarcodeList` block.

> This is a valid block sequence even with the `make a list` block empty. This reminds you **NOTE**
> during troubleshooting or clearing the variable that this variable is a list.

Next, start building the `.AfterScan` event handler to store the scanned code in the variable
and the variable in TinyDB under a single keyword:

1. Typeblock the `BarcodeScanner1.AfterScan` event handler. Notice the prepopu-
   lated `result` socket. An accompanying `value` block is created and placed in the My
   Definitions drawer.

2. Typeblock the `Add Items to List` block and snap it into the `.AfterScan` event
   handler. The `Add Items to List` block allows you to add multiple items to a variable list you specify.

3. Typeblock the `varBarcodeList` global variable block and snap it into the `list`
   socket on the `add items to list` block.

4. Typeblock the `result` value block and snap it into the first `item` socket on the `add items to list` block. Remember, the `result` block was created in your My Definitions drawer when you used the `.AfterScan` event. You can change the name `result` to whatever you like by changing the name block on the `.AfterScan` event handler.

5. Typeblock the `txtBarcode.Text [to]` block and snap it in the `.AfterScan` event under the `add items to list` block. Typeblock another `result` value block and snap it into the `.txtBarcode.Text` block. This sets the scan result into the `Textbox` when the scan completes. This gives your user visual feedback on the scan.

6. Typeblock the `TinyDB1.StoreValue` block and snap it in next.

7. Use a `text` block to set the `tag` socket to `barcodelist`.

8. Typeblock the `varBarCodeList` global variable and snap it into the `valueToStore` socket.

The completed `btnAddItem.Click` event and the `BarcodeScanner1.After scan` event should look like Figure 8-3.

FIGURE 8-3:
The
btnAddItem.
Click and
Barcode
Scanner1.
AfterScan
events

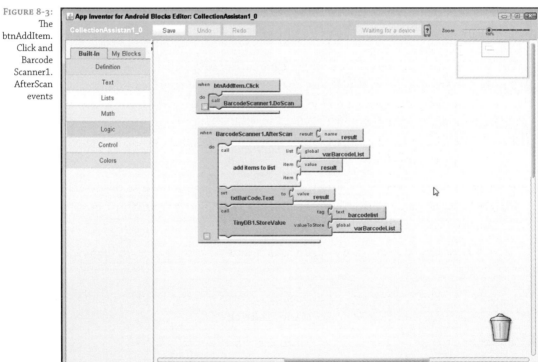

At this point, you have a variable that contains all the barcodes that have ever been scanned *and* stored in TinyDB under the tag barcodelist. You have stored the barcodes in TinyDB so that you can load the preload the variable with all the previous scan data when the application is started. The list of barcodes is your key to pulling the data stored in TinyDB. Because you stored data with the barcodes as tags, the barcodes are your list of tags. You could use the list in a list picker or to pull the data out of the database programmatically. In this application, you use the list of barcodes as a way to iterate through all items stored in TinyDB. Each barcode is pulled out of the list and used as a tag to pull the information stored in the TinyDB component with that barcode.

After a barcode has been scanned and an item name and location has been entered by your user, you need to save the entered info in TinyDB with the barcode as the tag. You use the Save Item to Database button as the event to save to the database. You use a little trick when you store the data so that it can be retrieved and parsed with a ForEach block. The name and the location data is stored under the barcode, separated by commas. When you retrieve the data, you use the comma as a split point. This is roughly equivalent to a multidimensional array in traditional programming languages.

1. Typeblock the btnSave.Click event handler and drag it to a clear workspace.

2. Typeblock the TinyDB1.StoreValue block and snap it into the event handler.

3. Typeblock the BarcodeScanner1.Result block. Be careful not to confuse it with the result local value block that is in your My Definitions drawer. That block only works inside the context of the BarcodeScanner1.AfterScan event as it is a local parameter value. The BarcodeScanner1.Result block has the same contents but is located in the BarcodeScanner1 drawer. Snap this block into the tag socket on the TinyDB1.StoreValue block.

4. Typeblock a make text block and snap it into the valueToStore socket on the TinyDB1.StoreValue block. You use the make text block to join the name and location text fields, separated by a comma.

5. Typeblock the txtName.Text block and snap it into the text socket on the make text block.

6. Typeblock a text block and replace the default text with a comma. Snap the comma block in the text socket under the txtName.Text block.

7. Typeblock the txtLoc.Text block and snap it into the next text socket.

A scanned barcode of 123456789, a name of "Boba Fett action figure," and a location of "Hall closet" are stored as shown in Table 8-2.

Table 8-2   Name, Location

Tag	Value
123456789	Boba Fett action figure, Hall closet

You can store as many values as you like under the tag separated by commas. Later in this chapter, I show you how to separate the data in the values. You can also use any delimiter you like, but a comma is usually fairly easy to use and see.

After you have stored the scanned item with its name and location, you can clear all the text boxes on VirtualScreen1 by setting their `.Text` property to a blank `text` block.

1. Typeblock the `txtBarCode.Text  [to]` block and snap it in under the `TinyDB1. StoreValue` block.

2. Typeblock the `txtLoc.Text  [to]` block and snap it in next.

3. Typeblock the `txtName.Text  [to]` block and snap it in next.

4. Place an empty `text` block in each of the `text` blocks.

Your `btnSave.Click` event handler should look like the one in Figure 8-4. The scanned code and the text boxes are stored in TinyDB and the text boxes are cleared for the next scan.

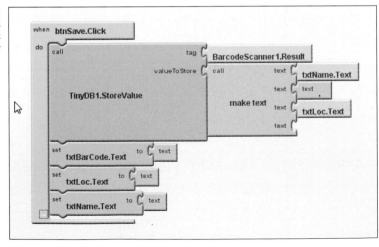

FIGURE 8-4: The completed btnSave.Click event handler

The next event you need to handle is the user tapping the Display Items button on VirtualScreen1. This button makes VirtualScreen2 visible, loads all the barcodes from TinyDB, and then parses the multi-dimensional array out into its separate values and formats it for display.

Your algorithm for loading each barcode and then formatting the data stored with the **REMEMBER** barcode is a little bit complex. After you understand the process, you can reuse this logic for multi-dimensional arrays of your own.

First you load the varBarcodeList into a ForEach block. Then you build the following logic: "For each barcode in the varBarcodeList, split the value stored under the barcode into a variable called tmpList." The split block divides any string of text into a list at the character you choose. So, you split the name, location string stored with the barcode into a temporary list. You can then use a nested ForEach block to format the tmpList into a formatted piece of text to display. You create the formatted text from the tmpList by selecting the first item in the tmpList and writing it to a temporary variable, and then selecting the next item and joining it with the previous item with formatting such as newlines. Finally, you write the barcode and formatted text to a temporary formatted variable for holding while you go on to the next barcode stored in the varBarcodeList.

This whole process sounds confusing and convoluted, I know. It is complex, but you can understand it by flipping ahead to Figure 8-5 and reading through the blocks in plain English.

For each item in varBarCode, do the following:

1. Set tmpList to a simple two-item list (using split) from the contents of TinyDB using the barcode loaded into var by the ForEach block.

2. Set tmpvar1 to the item at index 1 in tmpList. This is the Name value stored under the barcode.

3. Set tmpvar2 to the following formatted text:

   Item Name:

   \n (newline character)

   Name

   \n

4. Now set `tmpvar1` to the item at index 2 in `tmpList`. This is the location stored under the barcode.

5. Join the contents of `tmpvar2` with the following formatted text back into `tmpvar2`:

   Location Name:

   \n

   Location (in tmpvar1)

   \n

   ================= (separator characters between entries)

   \n

6. Join in `tmpvar3` the contents of `tmpvar3` and `tmpvar2`.

7. Go back to the top and do it again for each barcode.

8. Finally set the `lblDBDisplay.Text` to the contents of `tmpvar3`, which is all the formatted text created by each pass through the nested `ForEach` blocks.

As you build up each set of blocks, refer to Figure 8-5 for guidance.

First, create all the temporary variables and the temporary list that you will use through the `btnDisplay.Click` event handler:

1. Define a variable named `tmpList`. Snap in a `Make a List` block.

2. Define a variable named `tmpvar1`. Snap in an empty `text` block.

3. Define a variable name `tmpvar2`. Snap in an empty `text` block.

4. Define a variable named `tmpvar3`. Snap in an empty `text` block.

The `var` and `var1` value blocks are defined when you create the `ForEach` blocks. The `var` value blocks show up in the My Definitions drawer. They can be typeblocked because they appear at the top of the list when you typeblock the text `var`.

Typeblock the `btnDisplay.Click` event handler and place it on a clear workspace on the Blocks Editor. The `btnDisplay.Click` event is quite long when you are finished with it, so make sure you have room for it.

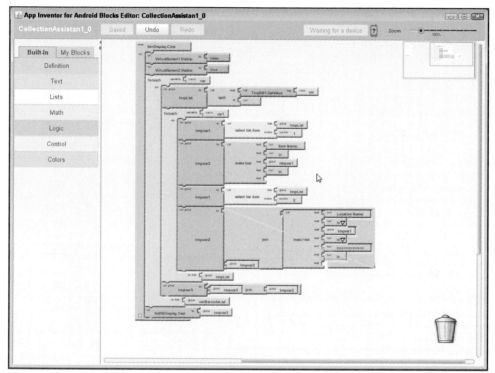

FIGURE 8-5:
The completed
btnDisplay.Click
event handler

The first thing that happens when the user taps the Display button is that VirtualScreen2 is
made visible and VirtualScreen1 is made invisible:

1. Typeblock the VirtualScreen1.Visible [to] block and snap a false block in it.

2. Typeblock the VirtualScreen2.Visible [to] block and snap a true block in it.

3. Typeblock the tmpVar3 [to] block and snap it in under the VirtualScreen blocks.
   Snap in a blank Text block. This clears the temporary formatting variable so it can
   will be fresh and shiny for each press of the Display button.

Next, start building the logic for the ForEach blocks shown in Figure 8-5.

1. Typeblock a ForEach block and snap it in the event handler.

Remember that App Inventor usually prepopulates the var socket on the ForEach block.
If the var socket is unpopulated, you need to snap in a name block from the Definitions
drawer and rename it to the next sequential var name/number combination.   **NOTE**

2. Typeblock the `varBarcodeList` value block and snap it into the `in list` socket at the bottom of the `ForEach` block.

3. Typeblock the `tmpList [to]` and snap it into the `ForEach` block.

4. Typeblock a `split` block and snap it into the `tmpList` block.

5. Typeblock a `TinyDB1.GetValue` block and snap it into the `text` socket on the `tmpList` block.

6. Typeblock the `var` block and snap it into the `.GetValue` block. This uses the barcode currently loaded from the TinyDB as the tag for the `.GetValue` block.

7. Typeblock a `text` block and replace the text with a comma. Snap the comma block into the `at` socket on the `split` block.

This series of blocks loads the contents stored under the currently loaded barcode and splits it at the comma. The `split` block is a very handy block that turns any string of text into a list of elements divided at the character that you snap into the `at` socket. You can use the `split` block to temporarily turn a line of text into a list so you can deal with each word in the line of text by its index number in the list. Remember that lists in App Inventor have an index number that is equal to its place in the list.

Next you build the `ForEach` block that processes the `tmpList` list variable into formatted text for display. Nested `ForEach` blocks can be confusing: Keep in mind that the outside `ForEach` block loads a temporary list and the inside `ForEach` block processes that temporary list. The outside `ForEach` loads another temporary list to do it all again:

1. Typeblock a second `ForEach` block and snap it under the `tmpList [to]` block.

2. Typeblock the `tmpList` global value block and snap it in the `in list` socket at the bottom of the `ForEach` block.

This is the inside `ForEach` block that processes the items in the `tmpList` variable. You use the temporary variables to select the items out of the temporary list and format the final display text. This logic could be made tighter and more graceful by using the `select list item` in the second set of blocks and not using `tmpvar1`. However, it would be a little harder to understand what you are doing. After building this series and getting it to work on your phone, you may want to come back and try to think through how the same goal could be accomplished with fewer blocks.

The `select list item` block allows you to pull a single item out of a list by its index number. You know that the `tmpList` has the format of name, location, so you pull out the first index item and place it in `tmpvar1`:

1. Typeblock the `tmpvar1 [to]` block and snap it in the inside `ForEach` block.

2. Typeblock the `Select List Item` block and snap it into the `to` socket on the `tmpvar1` block.

3. Typeblock the `tmpList` global value block and snap it into the `list` socket on the `Select List Item` block.

4. Typeblock a numeral 1 block and snap it into the `index` socket.

Now you use `tmpvar2` as a temporary holding place to format the text around the `Name` that you placed in `tmpvar1`. The `join` or `make text` blocks could be used for this task. For formatting text, it's a little easier to envision what the finished result will look like when you use the `make text` blocks:

1. Typeblock the `tmpvar2 [to]` block and snap it in below the `tmpvar1` block.

2. Typeblock the `make text` block and snap it into the `tmpvar2` block.

3. Typeblock a `text` block with the text `Item Name:` and snap it in the `text` socket. Be sure to leave a trailing space.

4. Typeblock a `text` block with the newline character (\n) and snap it into the next `text` socket.

5. Typeblock the `tmpvar1` value block and snap it in the next `text` socket.

6. Typeblock a `text` block with the newline character and snap it in last.

Now you reuse the `tmpvar1` to extract the next item in the `tmpList` for formatting:

1. Typeblock the `tmpvar1 [to]` block and snap it in below the `tmpvar` formatting blocks.

2. Typeblock the `select list item` block and snap it into the `tmpvar1` block.

3. Typeblock the `tmpList` value block and snap it into the `list` socket on the `select list item` block.

4. Typeblock a numeral 2 block and snap it into the `index` socket.

Next, join the current contents of tmpvar2 with new formatted text built around the contents of tmpvar1. Using a join block to join the contents of a variable with new text and place it back in the same variable is a lot like using the addition (+) block to increment a numeric value in a variable. You take what is in the variable, add something to it, and then place it back in the variable.

1. Typeblock the tmpvar2 [to] block and snap it in next in the inside ForEach block.

2. Typeblock a join block.

3. Typeblock the tmpvar2 global value block and snap it into the first socket on the join block.

4. Typeblock a make text block and snap it into the second socket on the join block.

5. Typeblock a text block and set the text to Location Name: with a trailing space. Snap it into the text socket on the make text block.

6. Typeblock a text block and set the text to a newline character. Snap it into the next text socket.

REMEMBER   The newline character for App Inventor text is the \n combination.

---

7. Typeblock the tmpvar1 global value block and snap it into the next text socket. The tmpvar1 now contains the Location value from tmpList.

8. Typeblock a text block with a newline character and snap it in the next text socket.

9. Typeblock a text block with some separator text such as ========= and snap it in the next text socket.

10. Typeblock a text block with a newline character and snap it in the last block in the make text block.

Your next block series is placed in the outside ForEach block under the inside ForEach (see Figure 8-5). You need to take the formatted text that contains the scanned and stored barcode, name, and location with their formatting and store it in tmpvar3, where it is joined each time with the previously formatted items until all the scanned barcodes have been formatted and are ready to be displayed.

1. Typeblock the `tmpvar3` `[to]` block and snap it in under the inside `ForEach` block.

2. Typeblock a `join` block and snap it into the `tmpvar3` block.

3. Typeblock the `tmpvar3` global value block and snap it into the first socket on the `join` block.

4. Typeblock the `tmpvar2` global value block and snap it into the second socket on the `join` block.

The last thing that happens in the `btnDisplay.Click` event handler is the display of all the formatted items in the `tmpvar3` variable in the lblDBDisplay label on VirtualScreen2:

1. Typeblock the `lblDBDisplay.Text` `[to]` block and snap it in the `btnDisplay.Click` below the nested `ForEach` blocks.

2. Typeblock the `tmpvar3` global value block and snap it into the `text` block.

Your `btnDisplay.Click` event handler should now look like Figure 8-5. It loads the contents of the `varBarcodeList` and starts using the barcodes as tags to populate a temporary list that is then used to format items for display. It then populates the large database display label on VirtualScreen2.

After your user has perused the items displayed in the label, you need to handle the Back button from the VirtualScreen2.

1. Typeblock the `btnDisplayBack.Click` event handler.

2. Typeblock a `VirtualScreen2.Visible` `[to]` block and snap in a `false` block.

3. Typeblock a `VirtualScreen1.Visible` `[to]` block and snap in a `true` block.

The only event left to handle is the `Screen1.Intialize` event that occurs at application start-up. You need to load the barcodes stored in TinyDB into the `varBarcodeList` variable. However, if it's the first run or the user has cleared the data from the Android application settings, you need to make sure you do *not* load a `null` value into the list. If you load a `null` value into the list, the application errors out any time your application attempts to use the variable as a list. The first time the user attempts to add something with a scanned barcode, the application would crash. This is a result of the `make list` block actually changing the structure of a variable. Writing a `null` value to the variable removes its essential "listy-ness." Because App Inventor uses only a single "kind" of variable, the variable takes its type or "kind" from the data currently stored in it. You use a simple `If` block to see whether any data is stored in TinyDB. If the TinyDB is empty, you don't load anything into the variable, avoiding the `null` value. If TinyDB does in fact have user data stored in it, it will be loaded into the variable.

1. Typeblock the `Screen1.Initialize` event handler.

2. Typeblock an `If` block and snap it into the `.Initialize` event.

3. Typeblock a `not` block and snap it into the `test` socket on the `If` block.

4. Typeblock an equals comparison operator (=) and snap it into the `not` block.

5. Typeblock a `TinyDB1.GetValue` block and snap it into the first socket on the comparison operator.

6. Typeblock a `text` block and change the text to `barcodelist` and snap it into the `TinyDB1.GetValue` block.

7. Typeblock a `text` block and remove the default text, leaving a blank `text` block. Snap it into the second socket on the comparison operator.

8. Typeblock the `varBarcodeList [to]` block and snap it into the `If` block inside the event handler.

9. Typeblock a `TinyDB1.GetValue` block and snap it into the `varBarcodeList` block.

10. Typeblock a `text` block and make the text `barcodelist`. Snap the `text` block into the `tag` socket on the `.GetValue` block.

These blocks first check to make sure that the `.GetValue` block is not returning a null value. If the value is not `null`, the `varBarcodeList` is populated with the contents of the tag `barcodelist`.

In the next version of Collection Assistant, you add search capability to pull individual items from the database and display the stored data.

By creating Collection Assistant 1.0, you learned

❍ The Barcode Scanner component can be used to change the mysterious lines and dots of UPC and matrix QR codes into text that can be used in your apps.

❍ You can use text iterative text parsing to create multi-dimensional arrays in TinyDB or a variable.

Now you're ready to move on to add even more complexity in the Collection Assistant 2.0.

Creating Collection Assistant 2.0

The 2.0 version of the Collection Assistant adds some powerhouse functionality to the application as well as teaching you how to search for data stored in TinyDB. The data formatting and structuring from the 1.0 version is reused for displaying the search results. There are three basic pieces of information that your application stores in TinyDB: the barcode, a name, and a location. You need to add the ability to search on all of these elements and return any results. The method I show you to you use for searching is slightly more complex than you really need for such a simple application. However, I use it to teach you a method that scales well into other applications. You can use the search methodology you deploy in the Collection Assistant to search through data that is stored in TinyDB, TinyWebDB, or global variables regardless of the amount of data. Keep in mind that the projects in this book are not prescriptive but rather descriptive. In other words, this project doesn't illustrate how you *should* implement a search routine, but rather how you *could* implement a search routine. One of the joys of programming is coming up with new and unique ways to solve problems more efficiently.

Your design

Figure 8-6 shows the design sketches for Collection Assistant 2.0.

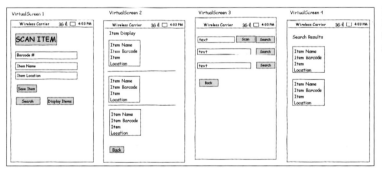

FIGURE 8-6:
Design sketches
for Collection
Assistant 2.0

In this version, you add a third virtual screen as a search home and a fourth virtual screen as a search results screen. You also add new interface elements to each of the existing virtual screens. The overall functionality for the 2.0 version includes adding items by scanning a barcode and entering metadata, and searching for items by scanning an item or typing in a search term.

Your primary design challenge is adding the search functionality to enable a user to search by scanned barcode or name or location.

Your primitives

These are the basic algorithms and logic pieces for the additions to your application:

○ Two new screens for search and results

○ New navigation elements in existing screens

○ A method for loading and searching the stored data

New components

No new components are introduced in this application.

New blocks

Only one new block is used in version 2.0 of Collection Assistant:

○ `Is in list?`

Your progression

These are your high-level steps you need to take as you move through your primitives. In reality, you build the search algorithm once for the barcode search and then reuse that code through the next search events. You also use a second barcode scanner to keep the `.Result` blocks distinct in case your user is both adding and searching in the same session. This also gives you the opportunity to see how to use multiple occurrences of the same event. Although the `.AfterScan` is the same real-world event, whether it is called from the Add Item button or the Search button makes for very different App Inventor events.

1. Add the new VirtualScreens.

2. Add the new navigational elements.

3. Add new Search text boxes and Search buttons for barcode, name, and location.

4. Add new Search results elements.

5. Build navigational elements for switching screens.

6. Handle barcode scan and search events.

7. Handle name search events.

8. Handle location search events.

Getting Started on Collection Assistant 2.0

Start by using the Save As button on the Design view to save a new copy of your Collection Assistant. Change the name to `CollectionAssistant2_0`. You are creating a copy of Collection Assistant 1.0 named Collection Assistant2_0. Make sure the Display Invisible Components in Viewer check box is selected at the top of the design view.

For the revision, you need to add search functionality to your application. This requires two new VirtualScreens in addition to the two found in Collection Assistant 1.0. The third VirtualScreen is activated by tapping a Search button from the main screen. The fourth VirtualScreen is activated when the search process displays the results (or lack of results).

In this revision, you add two new VerticalArrangements to use as VirtualScreens. Remember to leave the `Visible` property checked until you've made the very last adjustment to the user interface:

1. Drag two new VerticalArrangements to Design view.

2. Rename the first VerticalArrangement `VirtualScreen3`.

3. Rename the second VerticalArrangement `VirtualScreen4`.

Your user needs to be able to navigate from screen to screen, so you need to place Back buttons that return a user to the main screen, which is VirtualScreen1. You also use a new button on the main screen to take the user to the search screen.

First, indicate to your user what the overall purpose of this screen is:

1. Drag and drop a label into VirtualScreen3. Rename it `lblSearchBanner`.

2. Set the `Text` property of lblSearchBanner to read `Search for Item in Database Using One of the Following:`.

Next build up the search interface elements:

1. Drag a HorizontalArrangement onto the VirtualScreen1 below the Save Item to Database button.

2. Drag a new button into the HorizontalArrangement and rename the button `btn-Search`.

3. Set the `Text` property of btnSearch to `Search`.

4. Drag the Display Items button from the VirtualScreen1 into the HorizontalArrangement to the right of the new Search button.

The user interface of VIrtualScreen3 will be composed of a series of text boxes followed by Search buttons. The three fields and buttons correspond to barcode search, name search, and location search. The barcode search is unique in that it will allow the user to either scan a barcode for search or manually enter the numbers for search.

First, build up the barcode search user interface in VirtualScreen3:

1. Drag a HorizontalArrangement into VirtualScreen3. This holds the TextBox component and the two Button components.

2. Drag a TextBox component into the HorizontalArrangement. Rename the text box `txtSearchBarcode`.

3. Set the `Hint` property of txtSearchBarcode to `Enter or Scan Barcode`.

4. Drag and drop a button to the right of the txtSearchBarcode text box. Rename it `btn-SearchBarcode`. This is the button used to trigger the event you use to initiate a barcode search in TinyDB.

5. Set the `Text` property of the btnSearchBarcode to `Search`.

6. Drag and drop another button to the right of the last button. Rename it `btnScan-BarCodeForSearch`. This is the button a user can tap to scan an existing barcode to populate the txtSearchBarcode text box.

7. Set the `Text` property of btnScanBarcodeForSearch to `Scan`.

Using these interfaces items and a gentle hint from your `Hint` property, the user knows that they can either enter or scan a barcode into the text box.

Next, build the user interface elements for searching TinyDB by name:

1. Drag and drop a HorizontalArrangement under the previous horizontal arrangement in VirtualScreen1.

2. Drag and drop a TextBox component into the HorizontalArrangement. Rename it txtSearchName.

3. Set the Hint property for txtSearchName to Enter Name to Search.

4. Drag and drop a button to the right of the txtSearchName text box. Rename it btnSearchName.

5. Change the Text property to Search.

Place all of the user interface components for searching TinyDB data by location:

1. Drag and drop a third HorizontalArrangement in VirtualScreen3 beneath the previous search components.

2. Drag and drop a TextBox component into the HorizontalArrangement. Rename it txtSearchLoc.

3. Set the Hint property of txtSearchLoc to Enter Location to Search.

4. Drag and drop a button to the right of the txtSearchLoc text box. Rename it btnSearchLoc.

5. Set the Text property of btnSearchLoc to Search.

Finally, you need a navigation element to allow users to return to the main screen without completing a search:

1. Drag and drop a button as the last component in the VirtualScreen3. Rename it btnSearchBack.

2. Set the Text property to Back.

These are all the components for your search screen, which is VirtualScreen3. You should have a component list and layout that looks like Figure 8-7.

VirtualScreen4 is much like VirtualScreen2 in that it is a simple place to display any results of the search algorithm. Two labels indicate to the user what it is they are looking at and then display the results:

1. Drag and drop a label into the VirtualScreen4. Rename it `lblSearchResults-Banner`.

2. Set the `Text` property to `Search Results Screen`.

3. Drag and drop a second label below the first. Rename it `lblSearchResults`.

4. Set the `Text` property to some placeholder text such as `Results Here`.

Finally, set a navigation component to take the user back to the main screen.

1. Drag and drop a Button component as the last component in VirtualScreen4. Rename it `btnResultsBack`.

2. Set the `Text` property of the btnResultsBack to `Back`.

The btnScanBarcodeForSearch button activates the barcode scanner so that your user can scan the barcode they want to search for. However, you don't want to use the same Barcode Scanner component that is being used by the Scan and Add Item button. This is because each scan generates not only an event but also a block with the last scans results stored in it. You want to makes sure that your user's last "store item" scan is never confused with the "search item" scan result. To get around this, you add a second Barcode Scanner component and utilize the second component's events and blocks.

Drag and drop a new Barcode Scanner component from the Other Stuff palette.

Make sure the `Visible` property for VirtualScreen3 and VirtualScreen4 is deselected.

Your completed Collection Assistant 2.0 user interface should look like Figure 8-7.

Now, on to building the logic and algorithms for your Collection Assistant 2.0 application in the Blocks Editor. You set each of the Back buttons on VirtualScreen3 and VirtualScreen4 to return the user to the main screen. The Search button event activates VirtualScreen3. VirtualScreen4 is activated after the search algorithm has been run.

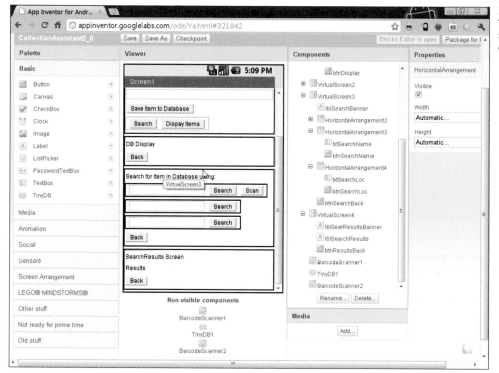

FIGURE 8-7:
The new user
interface
components

First, set up the Back button for moving the user from VirtualScreen3 back to the main
screen. VirtualScreen3 is the primary search screen, so name the button btnSearchBack:

1. Typeblock the `btnSearchBack.Click` event handler and drag it to an empty workspace on your Blocks Editor.

2. Typeblock the `VirtualScreen3.Visible` [to] block and snap it into the event.
   Snap in a `false` block.

3. Typeblock the `VirtualScreen1.Visible` [to] block and snap it in below the
   `VirtualScreen3` block. Snap a `true` block into the `VirtualScreen1.Visible`
   [to] block.

This event fires when the Back button is tapped and directs the user back to the main screen.
The next blocks handle the results page Back button on VirtualScreen4:

1. Typeblock the `btnResultsBack.Click` event handler.

2. Typeblock the `VirtualScreen4. Visible [to]` block and snap it in the event handler. Snap in a `false` block.

3. Typeblock the `VirtualScreen1.Visible [to]` block and snap it in under the `VirtualScreen4` block. Snap a `true` block into the `VirtualScreen1 [to]` socket.

Now set up the Search button event for VirtualScreen1.

1. Typeblock the `btnSearch.Click` event handler.

2. Typeblock the `VirtualScreen1.Visible [to]` block and snap it into the event handler. Snap in a `false` block.

3. Typeblock the `VirtualScreen3.Visible [to]` block and snap it next in the event handler. Snap in a `true` block.

This brings up the search screen when the user taps the Search button.

The next event you need to handle is the Scan button on the search screen. When the user taps the scan button, it should bring up the barcode scanner. When the user scans a barcode successfully, the result of the scan should be loaded into the txtSearchBarcode and used to search TinyDB. If your user manually types in a code for search, the Search button uses the number from the txtSearchBarcode.

1. Typeblock the `btnScanbarcodeForSearch.Click` event handler.

2. Typeblock the `BarcodeScanner2.DoScan` method call and snap it in the event handler. Make sure that it is the `.DoScan` from the second barcode scanner.

The barcode scanner generates an event when there is a successful scan. The `BarcodeScanner2.AfterScan` event calls the same procedure that the `btnBarcode-Search` event calls.

You build a procedure to be used for both events. The `procBarcodeSearch` is called from the `BarcodeScanner2.AfterScan` and also from the `btnSearchBarcode.Click` event. Whichever event calls the procedure, it takes as its search term the contents of txtSearchBarcode text box. Set the `.AfterScan` event to populate the txtSearchBarcode text box with the results of the scan. You place the procedure call in both these events in just a moment:

1. Typeblock the `BarcodeScanner2.AfterScan` event handler.

2. Typeblock the `txtSearchBarcode.Text` [to] block and snap it into the
   `.AfterScan` block.

If App Inventor does not automatically populate the `result` socket on the `.AfterScan`   **REMEMBER**
event handler, you need to plug in a `name` block.

---

3. Typeblock the `result1` value block and snap it into the `txtSearchBarcode.Text`
   block.

4. Typeblock the `btnSearchBarcode.Click` event handler.

Set these two events aside for a moment. You place the procedure call in them as soon as you
create it.

The search procedure loads the contents of the varBarcodeList one item at a time using a
ForEach block. It then checks to see whether the search term is equal to the currently loaded
barcode. If the currently loaded barcode is the same as the search term, it will be formatted
and output to search results. This algorithm is achieved with an IfElse block in the
ForEach that checks the local variable against the search term. The formatting is handled by
the same logic that you used for formatting in the 1.0 version.

First, define the variables you will be using in the procedure. You need a variable for the
search term and another for the search results:

1. Typeblock a new variable and rename it `varSearchTerm`.

2. Plug an empty `text` block into it.

3. Typeblock a new variable and rename it `varSearchResults`.

4. Plug in an empty `text` block.

These two variables are used through the procedure to provide clarity in understanding what
is going on. They are not strictly necessary and the routine could be made more efficient
without them. However, clarity is of first importance when dealing with something as complex as these blocks. You also reuse the temporary variables utilized by the formatting routine in the `display` event.

Start by creating the procedure and setting the varSearchTerm to the number that has been entered into the txtSearchBarcode by the user or a scan. As you build the procedure, refer to the completed blocks in Figures 8-8, 8-9, and 8-10.

1. Typeblock the new procedure and rename it procBarcodeSearch.

2. Typeblock the procBarcodeSearch call and snap it into the BarcodeScanner2. AfterScan event handler.

3. Typeblock another procBarcodeSearch call and snap it into the btnSearchBarcode event handler.

4. Typeblock the varSearchTerm [to] block and snap it into the procedure.

5. Typeblock the txtSearchBarcode.Text block and snap it into the varSearchTerm block.

Now you place the nested ForEach and IfElse blocks to check all the barcodes in the varBarcodeList:

1. Typeblock a ForEach block and snap it in below the varSearchTerm block.

2. Typeblock the varBarcodeList and snap it into the bottom of ForEach block in the in list socket.

This loops through the varBarcodeList and loads each item one at a time into the local variable, var2, which was defined when you created the ForEach block.

 NOTE   If the var2 variable isn't created, you can snap a name block into the var socket on the ForEach block and rename it.

Now you need to test if the currently loaded item is the same as the search term that you saved into varSearchTerm. You use an IfElse block to build the logic that says, "If the contents of var2 are not the same as the contents of varSearchTerm, do nothing; if they are the same, format the contents."

1. Typeblock an IfElse block and snap it into the ForEach block.

2. Typeblock a not block and snap it into the test socket on the IfElse block.

3. Typeblock an equals (=) comparison operator and snap it into the not block.

4. Typeblock the var2 value block and snap it in the first socket on the comparison operator.

5. Typeblock the varSearchTerm global value block and snap it into the second socket on the comparison operator.

The procedure for the barcode search should look like Figure 8-8 at this point. Leave the then-do socket empty on the IfElse block. If the contents of the temporary variable and the search term variable are not the same, you don't want to do anything yet. That is the first case in which the test evaluates to true, meaning that var2 is *not* equal to the search term. The ForEach loop loads another barcode into the var2 variable and its contents will be evaluated in the same way.

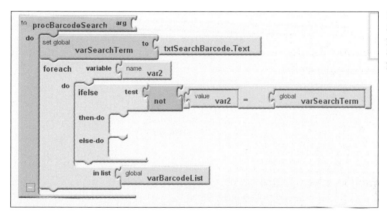

FIGURE 8-8: Starting the procBarCode Search procedure

If the test evaluates as *not* true, you want to take the barcode in var2 and use it as a tag to retrieve the contents stored under that barcode. You then format that content with the same ForEach loop you used in the btnDisplay.Click event.

For the second case, when the test evaluates *not* true, you first clear the varSearchResults of any previous search results. Then pull the contents stored under the barcode and store it in the tmpList you used previously:

1. Typeblock the varSearchResults [to] and snap it into the else-do socket on the IfElse block.

2. Typeblock a text block and set it empty. Snap the empty text block into the varSearchResults.

3. Typeblock the tmpList [to] and snap it in next in the else-do socket.

4. Typeblock a `split` block and snap it into the `tmpList` block.

5. Typeblock a `TinyDB1.GetValue` and snap it into the `text` socket on the `split` block.

6. Typeblock the `var2` value block and snap it into the `.GetValue` block.

7. Typeblock a `text` block and set the text to a comma. Snap it into the `at` socket on the `split` block.

These blocks retrieve contents stored under the barcode currently in the `var2` local variable and split it into a list stored in the `tmpList` variable. After the `tmpList` is loaded with the contents stored under the barcode that the user searched for, you need to use a `ForEach` to iterate through the `tmpList` and format it:

1. Typeblock a `ForEach` block and snap it in below the `tmpList` block.

2. Typeblock the `tmpList` global variable block and snap it into the `in list` socket at the bottom of the `ForEach` block.

WARNING　After a few `ForEach` blocks, App Inventor sometimes fails to auto-populate the `variable` socket on the `ForEach` blocks. To fix this, use a `name` block from the Definition drawer on the Built-In tab. Snap the `name` block into the `variable` socket on the `ForEach` block. You need to change the text name on the `name` block. Use the next sequential number `var` combination (in other words, the previous `ForEach` you created defined the `var2`, so you should use `var3` in the `name` block).

Next, use the old programmer's trick of borrowing code from yourself. You already put together the blocks for formatting and outputting the data from TinyDB, so why build it again? Locate the `btnDisplay.Click` event handler. Find the inside `ForEach` block in the nested `ForEach` blocks. The blocks that format the TinyDB1 data are the ones you need to copy. The easiest way to do this is to copy the entire `ForEach` block and then drag out the blocks it contains. Do not use the copied `ForEach` — the issues that this can cause are irritating and hard to fix. Instead, just pull out the "guts" of the `ForEach`: all of the formatting blocks that use the temporary variables.

1. Locate the `btnDisplay.Click` event handler.

2. Click the inside `ForEach` nested block.

3. Use the Ctrl+C to copy and Ctrl+V to paste it.

4. Drag the copy next to your `procBarcodeSearch` procedure.

5. Click on the top block in the copied ForEach block and drag all the interior blocks and snap them into your ForEach block in your procBarcodeSearch (see Figure 8-9).

6. You can delete the old copied and unused ForEach block.

Now add the barcode that was searched to the formatted results from the var2 local variable:

1. In the last tmpVar2 [to] block, remove the separator characters (you used a series of equals signs to separate the formatted results when you built the formatting logic) and last newline character and set them to one side.

2. Typeblock the var2 value local variable block and snap it into the open text socket on the make text block.

3. Copy the newline character block. Snap the copy into the next text socket.

4. Resnap in the separator characters in the next text socket.

5. Snap your final newline character into the next text socket.

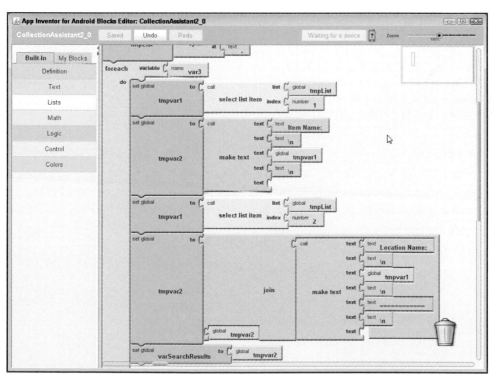

FIGURE 8-9:
The formatting blocks taken from btnDisplay.Click event handler

Now that you have formatted any matches from the `tmpList`, you need to write out the `tmpVar` to the results variable. Then you can make a decision about whether the search was successful based on the contents of the `varSearchResults` variable.

1. Typeblock the `varSearchResults` `[to]` block and snap it in below the last `tmpVar` formatting block.

2. Typeblock the `tmpvar2` value global variable block and snap it into the `varSearchResults` block.

Finally, you need to test the `varSearchResults` to see if anything matched and was written to the variable. If not, you write `Not Found` to the search results. If there are results in the search results variable, you write the results to the display label on VirtualScreen4.

1. Typeblock an `If` block and snap it in below the outside `ForEach` block in the `procBarcodeSearch` procedure.

2. Typeblock the equals (=) comparison operator and snap it into the `If` block.

3. Typeblock the `varSearchResults` global value block and snap it in the first socket on the comparison operator.

4. Typeblock a `text` block and delete the text for an empty block. Snap it into the second socket on the comparison operator.

5. Typeblock the `varSearchResults` `[to]` block and snap it into the `then-do` socket on the `If` block.

6. Typeblock a `text` block and change the text to `Not Found`. Snap this `text` block into the `varSearchResults` block you just placed.

If the `varSearch` results variable is empty, the text string `Not Found` is written to the variable. Now you just need to write the contents of the `varSearchResults` variable to the display label and enable the VirtualScreen4:

1. Typeblock the `lblSearchResults.Text` `[to]` block and snap it in below the `If` block.

2. Typeblock the `varSearchResults` value block and snap it into the `lbl-SearchResults.Text` block.

3. Typeblock the `VirtualScreen3.Visible` `[to]` block and snap it in below the `varSearchResults`. Snap in a `false` block.

4. Typeblock the `VirtualScreen4.Visible [to]` block and snap it in below previous block. Snap in a `true` block.

Your completed `procBarcodeSearch` procedure should look like Figure 8-10.

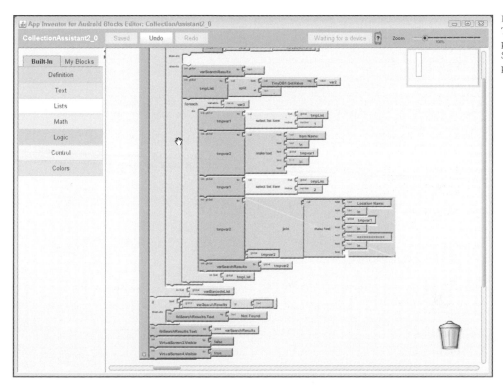

FIGURE 8-10:
The completed
procBarcode
Search
procedure

This procedure is called by the `BarcodeScanner2.AfterScan` event and the `btn-SearchBarcode.Click` event.

1. Locate the `BarcodeScanner2.AfterScan` event handler.

2. Typeblock the `procBarcodeSearch` call block and snap it into the `.AfterScan` event handler.

3. Locate the `btnSearchBarcode.Click` event handler.

4. Typeblock the `procBarcodeSearch` call block and snap it into the `.Click` event handler.

Now the Scan and Search events are handled for the barcode search functionality on the search screen. Now to handle the Search button event for the Name Search text box, you build out a similar logic. The name search event tests each barcode in the varBarcodeList to see whether the text string entered into the txtNameSearch text box is stored in TinyDB. If the text string is matched, it loads and formats that barcode into the Search results variable.

First, place the btnSearchName.Click event and load the text entered into the text box into the Search term variable. Then you place the outside ForEach block that loads each barcode in the varBarcodeList:

1. Typeblock the btnSearchName.Click event handler and place it on an empty workspace of the Blocks Editor.

2. Typeblock the varSearchTerm [to] block and snap it into the btnSearchName.Click event.

3. Typeblock the txtSearchName.Text block and snap it into the varSearchTerm block.

4. Typeblock a ForEach block and snap it in under the txtSearchName.Text block.

> **WARNING**   Make sure that there is a name block in the variable socket at the top of the ForEach block. Sometimes App Inventor fails to populate it. If there is no name block, drag one from the Definition drawer and snap it into the variable socket on the ForEach block. Change the name block to the next sequential var number. In this case, you would name it var4.

5. Typeblock the varBarcodeList value block and snap it into the in list socket at the bottom of the ForEach block.

Just as it did previously, this ForEach loads each barcode stored in TinyDB into a temporary list for evaluation or formatting:

1. Typeblock the tmpList [to] block and snap it into the ForEach block.

2. Typeblock a split block and snap it into the tmpList block.

3. Typeblock a TinyDB1.GetValue and snap it into the text socket on the split block.

4. Typeblock the var4 value block (the local variable from the ForEach block) and snap it into the .GetValue block.

5. Typeblock a text block and set it to a single comma. Snap it into the at socket on the split block.

These blocks set the tmpList up to be queried by an IfElse block. The IfElse block tests whether the contents of varSearchTerm are in the tmpList. If not, the IfElse block does nothing and the ForEach loads the next set of data in the varBarcodeList:

1. Typeblock an IfElse block and snap it in below the tmpList block.

2. Typeblock a not block and snap it into the test block of the IfElse block.

3. Typeblock a Is in List? block and snap it into the not block.

4. Typeblock the varSearchTerm value block and snap it into the thing socket on the Is in List? block.

5. Typeblock the tmpList global value block and snap it into the list socket on the Is in List? block.

The Is in List? block allows you to check whether a string is in a specified list. In this case, you are checking the tmpList that is created from the data stored under a barcode tag. If the search term is not in the list, nothing is done and the next barcode is used as a tag to reload the tmpList. Now you handle the second case. If the search term is in the tmpList, you need to format and output the list.

First, clear out any leftover results in the varSearchResults and place a new ForEach block to handle the formatting of the found data from TinyDB:

1. Typeblock the varSearchResults [to] and snap it into the else-do socket on the IfElse block.

2. Snap in a blank text block into the varSearchResults block.

3. Typeblock a new ForEach block and snap it in next in the else-do socket.

4. Typeblock the tmpList global value block and snap it into the in list socket on your new ForEach block.

Because App Inventor sometimes forgets, make sure the variable socket is populated with a name block named var5.

TIP

You use the formatting from the `btnDisplay.Click` just as you did previously. Remember that it is easier to copy a containing block such as the `ForEach` because when you copy and paste a containing block, the internal blocks are copied as well. You will copy and paste the formatting blocks from the inside `ForEach` from the `btnDisplay.Click` event, and then you use the formatting blocks in your `btnSearchName.Click` event, thus saving yourself the tedious task of building the same thing. You then discard the copied `ForEach` block.

1. Locate the `btnDisplay.Click` event.

2. Click the inside `ForEach` block in the event.

3. Use the Ctrl+C and Ctrl+V keys to copy and paste the `ForEach` and all its contained blocks. Drag it over by your `btnSearchName` event.

4. Click and drag the first block in the copied `ForEach` blocks. All the attached blocks are dragged. Drop the connected formatting blocks into the `ForEach` block located in the `then-do` socket on your `IfElse` block located in the `btnSearchName.Click` event.

5. Delete the unused old `ForEach` block.

You should add which barcode the search was found under to the formatted text. To do this, add the `var4` local variable from the outside `ForEach` block to the last formatting step. You plug it in right above the line of separator characters:

1. Locate the last `tmpvar2` block in the formatting blocks.

2. Remove the last newline character block from the `make text` block and set it aside.

3. Remove the separator character's text block and set it aside.

4. Typeblock the `var4` local variable from the outside `ForEach` block. This contains the barcode that was used to pull the data from TinyDB.

5. Snap the `var4` block into the open text block on the `make text` block.

6. Select the `newline` block and create a copy of it using Ctrl+C and Ctrl+V.

7. Snap in a newline character below the `var4` block.

8. Snap in the separator character's `text` block below the newline character block.

9. Snap in the last newline character block.

Finally, set the `varSearchResults` contents to the formatted text in `tmpvar2` and then display the variable on VirtualScreen4 and make the screen visible:

1. Typeblock the `varSearchResults` [to] and snap it in after the last formatting block (see Figure 8-11).

2. Typeblock the `tmpvar2` global value block and snap it into the `varSearchResults` block.

3. Typeblock the `VirtualScreen3.Visible` [to] block and snap it in below the outside `ForEach` block. (It should now be the last block in the `.Click` event.)

4. Snap a `false` block into the `VirtualScreen3` block.

5. Typeblock the `VirtualScreen4.Visible` [to] block and snap in a `true` block.

6. Typeblock the `lblSearchResults.Text` [to] block and snap it in under the VirtualScreen4 block.

7. Typeblock the `varSearchResults` global value block and snap it into the `lblSearchResults.Text` block.

Your completed `btnSearchName.Click` event handler should look like Figure 8-11 and Figure 8-12.

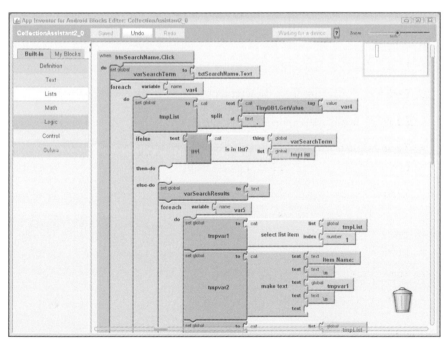

FIGURE 8-11:
The completed
btnSearchName.
Click event
blocks (top)

FIGURE 8-12:
The completed
btnSearchName.
Click event
blocks (bottom)

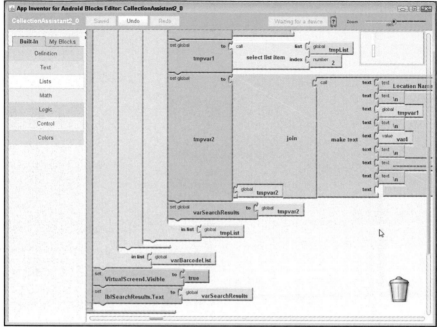

FIGURE 8-12:
The completed
btnSearchName.
Click event
blocks (bottom)

Challenging Yourself

This project ends with two challenges. The first is to complete the application using the exact same logic (and code blocks) to handle the btnSearchLoc event. You have built the logic and the blocks for the btnSearchName event. The location search should be identical with the exception of using the location text boxes and Search button. Try to build the event to look like the btnSearchName event.

The second challenge is more difficult. There is an area of redundant code in your application. Whenever the search routine produces a result, the resulting data needs to be formatted for display. To accomplish this, you copied the exact same blocks to every event. It would be far more efficient to have a procedure that could handle the text formatting for you. You could then call the procedure whenever you needed to format an entry from TinyDB1 and display it.

If you're up for a bonus challenge, use a procedure with result block and pass the barcode to the procedure for formatting and display.

BlueChat: A Bluetooth Chat Client

BLUECHAT IS A SIMPLE chat client/server. With it, two previously paired devices can send text messages to each other. As with the previous project, this project builds a base level of functionality and then challenges you to create added functionality. BlueChat can set up the client/server connection between only two devices — adding a third device is a whole different level of complexity.

The Bluetooth component in App Inventor is a low-level component. This means that it has a great deal of power and functionality, but also a great deal of complexity. Two Bluetooth components can be placed from the Not Ready for Prime Time palette. One is the Bluetooth server, the other the Bluetooth client. Only one of each is needed for two-way connectivity between your devices. However, in the BlueChat application, you use both components so that either device can initiate the connection.

Creating the BlueChat Application

While creating the BlueChat application, you will learn the basics of establishing a connection between two Bluetooth devices and then passing a basic text string between them. Many complexities are involved in Bluetooth communications. The functionality included with the App Inventor components can handle most common scenarios. However, in this project, you strip Bluetooth communication down to its simplest form and use it in its default mode. The default mode is the serial port profile, which emulates a serial connection in sending the data. The Bluetooth component is capable of more complex communications than you will use in BlueChat, including high byte, byte length, signed, and unsigned communications functions that are necessary to communicate with many Bluetooth devices. Generally speaking, you know when the device you are connecting to is expecting one of these functions by reading its documentation. However, for some devices, there just isn't any good documentation and some determined Googling to find the Bluetooth requirements for your device is necessary.

Your design

The design sketches (Figure 9-1) for BlueChat are fairly simple, depicting two screens: one for displaying chat messages and one for establishing connection to other devices. Use your design sketches while building your user interface.

BlueChat will have two screens. The first contains a text box for entering a message and a Send button to activate the Bluetooth send. The second screen contains a list of devices you have paired with using the Android Bluetooth settings. Your user can then establish a chat connection using a ListPicker component to select and connect with them. There is also a button to disconnect and a button to take the user back to the main screen.

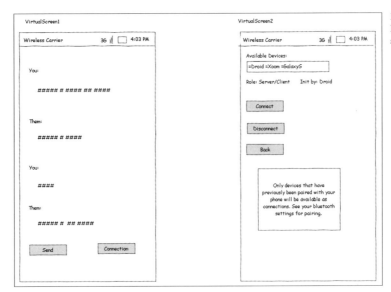

FIGURE 9-1: BlueChat design sketches

You use a clock to check the connected device for any messages cued up and waiting to be sent. With Bluetooth SPP (Serial Port Profile), you can specify the amount of data to be sent and received. You leave the data amount open-ended and continuously poll for data. As long as data is available to be sent, it is sent.

Your primitives

These primitives are the high-level tasks you have to achieve to fulfill your design goals:

- ◯ Two VirtualScreens for the user interface elements
- ◯ A label for displaying incoming messages and outgoing messages in conversational form
- ◯ A text box for accepting user input for messaging
- ◯ A Send button to send the message
- ◯ A method for handling sending the text message
- ◯ A method for handling incoming messages
- ◯ A method for formatting the text for the message display

○ A method for displaying available clients and allowing them to be selected

○ A method for connecting and disconnecting from available clients

New components

○ BluetoothServer

○ BluetoothClient

New blocks

○ Segment

Your progression

These are the high-level logical steps for accomplishing your design goals. For a really advanced challenge, see if you can build the user interface and some of the events just following the progression steps without the detailed steps later in the chapter:

1. Build the VirtualScreens.

2. Place the user interface elements as shown in the design sketches.

3. Create the event handlers for the Friend Connections button to open VirtualScreen2.

4. Create the event handler for the Back navigation button on VirtualScreen2.

5. Use the `Screen1.Initialize` to initialize the Connect ListPicker with the available devices and initialize the Bluetooth server.

6. Build the `ListPicker.AfterPicking` event to handle the selection of and connection to paired devices.

7. Build the `.ConnectionAccepted` event in case the device receives a connection.

8. Build the Disconnect button event handler and a procedure for handling interface reset.

9. Build the procedure for processing messages to the display label.

10. Build the clock timer for polling the connection for messages.

11. Build the event handler for the Send button.

Getting Started on BlueChat

Create a new project and name it BlueChat.

1. Change the Title property of Screen1 to BlueChat.

2. Make sure the Display Invisible Components in Viewer check box is selected.

3. Set the Icon property of Screen1 with the icon file from the chapter project files you downloaded from the companion Web site. (See this book's Introduction if you need more information on the companion Web site.)

Build the user interface first. Place the VirtualScreens on the Design view and set the Visible property unchecked. Begin by creating your VerticalArrangements and setting their properties to set be used as VirtualScreens.

1. Place two vertical arrangements on the Viewer. Change their names to VirtualScreen1 and VirtualScreen2.

2. Set the Width and Height properties to Fill Parent.

3. Uncheck the Visible property for both.

Now place the two main elements of interest to your users. The large label displays incoming and outgoing messages. The challenge is to present both incoming and outgoing messages in the order they occur. Chat programs need to display a running conversational view. The other main element is the text box where the user enters the message to be sent.

1. Drag and drop a Label component in VirtualScreen1. Rename it lblMessageDisplay.

2. Set the Height and Width to Fill Parent. Remove the default text from the Text property.

3. Drag and drop a TextBox component into VirtualScreen1 below the lblMessage-Display.

4. Rename the TextBox component txtMessage and set the Width (but not the Height) to Fill Parent.

5. Set the Hint property to Enter Message.

Next, place a HorizontalArrangement to hold the Send button and the button to open the connection settings screen. The Send button is used fairly frequently by the user and you want it separated from the Connections button so that it isn't accidently activated by the user. Use a blank label as padding between the two buttons to keep them separated:

1. Drag and drop a HorizontalArrangement below the TextBox component. Set its `Width` to `Fill Parent`.

2. Drag and drop a button in the HorizontalArrangement.

3. Rename the button `btnSend`. Change the `Text` property to `Send`. Uncheck the `Enabled` property. You enable the Send button when a connection is available.

4. Drag and drop a label to the right of the btnSend button. Rename it `padLabel1`. Remove the default text and set the `Width` to `Fill Parent`. This keeps the buttons apart regardless of screen width or orientation.

5. Drag and drop a button to the right of the padding label. Rename the button `btnConnections`.

6. Change the `Text` property to `Friend Connections`.

The VirtualScreen1 components allow viewing and sending of messages after a connection has been established. VirtualScreen2 displays any devices that have been paired with your device. It has a list picker that allows your user to then select the device they wish to connect with. It also has a Disconnect button that enables your user to disconnect. It also displays some important pieces of information to your user. When a connection is initiated between two devices, one of the devices is initiator of the connection, the other device receives. The device that receives the connection is considered the server: the initiator, the client. The Connections screen shows whether the user's device is a server or client and to which device it is connected.

1. Drag and drop a HorizontalArrangement into VirtualScreen2.

2. Drag and drop a Label into the HorizontalArrangement. Rename it `lblAvailDevices Label`.

3. Change the label `Text` property to `Available Devices`.

4. Drag and drop a Label to the right of the `lblAvailDevicesLabel`. Rename it `lbl AvailDevicesDisplay`. Remove the default text.

5. Drag and drop another HorizontalArrangement below the first.

6. Drag and drop a Label. Rename it `lblRoleLabel`.

7. Change the `Text` property to `Role:`. Be sure to leave a trailing space.

8. Drag and drop a second label to the right. Rename it `lblRoleDisplay`. Remove the default text.

9. Drag and drop a third label to the right of the previous label and rename it `lblInitiatedLabel`.

10. Change the `Text` property to `Initiated Connection to:`.

11. Drag and drop another label to the right of the previous label and rename it `lblInitiatedDisplay`. Remove the default text.

Now place the connection and navigation controls.

1. Drag and drop a ListPicker beneath the previous HorizontalArrangement.

2. Change the `Text` property on the ListPicker to `Connect`.

3. Drag and drop a button below the ListPicker. Rename the button `btnDisconnect`.

4. Set the `Text` property on the button to `Disconnect`. This button disconnects the Bluetooth connection and resets the user interface.

5. Drag and drop another button below the previous button. Rename it `btnBack`.

6. Set the `Text` property to `Back`. This button navigates from the Connections screen back to the main screen.

Finally, place a short message to the user to clarify what devices they can in fact connect to. Only devices that have been paired using the Android system Bluetooth settings are available as a Connection option:

1. Drag and drop a label below the Back button. Rename it `lblNotice`.

2. Set the `Text` property to `Only devices that have been paired with your device will show up as connections. Open your Bluetooth wireless settings to pair devices with your phone.`

The visible user interface elements should now look like Figure 9-2.

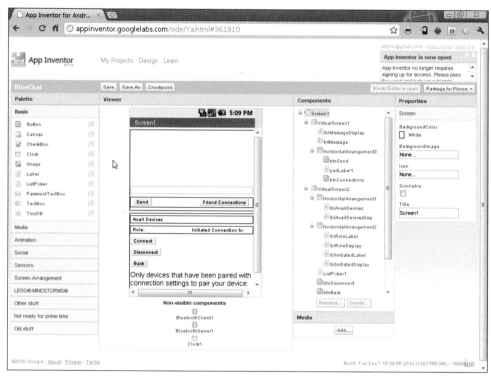

Now make the VirtualScreen2 invisible until it is needed and place the Bluetooth components. The Bluetooth components are non-visible components:

1. Drag and drop a BluetoothServer component from the Not Ready for Prime Time palette.

2. Drag and drop a BluetoothClient component from the same palette.

3. Drag and drop a Clock component from the Basic palette. This component polls for messages.

Now move on to building the blocks and procedures for your application. As usual, follow along with the progression but allow the process of building to change the progression. Also use the primitives as a checklist of events and interim goals needed to attain your end goal.

First, create the navigation elements to move back and forth from the main screen to the Friend Connections page. The user might want to open the connections page to verify an existing connection and then navigate back to the main messaging screen:

1. Typeblock the `btnConnections.Click` event handler.

2. Typeblock the `VirtualScreen1.Visible [to]` block, snap it in the event handler, and set it with a `false` block.

3. Typeblock the `VirtualScreen2.Visible [to]` block snap it in next and set it with a `true` block.

Next, create the Back button from the Friend Connections screen.

1. Typeblock the `btnBack.Click` event handler.

2. Typeblock the `VirtualScreen1.Visible [to]` block and snap it into the event handler set it with a `true` block.

3. Typeblock the `VirtualScreen2.Visible [to]` block and snap it in next under the VirtualScreen1 block. Set it with a `false` block.

As soon as the application starts, you need to populate the Connect button ListPicker with the options available to be connected to. You use the `Client1.AddressesAndNames` block to report what devices the Android device has been paired with. That returns an App Inventor-formatted list of all the devices currently paired with the phone. The list is formatted in "address space name" format so that each item in the list looks like 00:23:76:9F:E8:BE Nexus One. The Bluetooth hardware address is a 17-character unique address that allows messages to be sent to the device. The address length is constant, which is something you will use later to your advantage. Use the `Screen1.Intialize` event to populate the ListPicker elements and populate the available devices label.

1. Typeblock the `Screen1.Initialize` event handler.

2. Typeblock the `ListPicker1.Elements [to]` block and snap it into the event handler.

3. Typeblock the `BluetoothClient1.AddressesAndNames` block. Snap it into the `.Elements` block.

4. Typeblock the `lblAvailDevicesDisplay.Text [to]` block and snap it in below the `ListPicker` block.

5. Typeblock the `BluetoothClient1.AddressAndNames` block. Snap it into the `lblAvailableDevicesDisp` block.

You need to accomplish another task in the `.Initialize` block. The Bluetooth server component needs to be told to accept incoming connections. If someone else attempts to connect to your phone after having been paired with your device, your device needs to be expecting that connection and allow it. You use the `.AcceptConnection` block to tell the BluetoothServer component what services it should accept incoming connections from. For the purposes of your application, you don't use the service socket to specify a service. This allows a connection from any pair device.

1. Typeblock the `BluetoothServer1. AcceptConnection` block and snap it into the `.Initialize` event handler block below the `lblAvailDevicesDisp` block.

2. Typeblock a `Text` block and remove the default text. Snap the empty `Text` block into the `serviceName` socket on the `.AcceptConnection` block.

This tells the Bluetooth server to accept connections but does not specify that they must be only from a specific service. You can use this as a security feature or to run multiple Bluetooth servers listening for incoming connections.

When the Bluetooth component receives an incoming connection, it generates the event `BluetoothServer1.ConnectionAccepted`. You need to track whether a device is the server or the client for every session. To do this, use a variable with a simple Boolean (true or false) value. When the device is the Bluetooth server, it uses a completely different set of methods to send messages, receive messages, and disconnect than does a client. In other words, a `Server` block for sending a message only works if the device is a server and a `Client` block only works for sending messages when the device is the client. You use the `.ConnectionAccepted` device to set the `varIsServer` variable to `true`, and then refer back to that variable when you have to decide which blocks to use in any given instance.

First, define the variable:

1. Typeblock a variable and rename it `varIsServer`.

2. Typeblock a `text` block and set it `empty`. Snap it into the `varIsServer` block.

Next, handle the `.ConnectionAccepted` event:

1. Typeblock the BluetoothServer1.ConnectionAccepted event handler.

2. Typeblock the `varIsServer [to]` block and snap it into the event handler.

3. Typeblock a `true` block and snap it into the variable block.

Now you have set the variable value to `true` whenever a client makes a connection to your application. Next you need to disable the ListPicker because a connection is already set. That way, your user cannot attempt a connection if there is already a connection made between two devices:

1. Typeblock the `ListPicker1.Enabled [to]` block and snap it beneath the variable block.

2. Typeblock a `false` block and snap it into the `ListPicker1` block.

Because the device is now the server you need to set the role display to represent the Server role.

1. Typeblock the `lblRoleDisplay.Text [to]` block and snap it in beneath the `ListPicker1.Enabled` block.

2. Typeblock a `text` block and set the text to `Server`. Snap it into the `lblRoleDisplay` block.

Now enable the Send button so that your user can start sending messages to the connected device. You will also enable the `Clock1.Timer` block so that the device starts polling the connected device for any incoming messages. (*Polling* is the process of checking for expected data on a regular basis.) I show you how to build out the `Clock1.Timer` later.

1. Typeblock the `btnSend.Enabled[to]` and snap it in to the `.ConnectionAccepted` event handler. Set it with a `true` block.

2. Typeblock the `Clock1.TimerEnabled [to]` block and snap it in below the previous block. Set it with a `true` block.

That's everything for the `BluetoothServer1.ConnectionAccepted` event. Yours should resemble Figure 9-3. When the server component accepts a connection, it sets the `varIsServer` to contain the value `true`, disables the LisPicker1, sets the role display to display the text `Server`, and enables the Send button and the `Clock1.Timer`.

FIGURE 9-3:
The completed
.Connection
Accepted event
handler

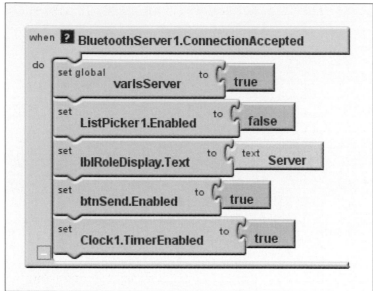

You need to give your user control over the connection. Your Disconnect button allows your user to terminate the Bluetooth connection. There are two different ways to disconnect depending on whether the device is server or client. You need to use an IfElse block to query the varIsServer variable and determine how to disconnect when the user taps the Disconnect button:

1. Typeblock the btnDisconnect.Click event handler block.

2. Typeblock an IfElse block and snap it into the event handler.

The test for the IfElse block is different from any other you have built up to this point. Because the IfElse looks for a return of true to execute the first case, and your variable is a Boolean value, you can plug the global variable reporting block directly into the test socket. If the varIsServer is reporting the value as true, the first case is executed. Otherwise, the else-do blocks are executed. This is different from previous tests where you used a comparison operator to evaluate two values and then return a true or false. It may look funny this way because you are used to using a comparison operator such as an equals block, but it works just as well if your variable contains a Boolean value.

1. Typeblock the varIsServer global value block and snap it into the test socket on the IfElse block.

2. Typeblock the `BluetoothServer1.Disconnect` block and snap it into the then-do socket on the `if-else` block.

3. Typeblock the `BluetoothClient1.Disconnect` block and snap it into the else-do socket.

Now your `IfElse` block evaluates the contents of the `varIsServer` variable and activates the appropriate disconnect method when the Disconnect button is tapped.

When the Disconnect button is tapped, you need to reset the user interface back to its pre-connected setting and clear all the text labels in preparation for another connection and chat session:

1. Typeblock the `lblRoleDisplay.Text` [to] block and snap it in beneath your `IfElse` block in the `btnDisconnect.click` event. Snap in a blank `text` block.

2. Typeblock the `ListPicker1.Enabled` [to] block and snap it in next below the `lblRoleDisplay` block. Snap in a `true` block.

3. Typeblock the `btnSend.Enabled` [to] block and snap it in next below the `ListPicker` block. Snap in a `false` block.

4. Typeblock the `Clock1.TimerEnabled` [to] block and snap it in next below the `btnSend` block. Snap in a `false` block.

5. Typeblock the `lblMessageDisplay.Text` [to] block and snap it in next below the `Clock1` block. Snap in a blank `text` block.

Now when the phone is disconnected using the Disconnect button, it clears the text from the Role display and the messages from the main message display. It disables the Send button and the `Clock1.Timer` also enables the ListPicker so that a new connection can be initiated.

The Connect button on the Connections screen is tied to a ListPicker that allows the user to select from paired devices to connect to. When the user taps the Connect button, the ListPicker displays the available devices. When the user selects a device from the ListPicker, the `.AfterPicking` event is generated. You use that event to initiate a connection. The `.BluetoothClient1.Connect` block is a different kind of method call. Most method calls are standalone or standalone with argument-type blocks. This block is a Boolean reporting method call with an argument. In other words, you supply the address you want to connect to, and the `.Connect` block attempts the connection. If that connection is successful, the `.Connect` block returns `true`. If the connection fails, the `.Connect` block return `false`. You can then use the `.Connect` block in an `IfElse` block. When the test is run, it attempts to connect to the address you plug into the `address` argument socket.

1. Typeblock the `ListPicker1.AfterPicking` event handler block.

2. Typeblock an `IfElse` block and snap it into the event handler.

3. Typeblock the `BluetoothClient1.Connect call` block and snap it into the `test` socket on the `IfElse` block.

4. Typeblock the `ListPicker1.Selection` block and snap it into the `address` socket on the `.Connect` block. The `Selection` block contains the address that the user chose from the ListPicker list.

Now when a user taps a selection in the ListPicker, the `.AfterPicking` event attempts to connect to the selected address. If the connection is successful, the `.Connect` block returns `true` and the `IfElse` executes the `then-do` blocks. If the connection fails, the `IfElse` executes the `else-do` blocks. If the connection is successful, you need to indicate that the device is the client in the `varIsServer` variable, set the user interface to reflect the successful connection, and set up for sending and receiving messages.

1. Typeblock the `varIsServer` `[to]` block and snap it into the `then-do` socket on the `IfElse` block.

2. Snap a `false` block into the `varIsServer` block.

3. Typeblock the `BluetoothServer1.StopAccepting` block and snap it in below the `varIsServer` block. This keeps the server from accepting new connections when a connection is already set up.

4. Typeblock the `lblRoleDisplay.Text` `[to]` and snap it in below the `BluetoothServer1` block. Snap in a text block with the text `Client`.

5. Typeblock the `btnSend.Enabled` `[to]` and snap it in below the `lblRoleDisplay` block. Set it with a `true` block.

6. Typeblock the `Clock1.TimerEnabled` `[to]` and snap it in below the `btnSend` block. Set it with a `true` block.

To allow your user to easily see who they have initiated a connection to, use the `ListPicker1.Selection` to display the connected device name. You need to trim the results of the `.Selection` to just the name portion. As you may recall, it contains a

Bluetooth address and a name. You use the `text` block `segment` to chop the selection text and select only the name for display.

1. Typeblock the `lblInitiatedDisplay.Text [to]` block and snap it in below the `Clock1.TimerEnabled` block.

2. Typeblock the `segment text` block and snap it into the to socket on the `text` block.

The `segment` block allows you to select some text from a string of text. It does this by having you define at which character to start and then how far to proceed in terms of numbers of characters. Put another way, you can select all the characters starting at the nineteenth character, for example, and stop selecting at the twenty-fifth character. The character to start at is plugged into the `start` socket in numeric form. The length is a number as well and indicates how many characters to select after the `start` character.

You know that the first 17 characters of the address/name combination make up the Bluetooth hardware address. Everything after the nineteenth character is the name. (You don't want to count the space between the address and the name.) You can find out how many characters to select past the nineteenth character by subtracting 18 (the address plus the trailing space) from the total length of the text.

1. Typeblock the `ListPicker1.Selection` block and snap it into the `text` socket on the `segment` block.

2. Typeblock a numeral 19 number block and snap it into the `start` socket on the `segment` block.

3. Typeblock a minus math operator block and snap it into the `length` socket on the `segment` block.

4. Typeblock the `length` block and snap it into the first socket of the minus operator block.

5. Typeblock the `ListPicker1. Selection` block and snap it into the `length` block. The `length` block returns the total number of characters in the `ListPicker1. Selection` block.

6. Typeblock a numeral 18 number block and snap it into the second socket on the minus block.

The number of characters that you want to select is the total length of the text in the `ListPicker1.Selection` block minus 18 characters.

These blocks display the name of the device you have connected to on the lblInitiatedDisplay label.

You need a way to indicate to your user if the connection fails. Place a simple text string in the InitiatedDisplay label to indicate a failed connection attempt:

1. Typeblock the lblInitiatedDisplay.Text [to] block and snap it into the else-do socket on the IfElse block in the .AfterPicking event handler.

2. Typeblock a text block and set the text to Connection Attempt Failed. Try Again. Snap this block into the .Text[to] block in the else-do socket.

If the connection attempt fails, the label displays the preceding message.

Your completed ListPicker1.AfterPicking event should resemble Figure 9-4.

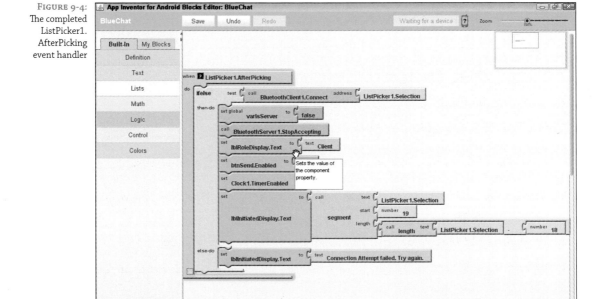

FIGURE 9-4: The completed ListPicker1. AfterPicking event handler

Both sent and received messages have to be displayed in conversational form in the message display label on the main screen. Instead of trying to write to the label from multiple events, you build a procedure that takes as argument the text you wish to format on the label. This is using a procedure as a sort of hand-off routine. You hand data to the procedure whenever you want something done to the data for your application, but don't particularly want information back or some other event or procedure called.

You use the same procedure to make sure that the length of the displayed messages stays manageable. You build simple logic to keep only the last four messages displayed in the display label. You also increment a counter variable every time you post a new message to the display label. Before you post to the label, you check the counter variable to see how many times it has been incremented. If it has been incremented four times, it means that four messages are displayed on the display label and you will clear it.

The procAddMessage takes two arguments each time you call it. You will feed to the procedure the message to be processed and who the message is from, the local user or the remote user ("you" or "them").

1. Typeblock a new procedure. Rename it procAddMessage.

2. Typeblock a name block. Change its text to message.

3. Snap the message block into the arg socket on the procAddMessage block.

4. Typeblock another name block and change its text to who.

5. Snap the who name block into the next arg socket on the procAddMessage procedure.

Now build the blocks for keeping track of the displayed messages on the display label.

1. Define a new variable and rename it varMessageCount. Set its default value with a numeral 0 number block.

2. Typeblock an If block and snap it into the procAddMessage procedure.

3. Typeblock a greater than comparison operator and snap it into the test socket on the If block.

4. Typeblock the varMessageCount global value block and snap it into the first socket on the comparison operator.

5. Typeblock a numeral 4 number block and snap it into the second socket on the comparison operator.

Now the If block tests to see if the message counter is greater than four. If it is, you need to set the lblMessageDisplay.Text blank in preparation for a new message:

1. Typeblock the lblMessageDisplay.Text [to] block and snap it into the If block.

2. Typeblock a text block and delete its text. Snap it into the lblMessageDisplay block.

Now the block to set the message display concatenates whatever is currently displayed on the label along with the new message. You use a make text block along with the value blocks for the procedure:

1. Typeblock the lblMessageDisplay.Text [to] block and snap it into the procAddMessage procedure below the If block.

2. Typeblock a make text block and snap it into the lblMessageDisplay block.

3. Typeblock the lblMessageDisplay.Text and snap it into the text socket on the make text block. This block contains whatever the current contents of the lblMessageDisplay.

4. Typeblock the who value block. This is the block created when you plugged a name block into the arg socket on the procedure.

5. Snap the who value block into the next text socket on the make text block.

6. Typeblock a text block and change its contents to a newline (\n) character.

7. Snap the newline character block in below the who block in the make text block.

8. Typeblock the message value block. Again, this is the value passed to the argument you created by populating the arg socket on the procedure.

9. Snap the message block into the make text block.

10. Snap another newline character block into the make text block.

This series of blocks takes whatever the current contents of the display label is, add, the message passed to the procedure, and rewrites it all to the display label.

Every time you write a message to the lblMessageDisplay label, you need to increment the varMessageDisplay variable to indicate how many messages are currently in the label:

1. Typeblock the `varMessageCount [to]` block and snap it into `procAddMessage` below the `lblMessageDisplay.Text` block.

2. Typeblock an addition operation block and snap it into the `varMessageCount` block.

3. Typeblock the `varMessageCount` global value block and snap it into the first socket on the addition operation block.

4. Typeblock a numeral 1 number block and snap it into the second socket on the addition operator block.

Now the `varMessageCount` increments each time a message is written to the label. This allows you to control the number of messages in the label with the previous `If` block.

Your `procAddMessage` procedure should resemble the one in Figure 9-5.

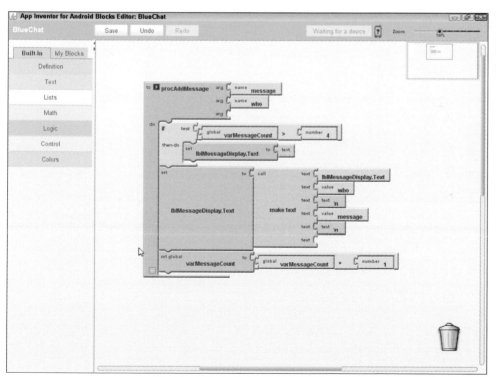

FIGURE 9-5: The completed procAdd Message procedure

Now that you have the procedure for adding messages to the display label, you can handle the Send button event and the receive data event handled by `Clock1.Timer`. The Send button event takes the text entered into the message text box and sends it across the established Bluetooth connection. If the device is the server, the server send method is used; if the device is the client, the client method is used. You use an `IfElse` block to test the `varIsServer` variable to determine if the device is the server:

1. Typeblock the `btnSend.Click` event handler.

2. Typeblock an `IfElse` block and snap it into the event handler.

3. Typeblock the `varIsServer` global value block and snap it into the `test` socket on the `If` block. Remember that this variable is a Boolean value, so it can be used without a comparison operator. If the value is `true`, the then-do blocks are executed. Otherwise, the `else-do` is executed.

4. Typeblock the `BluetoothServer1.SendText` block and snap it into the then-do socket on the `IfElse` block.

5. Typeblock the `txtMessage.Text` block and snap it into the `.SendText` block. The `txtMessage.Text` block contains the text entered in the `txtMessage` text box on the main screen.

You have sent the message via `BluetoothServer` if the device is the server. Now update the message display label:

1. Typeblock the `procAddMessage` procedure call and snap it into the then-do socket below the `BluetoothServer1` block.

2. Typeblock the `txtMessage.Text` value block and snap it into the message argument socket on the `procAddMessage`. This passes the text into the `procAddMessage` as the argument message.

3. Typeblock a `text` block and set the text to `You:`. Snap it into the who socket on the `procAddMessage` block. This message is displayed in the message display label as having come from the user.

4. Typeblock the `txtMessage.Text` [to] block and snap it in the then-do socket next.

5. Typeblock a `text` block and set its contents to empty. Snap it into the `txtMessage.Text` block. This clears the text box each time a message is sent so that your user can enter a new message to send.

Do the same steps for the else-do of the IfElse block except using the BluetoothClient method for sending the data:

1. Typeblock the BluetoothClient1.SendText method call and snap it into the else-do socket on your IfElse block.

2. Typeblock the txtMessage.Text and snap it into the BluetoothClient1.SendText block.

3. Typeblock the procAddMessage procedure call block and snap it in below the txtMessage.Text block.

4. Typeblock the txtMessage.Text block and snap it into the message socket on the procedure call.

5. Typeblock a text block, change the text to You:, and snap it into the who socket on the procedure call.

6. Typeblock the txtMessage.Text [to] block and snap it in below the previous block.

7. Snap an empty text block into the txtMessage.Text block.

Now whenever the Send button is tapped, the event checks whether the device is the client or server. It then calls the appropriate send method and updates the display label and the message text box.

Your completed BtnSend.Click event handler should look like the one in Figure 9-6.

The Clock1.Timer is the core of the application's ability to receive messages from the connected device. It polls the connected device and, as long as data bytes are available, it assumes the data is text and pulls that data as a text message to be added with the procAddMessage procedure.

Use two Bluetooth methods in the Clock1.Timer. The first is the .Bytes AvailableToReceive method. This method checks the attached device to see if there are any data bytes cued to be sent. The second is the .ReceiveText method. This is a built-in method for receiving text data across a Bluetooth connection.

FIGURE 9-6:
The completed
btnSend.Click
event handler

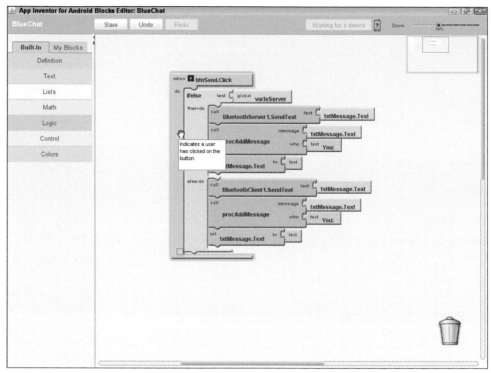

First, determine if the device is the client or the server, and then find out if data to be received exists. Finally, retrieve the data and pass it to the procedure for formatting:

1. Typeblock the `Clock1.Timer` event handler.

2. Typeblock an `IfElse` block and snap it into the event handler.

3. Typeblock the `varIsServer` global value block and snap it into the `test` socket on the `IfElse` block.

4. Typeblock an `If` block and snap it into the `then-do` socket on the `IfElse` block.

5. Typeblock a greater than comparison block and snap it into the `test` socket on the `If` block.

6. Typeblock the `BluetoothServer1.BytesAvailableToReceive` block and snap into the first socket on the comparison operator.

7. Typeblock a numeral `0` number block and snap it into the second socket on the comparison operator.

8. Typeblock the `procAddMessage` procedure `call` block and snap it into the `then-do` on the `If` block that is nested in the `then-do` of the `IfElse` block.

9. Typeblock the `BluetoothServer1.ReceiveText` block and snap it into the message socket on the procedure call. The `.ReceiveText` needs to be told how many bytes it can expect to receive. Use the previously used `.BytesAvailableToReceive` block to tell it how many blocks to receive.

10. Typeblock the `BluetoothServer1.BytesAvailableToReceive` block and snap it into the `numberOfBytes` socket on the `.ReceiveText` block.

11. Typeblock a `text` block and replace the text with `Them:`. Snap it into the `who` socket on the `procAddMessage` procedure call.

Now the Bluetooth server methods poll the connected device for any cued bytes. If any bytes are waiting, it pulls those bytes as text and passes them to the `procAddMessage` as being from `Them`.

You do the exact same thing in the `Else-do` socket of the `IfElse` block except with the client method calls instead of the server methods:

1. Typeblock an `If` block and snap it into the `else-do` socket on the `IfElse` block in the `Clock1.Timer`.

2. Typeblock a greater than comparison operator and snap it into the `test` socket on the `If` block in the `else-do` socket.

3. Typeblock the `BluetoothClient1.BytesAvailableToReceive` and snap it into the first socket on the comparison operator.

4. Typeblock a numeral 0 number block and snap it into the second socket on the comparison operator.

5. Typeblock the `procAddMessage` procedure `call` block and snap it into the `then-do` socket on the `If` block.

6. Typeblock the `BluetoothClient1.ReceiveText` block and snap it into the message socket on the `procAddMessage` block.

7. Typeblock the `BluetoothClient1.BytesAvailableToReceive` block and snap it into the `.ReceiveText` blocks `numberOfBytes` socket.

8. Typeblock a `text` block and change the text to `Them:`. Snap it into the `who` socket on the `procAddMessage` block.

Your completed `Clock1.Timer` event should look like the one in Figure 9-7.

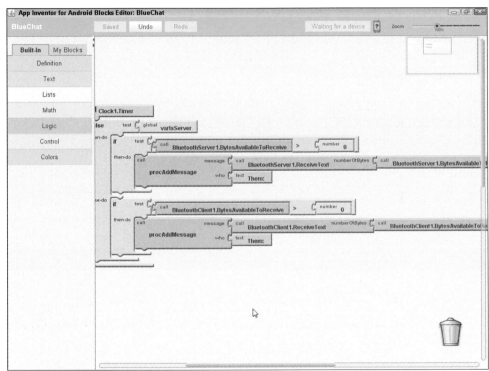

Download and install the app on two Android devices. Make sure the devices are paired using the system settings and fire up the BlueChat application on both devices. Check all the levels of functionality.

In the BlueChat application project, you have covered a couple of important concepts:

○ **Using the simpler aspects of the Bluetooth components from App Inventor:** A whole world of Bluetooth connectivity for other devices exists. Realize that many devices require some of the control communication blocks such as byte control (delimiter byte, high byte and so). You need to research the documentation for the device you are attempting to connect with.

○ **Using the** `segment text` **block to select a certain part of a text string:** This can be very useful when your application or return data has the data you need embedded in a fixed-length text string.

○ **Formatting and displaying text in a controlled manner:** You often need to control the contents of a label that is frequently populated. You can use a counter or the length blocks to check the contents of a label and clean up after your application.

○ **Polling when you have no control over a remote method or procedure you may need to poll:** Polling can be processor- and network-intensive, so make sure that your polling interval is reasonable.

○ **Using a procedure to process data from your application:** Use a procedure with defined arguments when you want to process data without a return. This can be useful when you are updating labels, formatting text, and related tasks.

Challenging Yourself

The BlueChat application has a lot of room for feature addition and improvement. Try using your App Inventor knowledge to add some of the following features:

○ A time stamp for messages

○ A chat log so that your user can scroll back through the conversations

○ Multiple connections to multiple devices using multiple Bluetooth components and the service argument

○ A method to pass a user name as a part of the text message

TwiTorial: A Twitter Application

TWITTER HAS BEEN at the cutting edge of the social media revolution ever since the company started. The micro blog enabling users to send 140-character messages to the world has become an integral part of the Internet presences of people and corporations alike.

App Inventor includes a Twitter component that has many features required to create your own complete Twitter application. The App Inventor Twitter component has its limitations, which I note as you move through this project.

The value of this project is not just in putting together a Twitter application, but also in exploring how Twitter can be integrated into other applications. You should consider social network integration in many types and categories of applications. Posting statuses or updates to a Twitter feed can be an excellent way to create brand exposure. Status updates can also be used as triggers for your applications. For instance, your App Inventor application can be monitoring a Twitter account for a certain text string as a trigger event.

Creating the TwiTorial Application

The TwiTorial application is quite complex. In terms of number of events and processes, it may be one of the most complex in this book. The instructions for TwiTorial exclusively use typeblocking to create blocks in the Blocks Editor. Because of the sheer number of events and user interactions, I show you a couple of new tricks for maximizing your user interface space and create pleasing design elements. Here are some of the things I cover in this chapter:

- ❍ Using the Twitter components
- ❍ Truncating very long lists
- ❍ Using procedure with result as a text formatter
- ❍ Using dynamically sized arrangements to maximize the screen area
- ❍ Using a Notifier component as a text input mechanism
- ❍ Setting custom Android colors with numbers

Your design

The TwiTorial design specifications contain three screens, as shown in Figure 10-1. A lot goes on with a Twitter application, so you need to use some clever tricks to maximize your screen real estate and make sure the busy interface is pleasing.

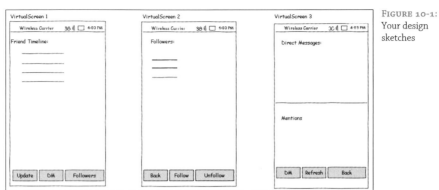

FIGURE 10-1:
Your design
sketches

Your primitives

These are the basic building blocks of functionality that will be required to meet your design goals:

- ○ Buttons/events for requesting timelines (streams of collected messages in chronological order), direct messages (DMs), mentions, and followers (those who choose to receive your tweets)

- ○ Method for formatting for display any list returned by the Twitter component

- ○ Buttons/events/methods for viewing, following, and unfollowing

- ○ Method for creating single color dividing visual elements

- ○ Method for setting custom colors

- ○ Method for truncating extremely long lists

- ○ Method for accepting input from user without wasting screen space for text boxes

New components

This is the primary new component for the TwiTorial project.

- ○ Twitter component

New blocks

These are the new blocks you will be using for the project:

- ⭕ Length of list
- ⭕ Add items to list

A lot of primitive concepts and basic capabilities that you use for this application have already been covered in earlier chapters. The preceding list includes only new or unique primitives: A complete list of primitives would probably be three times as long.

Your progression

There is a lot going on in the TwiTorial application. The following logical steps will help you build the primitives up in a fairly progressive way:

1. Set up the user interface elements for VirtualScreen1.

    a. Place the Timeline label and display elements.

    b. Place the Status, Message, and Followers buttons.

2. Set up the user interface elements for VirtualScreen2.

    a. Place the Followers label and display elements.

    b. Place Back, Follow, and Unfollow buttons.

3. Place the VirtualScreen3 user interface elements.

    a. Place the Direct Messages and Mentions labels and display elements.

    b. Place the DM, Refresh, and Back buttons.

4. Place the non-visual components:

    a. Three notifiers: TinyDB, Clock, and Twitter components.

5. Set up `.Initialize` with authorization and formatting logic.

6. Set up the timeline polling.

7. Set up the timeline received logic.

8. Build procedures for formatting incoming lists from the Twitter API.

9. Build status update button event using a Notifier component.

10. Set the DMs and Mentions button event logic.

11. Handle the DMs received event.

12. Handle the Mentions received event.

13. Set up the Followers button event.

14. Handle the Followers received event.

15. Handle the Followers Back button event.

16. Handle the Follow Tweep button event.

17. Handle the Unfollow Tweep button event.

18. Handle the DM Send button event.

19. Handle the Refresh DMs and Mentions button events.

20. Handle the DM and Mentions Back button event.

As of this writing, the direct message functionality of the Twitter component is not working,   **WARNING**
but Google is working on a fix that may be done by the time this book is available. I show you
how to build the Direct Message functionality and disable it. When Google releases the fix,
you can reactivate the blocks for the Direct Message functionality.

Getting Started on TwiTorial

Start a new application project and name it TwiTorial.

1. Make sure the `Scrollable` property for Screen1 is checked. Lots of information can come in via Twitter and your user may need to be able to scroll the Android screen.

2. Upload the icon from the Chapter 10 project files and set the `Icon` property.

3. Set the `Title` property to `TwiTorial`. You set this property here, although it changes as soon as a user authenticates with the Twitter application programming interface (API). The `Title` property shows not only the title of the application but the user name who is currently authenticated.

NOTE The Twitter API is the command's returned data that Twitter exposes from their servers to allow developers to create Twitter applications. All of the Twitter API programming has been done for you with the App Inventor Twitter component. When you use the Twitter component, all of the blocks, methods, and function calls send commands to the Twitter servers via the Twitter API.

The TwiTorial project is long enough that you may want to create checkpoints along the way. Refer back to Chapter 1 for a refresher on using the Checkpoints as version control.

Start by building up the user interface elements. The TwiTorial application has three screens. The first, VirtualScreen1, is the default screen and contains the Twitter follower timeline. The follower timeline is all of the status messages that are recent from the people you have followed. The VirtualScreen1 also provides buttons for updating your status message on Twitter. The update status or tweets are handled, like most of the other Twitter API calls, by built-in component method calls. You call the methods by using events controlled by your buttons.

1. Drag and drop a VerticalArrangement and change its name to `VirtualScreen1`.

2. Set the `Width` and `Height` property to `Fill Parent`.

Next, place the timeline display labels. These labels indicate to the user that they are looking at the timeline from their friends. Set the size of the font a little smaller than normal to get more on the screen. Be careful not to make it too small to comfortably to view. Check the view on your connected Android device.

1. Drag and drop a label into the VirtualScreen1. Rename the label `lblTimelineLabel`. This label is static and indicates that the next label is displaying the timeline.

2. Set the `Text` property to say `Timeline from friends:`.

3. Drag and drop another label below the previous label. Rename the label `lblTimelineDisplay`.

4. Clear the default `Text` property.

5. Set the `Width` and `Height` property of lblTimelineDisplay to `Fill Parent`.

Now place the navigation elements and buttons in a HorizontalArrangement. You need a button to allow your user to send a tweet and buttons to access VirtualScreen2 and VirutalScreen3, which are the Direct Messages and Followers screens, respectively.

1. Drag and drop a horizontal arrangement below the display label.

2. Set the Width property to Fill Parent.

3. Drag and drop a button into the HorizontalArrangement. Rename it btnUpdate-Status.

4. Change the Text property to Update Status. Set the FontSize property to 12.0 pixels.

5. Drag and drop another button to the right of the previous button. Rename the button btnMessages.

6. Change the Text to DMs/Mentions and change the FontSize property to 12.0 pixels.

7. Drag and drop another button to the right of the previous button. Rename the button btnFollowers.

8. Change the Text to Followers. Change the FontSize property to 12.0 pixels.

The timeline display label is populated by the .TimelineReceived event that is generated after a request for the timeline. The timeline consists of status updates from all the tweeps you follow on Twitter in chronological order. (*Tweeps* are people who use Twitter. I think it's is a conflation of *Twitter* and *peeps*, but don't hold me to it.) When the application initializes and the authorization is completed, the Clock timer is enabled and the timeline is regularly refreshed with the request for the timeline.

Next set up the VirtualScreen2, which is the screen where you display followers and allow your user to follow and unfollow tweeps:

1. Drag and drop a VerticalArrangement below VirtualScreen1 and rename the VerticalArrangement VirtualScreen2.

2. Set the Width and Height property to Fill Parent.

3. Drag and drop a Label into the VirtualScreen2 and rename it lblFollowerLabel. Set the Text property to Followers:.

4. Drag and drop another label below the first. Rename it lblFollowersDisplay. Remove the default Text property text.

5. Set the Width and Height property on the second label to Fill Parent.

Use a HorizontalArrangement to hold all the navigation and follower action buttons at the bottom of the followers display:

1. Drag and drop a HorizontalArrangement above the display labels and set its `Width` property to `Fill Parent`.

2. Drag and drop a button into the HorizontalArrangement. Rename it `btnBack-Followers`.

3. Set the `Text` property to Back.

4. Drag and drop a new button to the right of the previous button and rename it `btn-Follow`.

5. Set the `Text` to `Follow Tweep`.

6. Drag and drop a ListPicker to the right of the buttons and rename it `lstpkrUnfollow`.

7. Set the `Text` property to `Unfollow Tweep`.

In the series of steps, you will be building the third VirtualScreen, which is used to display both direct messages and mentions from the Twitter API. You will learn a method to divide the screen with a visual element designed to differentiate between direct messages and mentions. I show you a new method for of maximizing the screen real estate without having to control the sizes of all the elements inside of a VirtualScreen. You place all of your components into a VerticalArrangement that you will call `AutoSizeArrangement`. Then you use Blocks Editor logic to set the size of the AutoSizeArrangement. This accomplishes the same result as merely setting the `VirtualScreen` to `Fill Parent`, with the difference that you can select which parts of the VirtualScreen will be considered free for expansion. In other words, you don't want the entire VirtualScreen to expand out to accommodate the incoming messages and mentions — this would push the navigation buttons well below the visible screen. This would force your user scroll to the bottom of all the incoming messages to reach the navigation buttons. Instead, you want just the labels displaying the incoming data to actually expand to maximum size.

TIP   This is a little bit of an academic exercise, but it teaches you how to make a dynamic arrangement that is not dependent on *all* of your elements expanding to fill the screen. When you're designing for larger than average screen sizes such as tablets, this can be even more useful.

The method you use sets the AutoSizeArrangement to be as tall as all of the available Screen1 size, less the size of the HorizontalArrangement holding the navigation elements. The algorithm for making dynamically sized elements is to use `Width` and `Height` properties blocks to set the size, using a minus block to remove the size of elements you wish to exclude. You will build the blocks later. For now, just place the required component pieces:

1. Drag and drop a new VerticalArrangement below the existing virtual screens. Rename it `VirtualScreen3`.

2. Set the `Height` and `Width` properties to `Fill Parent`.

3. Drag and drop another VerticalArrangement into the VirtualScreen3. Rename it `AutoSizeArrangement`.

4. Drag and drop a label into the AutoSizeArrangement and rename `lblDMLabel`.

5. Set the `Text` property to `Messages:`.

6. Drag and drop a Label component beneath the previous label and rename it `lbl-DMDisplay`.

7. Remove the default text.

Now you use a clever trick to create a visible element similar to HTML horizontal lines or bars that are used to build web page design elements. Use a horizontally expanding Label with its background color set to `black` and its `Height` property statically defined. This creates a horizontal line separating the direct messages from the mentions.

1. Drag and drop a label into the AutoSizeArrangement and rename it `lineLabel1`.

2. Remove the default text.

3. Set the `BackgroundColor` to `Black`.

4. Set the `Width` property to `Fill Parent`.

5. Set the `Height` property to 5 pixels.

This creates a horizontal line 5 pixels high that expands to fill the AutoSizeArrangement and separates the direct messages and mentions. Now place your mentions display elements and the navigation elements below the separator line.

1. Drag and drop a Label component below the horizontal line and rename it `lbl-MentionsLabel`.

2. Change the Text property to Mentions.

3. Drag and drop another Label component below the previous label and rename it lbl-MentionsDisplay.

4. Remove the default text.

Now place a HorizontalArrangement in the VirtualScreen3 below the AutoSizeArrangement:

1. Drag and drop a HorizontalArrangement below the AutoSizeArrangement.

2. Drag and drop a ListPicker into the HorizontalArrangement. Rename it lstp-krSendDM.

3. Change the Text property to DM and the FontSize to 10.

4. Drag and drop a Button component to the right of the ListPicker. Rename the button btnRefreshDM.

5. Set the Text property to Refresh DMs and the FontSize to 10.

6. Drag and drop another Button component to the right of the previous button. Rename it btnRefreshMentions.

7. Change the Text property to Refresh Mentions and the FontSize to 10.

8. Drag and drop another button to the right of the previous button. Rename it btn-BackDM.

9. Set the Text property to Back and the FontSize to 10.

All of the visible user interface elements should be in place at this point. Now place the non-visible components. The TwiTorial application makes use of multiple Notifier components for its text entry pop-up. The app also uses the Clock component, the TinyDB component, and, of course, the Twitter component.

1. Drag and drop a Clock component to the Viewer.

2. Drag and drop three Notifier components.

3. Drag and drop a TinyDB component.

4. Drag and drop the Twitter component from the Social palette.

Twitter uses OAuth for communication with its API. OAuth stands for *Open Authorization*, a standard for authorizing and authenticating applications and users across the Internet. You can read more about OAuth at the OAuth Web site at `ouath.net`. Because Twitter requires that all third party applications use OAuth to use the API, your application must be authenticated with their system before it can be used. When a user first fires up your application, it asks the user to authorize your application to access their Twitter account via the Twitter API.

There are two parts of the OAuth transaction. First, your application has to be authenticated with Twitter by you, the developer. That's what the Consumer Key and Consumer Secret you get a little later are for. Second, your user needs to authorize the application to be used with their account. They do this by entering their username and password at the Twitter Web site when they are prompted by your application.

For this to work, you need to register your application with the Twitter OAuth mechanism. The process is fairly easy, but requires some attention to detail. The end result of registering your application is two pieces of information that you must plug into the Twitter component: the *Consumer Key* and *Consumer Secret*. Follow the steps below to get your key and secret.

1. Log into your Twitter account or the account that will represent your company, application, and so on. The account doesn't have to be your personal one but should be an account that will have the information that Twitter and possible users need to contact you.

2. Navigate your browser to `http://twitter.com/oauth_clients/new`.

3. Fill out the following fields on the New Clients form:

   a. Application Name: This must be a unique name for your application. You can't name the application `TwiTorial` because I've already used that name. You might use something like "Jason's TwiTorial" instead. The name you choose is what the user sees when they are asked to verify that they want your application to access their Twitter account. In this case, it asks the user if they want the Jason's TwiTorial application to have access to their account.

   b. Description: Enter text here to indicate what your application does to any user that is authenticating. Such as "The TwiTorial application is a simple Twitter client that is used to demonstrate the Twitter API integration with App Inventor."

   c. Application Web Site: This is a required field. This is the URL of a Web site where your users can access more information about your application. If you don't have such a Web site, enter the URL for your home Web site or some other Web site. This field can't be left blank.

d. Application Type: Set this to Browser.

e. Callback URL: This must be a valid URL; however, it doesn't matter what URL you put here because the App Inventor Twitter component populates the correct value here. Just use the same URL you used for the Application Web site field. For developers creating Web or desktop integration, this is the return URL after the user authorizes.

f. Default Access Type: Set this to the Read/Write option.

You can leave the other fields blank.

Make sure you fill out the CAPTCHA at that bottom of the form — you know, the stretched-out twisted series of numbers and letters. The CAPTCHA is to make sure that you are a human filling out the form and not a robot.

4. When your application is registered, you see a page that displays your Consumer Secret and Consumer Key. Write these down and transfer them to the appropriate `Consumer-Key` and `ConsumerSecret` properties of the App Inventor Twitter component.

5. From the Design view of your TwiTorial project, click the Twitter component to make it active.

6. In the Properties column, copy the Consumer Key and Consumer Secret to the appropriately labeled property fields.

Your TwiTorial user interface should look like the one in Figure 10-2. Take special note of the dark horizontal line on VirtualScreen3 and the Consumer Key and Consumer Secret in the Twitter component properties.

Now on to building the logic and flow of your Twitter client. Try to keep in mind that this project is more to familiarize yourself with the options available for Twitter integration than it is to make yet another Twitter client. Many Android Twitter clients already do an incredible job. But is there an application that tweets the score and schedule of your PeeWee football league to all the parents? There can be, with the Twitter component and App Inventor.

Begin your Blocks Editor work by setting up the `Screen1.Intialize` event handler. The `.Initialize` event has quite a bit to do in the TwiTorial Application. It sets the color of the `Screen1.Background` to an appropriate Twitter blue. You are familiar by this point with the preset color blocks available in the Colors drawer on the Built-In tab of the Blocks Editor. However, those are all primary and rather non-nuanced colors. Android is capable of displaying millions of colors and App Inventor is capable of using them. All colors in App Inventor are set using numbers that indicate the channel value of the RGBA. The maximum value of each channel is 255. For the R or Red channel, a setting of 255 indicates maximum red. The same is true of all the channels: Red, Green, Blue, and Alpha.

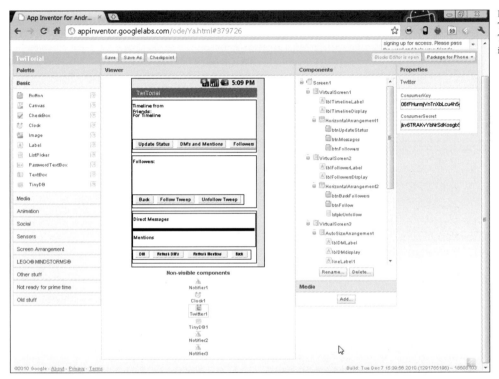

FIGURE 10-2:
The completed TwiTorial user interface

NOTE

You can read more about Android colors on the Android Developer Web site. Learn how to find the right number for the color you want at some of the App Inventor color mixing Web sites listed in the App Inventor Resources site at `https://sites.google.com/site/appinventorresources/home/tutorial-topics/colors`.

Use a custom number value to set the color of the Screen1 background to be a light blue color:

1. Typeblock the `Screen1.Initialize` event handler.

2. Typeblock the `Screen1.BackgroundColor [to]` block and snap it into the event handler.

3. Typeblock a number block with the number -7164945.0 and snap it into the `.BackgroundColor` block. You have to type the numbers first and then add the negative sign after the numbers are in the number block.

NOTE To test the color with your device attached, right click the `Screen1.BackgroundColor` block and click the Do It button. Your attached device's background color should turn the desired Twitter blue. A number, when plugged into a set color block, is interpreted as a color value.

The `Screen1.Initialize` event also has the logic for the AutoSizeArrangement in VirtualScreen1. You set the `Height` property of the AutoSizeArrangement to the Screen1 height minus the height of the HorizontalArrangement holding the buttons and navigation elements on VirtualScreen3.

1. Typeblock the `AutoSizeArrangement.Height [to]` block and snap it in below the `.BackgroundColor` block.

2. Typeblock a minus operation block and snap it into the `.Height` block.

3. Typeblock the `Screen1.Height` block and snap it into the first socket on the minus operation block.

4. Typeblock the `HorizontalArrangement3.Height` block and snap it into the second socket on the minus operation block.

NOTE The HorizontalArrangement you are using as a reference point should be the Horizontal Arrangement that contains your buttons on the VirtualScreen3. VirtualScreen3 should be your DM and Mentions screen if you created them in the order indicated previously.

These blocks then set the AutoSizeArrangement to maximize the screen space regardless of the screen size.

Twitter uses OAuth and you should have populated the Consumer Secret and Consumer Key in the Properties column in the Design view. Here I show you how to test to see whether any information is stored in TinyDB that would indicate that a user has previously authorized the TwiTorial application. If the user has previously started your application, they would have been prompted to enter their user name and password that process will authorize your application. If you find a token indicating authorization, your application loads that into a variable so it can be tested to see if authorization is current:

1. Define a variable and set its name to varIsAuth. Plug a blank text block into it.

   Your first set of blocks tests whether the TinyDB is empty. If it is not, it loads the contents of the TinyDB into a variable.

2. Typeblock an If block and snap it in below the AutoSizeArrangement in the Screen1.Initialize event handler.

3. Typeblock a not block and snap it into the test socket on the If block.

4. Typeblock an equals comparison operator and snap it into the not block.

5. Typeblock a TinyDB1.GetValue block and snap it into the first socket on the equals comparison operator.

6. Typeblock a text block and replace the default text with isauth. Snap it into the .GetValue block.

7. Typeblock a text block and remove the default text. Snap it into the second socket on the equals operator (=).

These blocks ask the question "Does the database contain a null value? If not, execute the following blocks."

1. Typeblock the varIsAuth [to] block and snap it into the If block.

2. Typeblock a TinyDB1.GetValue block and snap it into the varIsAuth block.

3. Typeblock a text block and replace the default text with isauth.

These blocks then load the contents stored under the isauth tag into the varIsAuth variable. If you attempt to load a null value from the database into a variable, you get an error that crashes the application. Although it may seem that you sometimes initialize a variable with a nothing or null value through these projects, a blank text block is a *zero-length* string and not a null value. In traditional programming, a zero-length string is frequently used as a placeholder for later data. You can think of it as a zero-length string being an empty CD but a null value being the absence of a CD.

Next, test the variable to see if it contains a true token to indicate that the application has been authorized. If it has, the application should enable the Clock1.Timer. If there is no true token, the Authorize method call needs to be called.

1. Typeblock an `IfElse` block and snap it into the `.Initialize` event handler under the `If` block.

2. Typeblock the `varIsAuth` block and snap it into the `test` socket on the `IfElse` block.

NOTE   You can use these kinds of tests if the contents of the variable is a `true` or `false` value.

If the variable is `true`, your app knows that the application has been authorized before and can get on with the business of being a Twitter client:

1. Typeblock the `Clock1.TimerEnabled` `[to]` and snap it into the `IfElse` block.

2. Typeblock a `true` block and snap it into the `.TimerEnabled` block.

3. Typeblock the `Twitter1.RequestFollowers` block and snap it in below the `.TimerEnabled` block. This requests the followers from the Twitter API, but you have to handle the actual data with the `.FollowersReceived` event handler.

4. Typeblock the `Screen1.Title` `[to]` block and snap it in below the `Twitter1. RequestFollowers`.

5. Typeblock a `make text` block and snap it into the `.Title` block.

6. Typeblock a `text` block and change the text to `TwiTorial, Logged in as:`. Make sure to leave a trailing space after the text.

7. Snap the `text` block into the `text` socket on the `make text` block.

8. Typeblock the `Twitter1.Username` block and snap it into the next `text` socket on the `make text` block. This block reports the user name of the authorized user. Thus the Title of Screen1 is changed to `TwiTorial, Logged in as: Jwtyler`, or whatever user name is authorized on the device.

9. Typeblock the `Twitter1.RequestFriendTimeline` and snap it in under the `Screen1` title block. This requests the status updates of your followed tweeps. The data is returned from the Twitter API and handled with the `Twitter1. FriendTimelineReceived` event handler.

If the `varIsAuth` indicates that the device has been authorized previously, the timer is enabled and a request for followers is sent. The `Screen1.Title` is set to indicate the authorized user.

If the varIsAuth does not contain true, the else-do socket is called, which in turn calls the authorization call from the Twitter component.

Typeblock the Twitter1.Authorize block and snap it into the else-do socket on the IfElse block.

Your completed Screen1.Initialize blocks should look like those in Figure 10-3.

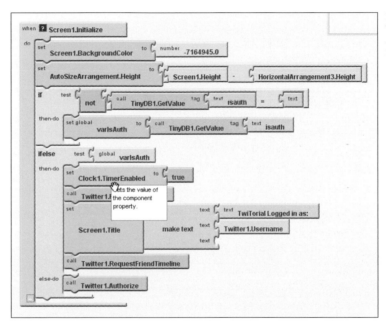

FIGURE 10-3:
The completed
Screen1.
Initialize blocks

The .Authorize block calls the Twitter OAuth Web site, where the user enters their user name and password to authorize your Twitter client. The authorization token is then recorded for your client.

When the .Authorize method is called and your client successfully authorizes, the .IsAuthorized event is generated. You use this event to record a true value to the TinyDB and the varIAuth. The .IsAuthorized event handler is also generated when you call the .CheckAuthorization method.

1. Typeblock the Twitter1.IsAuthorized event handler.

2. Typeblock the varIsAuth [to] block and snap it into the event handler. Snap a true block into the to socket.

3. Typeblock a `TinyDB1.StoreValue` block and snap it in next in the event handler.

4. Typeblock a `text` block and change the text to `isauth`. Snap it into the `tag` socket on the `.StoreValue` block.

5. Typeblock a `text` block and change the text to `true`. Snap the `true` block into the `valueToStore` socket on the `.StoreValue` block.

6. Typeblock the `Twitter1.RequestFriendTimeline` and snap it in the event handler under the `.StoreValue` block. This requests the status timeline after the user has been authorized by entering their username and password.

The `Clock1.Timer` component is the engine that keeps your Twitter client up-to-date. It is relatively simple, calling the `.RequestFriendTimeline` every few minutes.

1. Typeblock the `Clock1.Timer` event handler. Make sure the `TimerInterval` property is set to `120000` milliseconds in the Properties column of the Design view.

2. Typeblock the `Twitter1.RequestFriendTimeline` block and snap it into the event handler.

You have called both the timeline and followers data from the Twitter API, and now you need to handle the returning data events. However, for both of those events, you build a procedure to handle data returning from Twitter that is formatted as a list by the App Inventor Twitter component. This is very useful when you need to display data that comes in from Twitter. Almost all returned data from the Twitter API is a list. You save yourself lots of work by creating a subroutine that handles any inputted list and returns formatted data:

1. Typeblock a variable and rename it `varFormattedList`. Snap in a blank `text` block.

2. Typeblock a new `procedure with result` and rename it `procFormatAnyList`.

3. Typeblock a name block and rename it `List`. Snap the name block into the `arg` socket on the `procFormatAnyList`.

4. Typeblock the `varFormattedList` global variable block and snap it into the `return` socket at the bottom of the procedure.

Clear out the temporary formatting variable in preparation for formatting the incoming data passed to the procedure:

1. Typeblock the `varFormattedList` `[to]` block and snap it into the `procFormatAnyList`.

2. Typeblock a `text` block and sets its contents as blank. Snap it into the `varFormattedList` block.

Next use a `ForEach` block to format whatever list is passed to the procedure. Your `ForEach` block formats the text and writes it to the `varFormattedList` variable. When the `ForEach` has processed everything in the list, the `procFormatAnyList` returns the formatted data in the `varFormattedList` variable. It becomes more apparent how this works when you use it.

1. Typeblock a `ForEach` block and snap it into the `procFormatAnyList`.

2. Typeblock the `varFormattedList` value block and snap it into the `list` socket at the bottom of the `ForEach` block.

Make sure that the `variable` socket on the `ForEach` has a `name` block in it with a var **NOTE**
name. If you have previously placed `ForEach` blocks, or you have typeblocked the `ForEach`, the `ForEach` variable socket may not populate. If your `ForEach` block is created without a block in the `variable` socket, just typeblock a `name` block and change the name to var#, with the # being a sequential number.

---

3. Typeblock the `varFormattedList` `[to]` block and snap it into the `ForEach` block.

4. Typeblock a `make text` block and snap it into the `varFormattedList` block.

5. Typeblock the `varFormattedList` global block and snap it into the `text` socket on the `make text` block.

6. Typeblock a `text` block and change the default text to the newline character (\n).

7. Snap the newline character into the next `text` socket.

8. Typeblock the `var` value block and snap it into the next `text` socket.

9. Typeblock a new `text` block and change it into a newline character. Snap it in the next `text` socket.

10. Typeblock a `text` block and change the text to a line of separator characters like this: `----------`.

Your completed `procFormatAnyList` should look like Figure 10-4.

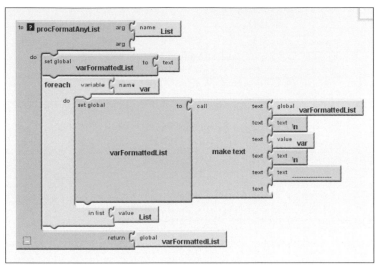

Now that you have a procedure for formatting incoming lists, you can start handling some of the Twitter components' received events.

The .FollowersReceived events not only populate the lblFollowersDisplay label, but are also used to populate the two ListPickers you have included in your interface. lstpkrSendDM allows users to select a follower to send a direct message to; lstpkrUnfollow selects a follower to unfollow.

1. Typeblock the Twitter1.FollowersReceived event handler. Notice the followers value that is generated for use in the event.

2. Typeblock the lstpkrSendDM.Elements [to] block and snap it into the event.

3. Typeblock the followers value block and snap it into the .Elements block.

4. Typeblock the lstpkrUnfollow.Elements [to] block and snap it in under the previous ListPicker block.

5. Typeblock another followers value block and snap it into the new .Elements block.

Now you use the procFormatAnyList to format the followers value list and then place that formatted list on the lblFollowersDisplay label.

1. Typeblock the lblFollowersDisplay.Text [to] and snap it in below the ListPicker element blocks.

2. Typeblock the `procFormatAnyList call` block and snap it into the `lblFollowersDisplay`.

3. Typeblock the `followers` value block and snap it into the `procFormatAnyList` block.

The data returned by the `.FollowersReceived` event is passed to the `procFormatAnyList` procedure and the returned formatted data is displayed in the label.

Your completed `.FollowersReceived` event should look like Figure 10-5.

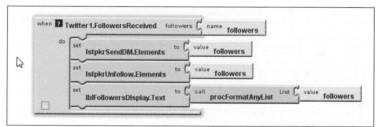

FIGURE 10-5:
The completed
Twitter1.
Followers
Received blocks

You do much the same thing with the `Twitter1.FriendTimelineReceived` event. However, because the data coming in with that event is likely to be a very long list, you need a method to truncate long lists. Use the `Add Items to List` block in conjunction with a series of `Select List Item` blocks to pull only the five most recent status updates from the incoming timeline list. You build a new list held in the `varTrimTimeline` and then pass that list to the `procFormatAnyList` to be formatted and then displayed in the timeline display label.

1. Define a new variable and name it `varTrimTimeline`.

2. Typeblock a `make a list` block and snap it into the `varTrimTimeline` variable.

3. Typeblock the `Twitter1.FriendTimelineReceived` event handler. Make sure there is a name block with the name set to "timeline" in the `timeline` socket.

First, clear anything in the `varTrimTimeline` variable from previous trim events:

1. Typeblock the `varTrimTimeline [to]` block and snap it into the event handler.

2. Typeblock a `make a list` block and snap it into the `varTrimTimeline` block.

3. Typeblock the `lblTimelineDisplay.Text [to]` block and snap it into the event handler.

4. Typeblock a `Make a List` block and snap it into the `lblTimelineDisplay.Text` block.

Next build an `IfElse` block that tests to see whether the incoming list is longer than five items. If it is longer than five items, the `IfElse` calls the truncating blocks in the then-do socket. If not, it just sends the list straight to the `procFormatAnyList` and then to the display label.

1. Typeblock an `IfElse` block and snap it in next in the event handler.

2. Typeblock a greater than (>) comparison block and snap it into the `text` socket on the `IfElse` block.

3. Typeblock a `Length of List` block and snap it into the first socket on the comparison operator. The `Length of List` block returns a number that is the number of items in the list snapped into the `list` socket.

4. Typeblock the `timeline` value block from the `.FriendTimelineReceived` event and snap it into the `Length of List` block.

5. Typeblock a numeral 5 number block and snap it in the second socket on the comparison operator.

Now build the trimmed timeline to use if the timeline list is longer than five items:

1. Typeblock an `Add Items to List` block and snap it into the then-do socket on the `IfElse` block.

2. Typeblock the `varTrimTimeline` global variable block into the `list` socket on the `Add Items to List` block.

3. Now typeblock a `Select List Item` block and copy it four times so that you have a total of five `Select List Item` blocks.

4. Plug each `Select List Item` block in an `item` socket on the `Add Items to List` block. It creates a new socket for each one used.

5. Typeblock a `timeline` value block that is generated when you create the `Twitter1.FriendTimelineReceived` event. Copy it and paste it five times to create a total of five `value timeline` blocks.

6. Snap each of the `timeline` blocks into the `list` sockets on the `Select List Item` blocks.

7. Create five number blocks with the numbers one through five on them so that you have 1, 2, 3, 4, and 5 blocks.

8. Snap each of the sequential blocks into the `Select List Items` blocks' `index` sockets. Starting with the number one block in the first `Select List Items` block, go down through the blocks snapping the next sequential number into the `index` sockets.

9. Typeblock the `lblTimelineDisplay.Text [to]` block and snap it in below the `Add Items to List` blocks.

10. Typeblock the `procFormatAnyList` procedure call and snap it into the `lblTimelineDisplay.Text` block.

11. Typeblock the `varTrimTimeline` global variable block and snap it into the `procFormatAnyList` procedure call.

Now create the `else-do` case blocks for the `IfElse` block. These blocks are called if the incoming list is less than five items. If you attempt to do the `trim` event on a list smaller than five items, it returns a nasty error and crashes the application:

1. Typeblock the `lblTimelineDisplay.Text [to]` block and snap it into the `else-do` socket on the `IfElse` block.

2. Typeblock the `procFormatAnyList` procedure call and snap it into the `text` block.

3. Typeblock the `timeline` value block and snap it into the procedure `list` socket.

Your completed `.FriendTimelineReceived` event handler should look like Figure 10-6.

FIGURE 10-6:
The completed
Twitter1.
FriendTimeline
Received blocks

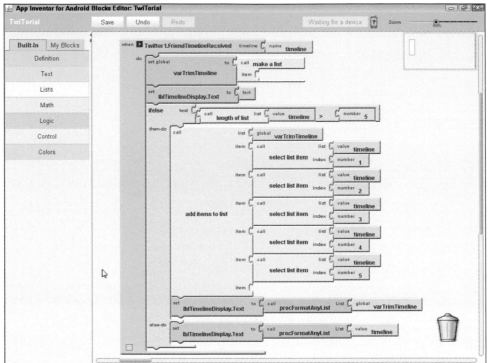

At this point, you have handled incoming followers and incoming timeline events. You have also handled timeline polling and text formatting. Now you need to start taking care of some of the button events on your user interface. The Update Status button on your VirtualScreen1 is used to send a status update to Twitter. To save screen real estate, you use a Notifier component with a text box pop-up instead of having a text box directly on the user interface. The Notifier component allows your user to input a message into a pop-up text box and then generates an event called .AfterText input. First you call the Notifier component with the button event, and then you handle the .AfterTextInput event for sending the status update.

1. Typeblock the btnUpdateStatus.Click event handler.

2. Typeblock the Notifier1.ShowTextDialog block. This is the block that pops up a text box for input.

3. Typeblock a text block and set its text to Enter   Status   update   <140 characters.

4. Snap the `text` block into the `message` socket on the `.ShowTextDialog` block.

5. Typeblock a `text` block and change its text to `Update Your Twitter status`.

6. Snap the `text` block into the `title` socket on the `.ShowTextDialog` block.

Now you need to handle the `.AfterTextInput` for Notifer1. Twitter status updates can be no more than 140 characters in length, so you need to test the user's input string to make sure it is within those parameters. You also need to test for a blank text field entry because that will cause an error:

1. Typeblock the `Notifier1.AfterTextInput` event handler. Make sure the `response` socket has a name block named `response` in it.

2. Typeblock an `IfElse` block and snap it into the event handler.

3. Typeblock an equals (=) comparison operation and snap it into the `test` socket on the `IfElse` block.

4. Typeblock the `response` value block from the `.AfterTextInput` event and snap it into the `length` block in the first socket on the comparison operator.

5. Typeblock a `text` block and set its contents blank.

6. Snap the blank `text` block into the second socket on the comparison operator.

7. Typeblock the `Notifier1.ShowAlert` block and snap it into the then-do socket on the `IfElse` block.

8. Typeblock a `text` block, set its text to `No Status Entered`, and snap it into the `Notifier1.ShowAlert` block.

If the user has entered some text into the text box, you need to test whether it is greater than the maximum 140 character limit and alert the user if it is. You use an `IfElse` block nested in the else-do socket:

1. Typeblock a second `IfElse` block and snap it into the else-do socket on the `IfElse` block already in the `.AfterTextInput` block.

2. Typeblock a greater than (>) comparison operator and snap it into the `test` socket of the new `IfElse` block.

3. Typeblock a `length` block and snap it in to the first socket on the comparison operator.

4. Typeblock the `response` value block and snap it into the first socket on the comparison operator.

5. Typeblock a number `140` block and snap it into the second socket on the comparison operator.

6. Typeblock the `Notifier1.ShowAlert` block and snap it into the `then-do` socket on the second nested `IfElse` block.

7. Typeblock a `text` block and set its text to `Status update must be less than 140 characters`.

8. Snap the `text` block into the `notice` socket on the `.ShowAlert` block.

9. Typeblock the `Twitter1.SetStatus` block and snap it into the `else-do` socket on the nested `IfElse` block.

10. Typeblock the `response` value block and snap it into the `status` socket on the `.SetStatus` block.

This last nested `IfElse` block checks to see whether the response from the user in the pop-up dialog box is greater than 140 characters and then appropriately either warns them or sends the status update to Twitter.

Your completed `btnUpdateStatus.Click` and `Notifier1.AfterTextInput` blocks should look like Figure 10-7.

The DMs and Messages buttons on the main screen are primarily navigation buttons in that they bring up VirtualScreen3, where the direct messages and mentions are displayed. However, they also make two Twitter API calls to prepare the display labels with content. The `.RequestDirectMessages` method and `.RequestMentions` method send a request to Twitter. When Twitter responds with the requested data, an event is generated and it is formatted as a list. You need to handle the `btnMessages.Click` event and then move on to handling the incoming data when a successful request is made.

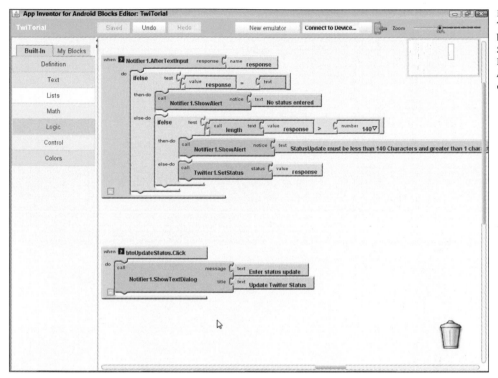

FIGURE 10-7:
The completed
btnUpdate
Status.Click and
Notifier1.
AfterTextInput
event handlers

> **NOTE**
>
> As mentioned at the beginning of this project, the Twitter Direct Messages functionality is currently broken in App Inventor. However, the issue is likely to be fixed very soon. I show you how to build the functionality and then use App Inventor's deactivate block function to keep the Direct Message request from being called. When the Google developer team announces a fix at `http://groups.google.com/group/app-inventor-announcements`, you can reactivate the blocks.

1. Typeblock the `btnMessages.Click` block.

2. Typeblock the `VirtualScreen1.Visible [to]` block and snap it into the event handler.

3. Typeblock and snap a `false` block in the `VirtualScreen` block.

4. Typeblock the `VirtualSceen3.Visible` [to], snap it in next, and set it with a `true` block.

Next make the calls to the Twitter API for the direct messages and mentions:

1. Typeblock the `Twitter1.RequestDirectMessages` block and snap it in next in the event handler. Right-click the `.RequestDirectMessages` block and select the Deactivate option from the right-click menu.

2. Typeblock the `Twitter1.RequestMentions` block and snap it in next.

Now you need to handle each of the events generated when the direct messages and mentions are returned from Twitter. Thanks to your `procFormatAnyList` procedure handling, the incoming lists are as simple as passing the incoming data to the procedure and placing the return result into the appropriate display label. Your `procFormatAnyList` procedure starts to pay off in spades at this point. Handling repetitive tasks with a subroutine like `procFormatAnyList` really speeds up development:

1. Typeblock the `Twitter1.DirectMessagesReceived` event handler. Make sure there is a name block snapped into the messages socket with the name set to messages.

2. Typeblock the `lblDMdisplay.Text` [to] block and snap it into the event handler.

3. Typeblock the `procFormatAnyList` procedure call and snap it into the text block.

4. Typeblock the messages value block into the List socket on the `procFormatAnyList` block.

5. Right-click the `Twitter1.DirectMessagesReceived` event handler and select the Deactivate option from the right-click menu. You can reactivate this event handler when the direct messages issue is resolved by Google.

Thanks to the work being done by your list processing factory, that's all you have to do. Now do the same for the .MentionsReceived event:

1. Typeblock the Twitter1.MentionsReceived event handler. Make sure a name block is snapped into the mentions socket with the name set to mentions.

2. Typeblock the lblMentionsDisplay.Text [to] block and snap it into the event handler.

3. Typeblock the prodFormatAnyList and snap it into the label block.

4. Typeblock the mentions value block and snap it into the list socket on the procedure call.

The btnMessages.Click, .DirectMessagesReceived, and .MentionsReceived events should look like the ones in Figure 10-8.

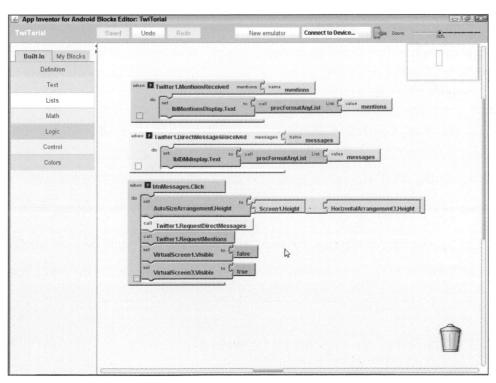

FIGURE 10-8: The btnMessages. Click, .Direct Messages Received, and .Mentions Received completed event handlers

Like the DMs and Messages button on VirtualScreen1, the Follower button on VirtualScreen1 is primarily a navigation button. It also sends a request to Twitter for a latest list of followers. As before, you handle the return data from Twitter in a separate event:

1. Typeblock the `btnFollowers.Click` event handler.

2. Typeblock the `VirtualScreen1.Visible` [to] block set it with a `false` block and snap it into the event handler.

3. Typeblock the `VirtualScreen2.Visible` [to] block, set it with a `true` block, and snap it into the event handler.

4. Typeblock the `Twitter1.RequestFollowers` block and snap it into the event handler.

You have already setup the `.FollowersReceived` event because it was called from the `Screen1.Initialize` block. You call the `.RequestFollowers` here to make sure that the locally displayed list is still fresh.

VirtualScreen2 has three buttons: Back, Follow, and Unfollow. The Back button is purely navigational, allowing your user to return to the main screen:

1. Typeblock the `btnBackFollowers.Click` event handler.

2. Typeblock the `VirtualScreen1.Visible` [to], snap it into the event handler, and set it with a `true` block.

3. Typeblock the `VirtualScreen2.Visible` [to] and snap it into the event handler. Set it with a `false` block.

The Follow button uses the same Notifier pop-up method we used previously. It allows your user to input a Twitter user's (or *tweep's*) name and follow that person:

1. Typeblock the `btnFollow.Click` event handler.

2. Typeblock the `Notifier2.ShowTextDialog` block and snap it into the event handler.

NOTE   This is the Notifier2 component. You are using separated Notifier components because you need unique `.AfterTextInput` event handlers.

3. Typeblock a text block, set the text to Enter User Name to Follow, and snap it into the message socket on the Notifier2 block.

4. Typeblock a text block, set the text to Follow Tweep, and snap it into the title socket on the Notifer2 block.

Now you need to handle the event generated by the user entering text in the pop-up dialog box:

1. Typeblock the Notifier2.AfterTextInput block. Make sure there is a name block snapped into the response socket and that it is named response1.

2. Typeblock the Twitter1. Follow block and snap it into the event.

3. Typeblock the response1 block that is generated by the event handler and snap it into the user socket on the Twitter1 block.

The Follow blocks should look like those in Figure 10-9.

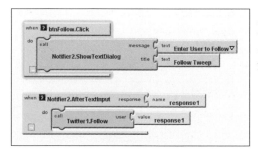

FIGURE 10-9:
The completed
btnFollow.Click
and Notifier1.
AfterTextInput
blocks

The Unfollow button is a ListPicker that is populated by the follower's returned event. Your logic blocks allow the user to select a user and unfollow them using the ListPicker. Because the elements are already populated, all you need to do is handle the .AfterPicking event to unfollow the selected user:

1. Typeblock the lstpkrUnfollow.AfterPicking event handler.

2. Typeblock the Twitter1.StopFollowing block and snap it into the event handler.

3. Typeblock the lstpkrUnfollow.Selection block and snap it into the user socket on the .StopFollowing block.

VirtualScreen3 has four buttons on it. Refresh DMs and Refresh Mentions are for refreshing the display. Their event handlers access the Twitter component `.RequestDirectMessages` and `.RequestMentions` methods. The Direct Message button is for sending a DM to another Twitter user. The Direct Message button uses the same method as you have used previously, except with a ListPicker to populate the user field. Tapping the DM button brings up a list of followers. After a follower is selected, a Notifier dialog box appears with a text box that allows the user to enter a text message. You then handle that text with the `.AfterTextInput` event. The Back button returns your user to the main screen.

First use the `.AfterPicking` event to call the notifier:

1. Typeblock the `lstpkrSendDM.AfterPicking` event handler.

2. Typeblock the `Notifier3.ShowTextDialog` block.

 NOTE   This is Notifier3. You do not want to create duplicate `.AfterTextInput` events from a previously used notifier. Duplicate events from the same component cause your application to error out and force close.

3. Typeblock a `text` block and replace the text with `Enter Text for DM`. Snap the text block into the `message` socket.

4. Typeblock a `text` block and replace the text with `Enter Message`. Snap it into the `title` socket.

Now you need to handle the `.AfterTextInput` event generated when your user enters some text and taps the OK button:

1. Typeblock the `Notifier3.AfterTextInput` event handler block. Make sure there is a `name` block snapped into the `response` socket and that its name is set to `response2`.

2. Typeblock the `Twitter1.DirectMessage` block and snap it into the event handler.

3. Typeblock the `lstpkrSendDM.Selection` block and snap it into the user socket.

4. Typeblock the `response2` value block and snap it into the `message` socket.

Your user taps the DM button and is presented with a list of followers. After the user selects one of the followers, the Notifier dialog box appears with a text field for text entry. The user types their DM text, taps OK, and sends the message to Twitter. Your completed Direct Message events should look like the ones in Figure 10-10.

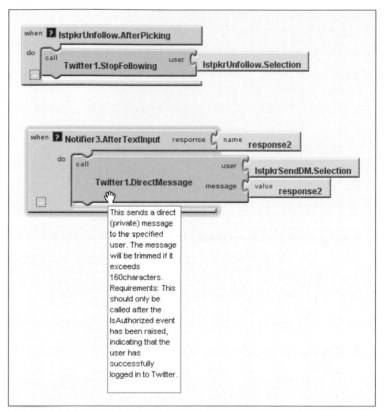

FIGURE 10-10:
The completed
lstpkrUnfollow.
AfterPicking and
Notifier3.
AfterTextInput
events

The Refresh buttons on VirtualScreen3 are fairly simple. They call the Twitter API to send the mentions and DMs to the device. This, of course, generates the .Received events that you have already handled. The Back button is strictly navigational and takes the user back to the main VirtualScreen1:

1. Typeblock the btnRefreshDM.Click event handler.

2. Typeblock the Twitter1.RequestDirectMessages and snap it in the event handler.

Next, handle the Mentions refresh:

1. Typeblock the btnRefreshMentions.Click event handler.

2. Typeblock the Twitter1.RequestMentions and snap it into the event handler.

The Back button is navigational and takes the user back to VirtualScreen1.

1. Typeblock the `btnBackDM.Click` event handler.

2. Typeblock the `VirtualScreen3.Visible [to]` block and snap it into the event handler. Set the block with a `false` block.

3. Typeblock the `VirtualScreen1.Visible [to]` and snap it in to the event handler next.

4. Set it with a `True` block.

With all of your events and all of your design goals met, it's time to package the TwiTorial application for your phone. If you generate any errors, look back over the figures and double-check your blocks. Refer to Chapter 1 for a refresher on how to package your application.

The TwiTorial application is large and has a lot of events going on. The primary purpose of developing the TwiTorial app is to help you understand the Twitter integration that is possible for App Inventor applications. As I mentioned earlier, you can use Twitter integration in many applications that are not primarily Twitter clients.

Part III

Part III contains some important reference materials, starting with the Blocks and Component Reference. This is not a comprehensive reference: Instead, it explains the most important and most complex blocks and components in App Inventor.

Appendix A tells you how to set up your phone and computer to get started with App Inventor, and Appendix B shows you how to set up your own TinyWebDB Service.

Blocks and Component Reference

THIS BLOCKS AND COMPONENT REFERENCE explains App Inventor's important blocks and components and those not used or explained in the main projects throughout this book. This is not a comprehensive reference. Refer to the index to discover where you can find more information on any component not referenced here. App Inventor is growing and improving all the time. Be sure and check out the online documentation for App Inventor at `http://appinventor.googlelabs.com/learn/reference/index.html`.

Built-In Blocks

All of the drawers for the built-in App Inventor blocks are located on the Built-In blocks tab of the Blocks Editor. The following is not a comprehensive list of drawers or blocks. Each drawer that is listed has a select few important or unreferenced blocks. Each block is named and then explained and demonstrated.

The Definitions drawer

The following blocks can be found in the Definitions drawer.

ProcedureWithResult

The `ProcedureWithResult` block allows you to create a subroutine of blocks to which you can pass data using arguments. You can then have blocks in the `ProcedureWithResult` process the data and return the output to the block that initially called the procedure. The arguments are optional.

When you create a `ProcedureWithResult`, a `call` block with the same name is created in the My Definitions drawer. The `call` block has sockets with names to match any `name` blocks placed into the `ProcedureWithResult` block.

When you place a name block in an `arg` socket on the `ProcedureWithResult`, a `value` block with the same name is placed in the My Definitions drawer. The `value` block always holds whatever is placed in the sockets on the `call` block.

In Figure R-1, two numbers are passed in the initial `call` block that calls the `EuclidsGCD` (Euclid's Greatest Common Divisor) procedure. The `EuclidsGCD` procedure processes the two numbers and returns the result to whatever the initial `call` block was plugged into. Euclid's Greatest Common Divisor is used in RSA encryption and other mathematic formulae.

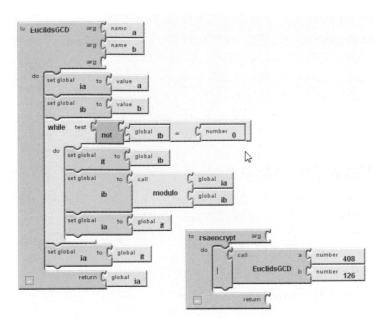

FIGURE R-1:
The Procedure
WithResult
blocks used to
calculate Euclid's
GCD algorithm

The ProcedureWithResult uses name blocks plugged into its arg sockets to create the call block with the required sockets. When a name block is placed into an arg socket, an accompanying value block is placed in the My Definitions drawer. The call block is placed in the My Definitions drawer with sockets that represent the name blocks. In the example in Figure R-1, you can see the a and b name blocks plugged into the arg sockets at the top of the procedure. Doing this creates value blocks that report the value of whatever was passed to the call block. In the example, the call block is given the value 108 for the a socket and 133 for the b socket. The value a and value b blocks used inside the procedure contain the numbers 108 and 133, respectively.

What ProcedureWithResult returns is determined by what is placed in the return socket at the bottom of the procedure. You can plug in a variable that holds the results of whatever was done in the procedure. You can also use any block that returns a value, such as a modulo math block and so on.

The ProcedureWithResult should be used anytime you want a subroutine to process data and return the result directly to where it is called. See Chapter 6 on the AlphaDroid project and Chapter 7 on the PunchDroid project for more information about using the procedure with result.

Procedure

A procedure allows you to create a subroutine of blocks to be executed when its `call` block is used in an application. You can also send data to the procedure using arguments if you do not need the procedure to return data. (See the previous section on `ProcedureWithResult`.) The arguments are optional.

When you create a procedure, a `call` block with the same name as the procedure is created in the My Definitions drawer. Whenever you want the blocks in the procedure executed, you place its `call` block.

When you place a name block in an `arg` socket, a `value` block with the same name is placed in the My Definitions drawer.

The example in Figure R-2 shows the use of a procedure with a single argument. The `call` block is passed the value of `true` or `false`. The `ResetGame` procedure executes one of the two cases in the `IfElse` block based on the contents of the `value` `WinState` block.

The `procedure` block can be used to execute a series of blocks with no argument, in which case the procedure can be used as a simple subroutine.

FIGURE R-2: The procedure block example

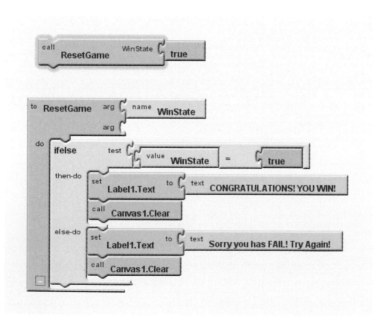

Variable

A variable is a storage and container mechanism. Text, numbers, and Boolean data can be placed in a variable to be retrieved later or acted on.

When a variable is created, it is said to be *defined*. In App Inventor, no distinction is made between the types of data stored in a variable. Text, numbers, and Boolean data can all be stored in any variable.

When defined, variables are given a unique name. Variables cannot be defined without having an initial value, even if that value is null. If you expect to use the variable for text, initialize it by placing an empty text box in it. If you expect to be using numbers in it, initialize it with a zero. Be sure that your initial value does not affect your program.

You can see the current value of a variable by right-clicking it and selecting the Watch option from the right-click menu.

When a variable is created, a set-to block is created in the My Definitions drawer. The set block is referred to with the word to in brackets in the project texts. Therefore, the variable defined with the name MyVariable would have the block MyVariable [to] as its set-to block. The [to] block allows the contents of the variable to be defined. Anything placed into the to socket on the MyVariable [to] block would be stored in the variable.

When a variable is created, a value block is created in the My Definitions drawer. The value block reports the contents of the variable wherever it is snapped in.

The example in Figure R-3 shows the variable MyVariable with its contents set to the text string My awesome data and a label with its text set with the MyVariable value block.

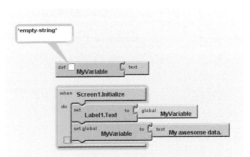

FIGURE R-3:
The variable
example blocks

Name

A name block is used whenever you need to give an argument or parameter a name (see Figure R-4). A name block can be dragged out from the Definitions drawer or typeblocked with name. The default text on the block is its name, which should be changed to represent whatever argument you are naming. See the "Procedure" and "ProcedureWithResult" sections for examples.

It is important to note that all arguments must have unique names across all names in App Inventor.

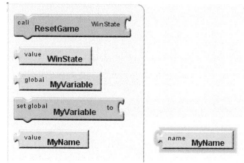

FIGURE R-4: The renamed name block and its associated value block

This block is a dummy `call` block. It allows to you call a procedure and have the procedure blocks execute, but ignore the return.

Taking the `ProcedureWithResult` used previously, if you wanted to populate the variables with a previous calculation's values but do not need the return value, you could use the `call` block for the EuclidsGCD in the dummy block, as shown in Figure R-5. All of the variables would be populated, so you could use them in other places. Without the dummy block, it's impossible to call the EuclidsGCD procedure on its own with no return.

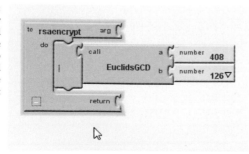

FIGURE R-5: The dummy block being used with a Procedure WithResult to execute and ignore the return result

The Text drawer

The following blocks can be found in the Text drawer.

Text

The basic `text` block allows you to place any length of text into a block, as shown in Figure R-6. That block plugged into any socket reports the string on the `text` block. `Text` blocks can be used to set the value of a variable, or to set the value of a `property` block. The default on a `text` block is the string `text`. Clicking the string or pressing Enter while the block is selected makes the block text editable.

FIGURE R-6:
A default text block and a text block with a very long string of text

Equals (=)

The `equals` block test whether two string values are equal. If they are equal, it returns `true`; if they are not equal, it returns `false`. The example in Figure R-7 shows the `equals` block testing text strings. This is the same block that is located in the Logic and Math drawer — it's been placed here for convenience. The values do not have to be text.

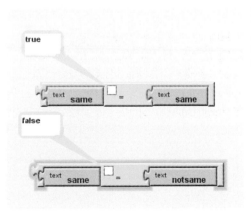

FIGURE R-7:
The equals block comparing text strings for sameness

Join

The join block joins two separate strings and creates one string from the two. It can also join text from variables to create strings of text from generated text. Figure R-8 shows a join block with the Watch function turned on. The join block is turning Two short strings and into one long string into Two short strings into one long string. The second example is doing the same thing, only using the contents of VariableA and VariableB.

FIGURE R-8:
The join block
being used to
join strings

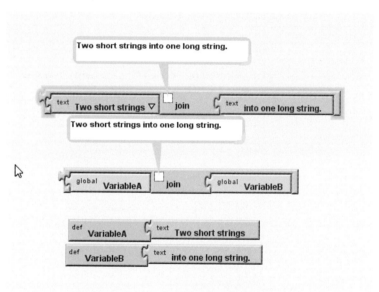

Text Less Than (<), Text Greater Than (>), and Text Equals (=)

These blocks are alphabetic arrangement blocks. They test whether a text string is greater or lesser than the compared block. If the strings start with the same letter, the shorter string is considered lesser. So, if you compared dog and dogs, as in Figure R-9, the dog string would be considered less alphabetically. Also, lowercase letters are considered lesser value.

The text= blocks compares two text strings for sameness. If two strings are the same, it returns true. The text= is slightly different than using a simple equals (=) comparison operator. An equals block returns the strings 0123 and 123 as equal, whereas, the text= block returns that those two strings are not equal because it evaluates the two strings as text.

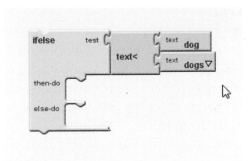

Trim

The trim block takes a string and removes any preceding or trailing spaces. The example in Figure R-10 shows a string with a bunch of spaces in front of and trailing it. The Watch bubble shows that the trim block has removed all the spaces and is returning only the string.

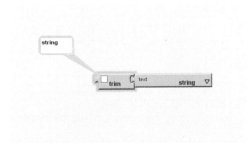

Upcase and Downcase

The upcase and downcase blocks put the entire plugged-in text string in either uppercase or lowercase, as shown in Figure R-11.

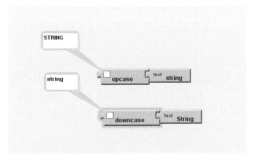

Starts at

The starts at block allows you to locate which index the first occurrence of a given character occurs at. Figure R-12 shows that the character y exists at the index (character number) 21. If the character does not exist in the string, the block returns 0.

FIGURE R-12:
The starts at
block finding the
index of y and z

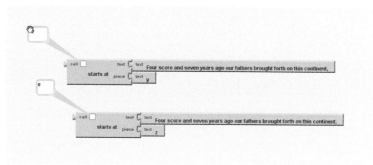

Contains

The contains block return true if the piece is located in the text. It returns true even if the piece is embedded.

Split at First

The Split at First block creates a two-element list whose two parts will consist of the string before the character in the at socket and the string after the character in the at socket. Notice in the Figure R-13 that the list that is created removes the first comma and includes the second comma in the second element of the list. You can see the split has occurred at the first comma.

Split at First of Any

The Split at First of Any block returns a two-element list based on the first occurrence of any of the characters in the list plugged into the at socket, as in Figure R-14. In the given example, because and exists before the comma, the two-element list has removed the and and included the comma in the second element. If you do not know which of a series of characters or strings may occur in the text you wish to split, include each possibility in the list, socketed in the at socket.

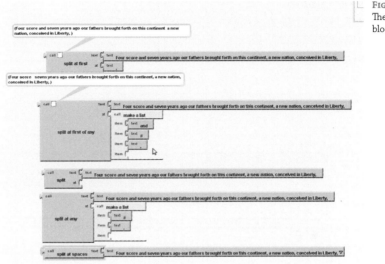

FIGURE R-13:
The Split at First
block

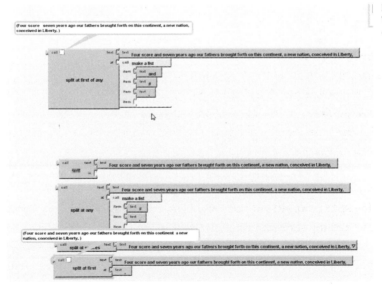

FIGURE R-14:
The split at first
of any block

Split at Any

The Split at Any block is similar to the previous block except the string is turned into a multi-element list based on all occurrences of the characters listed in the list attached at the at socket. In Figure R-15, you can see that the list created in the Watch bubble is three elements consisting of the segments of text divided by hash symbols and commas. This block, like all the split blocks, is very useful for parsing data.

FIGURE R-15:
The Split at Any block creating a list based on hash symbols and commas

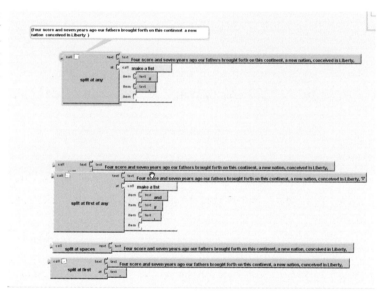

Split

The split block creates a multi-element list based on the character plugged into the at socket. You can see the way split works in Figure R-16. The list is created based on the comma character (,) and is seven elements long.

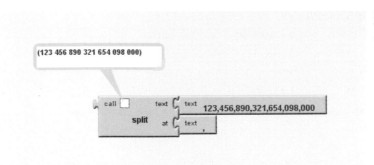

FIGURE R-16:
The split block
creates a list

Split at Spaces

The Split at Spaces block behaves exactly as the split block does, but splits only spaces, creating a multi-element list.

The Math drawer

The Math drawer contains typical math operations from simple to very complex. Most of the blocks are fairly self-explanatory, but you can hover your mouse cursor over any block to get a quick description of its function.

Random Integer

The Random Integer block returns a random number inclusive of the two numbers you indicate in the From and To sockets. This block can be very useful for providing some level of randomness to applications from games to semi-secure transactions or unique numbers for session identification.

Random Fraction

The Random Fraction call returns a decimal integer between 0 and 1. Again, this block is useful for pseudo randomization of events and math functions for your applications.

The Control drawer

The Control blocks have been used extensively throughout the projects to control the application flow and process. It is important that you understand and are able to use the control blocks. If you are unsure of a Control block's functionality, try creating an example for yourself that specifically uses the desired block.

While

The while block executes as long as the test condition is true.

 NOTE   You must be very careful when using the while block. Any condition that lasts for longer than about five seconds makes the Android operating system assume that your application has frozen and present the user with the force close option.

Close-Screen-with-Result

The Close-Screen-with-Result block closes the application with a result that can be picked up by another application. Your application closes gracefully with whatever you plug into the result socket. This can be used with the get start text block to close one program and open another, with some piece of information being passed between the two applications.

Get Start Text

The Get Start Text block is used in conjunction with the Close-Screen-with-Result block. This block retrieves whatever was in the result socket when the application closed.

For Range

The For Range block is an extremely useful block for performing a set of instructions a known or given number of times. The parameter variable is a local variable that increments each time the instructions are executed. This allows for local control of the number of iterations. In other words, you can use the variable to "break out" of the steps when the variable increments to a certain number. You can think of the For Range block in terms of the sentence "Do these things (do) for the number of times specified (start, end) and each time you do it, increment the number in variable by this number (step)."

My Blocks

The drawers on the My Blocks tab are created when you place a component in the Design view of App Inventor. Each drawer takes its name from the name it has in the Components column on the Design view. The component default name can be changed by selecting the component and clicking the Rename button in the Components column on the Design view. The Blocks drawer represents the name the component is given or its default name. In this reference, I refer to the components by their default names.

My Definitions

Any block created by defining one of the blocks in the Definition drawer on the Built-In tab creates blocks in the My Definitions drawer. Parameter and argument blocks also show up here when components such as the Canvas have blocks with parameters, arguments, or name blocks on the workspace. Variables create the blocks to set the value of the variable as well as blocks to report the value of the variable. Refer to the Definitions section of the Built-In blocks reference for any block that appears here.

Component blocks

Any component that is created by dragging it onto the Design view creates a drawer on the My Blocks tab. Each drawer has blocks that specifically affect that component. Some of the blocks are the same from component to component. The `property` blocks usually do the same thing from component to component. For instance, a `set Label1.Text to` block does the same thing as a `set Button1.Text to` block. The `Text` portion is the property that is being set. Through this section, I take the Button1 component as an example. Most blocks with the following properties have the same blocks but with their own names prepended. Remember that the important part to pay attention to throughout this section is the part after the dot (.), as in `Button1.Text`.

In this section, I won't address `property` blocks. Because this isn't a comprehensive reference, I explain only blocks that are unique or difficult.

Basic palette components

These are some of the components from the Basic palette.

Button1

The following are some of the important blocks for the Button component.

Button1.Click do

The `Button1.Click` block shown in Figure R-17 is an event handler. Anytime the event that this block describes occurs, the blocks contained in it execute.

The event is the click or tap on the component, known in this case as Button1. Button click events are used anytime you want something to occur or be activated by a user tapping a button. In the Figure R-17, when the `Button1.Click` event occurs, the event handler sets the variable to the value `My awesome data`.

FIGURE R-17:
The .Click event
handler

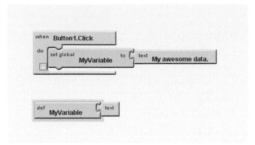

Button1.GotFocus do and Button1.LostFocus do

Most of the user interaction components have .GotFocus and .LostFocus events. The .GotFocus event handler is a special-case event handler. The only time the .GotFocus event occurs is when the button is highlighted with a trackball or D-pad (directional pad) and not pressed. In other words, this event cannot be used with any touch events. A button is not considered to have got or lost focus with a touch event. The Button1.GotFocus and Button1.LostFocus event handlers can be used when you know the button will be highlighted with use of a trackball or other non-touch pointer.

Component Button1

All components have the Component Button1 block. This is the component report block. It doesn't currently have much functionality. It can be used to check for sprite identity in collision events. In future App Inventor releases, it will be used to refer programmatically to a particular component. When watched, it returns a string such as com.google.dev-tools.simple.runtime.components.android.Button@44a69aa0. The alphanumeric characters after the @ symbol are the unique reference to the component used by the application manifest at build time. The application manifest is an XML file that tells the Android operating system what to expect from your application.

PasswordTextBox

The PasswordTextBox block is located in the Basic Palette and has many of the same properties as the Button and other Basic components.

The PasswordTextBox block behaves just like a normal text box and can be used in all the same ways. The difference is that the user cannot see entered text. A row of stars appears onscreen as you would expect in a password entry field.

Media palette components

These are some of the components from the Media palette that are important or not covered in previous project chapters.

Camera

The Camera component provides access to the camera functionality on your device. The two basic calls are `.Take Picture` and the `.AfterPicture` event handler.

Camera1.TakePicture

The `.TakePicture` call makes the camera interface active when it is called. The interface that is launched is external to your application. After the user snaps a picture, they are presented with the opportunity to approve the picture or retake it. If the user taps the OK button to approve the picture, the user is returned to the application and the `.AfterPicture` event is generated.

Camera1.AfterPicture

The `.AfterPicture` event is generated whenever the user approves a picture taken with the launched camera interface. The example in Figure R-18 shows the camera component being used to take a picture with a button click and then the `.AfterPicture` event being used to set the `Screen1.BackgroundImage` to the picture. The `image` parameter on the `.AfterPicture` event handler returns a path such as `tile:///mnt/sdcard/Pictures/app_inventor_1294364859308.jpg`. That path can be stored in a list, variable, or TinyDB and be referenced later. It can also be used to set the `image` property for any component with an `image` property.

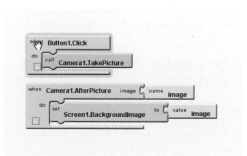

FIGURE R-18:
The Camera component example

ImagePicker

The ImagePicker component allows the user to select an image from the phones gallery. The image picker works much like the ListPicker component. It's appearance is that of a button. When it is tapped, it launches the device gallery. When the user taps an image in the gallery, the user is returned to the application and the `.AfterPicking` event is generated.

The path to the image that has been selected is returned in the `.ImagePath` block. The example in Figure R-19 shows the `.AfterPicking` event being used to set the Screen1 background image to the user-selected image using the `.ImagePath` block.

FIGURE R-19:
The ImagePicker
being used to set
a background
with the
ImagePicker

NOTE Be careful not to confuse the `ImagePicker.Image` and the `ImagePicker.ImagePath` blocks. The `.Image` block simply returns what the current value of the `Image` property is on the ImagePicker component. This is equivalent to the image on the ImagePicker button.

VideoPlayer

The VideoPlayer component works as you would expect, with a couple of caveats. The source for the video to be played must be uploaded to the Media column. The `.Start` and `.Pause` events perform as you would expect.

`.GetDuration` returns the total number of milliseconds that the video clip that is set in the source property. The video source can be set in the Properties column or via the `.Source` block. The `.GetDuration` time can then be used as a reference for using the `.SeekTo` block.

The `.SeekTo` block lets your user start play at a certain point in a video. The blocks can be used to play the video from a certain point forward. This can be used to have multiple clips in the same file. For instance, your uploaded file could contain a Start Game clip, a Win Game clip, and a Lose Game clip. You could play the desired clip by starting the video from the appropriate millisecond location using the .SeekTo block.

The .Completed event is triggered when the source video clip has finished playing.

The Social palette

The Social palette contains the components for interaction outside of your device such as phone calls, text messages, and Twitter. Many of the components have been covered in the project chapters. I don't cover the components used in a project here.

ContactPicker

The ContactPicker is not a picker in the same way as the ListPicker. The ContactPicker is more like the ImagePicker. The ContactPicker allows the user to pick a contact from the user's contacts. After this is done, the .AfterPicking event is generated and your application can do something programmatic with the .ContactName or .EmailAddress.

The .ContactName block contains the name from the user contact selection. The example shown in Figure R-20 shows the .ContactName and .EmailAddress being used to populate text fields. The same blocks could also be used to populate a series of text entries to e-mail text or call the ActivityStarter.

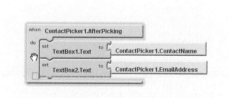

FIGURE R-20:
The
ContactPicker
in use

EmailPicker

The EmailPicker is not a picker like the ListPicker, ImagePicker, or even the ContactPicker. It acts more of a filter picker for e-mail addresses. It is an autocompletion text box. It behaves and can be used exactly like a text box that autocompletes e-mail addresses from the user's contacts, as shown in Figure R-21. A button or other event can then use the address from the EmailPicker.

NOTE   The EmailPicker is a fairly persnickety component. Many devices do not support its use and return a "This application uses functionality not supported by this phone" error. As with all components, test your application on the devices you intend to target.

PhoneCall

The PhoneCall component allows you to pass a number to the phone and have it dialed. The number can come from a PhoneNumberPicker or a number entered by the user.

The .MakePhoneCall block calls the phone functions of the Android device with whatever number is set in the .PhoneNumber property in the Properties column or in the .PhoneNumber property block.

Figure R-22 shows a PhoneNumberPicker.AfterPicking event block being used to call a number that has been selected by the user. First the .PhoneNumber block is used to set the number to be called and then the .MakeCall initiates the phone component on the device.

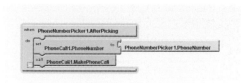

FIGURE R-22:
The PhoneCall
device used in
conjunction
with the
PhoneNumber
Picker

PhoneNumberPicker

The PhoneNumberPicker presents a list of phone numbers from the user's contacts. The list usually contains only numbers that exist in the user's Google contacts.

PhoneNumberPicker is finicky and you should test it well before using it. **NOTE**

The Sensors palette

The Sensors palette gives you access to all of the sensors on your device. If your device does not have one of the sensors, such as the accelerometer, your application generates an error.

AccelerometerSensor

The AccelerometerSensor reports the acceleration of the device in X/Y/Z axis. The AccelerometerSensor has two event handlers that can be used to trigger and execute blocks.

.AccelerationChanged is triggered whenever the device is moved. The event has three parameters: XAccel, YAccel, and ZAccel. Each of the parameters contains a value (in SI units of m/s2 or meters per second, squared) that measures the amount of movement.

XAccel has a positive value when the device is tilted to the right. It has a negative value when the device is tilted to the left. YAccel has a positive value when the bottom is up and a negative value when the top is up. ZAccel has a positive value when the device is face up and has a negative value when it is face down.

Figure R-23 shows a sprite having its heading changed based on the device being tilted. The XAccel is used to determine whether the right or left side of the device is being tilted.

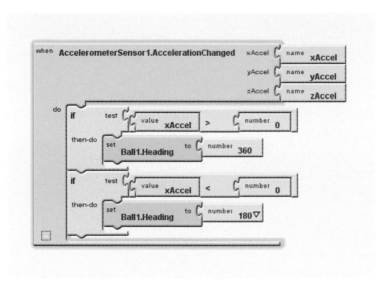

The `.Shaking` event handler is triggered when the device is shaken. It can be used as a trigger to execute blocks for your user interface.

Figure R-24 shows the `.Shaking` event handler being used to trigger a sound. Whenever the device is shaken, the contained blocks are executed.

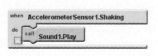

Orientation Sensor

The Orientation Sensor component has one event handler and two important method calls. The event handler can be used to measure the yaw, pitch, and roll of the device when it is changed. Yaw is the rotation around the vertical axis, pitch is the rotation around the horizontal axis and pitch is the angle from level.

The .OrientationChanged event handler is triggered whenever the device's roll, pitch, or yaw changes. The three parameters are updated with the numerical angle of the device with every change. You can use the orientation change to influence sprite movement or to record telemetry data. Figure R-25 shows the .OrientationChanged event being used to change the heading for a sprite.

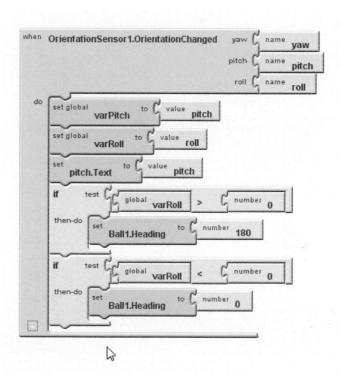

FIGURE R-25:
The .Orientation
Changed event

The .Magnitude block reports the severity or amount of angle that the device currently is registering with a numerical value between 0 and 1.0. Another way to think of this measurement is how fast a ball would roll down an incline of the same angle. Figure R-26 shows the .Magnitude being used to change the speed of a sprite.

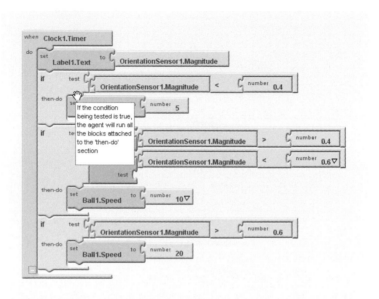

The .Angle block reports the angle of the phone, as shown in Figure R-27. The block reports in units of degrees the rotation of the phone:

○ 270 degrees indicates the top of the phone is angled directly up.

○ 0 or 360 degrees indicates the top of the phone is angled directly right.

○ 180 degrees indicates the top of the phone is angled to directly to the left.

○ 90 degrees indicates the top of the phone is angled directly down.

The example in Figure R-27 only shows when the device is pointed in a direction that is not up. Showing "up" would require further logic, cutting the degrees into smaller segments.

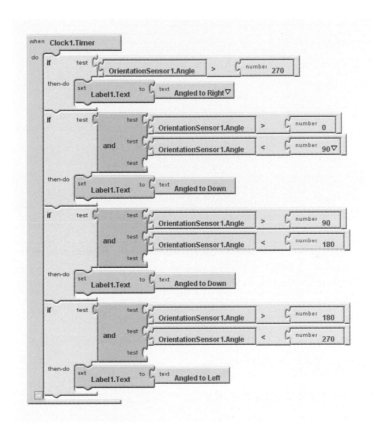

FIGURE R-27:
The .Angle block
being used to
report the
direction of the
top of the phone

The Lego Mindstorms palette

The Mindstorms palette provides direct access to the Lego Mindstorms robots through the Bluetooth client. The components and blocks usage are well beyond the scope of this book. To use this palette, you need a Bluetooth client for communication as a part of your project. Refer to the Google documentation and the App Inventor forum for examples on using the Mindstorms blocks to control your Lego robot. You can find reference materials and help at the following links:

```
http://appinventor.googlelabs.com/learn/reference/components/
  legomindstorms.html
http://appinventor.googlelabs.com/forum/index.html
```

The Other Stuff palette

The Other Stuff palette is the catch-all palette for components that don't fit neatly in the other palettes.

SpeechRecognizer

The SpeechRecognizer uses Google's network-dependent voice-to-text system to transcribe a user's vocal input. The component requires network connectivity to function.

The .GetText call initiates the Android speech component, which prompts the user for speech input and then sends the sound clip to Google's speech-to-text system. The resulting text is sent back to the device and the .AfterGettingText event is triggered.

The .AfterGettingText event is triggered when the Google servers send back the text from the speech input. The result parameter contains the text for use in your application. The .BeforeGettingText is called after the .GetText call is made but before the .AfterGettingText is triggered by the returning text.

Figure R-28 shows a button calling the speech components and a label being populated with a text result.

FIGURE R-28:
Speech
recognition

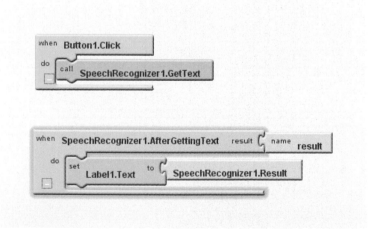

TextToSpeech

The TextToSpeech component turns any string into audible text. The speech is based on the Android device's Speech settings. However, you can set the language and country using the .Country and .Language blocks.

The .Speak block takes whatever text is input in the message socket and turns it into audible spoken words. You can place either a text block or input from a text box field into the message socket.

The .BeforeSpeaking event is called after the .Speak block but before the .AfterSpeaking block. You can use it to execute blocks before the .AfterSpeaking event occurs.

The .AfterSpeaking event is triggered after the text has been rendered to speech.

The example in Figure R-29 shows a button being used to call the .Speak block to speak text that has been entered into a text box. The .AfterSpeaking event then calls a procedure to reset the application.

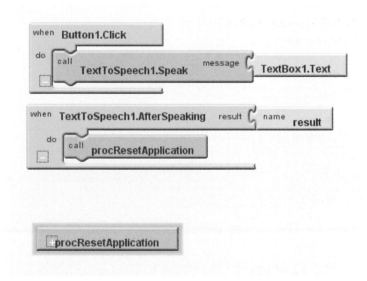

FIGURE R-29:
The TextToSpeech blocks

Not Ready for Prime Time Palette

The Not Ready for Prime Time components are components whose functionality is currently limited, in testing or has incomplete documentation. When you use a component from this palette you should expect some difficulty and perhaps more bugs and errors. The App Inventor development team is moving components from the Not Ready for Prime Time to their own palettes on a regular basis. While the component is still in testing it will be here in this palette.

GameClient

The GameClient component is an experimental component that is not currently fully functional. Some power users from the Google App Inventor forum are experimenting with it currently.

It was designed and created by an MIT student as a part of a thesis. You can find the thesis by searching the Google App Inventor documentation and forum at `http://appinventor.googlelabs.com/learn/reference/components/notready.html` and `http://appinventor.googlelabs.com/forum/index.html`.

SoundRecorder

The SoundRecorder allows your application to record sound clips to the SD card. It also generates events to allow you execute blocks during and after recording.

The `.Start` block starts recording to the SD card. It also generates the `.StartedRecording` event handler.

The `.Stop` block stops the recording and generates the `.StoppedRecording` and the `AfterSoundRecorded` events.

`.AfterSoundRecorded` event handler has one parameter, `sound`, which contains the full path to the recorded sound. This event can be used to store a local listing referring to the sound or handling the sound. You do not have to do anything with the `.AfterSoundRecorded` event because the sound is written to the sound card regardless of what is done in the generated events.

`.StoppedRecording` is generated when recording stops and allows blocks to be executed immediately when recording stops. `.StartedRecording` is generated when the recorder is invoked and allows blocks to be executed while the sound is being recorded.

The example in Figure R-30 shows the SoundRecorder component being used to record a sound with a SoundPlayer component source set to the newly recorded sound. The picture blocks follow this logic.

When Button1 is pressed, if the varRecording variable is true, the .Stop block is called and the variable is set to False. If the varRecording is false, the .Start block is called to start recording and the varRecording is set to true.

In Figure R-30, the .StartedRecording and StoppedRecording event handlers are shown being used to change the color of the record/Button1 button during recording and when recording is stopped.

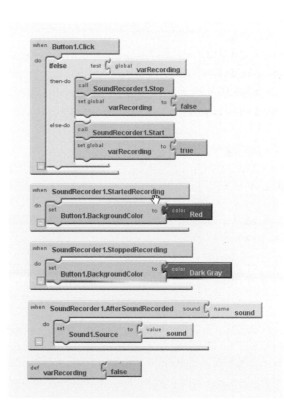

FIGURE R-30:
The
SoundRecorder
component used
to create a
simple recording
application

Appendix A
Setting Up Your Phone and Computer

BOTH YOUR PHONE and your computer require some prep work before you can get started using App Inventor. None of the requirements are unusual or exotic, but you do have to make sure that everything is set up before you jump into making your first application. You need to install Java and the App Inventor Extras and verify both are working before you can get started.

These steps are all easy, and you don't have to have any special knowledge or extra nerd cred to be able to get started. I show you how to set up your computer with the correct version of the Java software that App Inventor requires. I also show you how to set up the App Inventor specifics you need to connect your phone to your computer and run App Inventor.

I show you how to set each item up and test it to make sure it is where it needs to be and is working.

Setting Up Your Phone

Your phone needs to have three main settings enabled to work with App Inventor. It needs to be in Debug mode to allow the Android Debug Bridge (ADB, more on it later) to detect and communicate with the phone. Your phone won't communicate with App Inventor without the Debug mode turned on.

Your phone also needs to be told to trust external application sources. By default, Android only allows applications to be installed that come from the Android App Market. You need to tell your phone, "It's okay, you can trust me. Really." This is a setting that you can turn on while working with App Inventor and then turn back off when you are no longer connected to App Inventor.

You also need to set the phone to not turn off the screen while you are programming it with App Inventor. If the screen goes to sleep, Android stops whatever app is currently running and puts it in a paused state. If that happens, your phone loses contact with App Inventor and you have to reconnect it.

These last two settings, the screen timeout and external trust, are two settings you will want to change back to their default settings when your phone is not connected to your computer. If you leave the screen timeout off, it has a very negative effect on your phone's battery life. If the screen stays on all the time unless you explicitly turn it off, you can cut your battery life in half. You should also disable the Trust External Installation Locations setting to protect your phone from accidently installing an application from an untrusted location such as a Web link. To put your phone in Debug mode and keep it awake, follow these steps:

1. From your Home screen, tap the Menu button or hotspot on your phone to bring up the pop-up menu at the bottom of your screen. The Menu button is usually near the Home button or icon.

2. Tap the Settings button.

3. Tap Applications in the list that appears.

4. Tap Development in the list that appears.

5. Tap the OK button on the verification notifier, if you get one.

6. Tap the check box next to USB Debugging to select it.

7. Tap the check box next to Stay Awake to select it.

8. Tap the Home button or hotspot on your phone to return to your Home screen.

When you connect your phone to your computer with a USB cable, you should see two icons in the notification bar at the top of the phone, as shown in Figure A-1. These are the Debug and USB connected icons.

FIGURE A-1:
The USB and
Debug icons

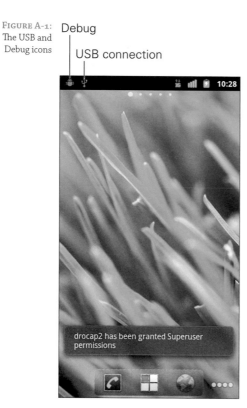

Do *not* mount your SD card so that it is accessible as a storage drive on your computer. App Inventor has to have access to the SD card to store pictures and other media. If your computer sees the SD card as a drive that you can access, you will need to change the USB mode of your phone. (There are a number of different USB modes, depending on the manufacture of your handset.) Some Android phones such as the original Droid from Motorola only have two modes: a USB Storage mode and a Not USB Storage mode. Other phones, such as the Samsung Galaxy S and some HTC phones, have four different modes. You may need to experiment with each mode to see which mode does *not* mount your SD card as external storage and therefore works with App Inventor. On most phones, you can access the storage options by selecting the USB Connected icon from the notification bar on your phone, which brings up the USB Options screen. (See Figure A-2.) Many phones, such as the DroidX and HTC Desire, have a Charge Only mode. If your phone has a Charge Only mode available, it will likely work with App Inventor.

The SD card must *not* be available to your computer as a storage option.

If there is no USB symbol at the top of the phone screen as shown in Figure A-1, your phone is likely not physically connected to the computer. Check the cable where it enters the phone and where it enters the computer to make sure it's tightly connected. Try a new USB port on your computer or a USB hub. If you still don't get the USB icon in the notification bar of your phone, try a different USB cable. It is generally a good idea to connect directly to a USB port on your computer. Hubs and especially unpowered hubs are notorious for causing phone connection issues.

Installing Java on Your Computer

Java is a programming language that, among many other things, allows developers to create programs that run on your local computer but are hosted on a Web site. You need to have the latest version of Java installed on your machine. Here's a quick look at what I'm going to show you how to do:

1. Go to the Java Web site and check whether you have the latest version of Java.

2. If you don't, install the latest version of Java.

3. Check that the Java Web Start programs launch correctly.

4. Optimize your browser for Web Start programs.

TIP   Linux users need to have the Sun Java packages installed. App Inventor doesn't work with the OpenJDK that most Linux distributions come with by default.

Even if you are absolutely certain that you have the latest Java installed and that it works exactly as it should, I would still complete at least the first three steps to verify that you have the recommended Java version installed and then jump forward to the Web Start test.

1. Open a standards-compliant Internet browser. Internet Explorer 7 or later is standards-compliant enough. Google's Chrome Web browser or Apple's Safari is a good choice as well. You can use most popular Internet Web browsers to access and use App Inventor.

2. Go to the Java Web site at www.java.com.

3. Click the Do I Have Java? link. Clicking this link takes you to a Java verification page.

   Mac users should note that Sun's Java page directs them to use their Mac's Software Update feature to verify that they have the most recent version — they should skip Steps 4 and 5 and run Software Update (accessible under the menu). If Software Update doesn't list Java as an item to update, you have the current version; otherwise, have Software Update update your Java software by selecting the check box next to Java and clicking the Update button.

4. Click the Verify Java Version button. This button starts a Java applet (a little program that runs inside your browser) that checks to see whether you have the latest version of Java installed.

   One of two things will happen:

   ○ If Java is *not* installed on your computer, your browser prompts you to install the Java plug-in. You can either follow your browser prompts or move on to manually installing Java.

○ If Java is installed on your computer, the browser reports that you have the recommended version or prompts you to upgrade.

To manually install Java on your computer, follow the steps for the browser you are using.

Chrome

To install Java on a computer using Chrome, do the following:

1. Go to the Java Web site at www.java.com.

2. Click the Free Java Download button.

3. Click the Agree and Start Download button. Your browser prompts you to save the Java installation program.

4. Run the Java installation program by double-clicking on the completed download at the bottom of your Chrome browser window. Alternatively, you can press Ctrl+J to bring up all your recent downloads.

5. When the Java setup program starts, click the install button.

6. When the setup is complete, close the Java setup program.

Mozilla Firefox

To install Java on a computer using Mozilla Firefox, do the following:

1. Go to the Java Web site at www.java.com.

2. Click the Free Java Download button.

3. Click the Agree and Install button. If you don't, the download can't continue.

4. Press Ctrl+J to bring up the Downloaded Files window.

5. Double-click the jxpiinstall.exe file.

6. Click the Run button on the Open File – Security Warning that pops up.

7. Click the Install button when the Java setup program starts. Don't change the default installation path.

8. When the Setup is complete, close the Java setup program.

Internet Explorer

To install Java on a computer using IE, do the following:

1. Go to the Java Web site at www.java.com.

2. Click the Free Java Download button.

3. Click the Agree and Install button (after thoroughly reading the License Agreement, of course!).

4. Click the Run button. A security dialog box pops up, asking, "Do you want to run or save this file?" Click the Run button.

5. When your download completes, the Java setup program runs automatically. Click the Install button that appears.

6. Close the Java setup program. When the setup completes, close the Java setup program.

Testing Java Web Start

Java is the language in which App Inventor is written. You need to test to make sure that your browser can detect and run Java standalone programs that are started from a Web page. These kinds of programs are called Java Web Start Programs. These Web Start programs consist of a file with a .JNLP extension that runs after download.

Your browser could do three possible things when you click on a link to start a Java Web Start program. How your browser acts when you click a link to start a Java Web Start program depends on how your browser is currently set up. Some of your browser's behavior is based on the particular browser you are using. How you have answered questions about downloads and running programs from the Internet determines how your browser treats these files as well. So, depending on the settings in your browser, it could do one of the following:

○ **Prompt you for a location to download a file.** After finishing downloading, your computer does absolutely nothing. This is usually true if you download a Java Web Start program via Chrome. Chrome users typically end up sitting staring at the screen for a while, patiently waiting for something to happen, and then clicking to try it again. When you repeatedly click a Java Web Start button such as the Open Blocks Editor button, your browser downloads another .JNLP file after prompting you for a location to store it. This can go on until you grow weary of playing this game and give up. Finding where the .JNLP file was downloaded and double-clicking it starts the program and helps stop the shouting at the computer that inevitably results.

○ **Automatically download the file to a default download location and then go on to do absolutely nothing.** Repeated clicking of the Java Web Start button just downloads another .JNLP file to the default download location. For Chrome and Mac users, the default download location is the Downloads folder under your user directory. In Windows Vista and Windows 7, you can find the default downloads directory by clicking your user name on the Start menu.

○ **Download the file and then execute it.** This is the desired behavior.

In the next section, I show you how to test which of the previous behaviors your computer is set up for and correct any bad behavior. If Java Web Start programs open just fine, you can skip the "Testing your Java Web Start behavior" section.

Testing your Java Web Start behavior

In these steps, you test your browser and computer's response to a Java Web Start request. If the Java Web Start applications do not start as desired, I show you how to correct the behavior.

1. Type `www.oracle.com/technetwork/java/demos-nojavascript-137100.html` into your browser to go to the Java Web Start demo and test page.

2. Click the first Java Web Start demo. The first demo is the Draw application, but any Java Web Start on this page will do. Your browser performs one of the three previously mentioned behaviors.

3. If your browser just downloads the file (most likely), you can manually launch the file:

   • Chrome: Press Ctrl+J keys (Shift+⌘+J in Chrome on a Mac) to bring up a list of downloaded files. Click the .JNLP file in the list.

   • Firefox: Press Ctrl+J (⌘+J on a Mac) to bring up a list of downloaded files. Double-click the .JNLP file.

   • Safari: Press Ctrl+L (Option key+⌘+L on a Mac) to bring up a list of downloaded files. Double-click the .JNLP file.

- Internet Explorer: IE is likely to just automatically launch .JNLP files with little or no fuss. If the JNLP does not automatically launch, click the Run option when prompted by Internet Explorer.

At this point, the selected Java Web Start program should be running. If you get an error or the .JNLP does not launch, flip ahead to "Troubleshooting Your Java installation" later in this chapter. You cannot use App Inventor until Java Web Start is functioning correctly.

To make your browser behave the way it should, you need to change the settings so that you are not prompted for a download location and so the .JNLP is started automatically after download. You are most likely to need to change these settings for Chrome and Firefox.

Follow the steps appropriate for your browser.

Chrome

These steps show you how to make Chrome to automatically open the .JNLP files from a Java Web Start application:

1. Open the Chrome browser options by clicking the Wrench icon in the upper right corner of your browser window, and then selecting Options (Preferences on the Mac) in the drop-down list.

2. Click the Under the Hood tab in the Google Chrome Options dialog box that appears.

3. Scroll down and deselect the Ask Where to Save Each File Before Downloading check box.

4. Click the Clear Auto-Opening Settings button.

5. Close the Google Chrome Browser Options dialog box.

6. Point your browser to `www.oracle.com/technetwork/java/demos-nojava script-137100.html`.

7. Click one of the Java Web Start demo applications such as the Draw program that is first in the list.

   The .JNLP should download. You will see the download at the bottom of your browser window.

8. Click the drop-down arrow beside the downloaded file at the bottom of your browser window, as shown in Figure A-3.

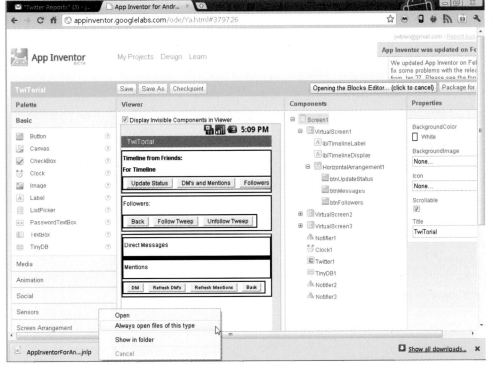

FIGURE A-3:
Downloaded
files pop up at
the bottom of
the Chrome
browser

9. Click the Always Open Files of This Type option.

10. Click on one of the Java Web Start demos again. The file should download and start
    automatically.

Firefox

The following steps guide you through setting up Firefox to auto-open the .JNLP files.

1. Click the Tools menu item.

2. Select Options from the drop-down list.

3. Click the General tab.

4. Click the Save Files To radio button. Make sure you know where the folder in the
   Download To dialog box is located. Alternatively, you could select a folder for Firefox
   to save all downloads by default.

5. Click the Applications tab.

6. Scroll down to JNLP File and verify that the Action column says Use Java Web Start Launcher. If it doesn't, click on the drop-down arrow and select Java Web Start Launcher. If the Java Web Start Launcher is not an option, you need to install Java from Firefox again.

7. Close the Options window.

8. Click on one of the Java Web Start demos. The file should now download. You may be presented with a dialog box asking you to verify that you wish to open the .JNLP. See Figure A-4. You may need to select and then deselect the Do This Automatically from Now On check box and then click OK.

FIGURE A-4: Select and deselect the Do This Automatically from Now On check box

Safari

The following steps guide you through setting up Safari to auto-open the .JNLP files.

1. Open Safari Preferences by choosing Preferences from the Safari menu or by pressing ⌘+, (comma) on the Mac or Ctrl+, (comma) in Windows.

2. Select the General tab if it's not already selected.

3. Select the Open Safe Files after Downloading check box.

Internet Explorer

Internet Explorer should not require any changes to its settings after Java is installed. You may be prompted to open or save the .JNLP. Click Open.

Troubleshooting your Java installation

If you get unexplained errors or your browsers asks what program to use to open .JNLP files, you need to reinstall Java. Uninstall Java from your computer's Control Panel. Here's how:

○ Windows XP: Select the Add Remove Programs component from the Control Panel, located on the Start menu. Find Java in the list of installed programs and uninstall it.

○ Windows Vista/7: Open the Control Panel and Select the Programs and Features component. Find Java in the list of installed programs and uninstall it.

Advanced troubleshooting requires some knowledge of Java. If you are still having trouble, mosey over to the App Inventor Getting Started Google Group at `http://appinventor.googlelabs.com/forum/` and ask for some help. Someone there may ask you to copy the contents of the Java console for error troubleshooting. Follow these steps to get the Java console open:

1. Click the Start button.

2. Click Control Panel.

3. If you're using Windows XP or Vista, click Classic View.

4. Double-click the Java icon.

5. Click the Advanced tab.

6. Expand the second category, Java Console. See Figure A-5.

7. Click Show Console.

8. When you try to launch any Web Start program such as the App Inventor Block Editor, a console window opens, as shown in Figure A-6. You can copy and paste text from that console window to assist anyone trying to help you with troubleshooting.

FIGURE A-5:
Enabling the
Java console for
troubleshooting

FIGURE A-6:
The Java console
after loading an
App Inventor
project into the
Blocks Editor

Installing the App Inventor Extras

The App Inventor Extras are a bundle of necessary USB drivers and software to make your computer aware of and connect to your phone. Many Android phones work with the USB drivers included with the Extras. When you get to setting up your phone and connecting it, you will be using the USB drivers included with the Extras or specialized drivers from your handset's manufacturer. The Extras include the Emulator, which allows you to create and test apps without having an Android phone. It also includes a piece of software called Android Debug Bridge, or ADB. ADB allows your computer to access and send data and commands to and from your connected Android phone. I tell you a little bit more about ADB and its uses later in this chapter.

To download the App Inventor Extras, point your browser to `http://appinventor.googlelabs.com/learn/setup/setupwindows.html`. Click on the Download link to download the installer. Save the installer where you can locate it. After downloading, run the installer.

1. Click Next when the installer starts.

2. Click I Agree on the License Agreement dialog box. (Unless of course you do not agree, in which case, you can't use the Extras.)

3. Click Next. Do not change the path of the extras. Make a note where you are installing them: You will need to navigate there if you need to troubleshoot your device connection.

4. Click Install.

5. Close the Extras installer.

After you have the App Inventor Extras installed, it is time to test them and make sure your phone can connect.

NOTE

Install packages for Linux can be downloaded at `http://appinventor.googlelabs.com/learn/setup/setuplinux.html`.

Install packages for Mac users can be downloaded at `http://appinventor.googlelabs.com/learn/setup/setupmac.html`.

Working with ADB (Android Debug Bridge)

The ADB is the core piece of software that lets your computer and your phone have a two-way conversation. ADB sends commands and files to your phone from App Inventor. ADB also allows you to test to see whether your phone is "visible" to your computer.

ADB is command-line software. That means that you can't just double-click it from Windows Explorer, the Mac Finder, or your Linux GUI and use it with a pretty point-and-click interface. To use ADB, you have to go back to your trusty DOS, Terminal, or Linux command-line skills, navigate to the App Inventor Extras install directory, and run ADB with some extra options attached.

First, check to see if it is there:

1. Open Windows Explorer or switch to the Mac Finder.

2. Expand the C:\ in the navigation tree on the left. See Figure A-7. On a Mac, navigate to the AppInventor folder inside your Applications folder and verify that the command-line tools are in the commands-for-AppInventor subfolder and skip the rest of these steps.

FIGURE A-7: Navigating to the Windows ADB and App Inventor files

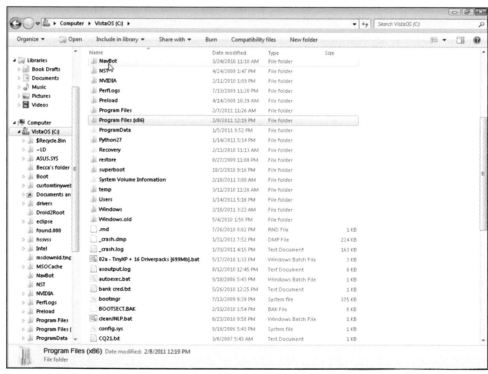

3. Expand the Program Files folder. You may need to click the Show Files in this Folder link. If you are using 64-bit Windows, you see a Program Files (x86) folder. Expand this folder instead of the Program Files folder. Remember that you saw the x86 — you'll need this information later.

4. Expand the App Inventor folder.

5. Expand the commands-for-appinventor folder. Verify that the folder contains the required files. See Figure A-8.

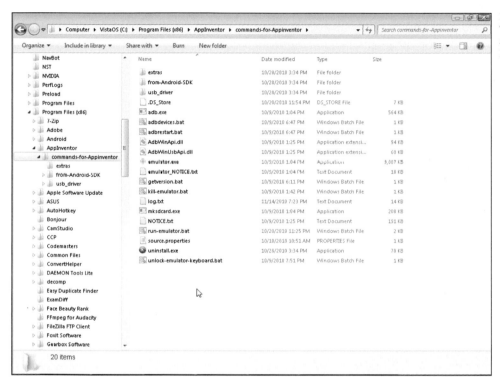

FIGURE A-8-:
The ADB.EXE
and App
Inventor Extras

If everything is well and you can see all the App Inventor Extras in that folder, you can move on to the really fun command-line stuff. First you have to open a command prompt and navigate to the App Inventor Extras directory. You can use these steps to return to the ADB directory for troubleshooting your phone's connection or applications later if you need to.

Opening a command prompt and navigating to App Inventor Extras

Now that you have verified ADB is installed, the following are optional steps for troubleshooting the connection between your Android device and App Inventor. If you have successfully connected to the App Inventor Blocks Editor, these steps are not necessary. Any connection issue or advanced application troubleshooting will require you to follow these steps to use the ADB for troubleshooting.

On Windows:

1. Press the Windows key (it's the one with the little Windows symbol) and the R key simultaneously. This brings up a Run box.

2. Type cmd in the Run box and press Enter. This launches a command prompt window, as shown in Figure A-9.

FIGURE A-9:
Navigating the
command
prompt to the
Commands for
AppInventor
directory

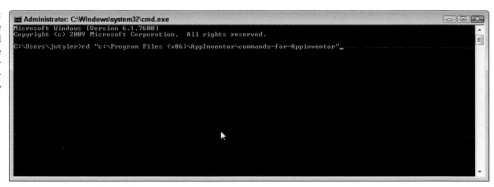

3. Type the following exactly as written, including quotes:

   ```
   Cd "c:\Program Files\AppInventor\commands-for-AppInventor\"
   ```

4. Press Enter. Your command prompt is now in the commands-for-appinventor context. Any commands you type will try to run in this directory.

On a Mac:

1. Launch the Terminal application (it's located in /Applications/Utilities, Shift+⌘+U).

2. Type the following exactly as written, including quotes:

   cd "/Applications/AppInventor/commands-for-AppInventor"

3. Press Return. Your command prompt is now in the App Inventor Extras context. Any commands you type will try to run from this directory.

Testing for device connectivity

1. Follow the steps in the previous section.

2. Type adb devices. If your phone is currently connected via USB and its drivers are installed, you see a device listing as shown in Figure A-10. The command for Mac is entered without spaces as adbdevices.

FIGURE A-10:
The adb devices command verifies that a device is connected

Adapting to Special Circumstances

After running the adb devices command, in some instances, you may see the device serial number followed by the words Offline. I have found that this usually occurs when there has been a conflict between your device and another Android device such as the Emulator.

1. Open a command prompt to the ADB command location as explained in the "Opening a command prompt and navigating to the App Inventor Extras" section.

2. Type adb kill-server to stop the ADB process and kill the listening sockets.

3. Reboot your computer.

4. Check with the ADB Devices command as in the "Testing for device connectivity" section to see if the device is still listed offline.

Using ADB to view the phone log in real-time

You may want to see a detailed log file from the Android phone if you are in the midst of advanced trouble shooting or if you are trying to run down information for the properties for the ActivityStarter component. Use the following steps to get a comprehensive log from your Android device:

1. Follow the steps in the "Opening a command prompt and navigating to the App Inventor Extras" section.

2. With your phone connected, type adb logcat. A log stream flashes very quickly across the command prompt screen. It continuously scrolls as events occur on your phone until you interrupt the logcat process.

3. To interrupt the logcat process, press Ctrl+C. The ADB command exits back to the command prompt.

Capturing the phone log to a file for notepad/textedit viewing

Sometimes it is very difficult to catch an error event when it occurs by looking at the real time log file. You can use the following steps to capture the Android log file to a text file so you can pore over it at leisure.

1. Follow the steps in the "Opening a command prompt and navigating to the App Inventor Extras" section.

2. Type `adb logcat >logcapture.txt` and press Enter. The log streams into a file called logcapture.txt until you interrupt it. You can use any name you want for the log capture file.

3. Press Ctrl+C to interrupt.

4. Type `notepad logcapture.txt` ("`textedit logcapture.txt`" on a Mac) to launch Notepad/TextEdit with your freshly captured logcat. If you use a different name for your log capture file, remember to change the name in this step as well.

ADB can be used to detect what Android devices are connected to your computer. If the ADB devices command lists a device serial number, it is very likely that it will work with App Inventor. The ADB command also lets you stop and start the Debug Bridge process. Advanced uses of the ADB include installing applications from your computer to the phone and messing around with the phone file system.

Working with the Android Emulator

You do not have to have an Android Phone or device to create and test applications with App Inventor. Part of the App Inventor Extras package is an Android Emulator. An emulator simulates or "pretends" to be another device. As far as App Inventor is concerned, when you have the Emulator running, you have an Android device connected to your computer. The Emulator allows you to play with the interface and applications on your computer desktop as you can see in Figure A-11.

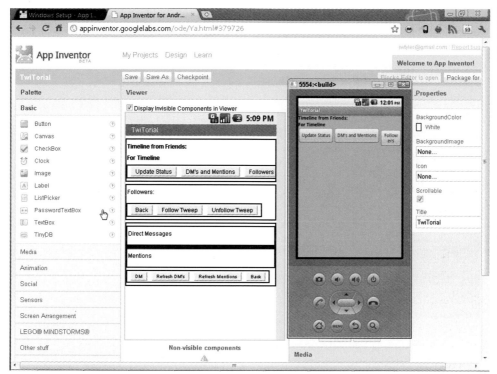

The Emulator allows you to use your mouse as a virtual "finger" to tap and drag on the simulated phone screen. It also uses your computer's Internet connection to create connections to the outside world, including to Web databases and the World Wide Web. The Emulator that comes with the App Inventor Extras is a prepackaged version of the Emulator that comes with the full Android SDK (Software Development Kit), with all the settings and configuration items preset.

To start the Emulator and connect App Inventor to the emulator, follow these steps:

1. Click the Open the Blocks Editor button from the Design view of App Inventor.

2. When the Blocks Editor is open, click the New Emulator button at the top of the Blocks Editor. It can take up to five minutes for the Emulator to start.

3. When the emulator has started, click on the Connect to Device button at the top of the Blocks Editor. All the Android devices connected to your computer, whether emulator or real devices, are shown in a drop-down list.

4. Select the device or Emulator you wish to connect App Inventor to from the drop-down list. See Figure A-12.

FIGURE A-12:
Connecting the
Blocks Editor to
an emulated
Android device

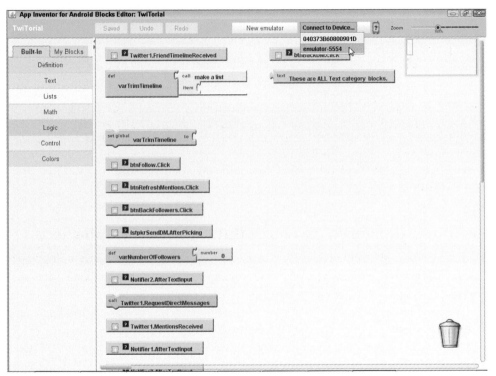

FIGURE A-12:
Connecting the
Blocks Editor to
an emulated
Android device

Exploring the Android SDK and Other Emulator Options

The Emulator that comes with App Inventor Extras is a base Android 2.1 install with typical screen size and options. If you want a customized emulated device or a different version of Android on your Emulator, you need to install Eclipse and the full Android SDK (System Developer Kit). The full SDK and App Inventor Extras can be installed on the same machine with no fear of conflict.

Troubleshooting Your Phone's Connection

Sometimes your Android device may appear to be detected by your computer and installed but ADB does not detect the device when the "adb devices" command is run. In almost every case this is caused by the default windows drivers being used to install the device rather than ADB specific drivers. If the connected but not detetected state happens to you you can follow these intructions for replacing your Android device drivers on your Windows computer.

Many phone require special drivers for connection with ADB. These drivers can be obtained variously from hardware manufacturers' Web sites (Samsung, LG, HTC, and so on) or from cell phone carrier Web sites (Verizon, Sprint, and so on). Your best bet for locating the drivers specific to your phone is to ask if anyone in the App Inventor Getting Started forum has a link to the drivers you need. You can access the forum at `http://appinventor.googlelabs.com/forum/`.

NOTE

Verifying device driver installation for your phone

Your computer needs the correct drivers installed to connect to App Inventor. The Extras you installed have a broad range of drivers for many phones. You need to verify that your computer has drivers installed for your phone.

Here's how to verify driver installation if running Windows:

1. Click Start.

2. Right-click Computer (or My Computer on Windows XP).

3. Click Manage.

4. Click Device Manager.

5. If your device is not installed correctly, you see a device or a generic uninstalled device with a little yellow icon with an exclamation point on it, as shown in Figure A-13.

6. If your device *is* installed, you see your device name or manufacturer name listed in the device tree, possibly with ADB Composite, as shown in Figure A-14.

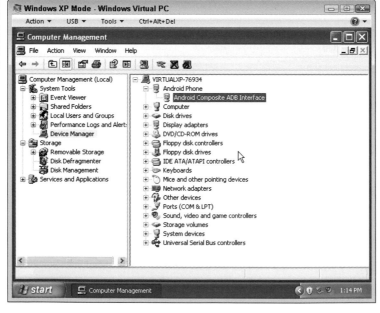

Here's how to verify driver installation if running on a Mac:

1. Press , then About This Mac

2. Click More Info in the dialog that appears.

   The System Profiler utility launches.

3. Click USB in System Profiler's Hardware section.

4. If your device *is* installed, you see your device name or manufacturer name listed in the USB Device Tree.

Installing or reinstalling drivers for your phone

You may need custom drivers for your phone that can only come from the manufacturer of the device. The best place to look for device drivers for your phone is on your handset's manufacturer's Web site. Note that the manufacturer of the device is not the same as the carrier from which you purchased the phone. In other words, although I purchased my Droid1 from Verizon, I have to download the drivers from the Motorola Web site because Motorola manufactured the Droid. Likewise, HTC drivers come from HTC's support Web site, and so on. A Google search is a good way to find where you can get drivers for your particular device. If you can't find drivers or are just tired of looking, try searching the App Inventor Google Group at `http://appinventor.googlelabs.com/forum/`. Most phones have been addressed there at one time or another, and helpful people are usually hanging around to assist you in finding drivers.

TIP

If your phone has some drivers installed but is still not recognized by ADB, you may need to uninstall the current drivers and install new or updated drivers. Your phone may have been installed initially with drivers that just won't work with ADB and App Inventor, in which case you need to uninstall the existing drivers and then follow the steps to install a different set of drivers. Follow the steps in the next section to uninstall your device's drivers.

Uninstalling your device drivers in Windows

You would only uninstall your device drivers if drivers are already installed and you still can't connect to App Inventor. If there is a yellow icon in the Device Manger after checking from the previous "Verifying device driver installation for your phone" section, and you uninstall, your device will likely just disappear from the list. You will need to unplug and replug the USB cable from your computer. It then redetects and asks you where drivers for the device can be located.

1. Click Start.

2. Right-click Computer (or My Computer on Windows XP).

3. Click Manage.

4. Click Device Manager.

5. Locate your device and right-click it.

6. Click Uninstall.

7. Click OK to verify you want to uninstall the device.

   You may be asked to reboot your computer. Go ahead and reboot.

Manually installing custom drivers in Windows

To apply the custom drivers from your manufacture or the drivers included with the App Inventor Extras, follow these steps:

1. Click Start.

2. Right-click Computer (or My Computer on Windows XP).

3. Click Manage.

4. Click Device Manager.

5. Locate your device and right-click it. It probably has a yellow icon with an exclamation point on it.

6. Click Update Driver.

7. Select the No, Not at This Time radio button on the Hardware Update wizard.

8. Click Next.

9. Select the Install from a List or Specific Location option from the next screen. Click Next.

10. Select the Include This Location check box.

11. Click the Browse button. Now you need to point the wizard to where your drivers are located. You can point to the file folder where you downloaded custom drivers from your manufacturer's support site or attempt to use the drivers that came with App Inventor Extras.

The App Inventor Extras drivers are located in the C:\Program Files\Appinventor\ commands-for-appinventor\usb_driver\ folder, as shown in Figure A-15. Remember that for Windows 64-bit systems, this is in Program Files (x86).

12. Click OK on the Browse for Folder window.

13. Click Next on the Hardware Update wizard.

14. Your computer attempts to install drivers from that location. If there are no drivers at the location you specified, the Hardware Update wizard fails. Click the Back button to check the path that you entered is where your drivers are located.

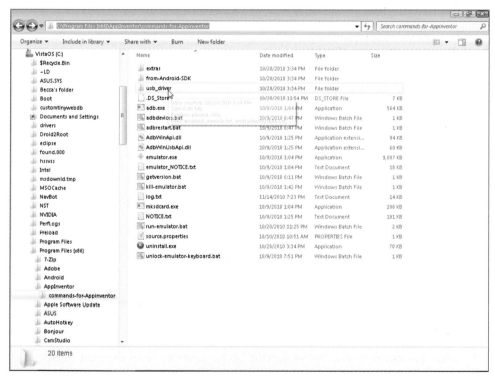

FIGURE A-15: The drivers that come with the App Inventor Extras are located in the commands-for-appinventor subfolder

When you have your phone set up, Java installed, and drivers for your phone installed, it's time to log in to App Inventor and start inventing some apps!

Appendix B
Creating Your Own
TinyWebDB

THE TINYWEBDB COMPONENT that is used in Chapter 7 stores and retrieves information across the Internet. An App Inventor application can use the TinyWebDB to maintain a database off of the Android device. This is accomplished by sending requests to store and get information from a database that resides on a Web server. The Web server where the TinyWebDB database resides must be running the TinyWebDB service. The TinyWebDB service listens for and responds to the GET and STORE requests.

These instructions help you install and configure the TinyWebDB service on a free Google Apps server. The instructions include downloading a version of the TinyWebDB service that has been built with the Python programming language. You can run the TinyWebDB service on your own Web service or your local computer. Instructions for customizing the Python code to run on your own server are beyond the scope of this book. If you are interested in customizing the TinyWebDB, research customizations on the App Inventor forum and the App Inventor Resources site at `http://appinventor.googlelabs.com` and `https://sites.google.com/site/appinventorresources/`.

Before beginning, download the following files:

❍ The Python App Engine for Google App Engine from `http://code.google.com/appengine/downloads.html#Google_App_Engine_SDK_for_Python`

❍ The Python code for the TinyWebDB Web service from `http://appinventor.googlelabs.com/learn/reference/other/tinywebdbassets/custom tinywebdb.zip`

The following steps allow you to run your own Web service to receive data and send data to your TinyWebDB component. You need to have a URL to point the component toward. The default URL for the component is a test database that is public and is regularly deleted.

NOTE   These steps guide you through setting up a service on Google's App Engine host service. However, Google's App Engine is not the only option for hosting the service: It can also be hosted on a server of your own. Hosting the service on your own server requires significantly more knowledge. The Python script that responds to TinyWebDB can be altered to run on your own Python framework.

A few Java ports exist for the Web service as well. You can find discussions about implementing the Java versions of the TinyWebDB service in the Google App Inventor forum at `http://appinventor.googlelabs.com/forum/`.

The high-level steps for the process are as follows:

1. Set up your free Google App Engine account.

2. Install the Google App Engine SDK (software development kit) on your local computer.

3. Create your application on Google App Engine.

4. Extract the Python code for the TinyWebDB service to your local computer.

5. Edit the Python code to be unique to your application on the App Engine.

6. Upload the customized Python code to your App Engine account.

Setting Up Your Google App Engine

I give more details on these steps in the remainder of this appendix. First, you need to sign up for a Google App Engine account:

1. Navigate your Web browser to `http://code.google.com/appengine/`.

2. Click on the Sign Up for an App Engine Account link. See Figure B-1.

FIGURE B-1:
The Google App
Engine sign-up

Next, install and set up the Google App Engine:

1. Install the appropriate Python SDK package from the App Engine download files. For Windows machines, the file is called GoogleAppEngine-1.#.#.msi. This step starts the Google App Engine Install wizard.

2. Click Next on the Welcome screen. If you do not have Python installed on your local computer, click the button to install Python and follow the prompts.

3. After the Python installation is complete, return to the Google App Engine SDK set up and Accept the license agreement on the end user license agreement page.

4. Click Next on the Destination Folder window.

5. Click Install on the Ready to Install page.

6. When the installation completes, run the Google App Engine launcher. (See Figure B-2.)

FIGURE B-2:
The App Engine
console

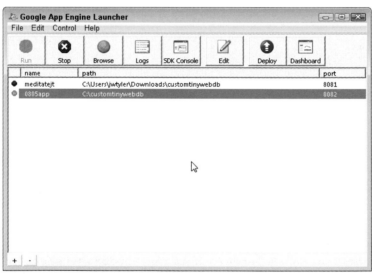

7. Click the Dashboard button on the console. This brings up the log-in for the Google App Engine.

8. Enter your Google credentials for the log-in.

For most people, their Google account is their Gmail username password. If you do not have a Gmail account or a Google Apps account, you need to sign up for Gmail. Both the App Engine and App Inventor require a Google account. You can use the same log-in to log in to both App Inventor and App Engine.

9. Click the Create Application button.

10. If you have not done so previously, you are asked to verify your account using an SMS message.

11. After you have verified your account, create an application.

12. Select an application identifier. This is part of your TinyWebDB service URL. The identifier you choose must be unique across all App Engine apps. Your URL is your application identifier followed by appspot.com. If you select an application identifier of 0805App, for example, your URL is 0805app.appspot.com.

13. Write down your application identifier for safekeeping.

14. Select an application title. Any descriptive text will do.

15. Scroll down and click the Create Application button.

Now you have a blank application ready to put your Python code into.

Customizing and Installing the TinyWebDB Service

Next, unzip the Python code, customize it, and load it to your App Engine account using the App Engine console:

1. Unzip the customtinywebdb.zip file you downloaded from http://appinventor.googlelabs.com/learn/reference/other/tinywebdbassets/customtinywebdb.zip into an easy-to-find location.

2. Locate the app.yaml file from the files you extracted from customtinywebdb.zip and open the app.yaml file with Notepad. You see the text shown in Figure B-3.

FIGURE B-3:
The app.yaml file

3. Change the `customtinywebdb` text to match your unique application identifier. Using the previous example, the app.yaml file would look like Figure B-4.

FIGURE B-4:
The customized
app.yaml file

4. Save the app.yaml file and close Notepad.

The next step is to upload the application to Google App Engine.

1. Open the Google App Engine launcher from either the desktop shortcut or your Start menu.

2. Click File on the toolbar and select Create New Application.

3. Enter your application identifier in the Application Name field. Using the previous example, you would enter `0805app`.

4. Click the Browse button next to the Parent Directory field.

5. Navigate to the customtinywebdb folder you extracted from the customtinywebdb.zip.

6. Select the folder and click OK.

7. Click Create.

Now you see your application in the main screen of the launcher.

8. Select your application in the main launcher window and click the Deploy button.

9. Enter your Google account credentials whether Gmail or Google Apps account in the pop-up dialog.

10. Click OK.

A deployment window appears and the deployment starts. When a message appears that says, `You can close this window` now, close the window and close the launcher.

Test to see whether the service is running:

1. Open a Web browser and enter your application identifier followed by `.appspot.com`. Using this example, you would enter `0805app.appspot.com` and press Enter.

2. Your app should serve a page like the one in Figure B-5.

3. If you get a Web page with Hello World, give the application a few minutes to deploy and try again. It may take a few minutes before it responds.

FIGURE B-5: The running TinyWebDB service

Now you can customize your App Inventor application to send and receive data from your custom TinyWebDB service:

1. Drag and drop the TinyWebDB component into your application.

2. In the Properties column, change the `ServiceURL` to point to your custom application. In this example, you would change it to `http://0805app.appspot.com`.

Now you can use the GET and SEND values to send and retrieve data.

NOTE   The data sent and received from the TinyWebDB service is not secured and a determined snoop could find your appspot.com URL and snoop through the data. Using a random string for the app spot name can help secure your data to some extent, but you should always think of the TinyWebDB service as not secured.

Index